First published in Australia by HiveMind Press 2023.

Copyright © HiveMind Press, 2023.

Jessica Sierra has asserted her moral right under the Copyright Act 1968, [2006], and Patents Act 1990, to be identified as the author of this work.

All rights reserved. No reproduction, copy or transmission of this publication may be made without written permission. No paragraph of this publication may be reproduced, copied or transmitted save with written permission or in accordance with the provsisions of the Copyright Act 1968, [2006]. Any person who does any unauthorised act in relation to this publication may be liable to criminal prosecution and civil claims for damages.

ISBN: 978-1-923053-09-0

Cover Design by - Wren Jessica Richards of Ancient Rhythms Art (@ancientrhythmsart)

Typeset by - HiveMind Press

THE UNRAVELLING JOURNEY

*A memoir spanning seven continents
and the transformation of wounds to wisdom.*

Jessica Sierra

Contents

PREFACE — 1

PROLOGUE — 2
THE CALLING — 2

PART I: — 30
BIRTH — 33
DEATH — 65
AWAKENING — 119
EXPANSION — 159
FLOW — 193

PART II: — 222
REBIRTH — 225
THE SEVENTH CONTINENT — 241
THE UNFURLING — 279
TRANSCENDENCE — 319

EPILOGUE — 357

ACKNOWLEDGEMENTS — 361

PREFACE

I acknowledge that the healing modalities I share are not mainstream, but I stand in my truth that they worked for me. My journey has been one of pondering and probing at the veracity and art of life. I found my way by questioning society's default, but the path I took will not work for everyone. Depression is a complex disorder with highly individualistic symptomology. What worked for me may be detrimental for you. Only you can choose your direction and trail your way forward.

My intention is to break the stigmas of mental illness and sexual assault by interweaving raw experiences with poetic storytelling. At times these pages may provoke strong emotions within you. I invite you to sit with the uncomfortable and see what it stirs. Being aware of your triggers is alchemy that allows trauma to be realised and released rather than stored as bundled-up knots of emotional energy within. With this awareness, the horizons of possibility widen.

Alive with vulnerability, I give my word to be real with you and let my truest voice carry you through each page. I have been faithful to my memory and the meaning forged from these experiences. I wrote this book in devotion to enriching and empowering you, not to cause harm. For this reason, most names have been changed and some identities blurred.

This book is a mix of grunge grit and soft emotion that peers inside the heart and mind of a young woman traversing the serrated terrain following sexual assault. In a world dominated by unrealistic expectations of what is it to be a woman, my hope is you will gain empathy and understanding, or maybe even resonance and healing.

Buckle on into my skin. Welcome to the unravelling journey.

PROLOGUE - THE CALLING

Tuesday 9th July 2013 - Buenos Aires International Airport

"Where are you from?" asks the middle-aged Latino man with a subtle Australian twang.

I look up from the dusty black conveyer belt. He wears a black suit that sits flat on his shoulders and hugs his body well. Around us, people chatter in Spanish as luggage is hauled and wheels roll on tiled floors.

His question is an innocent conversation starter that gives insight into my ethnicity and cultural beliefs. It's simple. But it makes my whole body cringe. Extensive travelling has eroded the novelty into an abrasive bite. I am sick of the prejudices attached to an answer I cannot—and will not—simplify. I travel to step outside the world's stereotypical prism, not to be pigeonholed inside four rigid walls.

But the man, like so many before him, doesn't understand my context with the question, so I offer a tired smile as I rub my eyes and reply, "El Mundo."

He nods slowly with a quizzical smile. "El Mundo? You are from *the world?*"

"Si," I murmur, diverting my gaze to the baggage wheel that will deliver the backpack containing everything I need for my one-way journey. Carrying my home on my back is normal for me. Minus a few weeks of work in Perth, I've been living and working on the road for over a year. With a topped-up bank account, I am stepping back onto another blank page and writing my own story.

The man laughs. "How are you from *the world?*"

For a moment, I forgot he was there. The flights from Perth to Sydney to Buenos Aires have been long. I haven't slept since I cocooned myself between feathered blankets in Perth two days ago.

With a deep breath I explain, "I was born in Hong Kong. My heritage is European. My accent is Australian, and I'm travelling on my UK passport. For an unknown amount of time."

Beneath lifted eyebrows, his eyes dot the puzzle together.

Just in case he doesn't get it, I summarise, "The world was made without borders. Everywhere I go is home."

His gaze trails along my world map tights. Suddenly I feel cramped inside the satin-smooth spandex where the seven continents float, so I direct the conversation back to him.

"De donde eres?" I ask, peering into his chocolate eyes.

"I am from Peru."

"Excelento," I chirp. "Peru is my favourite country."

He laughs. *"Excelento? Don't you mean excelente?"*

"Si. My friend and I joke that ending English words with 'o' makes them Spanish."

His brow furrows. I realise the notion is culturally insensitive, cringe at myself, and vow to be more aware.

Luckily the man shrugs and quizzes me with gleaming eyes. "You have been to Peru?"

"Si." I smile. "I spent cinco months in Sur Americano last year."

He chuckles. "You're talking to me in half English, half Spanish."

I nod. "It's the only way to *aprender*."

"Where in Peru did you go?"

Images of ancient stone cities, mysterious desert geoglyphs, and warm sunny beaches flash through my mind.

"Cuzco, Nazca, Mancora, Puno, Arequipa..."

The sight of my bumpy green backpack circulating the carousel amongst a dozen black suitcases tears me away. I skip off and strap my life onto my back, feeling the weight of what I've chosen to carry. Crammed between clothes apt for all four seasons, a dozen journals burden me with the potency of memory lane. Paper pages stew as inspiration to write this book brews. I approach the automatic sliding doors when the man appears again, small black suitcase in tow.

"My name is Luis," he introduces, extending an arm.

"Mucho gusto, Luis. Mi nombre es Jessica. Your accent has an Australian dialect. Is that where you learned English?"

Luis smiles. "Yes. I lived in Sydney for a year and go back regularly for business."

I ponder asking what his business is, but jet lag droops from the bags beneath my eyes. It will be twenty-three hours before my third and final boarding pass is scanned and torn. All I want to do is scrub my face, brush my teeth, and find a quiet place to rest for the night.

"Do you want to share a cab into town and get dinner? Buenos Aires is a fantastic city. The nightlife starts late and goes till morning."

His question jolts me back to the dusty airport terminal bustling with businessmen and backpackers. I pierce his gaze, looking beneath the surface. He gives a smile that warms his face but doesn't quite reach his eyes. Somewhere in my drowsy daze, an alarm bell sways. His invitation into the city seems slick and smooth, but something in the undercurrents looms.

"I'm not staying here," I explain. "Tomorrow I meet a friend in Lima."

He jams his hands in his front pockets. "Oh, you are on a layover?"

"Si," I assert, with an unrelenting stare.

He diverts his gaze to my left knee. "Me too. What flight are you on?"

"Ah…" I lift the flap of my handbag then close it, not wanting to disrupt the meticulous order inside.

"I fly at night," I deadpan.

He is lingering like a fly hovering over a decadent feast.

"I am on that same flight," he declares.

I doubt it. Surely there are other flights between the two capital cities that a businessman who does that trip regularly will take. He keeps changing his story to match mine.

"Mmmm, we have a long layover," I note, catching the time on a departure screen. Twenty-two hours, thirty minutes, and counting.

"Do you want to share a taxi to a hotel?" he suggests, glancing sideways.

His words knot in my stomach, jerking me out of my jet lag. Suddenly his aristocratic demeanour feels too deliberate. He is too eager, too subtly persistent, for me to get in a taxi with him.

"No. I'm staying here," I chirp with an intended naivety. The less he thinks I know, the more he will give away.

"You're going to spend an entire night and day at the airport?"

"Si."

In the distance, renovations clamour with drills that bore into my skull.

He cocks his head to the side. "Why?"

I answer with truth. "The money I save on a taxi and accommodation will stretch my travels into another week later on."

He nods slowly then pleads, "I can pay for the taxi?"

"No." My tone is firm. That's strike three.

"Maybe we can eat some food here then?"

My body stiffens as I study his polished black shoes. Entertained by the sharp edges, I nod slowly as I formulate a plan to lose his trail.

"I need to go to the toilet first."

I can lose him by hiding in the bathroom for half an hour.

"Okay. I need to go to the bank." He gestures to two ATM's. "Shall we meet back here?"

"Si," I affirm. "See you soon."

Pretending to play with my iPod, I watch him stride into the bank then I speed walk in the opposite direction. In a dark, dusty corner in an adjacent terminal, I wrap myself in a blue-and-green-striped blanket, curl into a ball on the floor, and succumb to my fatigue. Perhaps he doesn't have an ulterior motive with me. I'll never know for sure. All I can adhere to is what I feel in my body to be true. The next day, there is no sign of him at the departure gate as my boarding pass is scanned. Maybe he was on an earlier flight, or maybe he wasn't really from Lima and my instincts were right. I learned young to listen to my body and trust my intuition. Almost always, my hunches are dead-on.

As the plane taxies down the runway, warm sensations bounce from my torso and stimulate my entire body. My heart yearns for connection with strangers who will become friends. I am homesick for places I don't yet know exist. On a voyage without a compass or a map, I am ruled by my inner GPS. I brim with an insatiable desire to map the uncharted waters that are my comfort zone.

Out the plane window, my daydreams stretch into the horizon. In creamy tangerine puffs of sun-kissed clouds, I envision the day someone looks deep into my eyes and asks:

"In what language do you dream?
What makes your heart beam?
Is there more to this life than what can be seen?"

The journey begins with the decision to go.

February 2013, Four months earlier – Perth, Western Australia

My friend Laula lives in a loft above her parents' garage. Crickets click from towering marri trees as I clutch a cool metal rail and climb the wonky wooden stairs. The flowers effuse a soothing eucalyptus scent. I breathe it in as cars whiz along the nearby highway. Beyond them, a jarrah forest echoes with birdsong from Western Australia's oldest national park.

The funk rock of Incubus blasts through Laula's open door. The music gets louder with each uneven step, and I grin at the pitter-patter of Laula dancing. Since returning from a soul-stirring voyage through South America and Antarctica two months ago, I relish spending quality time with my six-foot-tall, bleached-blonde friend.

At the top of the stairs, dozens of potted plants adorn a large wooden balcony. With "The Warmth" as my soundtrack, I leap through the front door, chuck my bag of food beside the empty fireplace, and embrace Laula in a bouncy hug. An amused smile embellishes her beautiful face as she throws her head back and claps her hands.

Holding me by my elbows, she exclaims, "I have good news!"

In her eyes, golden nebulas explode from emerald pools. I hold my breath as she leads me to two thin, padded cushions on the floor.

"You found an octopus with nine legs?" I joke.

"No." She laughs. "I'm going to Peru."

My heart oozes with appreciation for the land that rekindled my passion for life. I express my joy then question why she's going.

"I want to drink San Pedro," she declares in a Latin accent. Her eyes shimmer with animated expression. Years of performing embellish Laula with the gift of instantly embodying a vast calibre of characters and captivating crowds with engaging stories. I adore this part of her.

"What's *San Pedro*?" I quiz.

"It's a plant medicine."

I lean closer. *"A what?"*

Laula explains that plant medicines are, literally, medicinal plants. For thousands of years, ancient remedies have been used to heal a range of physical and psychological disorders.

"Oh, I remember our guide talking about them when we were trekking through the Amazon. He pointed out a plant with cancer-curing properties. It's sad, though. He said that the natural remedies many shamanic healers know are being forgotten as young generations lose interest in their ancestral wisdom and turn to western ways."

"That's why I wanna drink some cactus," Laula bubbles as she strikes a match on what appears to be a tight bundle of tattered paper bound by a string. Smoke billows with an astringent aroma as she draws a figure eight in the air with the strange, burning bundle.

She is blasé to the safety hazard, so I enquire, "Babe...why are you burning paper?"

She bursts out laughing and explains it is white sage—an aromatic undershrub used to cleanse and detoxify spaces. Apparently the smoke changes the composition of air and neutralises the positive ions in our body.

"Oh..." I laugh. "Back to the cactus. How do you drink it?"

"The spikes are skinned, then the inside is boiled into a tea and brewed for eight hours."

My vision of sticking a metal straw inside the spiky succulent and guzzling green goo dissipates. I tilt my head to the side and ask, "Is it safe?"

"Yeah, babe. People have been using it for over two thousand years as a healing modality."

Over the years, I've noticed Laula refers to me as "babe" when she is absolute in her decisions. Whether intended or not, it is a signpost for me to step back and look at things from a higher perspective. She's aroused my curiosity. But scepticism underpins my bubbly nature that craves the excitement of new adventures. I think of a story I heard in the Amazon of a western girl being raped by a pseudo shaman after drinking ayahuasca. The story erects walls around my open mind and flings Laula's words into a cobwebbed corner where boxes of her dad's photography films collect dust. I don't doubt the truth in what she is saying. My concern is her being alone in Peru. I don't want to chuck a wet blanket on her fire though, so I hide my apprehension and probe for more information.

"Where are you going to do this?"

"With Lesley Myburgh." Her tone implies I should know the name.

No bells of familiarity chime. "Who?"

"Oh my gosh, she's an absolute Goddess," Laula raves. She rolls onto her back then swings up to face me. "She's a South African shaman who lives in Cuzco with her twin sons. She first drank San Pedro in 1991—the year you and I were born."

I imagine a toothless lady living in a ramshackle building drinking nothing but cacti all day. "How do you know she is who she says she is?"

"It's legit, babe. I'll show you."

Laula reaches for her laptop and clicks open a webpage titled "Casa De La Gringa".

"*Casa De La Gringa?*" I burst out laughing.

"Yeah, that's her hostel." Laula shoots me a smile. "Do you know it?"

"No, but gringa, or gringo, is a derogatory term that locals use to describe foreigners. It's interesting that's what she's named her hostel."

My speculations dissolve when Laula shows me a photo of Lesley. Long blonde locks cascade from her crown like a fountain of youth. Her sapphire eyes glisten above freckles forming constellations on her silky skin.

"She looks lovely," I admit. "How long are you going for?"

"I'm going for five months, like you did. It's massive for me. I've never left Australia for that long. Other than short trips to Bali and Thailand with my family, I haven't really left Australia…"

Our conversation ceases as she peers inside my bag of food. Chili and garlic waft from a container brimming with tomato salsa. A huge part of our friendship revolves around enjoying the flavours of hearty home-cooked meals. Rice cakes snap into the silence as we crunch and chew. Eating with Laula is something I treasure dearly. Entering a meditative trance, we stare into each other's eyes and savour. Sometimes I feel that Laula is the only one who sees me, the real me, unhindered.

After the salsa, we suckle on chocolate I've pinched from the continuously refilled stash in my parents' pantry. With our feast, I digest our conversation. I'm nervous for her to go alone. I pride my adaptability to flow into the unknown while maintaining an eagle eye, and I'm already planning on exploring my seventh continent later in the year. Swinging by Peru on the way to California would be easy.

"Maybe I'll come with you," I ponder.

"Really?" Laula's eyes sparkle. "I'd *love* that."

"Just for a bit. Maybe the first few weeks, to help you ease in."

"Will you take part in a ceremony with me?"

My stomach lurches. "I'm not sure, babe. Let me feel into it…"

In the weeks that follow, the dreams sailing into my psyche illuminate the storm raging in my unconscious mind. In one dream, I drink San Pedro in a dark hall. As the medicine kicks in, I levitate to the ceiling and drift through wooden rafters where I am suspended by a dark and invisible force.

A few weeks later, I dream of San Pedro again. This time I am in a spacious room. The dreamscape feels safe and sacred. As a doorway emerges from a blinding-white wall that leads to a small courtyard, Laula appears. She is smiling. Bricks and slabs then morph into a flourishing garden. My life radiates with joy because I have drunk the mescaline-bearing medicine.

San Pedro is calling to me. Knocking on the door to my heart, it seeps through the cracks in the walls I've stacked around me. I need the medicine, but my ego is getting in the way.

My subconscious is a sea
that drifts through my dreams,
deep on my eyelids.

Saturday 13th July 2013 - Arequipa, Peru

"Are you real?" I ask Laula, as I pinch the skin on my forearm.

The sharp nip tells me I'm not dreaming.

She tilts her head and shrugs. "I don't know, am I? *Are you real?* What is reality?" Bright-eyed, she catches my gaze and laughs.

Tipsy off a bottle of merlot we drank on the moonlit roof, we are brushing our teeth in the tiny hostel bathroom.

I sometimes wonder if Laula can read my mind, but she looks at me deadpan, so I reiterate, "Seriously, this is something I wonder. How can someone so cool be real?"

Her cheeks flush.

This compels me to profess more, "You're incredible, babe. You're open-minded, hilarious, deeply perceptive, and always happy. I feel so grateful to be here with you. Sometimes I wonder if I'm actually a crazy person and you're my invisible friend. I feel so connected to you it feels otherworldly."

The mustard-yellow walls intensify in colour as the vulnerability of my words deepens my presence to the world around me.

"I feel the same about you," she breathes.

Linking arms, we skip back to an empty dorm. The other travellers are out or yet to arrive on late-night buses and planes.

Our own journey from Lima to Arequipa was long, in front row seats on a double-decker bus. For sixteen hours, jagged cliffs and stormy coastlines loomed from rattling windows. Trusting the driver's keen navigation through mountainous terrain, I surrendered to the annoying whistle that accompanied us for the entire ride. The torturous roller coaster of South American bus rides was familiar to me. I had faith in our safe arrival. While I sank into short intervals of light sleep, Laula draped a blanket over her head as her stomach churned.

In the charming cobblestone city with buildings constructed from white volcanic rock, we caught up on sleep, wrote poetry, and settled into the rhythm of honking motorcycles whizzing through sillar stone streets. It was invigorating, exhausting, adventured-fuelled, and now we're here.

Laula motions to the empty dorm then turns to me with palms upturned.

After scanning the room, I leap onto the only non-bunk and start jumping. Up. Down. Boing. Boing. Between strands of my thick blonde mane, Laula doubles over laughing. Eventually I tire myself out and bounce off the bed. Just as I've smoothed out the blanket's creases, two Israeli men burst in, ranting in thick Hebrew. One throws his bag onto the bed that was my trampoline moments earlier. I shoot Laula a puckish look then sing hello.

"Hello. Hola. Shalom."

The greeting delves into us sharing worldly views. He asks what it's like living in Australia. With words slurred from merlot I admit my resistance to return. I feel like a foreigner in a land once familiar. Hearing Aussies dismiss the human rights violations occurring in lands that asylum seekers run from with derogatory phrases that stem from racist political discourses makes me ashamed to call myself Australian. It's privilege compounded with an ignorance that is downright embarrassing and disgusting. The Brits arrived on boats, then eradicated Indigenous traditions as they "founded" the young country on the very land the world's oldest continuing culture has walked for over 60,000 years.

Itai listens intently to my rant. After a reflective pause, he gives the sobering words: "To us, we see Australia as paradise."

The following evening, Laula and I board another overnight bus bound for Cuzco. Luxuriating on two spacious back seats, we prepare for an unbroken chain of bumps and jolts. Between the energizing soundscapes of rock and roll, the loudest snoring I've ever heard erupts from the fat man across the aisle. Only, it isn't snoring. It is roaring. At first, it's amusing. Then it's annoying. After ten hours we want to strangle the guy. I place a blanket over my head, hoping it will muffle the lion trapped in his throat, but each coarse inhalation severs my eardrum open. As morning imbues the sky with hope he'll wake, his obnoxious, grinding gravel snores continue.

Eventually, Laula throws a pillow at him and barks, "Shut up!"

For a moment it is still. He looks around with a perplexed expression and rubs his eyes. Then he plummets back into deep slumber, exhausting the rest of the bus as we pull into Cuzco.

His roars reverberate inside my skull like the engine of a jet plane as we bounce along patchy cobblestone roads in a taxi with an attractive Dutch couple. They too have been kept awake by the fat man's snores. Our annoyance morphs into awe as we contemplate the towering mountains fortifying what was once the beating heart of the Incan Empire. In the city centre's swarming plaza, locals hustle tours to Machu Picchu. A lavish Catholic church domineers over immaculate flower gardens, casting shadows with its baroque façade. It boasts Peru's largest altarpiece coated with gold. The splendour crumbles when I learn the stone church was erected on the foundations of an Incan Palace during the Spanish Inquisition. I empathise with ancient Incan sites being ravaged and ransacked for gold and glory. To me, the mountains are the real temple.

I think of tectonic plates shifting and lifting the earth as civilisations rise and fall through time. The mountains witnessed the logistical mystery of the Incas quarrying and transporting massive stones to create exquisite cities and temples with a precision that baffles historians. Nature knows the answers to the questions we seek. This renders a deep reverence for the mother who homes us. Without her, we wouldn't have sustenance to support our journey. We wouldn't have solid ground beneath our feet to bring rest when we are weary. We wouldn't have air to circulate life force with invigorating breath. And we wouldn't have water to replenish our cells and keep our bodies lively.

I feel a bizarre fusion of sadness and hope entombed within the earth, like the atrocities of the past have sunk into the sprawling vale. Yet in that same sediment is layer upon layer of ancient wisdom yearning to be remembered. I've barricaded my heart in a safe shell I think protects me, but my walls are slowly crumbling. And so, I get whiffs of a long-forgotten scent enchanting me with the memory of how we once lived in communion with the land.

Laula and I follow an uphill cobblestoned street with colonial architecture perched on Incan stone walls. The charm deepens as our walk steepens. Gasping for breath in the alpine air, we look back intermittently to admire the shrinking city. Tucked above the bustling city centre, the bohemian hub of San Blas comes to life with local artisans selling handicrafts and pedestrian-only streets veering up patchy inclines.

Laula knows Lesley's hostel is somewhere in San Blas, but the exact location is unknown. Midday sun weighs us down as we meander through winding lanes, searching for the big blue door that is our gateway to shade and slumber. Locals point us in different directions on a tiring wild-goose chase with every door in the district painted the same blue hue. We are lost puppies trying to find the scent of home. My smile wanes with heavy pants and sweat that collects under my bag strap, broiling my shoulders sunburned from lazing on the hostel roof. When we stumble upon the hostel an hour later, my enthusiasm has percolated into a sulky puddle.

Inside, the Andean lady at the front desk greets us with a warm smile. She leads us through two elegant French doors to a corridor drenched with sunlight from a massive skylight. I scuff along the white-tiled floor, brushing past ferns dangling from the ceiling. Halfway down the corridor, a Caucasian man lazes in a small sunny courtyard, gazing at life-sized fairies painted on the wall.

"Hello," Laula exclaims. "Are you Lesley's son?"

"Yes." The man smiles. "One of two. My name is Mark."

His rich South African accent startles me as he pushes reading glasses towards his sleepy eyes.

"Hello, Mark, my name is Laula." She extends her hand to shake his, then raises her arms and hugs him instead.

"Nice to meet you, Laula. Did you have a safe journey here?"

"Ah, yes. Safe, but not straight…"

I watch them from afar through narrow eyes. The weight of my backpack taxes my patience. "I'm going to the room," I huff at Laula. "See you there."

Their voices follow me down the breezeway.

"I've been so excited to come here and meet Lesley," Laula chirps. "Is she holding any San Pedro ceremonies this week?"

"Yes," Mark begins. "There's one tomorrow, and Friday."

The conversation mutes as I step into our turquoise room. I dump my bag on the floor then climb a wooden ladder to a double bed bathing in sunlight. Sinking into the luminous pool, I close my eyes. All I want is some rest but the skylight's warm shower agitates me.

I stomp down the ladder as Laula prances into the room.

"I'm going to explore the plaza and get a *café con leche*." She grins. The thought of a milky coffee electrifies her. "Would you like to come?"

"No, thank you," I mumble. "I'm going to have a shower."

Across the hall, I wrinkle my nose at the toilet's pungent stench. Shivers race under my goosebumped skin as I twist the metallic tap. My toes cower at the icy waterfall. I wait. South American showers often come chilled. I know this from my last visit. But the hostel promised hot water, and all I want is to bask beneath thousands of heated drops. I am so close to immersing with my steamy dream I can almost feel thermal sensations trickling down my spine and washing away the sweat, snoring, and fatigue. I'm on the verge of a reset. But the frigid downpour continues. I turn off the hot tap and twist the cold on full blast. Maybe they're marked incorrectly. I cradle the icy cascade. It does not warm.

My body quivers as I dress in our room. I need comfort of some kind and decide to find it through connection with friends back home. On first attempt, the WiFi connection fails. I try again, slowing my pace to ensure correct spelling.

The tab on my computer shakes. Another fail. Resentment rises from my lower belly, scrunching into an angry coil behind my brow. I'm pissed off at Laula's lack of planning that resulted in a long, uphill, sticky walk here. I'm irate at the fat man for keeping us up all night with his snores. I'm annoyed at the hostel for not providing the comfort and access to connection that I desire. Worse yet, I'm aware of my own entitlement and it disgusts me. I feel like I have no control over the irritation boiling within me. There's no clear path out or away from it. I want to leave.

Travelling to less privileged countries is not new to me. When culture shock presents me with ways of being that are not bound in privilege or wealth or ways that I am familiar, my mantra has been to adapt, for I will learn something new. I've not exhibited this kind of behaviour before, and I'm judging myself immensely. In hindsight, I discern that my discomfort is not about the sweat, snoring, lack of hot water and WiFi. It's feeling stretched beyond my comfort zone with my close proximity to plant medicines. My scepticism of the world and fear of the unknown is funnelled into frustration toward my current experience that acts as a scapegoat for what is really going on internally. I don't know who I can trust or what people want from me, for I've been burned before. It seems easier to barricade everyone and everything rather than open myself up to the soft process of healing.

I march into the large sunroom filled with sofas offering a relaxing retreat and plonk myself before the public computer. I am googling another hostel to stay in when Laula returns. Avoiding eye contact, I complain and project my problems onto her.

"We don't have to stay here," she assures, unresponsive to my cat claws that seek a fight. "If you want to go, we'll go."

With a deep breath she retreats to the courtyard where Mark lazes.

"Excuse me," she begins, searching for the words to convey my melodrama with grace. "I really, really love it here, but my friend doesn't dig it. Do you know if there's another hostel nearby?"

"Is she okay?" Mark's voice floats into my periphery.

"Um...I think... She just really wants a hot shower, and the water's not heating."

"Oh, sorry about that." He sounds genuinely concerned. "I'll get someone to look at it now. Where is she?"

I cross my legs and recoil into my sizzling centre.

"On the computer next door."

His chair scrapes. A moment later he squats beside me.

"Talk to me," he insists, inviting me out of my shell with a kindness safe to soften into. I don't want to be there, but I am too rigid to accept his help. It seems easier to burrow deeper into the drama than admit I am overreacting or have the courage to look within and take the first step toward healing by uncovering what really bothers me.

My teary eyes dart from his kind gaze. "The hot water's not working. Neither is the WiFi," I snap. "I understand these things happen, but I don't want to stay here."

He maintains a calm composure. "Got it. I'm sorry you feel this way. We'll look at the hot water now. Sometimes the WiFi doesn't work in the rooms because the modem is at reception. If there's anything I can do to help, let me know."

His courtesy makes me embarrassed for my behaviour. I am being the epitome of the traveller I loathe.

"Okay...thank you," I stammer, wishing to dissipate into the sunbeams swirling above his head.

Laula watches us from the door. "I'm so sorry..." she starts.

"It's okay. These things happen," he rationalises. "I hope you guys find a nice place to stay. I'll help direct you once you find somewhere new."

*

The silent whispers of your heart are calling you home.
Can you hear their song?

We sleep in a cold, unadorned hostel on a street we'd staggered upon on our quest to find Casa De La Gringa. It is booked out the following night, so we move to a room opposite four attractive Spaniards in a warmer hostel nearby. The friction soothes with Laula's wholehearted ability to accept my apology for hauling her away from the healing hub she's been so excited to immerse in.

"It's all good, babe. We've only got three weeks together. I can go back when you leave."

I've always admired Laula's easygoing attitude and her swiftness in letting things go. There are no nasty feelings left to ferment between us because she acknowledges the conflict at its roots and clears it through assertive communication. She doesn't enable passive-aggressive behaviour, so I have no choice but to be vulnerable and share what is really going on beneath my frenzied flames.

In between throwing an unripe avocado over the wall to our Spanish friends' room and giggling like schoolgirls when the boys fling it back, an all-encompassing feeling of love glides into my awareness. I can't shake Mark's genuine eyes or Casa De La Gringa's ethereal feel. A chasm cracks and grows within me at the thought of Laula returning without me. It overcomes me with an instinct to return to the hostel and apologise for overreacting. I voice this to Laula. She perks up from her single bed.

"Well, you don't have to go back if you don't want to. But if you feel that's what you want to do, I fully support you."

The avocado thuds beside my bed. I refrain from giggling. For the first time all night, neither of us seize it.

"So...San Pedro is heart medicine?"

"Yeah, babe," she encourages. "I'm sure there's plenty of information online if you want to read more."

Google enlightens me with a sea of information at the tip and tap of my fingers. Wikipedia reveals the name San Pedro is derived from Christian mythology after the Spaniards' failed attempt to suppress its use. The association with Saint Peter holding the keys to Heaven opens my mind to discover more. For 3000 years, the cactus has been used for healing and religious divination, with the visionary chemical mescaline present in its composition. My research detours briefly into the realm of exorcisms where I discover cacti with four spines are used.

My eyes strain from artificial light I hope will unlock the answers. Is this safe? Can it really heal me? How is the spiky succulent able to cure a broad range of mental, physical, and emotional disorders? An article titled "San Pedro, The Miracle Healer" reveals Lesley uses cacti with seven or nine spines in her ceremonies because they create the most gentle and beautiful brews. As the thick, bitter liquid boils for several hours, she offers it healing prayers.

Within me, a "fuck yes" brews at the thought of taking part in ceremony. It seethes in my heart then ripples through my cells in invigorating waves. Online blogs describe an awake, dreamlike state that lasts anywhere from seven to fifteen hours. During this time, an enhanced connection to Pachamama—the name for Mother Earth in Incan mythology—prevails and profound healing takes place. If I am to partake, what do I want to heal? I tear my eyes from the screen and find an answer in my six-month supply of antidepressants. Dozens of tablets plateau from silver blister packs in rows of two like soldiers marching into battle. Seven years ago, western doctors diagnosed me with depression. I believe it is a genetic illness based on dialogue from my mother. After I attempted suicide, my psychiatrist doubled my dosage and told me I need medication for life. Every day, I swallow a small pink pill, hoping it will devour my darkness, so I never have to feel the pain beneath the band-aid.

If San Pedro can sucker punch addiction and cure cancer, surely it can help my deep, dark density. Multiple sites report successful healings of depression and grief, but my research hurdles at Casa De La Gringa's website, where it advises not to drink the medicine if a history of mental illness is present.

I close my laptop and share the dilemma with Laula. My research has scaled me to a mountain peak that I stumble down when the question bubbles of whether I can even drink. There is something there, though. I feel it in every fibre of my being. Something urges me to break free from the fear that cages me. Laula listens intently and suggests we chat with Lesley. And so it is we return to the hostel the next day.

The lady at reception welcomes us back with a radiant smile. I try evading eye contact, but she captures me with a compassionate gaze. Sunlight swirls on the white-tiled corridor as we walk to our new room. In the courtyard, Mark dozes in the sun. I halt, hesitant to wake him from his reverie. A gentle breeze rustles a nearby vine. He stirs.

"Hello," I call.

He looks up with twinkling eyes. "Ah, you're back."

"Yes…" My gaze darts to my pink-and-white sneakers scuffed with years of adventures. "Sorry to interrupt. I just wanted to apologise for my behaviour the other day. And thank you for the way you handled…the situation."

His mouth drops, then he gives a forgiving smile. "That's okay, these things happen. How are you feeling now?"

"Better, thank you." I pause. "I've been researching San Pedro and…I think I might want to take part in a ceremony…but your website warns against drinking if a history of mental illness is present."

The distant murmur of chitchat fills our silence. I want to talk to Lesley, but I don't know how to ask for what I want without feeling like a burden.

Perhaps Laula senses my internal conundrum, because she chimes in, "Do you think it's possible for us to meet with Lesley to have a chat?"

Mark smiles. "Of course. I think she'll be floating around the hostel later today. I'll find out and arrange a meeting."

*

Change, like healing, takes time.

Up a wooden ladder, I dive onto one of two single beds. Laula excuses herself to shower, closing the door behind her. Not long after she leaves, a white cat with a missing ear saunters into the room and purrs.

"Meow," I reply, puzzled at how she got in. An ajar window opening to the roof is my answer. Peering out, I spot a sunny balcony adorned with potted plants and flowers. I look back at the cat, who suddenly pounces onto my chest and presses her paws into my heart. Her soft body finds solace on mine. I stroke her smooth ivory fur as her healing hums strum the invisible strings connecting us. When Laula returns, the cat and I are drifting into daydreams.

"I just bumped into Mark," she reports. "He's arranged for us to meet Lesley at 11:00 a.m."

I jolt awake. My stomach stirs, as though I absorbed sludgy caterpillars on our first visit that are now transforming into butterflies. Soon after, we climb a wooden staircase that leads to the sunny balcony I spotted out the window. At the top, Lesley appears like a full moon on a perfect summer day. Light drizzles from her long blonde mane onto a velour dressing gown wrapped around her petite body.

"Welcome," she sings in a silvery South African accent, then motions us inside to a white couch perched opposite a four-poster bed draped with silks. "I'll be with you in a moment. Please, make yourself at home."

As Lesley disappears into an adjacent bathroom, Laula basks in the delicious floral fragrance streaming from an oil burner beside a large, open window. Crystals and feathers adorn velvety shrines. I awe at the celestial art and affirmations coating the walls. The aesthetics remind me of my old bedroom in Perth.

Lesley emerges and glides to a nearby chair. I admire the freckles dotting constellations on her seamless skin.

"Can I get you anything to drink? Tea?"

"I'm okay, thank you." My voice is softer than usual, like we've been transported to Venus and the only way to be is sensuous and serene.

Lesley smiles with a resplendence that glows from within. "Now, Mark tells me you have some questions about participating in ceremony?"

I divert my gaze to the sunny balcony. She is so blissful. I don't know how to articulate my dilemma without ruffling the calm. "Well, I'm interested in the ceremony. But..."

I don't want to express the "but". But not doing so keeps me shackled. Only the truth will set me free.

"I have depression, and your website advises against drinking if a history of mental illness exists..."

She nods slowly, allowing me to continue.

"I'm on a high dose of antidepressants that—that I need to be on for life. I don't want to mess up any..." I circle my hands around my head.

Lesley examines me with sincerity. "My darling, you have nothing to worry about. I suffered from depression from the age of twelve to thirty-nine."

My eyes widen.

She continues in a gentle tone, "Yes, it's like a whole other life, like I was sleepwalking. There are entire years I can't remember. I was on very strong antidepressants. The day I drank Huachuma my life changed forever."

Why-choom-a—what?

Lesley notices my blank expression and clarifies, "Huachuma is San Pedro's original name."

"Oh."

"Huachuma, San Pedro, changed my life forever. It's like a veil lifted!"

The truth irradiates her vivid blue eyes.

"I began to see the world as it really is. I realised how beautiful it is. San Pedro taught me to believe."

I resonate with her story. Beneath my I'm-a-world-traveller exterior, I am living a half-life. The antidepressants aren't making me better. They numb me. On days I forget to take my medication, my creativity skyrockets and my dreams become lucid. Western doctors tell me I need the pills. Every day. For the rest of my life. But I sense there is another path.

Lesley gives a knowing smile and continues. "San Pedro is a very special medicine. And very gentle. You have nothing to worry about. You can walk and talk as normal. It is not a drug. Huachuma is a master teacher."

Her words anchor calm in my mind's flurry.

"It is medicine for the heart, helping us heal, grow, and awaken so we reach higher states of consciousness. It shows us life as it is, not how we think it is. I have experienced many miracles; people being cured of all sorts of illnesses. The day you meet Huachuma, your life is changed forever."

Her truth emanates hope as she talks of waking up from her depressive spell and embracing life.

"Maybe it'll help with my depression," I ponder. My own words yank at a knot in the centre of my forehead. Present to the tension, I wonder how long it's been there. "I think I want to take part in ceremony tomorrow."

"Really?" Laula squeals.

The ghost of a smile curves on my cheeks. "Yeah."

Lesley's eyes gleam like rare jewels. "Great. Today you must eat raw in preparation. No drinking, smoking, or eating meat. After dinner tonight, you must fast. Today, take your antidepressant as usual. Tomorrow, skip it. You will be consuming a different kind of medicine."

A rustling by the door has all our heads pivot. The white cat slinks inside.

"This is Angel," Lesley explains.

"Aww, she was just napping with me in our room!" I exclaim.

Angel swishes her tail as she catches my eye.

Lesley's hand rests on her heart. "Yes, she tends to do that with guests she likes..."

Angel takes a moment to absorb the three of us, then leaps off the balcony out of sight.

※

Descending the stairs feels like a passage connecting Heaven and Earth. Laula excuses herself to journal in the sunroom. I rest in bed, feeling the knot behind my forehead twist. It is a new sensation to feel my emotions tangling in real time. I try but fail to express them on paper. Breathing into the tension, I discern that analysing and articulating blocks aren't the only way to transmute them. My mere presence moves it through me. I'm in a state of surrender as Angel glides into the room and presses her tiny white face against mine. She kisses my forehead. I let the moisture permeate and breathe into the stillness. When Laula returns, afternoon shadows stretch across the room and Angel has long gone.

"I met some guys who are drinking with us tomorrow," Laula informs. "Four cute Canadians. They've just come from the jungle."

"Oh, cool," I mumble, remembering the Amazon's dense green.

"They've got some interesting things to say, but I got bored of hearing about ayahuasca after a while and came to find you... They're very good-looking."

I blink away the vision of a river flowing beside my bungalow balcony and catch Laula's eyes. Is life going to be the same after tomorrow?

"D'ya wanna go for a walk?" I propose. Moving my body gives clarity by moving thoughts through me.

"Sure, let's go."

Outside the hostel, three narrow streets trail in different directions.

"Shall we let our intuition guide us?" Laula asks.

"Yes," I beam, inhaling the crisp evening air.

Ahead is the San Blas plaza. Behind us is a maze of restaurants and hostels. To our left, steep stone stairs trail above the city. The path looks quaint and quiet. It is a way we haven't yet been.

"Let's go up here." My voice sounds husky in the soft alpine breeze.

We scale a few steps, then stop to catch our breath. Even locals huff and puff as they climb. At the top is a viewpoint. We watch orange roofs merge with the mountains beneath a setting sun. I feel clearer, witnessing the hustle from a higher perspective. I trust Laula. I trust the journey. Exhaling my anticipation, I surrender into the radiant tapestry of Incan ruins, colonial architecture, and snowless mountains interlacing before my eyes.

*

*We meet our destiny in different ways,
through different doorways, on different days.*

That night, we dine at a vegetarian restaurant overlooking the illuminated valley. Sitting at a booth built into the window, we sip on steaming soup as four attractive men amble in. Laula gives a friendly wave. It's the Canadians. As we depart after our meal, she introduces me. The guy closest to me introduces himself as Trey. With a chiselled face softened by dreamy brown eyes, he's handsome in a male-model-on-the-cover-of-a-magazine way with symmetrical features coated in light stubble.

"Yo," he muses in a chilled-out tone, as though tasting the corners of transcendent realms.

The lanky guy across the table examines the khaki-coloured continents floating on my legs beneath his thick, raised eyebrows.

"I like your world map tights," he notes, with lively brown eyes. He's introduced himself as Ben. Dimples dot his tanned face on either side of a light moustache that is the same colour as his wild, untamed hair.

"Thanks." I giggle, pointing to my left calf now serving as my cartography chart where Peru contours the sea. "We're here. Tomorrow, we're going..." I trail off as I dance my fingers above my head.

The guys all chuckle.

"Yes. We are."

I look at the speaker, mesmerised by his enigmatic green eyes. The rest of his features blur into a mystery I yearn to understand.

"What was your name again?" I ask.

"Riley."

I blink in his buzz-cut head and full lips then point to the middle of Canada on my left thigh.

"You guys are from here?" I ask as Laula excuses herself to the toilet.

"Yeah, but we're from Calgary. It's to the west."

Conner is slightly shorter than the others, with brawny shoulders. His rosy face beams as I peer into his deep-set hazel eyes that I will later associate with the philosophical musings engaging his visionary mind.

I refrain from furthering conversation as the waiter appears with four garlicky dishes. The guys drool like puppies eyeing a treat. It's my cue to go.

"Nice to meet you all," I sing. "Enjoy your meal!"

"Thanks."

"See you tomorrow."

"OOOOO, how exciting," I chime, then awkwardly dance toward Laula, who laughs at my goofy goodbye.

☙

"Good morning, Jessica." Laula's voice slithers across the room like silk being wound onto a spool.

"Good morning," I yawn, stretching my hands above my head.

"How are you feeling?" she asks.

Morning light drizzles through the window, wrapping me in a tranquil spell as sounds and sensations slowly ooze into my peaceful cocoon.

"Strangely calm."

"Great." Laula beams. "Today we're going on a magical journey."

In the hostel foyer, the Canadians stroll in with four other men. At ten o'clock, the ten of us descend steep cobblestone lanes to the taxi rank in San Blas Plaza. Laula and I find a tempo with Riley and Trey. They both wear macramé necklaces that cradle massive quartz crystals. Small talk veers into natal astrology with Laula enquiring after their birthdays. It is a common question I hear her ask new friends, and the topic tantalises the guys.

Prior to leaving Australia, Laula calculated my astrological natal chart online. Striding down Cuzco's steep streets, we pass sleepy shopkeepers tending small handicraft stalls and the odd stray dog following a scent to the next adventure. I drift in and out of the conversation as I remember Laula reading to me while I relaxed into fluffy aquamarine blankets on my queen-sized bed.

"Individuals with the sun in Aries are energetic, passionate, courageous, and pioneering. They can be impatient and act with impulse, but a genuine guilelessness gives them a noble air. The placement of the moon in Cancer gives a nurturing and creative nature bound by a striking depth of emotion and a strong intuition that allows you to read situations and people well…"

As Laula continued with the detailed account, my attention drifted to the world map on my wall. What awaited me in all those countries I had yet to explore? How much adventuring could I do before I settled down and started a family? Endless possibilities seduced me until Laula's sonorous tone swept me back into my bedroom.

"Oh, THAT makes sense!" she exclaimed, while I stretched my limbs to all four corners of the bed.

What made sense? A tang of shame swirled in my stomach for not being present with her while she read.

"I'm sorry, beautiful. I got distracted by the map, daydreaming where I want to travel next. Could you repeat that last bit?"

Laula looked from me to the map and settled on my blank expression. Then she burst out laughing and sighed. "That's exactly what I was just reading! Your sensitive moon in Cancer softens the Aries brashness, merging your adventurous nature with psychic abilities and a vivid imagination. Of course you'd tune out to contemplate the map!"

Her playful wink showed she wasn't offended, and for the first time in my life I wondered if there was more to astrology than ambiguous statements printed in glossy magazines.

﹆

The charm of San Blas Plaza is upon us when Trey responds in a low, dreamy tone. "I'm a Pisces."

"Oh, the fish," Laula muses. "Connecting us with other worlds."

She turns to Riley, who is casually attired in a grey T-shirt.

"I'm Scorpio." His voice is strong yet pleasantly silken. I soon learn he isn't one to waste words. When he does speak, he often expresses deep thoughts and sophisticated perceptions.

"Yeahhhh, boy!" Laula high-fives him. "I'm Scorpio moon and rising."

They share a knowing look, as though they both hold keys to—well, I'm not sure. The mystery is magnetising. I want to find out.

"What's your sun sign?" he enquires.

"I'm a Taurus," she responds.

I look from her to Riley, still curious to the enigmatic look they shared. In a yellow taxi, I take the backseat between Laula and Trey. On the fringe of the city, narrow cobblestone streets smooth into black asphalt, and I catch myself ogling Riley's attractive, angular jawline. His firm expression softens as his green eyes strike me in the rearview mirror like a bolt of lightning electrifying a clear blue sky. My breath tightens. Then the car pulls onto a dirt track.

I still feel giddy when we stop outside a tall stone wall and exit the taxi. Breathing into my stomach, I step through an open arched door like it is a portal into an enchanting garden. Inside, hundreds of cacti reach for the sun. A winding path leads to a stone home. Two gigantic cacti soar on either side of the front door towards prayer flags that dance from the second-storey balcony. I get the feeling they are the guardians of the garden, protecting all who enter the space.

Dragonflies buzz as we meander towards the house in single file. Halfway there, the path splits in two, and we veer towards an adjacent garden through a gap in a brown brick wall. My fingers tingle with excitement as the others *awe* and *wow* at a large stone teepee shadowing the lawn with its soaring straw roof. Windows encompass the entire structure, reflecting sunlight as though thousands of pixies prance in an unrestrained rhythm. I envision iridescent wings fluttering between clusters of San Pedro and beautiful clay pots adorning flowerbeds skirting the garden. Behind the teepee is a two-storey guesthouse. Prayer flags flap from wooden rafters, and metallic wind chimes jingle in mellifluous waves with the late-morning breeze.

We drizzle into the teepee, leaving our shoes beside a stack of mattresses by the door. A thick wooden trunk appears to lift the roof like a big-top circus tent, surrounded by four massive skylights. Sunshine illuminates a circle of cushions where Lesley sits before a tapestry festooned with crystals, large feathers, and beautiful ornate goblets.

"Welcome." She smiles and ushers us in.

I sink between Laula and Ben, comforted by Laula's knee kissing mine. A young Caucasian man sporting a cowboy hat sits beside Lesley. She introduces him as Gui. He is our go-to guy should we need anything. Lesley explains what to expect from the medicine then reaches into her altar and lights a bundle of sage. Swirling smoke into our sphere, she invites us to introduce ourselves and share any intentions and gratitude.

"Intention is very important," she affirms. "Everything is about energy. Contemplate on what it is you want to heal or learn."

A few of the guys share, then Laula chirps, "My name is Laula, and my intention is to receive what needs to be revealed. Gratitude is my attitude! I'm grateful to be here with my beautiful friend Jessica."

My rib cage expands with a warmth that drips to my feet and extends over my crown. The vulnerability in our collective sharing is like a dozen lotus flowers simultaneously opening.

"Hello, my name is Jess. I'm grateful to be here with my special friend Laula. For being blessed with this opportunity. My intention is to figure out where I'm meant to be, do some cleansing, and see each moment as new."

As the circle completes, I catch Ben's deep-brown eyes in a moment of reciprocated anticipation. His thin lips etch into a smile that feels strangely familiar, like I've seen it before in the far-off reaches of a dream within a dream.

Lesley pours the boiled cactus tea into ten glass goblets. My hands feel clammy as I press my thumbs evenly into the metallic ornamentation and hold the medicine to my chest. My heart pounds against my fingers. As she finishes serving Ben, an extra dollop of thick green goo glides from her canister into Ben's glass.

"The medicine knows how much we need," Lesley notes as she scrapes the spillage into his now-filled-to-the-brim cup.

"It's better to drink it all at once," she advises, then hands us lemon candies for the aftertaste.

We lift our goblets to our mouth. Thick, bitter grit engages my gag reflex. My stomach churns. San Pedro cactus is one of the hardest things I've ever had to swallow. It's like drinking pungent snot that's been fermenting in a giant slug's nose for a thousand years. I affirm the worst is over with my first gulp, then look despairingly at my half-full glass. I reach for my bottle, chug some water, and then take another swig. With an empty glass, I rip open a lemon candy and slide my tongue over the hard-glazed edges until the bitter cacti dissolves into a forgotten memory.

The more you know,
the more you know you don't know.

Lesley invites us to meditate with the medicine as the journey begins. I inhale deeply and close my eyes as a sweet, flowery scent fills the air. It smells like a big bowl of citrus punch spiced with cinnamon and clove. I later discover the smell is Agua Florida—a plant-based perfume to ground you into your body and balance energetic spaces. The quiet shuffle of the others scrambling towards the door blends with the sensation of my chest rising and falling before I open my eyes to a lone man meditating across the room.

Outside, I lay a mattress beneath the midday sun. A crisp mountain breeze sails through the garden as though searching for home. Goose bumps dot my arms. I clasp my stripy green travel blanket under my toes and stretch it over my head. Covering my body with woollen warmth, I lie on my stomach and close my eyes. Sleepy sensations seep into my being as my cells soak up the remedy. Footsteps pitter-patter on the winding stone path, and I feel Laula's nearby presence leave. I turn onto my back, wondering when the medicine will kick in.

Twisting onto my stomach, I lift my torso and brush my fingers through my silky ash hair. That's when I realise there is something different in my way of seeing. I am entirely coherent, but technicolour rays enrich the garden as life slows to witness its own blossom.

Then the medicine speaks. Not in words, but in the profound awareness I am exactly where I'm meant to be. I always was. I always will be. There is no then or there. There is only here and now. I'm not beginning my journey, nor am I ending the odyssey. I am in the journey. The journey is within me.

In an instant, I become at peace with where I am and no longer miss out on the beauty of the present moment by yearning for the next adventure. My quest of questioning where I am meant to be is answered, inviting me into a new way of being that is deeply fulfilling and enriching.

I am awakening from a long slumber while simultaneously seeing the world for the first time. With my deepening perception comes a gentle drowsiness that has me lie back down and cocoon myself in my blanket again. I close my eyes. A white light trickles into my being from the sun's golden glow. As I float between awake and asleep, random images hover on the surface of pools connecting my conscious and unconscious mind. Symbols flash in the reflection of still waters, giving clues to the codes running the operating systems hidden deep in my psyche. The formulas feel strangely familiar yet are hard to translate from a dimension that transcends words. Deeper and deeper, I journey through unknown territory in my inner terrain.

My closed eyes bind me to my internal state. Metaphorical nontoxic superglue smears my lids. It is difficult to tell how much time has passed since drinking the bitter potion, for time loses its limitation in ceremonial space. Sometimes, a single moment feels like an entire lifetime has birthed and died—a macrocosmic journey sliding by in the blink of an eye. Silent tears glide through my closed eyes with a warm trickle that curves at my jawline. I know the world beyond my cocoon is bright and beautiful. I feel the luminosity awaiting me to break through my darkness. But for all my knowing, I cannot open my eyes.

I am being shown the truth of my highly medicated, seven-year depression. The light is there but I cannot see it, because on some level, I have chosen to stay in the dark. The simplest action of lifting my lids suddenly becomes the hardest movement to make. The veil I have long-ago flung on my default state is being revealed. With its discovery, I have a choice to change. I lie there for a long time, processing the uncomfortable revelation that I can no longer neglect the responsibility of transforming my life and rising above my suffering.

It is up to me to open my eyes. No one else can do it for me. No more can I pass off my depression as a lonely disease beyond my control. In choosing to see the light, I can transcend the depressive spell that has been my norm. I must create a new default for my thoughts to run and enable my healing journey to begin.

If my brain is hardware, then my thoughts are software. They create beliefs that inspire my behaviour and impact my perceptions and thus shape my reality. Depression is a virus that has changed the hardware of my mind. It has shrunk my hippocampus and prefrontal cortex, causing a reduction in brain-derived neurotrophic factor that reduces my memory, ability to learn, and stress management with excessive cortisol levels impeding neuron development in my brain. This impacts my amygdala's function, making apathy, hopelessness, fuzzy thoughts, and disruptions to sleep and appetite my norm. Brain shrinkages in these regions combined influence my emotional responses and capacity to read other people's emotional cues.

Depression has also changed my mind's software. By activating parts of my brain that cause me to seek isolation, amongst other things, I have been caught in a downward spiral with heavy thoughts dominating my inner terrain. I want to update the software. Doing so will repair the hardware over time. For me to fire up new neural pathways that lead to bliss, I must courageously choose thoughts embedded with self-awareness and love.

This realisation becomes a pivotal point in my journey. Swiftly, it slices a before and after in its wake.

PART I

PART I

BEFORE

BEFORE

Chapter I
BIRTH

I am five years old when I ask Mama where I come from. She replies, "A little twinkle in Papa's and my eyes." It makes no sense until I learn that we're made of the same elements composed in the hearts of shooting stars. While nebulas nurture the potential for new constellations, our parents' genetic codes meet and merge in the most unique and intricate art. Carbon in our muscles, oxygen in our lungs, calcium in our bones, nitrogen in our DNA, iron in our blood, and hydrogen forming water in our cells intertwine into a mass of flesh and bones that become the tapestry of our existence. In a cosmic cauldron, our complex layers begin as a single cell.

Whilst divinity dances in a cosmic sea, an amazing hormonal rhythm enriches our fluid-filled womb with darkness. As we are nurtured and nourished by the umbilical cord, a stream of light from the centre of our galaxy ripples through our starry-eyed parents and threads into the fabric of our being. Written in the stars, or maybe our genetic code, is the inevitable pain that earthbound life entails. Whether we transform these wounds into wisdom is a daily choice we write. Twisting and churning across inky black skies, stars are twinkling enchantments of passion, hope, and resolve. We feel resonance with the night sky for it is a potent reminder of where we came from.

When the time comes for us to enter this world, powerful contractions pull us through the birthing portal and our mothers push through intense pain. It is the most painful and pleasurable experience of life. The first breath is a shock to our system. We are waking up from one dream and entering the next. Emerging from the darkness, we are birthed into the light.

On the 13th of October 1940, in a blacked-out midnight, incendiary air raids shake London for the thirty-fourth consecutive day. As German bombers stab the city with fire and angry yellow flames crackle, a baby is born under a piano. Sirens wail. Explosives descend upon the city in quick, bitter sounds. My father's mother takes her first breaths amid the longest and most sustained aerial bombing the world has ever known.

Grannie enters a world of pounding booms, black nights, and long queues for food rations. Planes come down in violent infernos, and streaks of smoke haze the sky. When the air raid warning sounds, my great-grandparents slide Grannie down the stairs in the drawer that is her cradle so they can evacuate to the Anderson shelter in their backyard faster. In the snug corrugated metal shelter buried four feet in the yard, she shakes in terror as dramatic aerial dogfights demolish nearby houses and blaze the sky with red and orange. Grannie doesn't realise Germans are people until she overhears her mother talking to her neighbour about a German pilot being shot down. Until then, she thinks Germans are monsters who will kill everyone.

In the south of Wales, when Grannie is two, an eight-year-old boy is at the cinema where a news item shows a German plane crashing in smoke and flames. As the pilot bails out, his parachute touches the plane as it opens, starting a small fire on the chute that plummets him to his death. Everyone shouts, laughs, and cheers. The boy does too.

Until his mum grabs him by the face and chides, "Don't you laugh and cheer when you see a brave man die."

"B-b-b-but it's a German, Mam."

"It's someone's son, someone's brother, someone's sweetheart, maybe someone's father..."

The young boy swallows as his dad chimes in. "All this hatred, it's not the way things should be. If circumstances were different, that's someone who we might be proud to call friend."

Decades later, the boy becomes my grandfather. He speaks of an ancient Welsh tradition in which a harmony played by the Hand of God pervades the universe. It is called "Y Delyn Aur"—"The Golden Harp". He swears he almost heard it in the cinema that day.

The following year, my great-grandfather's piano is carried into their London street for a party to celebrate the end of the war. Though it is scarce, everyone pools together food. On the same piano protecting Grannie's birth, my great-grandfather summons calming melodies with fingers dancing over black and white keys. With music, the truth of being human ripples through sonic waves intertwined with complex emotions that give hope and revitalization.

*

Twelve years later, Grannie meets the gentle, grown-up boy with deep-brown eyes. She asks her friend to tell him that she's afraid of walking home from church alone. She isn't really. Grannie is brave. Many decades later, Grandad reflects on that night. He says the harp of gold played just outside their range of hearing as he walked Grannie home.

Eventually they settle down in a two-storey home with my father and his three brothers. In 1969, they lose their youngest son to an acute, symptomless viral pneumonia. The grief is debilitating. It prompts them to move to Australia in hope of a better life.

Papa grows from an adventurous six-year-old boy who—unbeknownst to Grannie—catches a train ten minutes down the line to buy a toy car with his pocket money, to an intelligent and inquisitive young man with an infectious cheeky charm.

Mama grows up in Perth's virescent hills with three younger sisters. When she is twelve, a *bang bam smack* on the church roof has her glimpsing a group of boys running away down a narrow alley. Papa is one of those rock-throwing boys. Six years later, he appears at the local youth group. They become best friends before realising they are in love. At twenty-one years old, in the same church he once ran from, grey-eyed Papa marries gorgeous, auburn-haired Mama.

As newlyweds, Papa's telecommunication engineering work moves them to stinking-hot Port Hedland and then stunning Kununurra, where my sister is born. While red-haired, blue-eyed Emily starts walking, Papa scores with the Department of Defence, and they move to the UK for training.

On Papa's 28th birthday in 1990, Mama gifts him the conception of me. The following month, when I am the size of a grain of rice in Mama's belly, Papa's work relocates them again to Hong Kong.

At 12:27 a.m. on April 20, 1991—nine days early—I am born in a speedy two-hour labour. Later in life, Laula and I discover that we are born on each other's due dates. Nine days early, I am eager to pioneer and explore. Nine days late, Laula is content moving slowly while the umbilical cord nourishes her with sustenance. It's a typical Aries and Taurus combo.

In our top-floor apartment tiering down a mountain on Hong Kong Island, Mama watches hundreds of neon skyscrapers bank deep shimmering waters and illuminate the night sky. Seventeen million people congregate in the densely populated pocket. Each morning, thick fogs sweep in and blanket the city in white. Foghorns bellow warnings to gigantic tankers as ocean liners bob and creak with the backdrop of lush mountains and sprawling parks.

The confluence of Chinese history and British colonisation renders an intercontinental atmosphere with Eastern temples, Chinese wood carvings, and 20th century French windows opening into dirty streets. Night markets bustle with exotic textures, tastes, and smells. Some are mouth-watering. Mama describes others as "cooking with thousand-year-old oil". Cantonese fills the air. Businessmen, expats, and fishermen haggle at stalls offering cheap technology alongside live meat markets. The first years of my life are sheltered and happy.

In August 1992, we move again. This time to sun-drenched, windy Geraldton on Jambinu country in Western Australia's sparsely populated Mid West. Papa's work has relocated him to what locals call "the spy base".

Not long after moving, Mama trips on some buckled carpet on the stairs and drops me in a series of thudding tumbles. The white cockatoo in the front door's stained-glass window watches Mama slip towards where I've plonked in a crying pile. Milliseconds before squishing me, she somersaults over me and breaks a bone in her foot. Miraculously, I am okay. Actually, I'm better than okay. Without the constraints of Mama's hands which she needs to manoeuvre her crutches, I am free to run away and explore.

As I grow from a toddler to preschooler, gymnastics, jazz, and tap dance become a release for my limitless zest. Later in life I am diagnosed, but not medicated, for ADHD. My love of learning motivates a fierce focus, so long as I burn off my excess energy during schoolyard breaks.

Every Christmas and Easter, we venture to Guilderton—a small coastal town 100 kilometres north of Perth, originally known as Gabbadah, meaning "mouthful of water" to Yued Noongars—where my father's parents live in a handmade, two-storey wooden home. Grandad hires canoes to tourists and keeps some in the silver creek at the bottom of a bush track across the road for us to paddle across the river to the sand dunes we dub "the desert".

Our grandparents nurture us to grow with high morals and a peaceful disposition. At night, we walk their dog with Grandad. He teaches us the constellations twinkling in the night sky and encourages us to reach for the stars. By day, Emily leads my younger cousin, Stacey, and I through imaginary realms where paperbark trees and boogie boards became horses.

Upstream from my grandparents' home is the Moore River Native Settlement where, earlier in the 20th century, Aboriginal people were segregated into inhumane living conditions and forced to "assimilate" into society in attempted genocide that was against international law. As young children growing up in privilege and peace, we do not know our nation's cruel truth because the white-washed version of history we are taught in school ignores Indigenous worldviews and the rich, sophisticated, diverse culture of our First Nations peoples who have called Australia home for over 65,000 years. It is many years before I fathom the importance of truth-telling on a national scale to enable Australia to make amends for its past and move towards a fair and reconciled future.

*Music is a universal language
conveying our soul's expression.*

One day Mama brings a drum kit home to repair the skins. She is teaching woodwind instruments at schools around town. The kit calls to me. Perched in the centre of our playroom, it compels me to pick up two sticks and bang out what Mama proclaims is a professional synchronizing a beat. I soon have my first piano lesson and win competitions on the same wooden stage that I prance and pirouette on in my end of year dance performances.

Our two-story, white-brick-fenced home is enriched with sound. Mama's flute hums poetry in soft, high-pitched winds. Sometimes the golden keys of her saxophone wrap me in deep, sultry spells. Emily's shrill clarinet smooths into reedy, mellow tones. And Papa's trumpet tootles a metallic brilliance in the Sierra band that marches around Guilderton playing carols at Christmas.

I am my mother's empathy, my father's hyperactivity, and both of their playfulness, studiousness, and curiosity for life.

I am seven years old at the beginning of 1999. My best friend, Zane, is a scruffy brown-haired boy with a mischievous smile. He is always absent from school photos. I question why this is so as we play Lego one weekend. His mum—a crusty, tattooed, cigarette-reeking woman—pokes her head around the corner, stretching the telephone's spiral wire until it is straight as she observes us play with pirate ships while she yarns. He says she doesn't want visual traces of him at school. She barks at him to never say that again, then asks me to keep the knowledge quiet.

Later that afternoon, Zane and I play in a hollowed-out, cement cylinder sand pit in the empty school playground. A young teen marches our way. Zane waves hello. They are friends. I usually like Zane's friends. Sometimes I hang with his neighbourhood pals. They are cheeky and rough, but always kind. I don't recognise this boy. Nor does he seem nice. The boy taunts Zane because he is playing with a girl. Zane says that I am his best friend and he likes playing with me. This seems to provoke the boy.

"Awwww yeah, is that so? If you like playing with her so much, then why don't you have sex with her?"

He spits the words like they taste bad. I don't understand what he's saying, but my heart pounds like a war drum. I peer at Zane, wide-eyed.

He looks at me tenderly, then faces the boy. "No," Zane declines. "I'm not going to do that."

The boy scoffs, then demands that Zane does as he says.

Eventually Zane throws sand at the boy, and he walks away.

Zane takes my hand in his, and reassures, "Don't worry. You're safe with me."

I don't understand what sex is, but my heart explodes with appreciation for Zane's reverence to me and refusal to do me harm. Years later I comprehend the potency of my friend sticking up for what he believes is right and respecting my rights to my body.

At seven years old, Zane shows me more manhood than some adults ever will.

Around the same time, in our new cul-de-sac rental, a troubled student bombards Mama with abusive phone calls because she didn't receive the loan saxophone that she wanted from the school's music program. As the phone calls escalate into threatening letters, Mama's doctor prescribes her a concoction of pharmaceuticals and labels her depressed. Mama later admits that she never felt depressed. She is medicated to control the panic attacks that make her feel like she is dying.

One morning, I watch Mama swallow her daily dose from the kitchen bench.

Her brow is furrowed beneath her waist-length hair. I love the way it falls down her slender frame and covers her heart like a thick curtain. At church, I used to flick her auburn drapes over her shoulders and press my ear against her chest while she sang. Her angelic voice echoed and vibrated inside her rib cage like a joyous choir. With her heartbeat holding the beat, I was cocooned in her safe hold.

I wonder how her insides are doing these days.

"If you jump up and down, will you rattle?" I ask, scooping Coco Pops into my mouth.

Her solemn expression bursts into a radiant smile she has lost but neither of us have forgotten.

As autumn cools to winter, anxiety spirals Mama further into a dense and shaky confine. Her world is unruly. For Mama, this is terrifying. Without her safety net of feeling in control, she struggles for balance on a frayed tightrope with nothing to catch her.

One day, she returns from the grocery store a hyperventilating mess after spotting the mother of the girl who is abusing her. The aggression has developed into legal threats for defamation. Mama is trembling. She feels unsupported by the education system, and this demeans her self-worth and passionate work ethic into feeling like a failure. Mama later learns skills to resolve conflict and manage her emotions. At the time, her support network is thin with her best friend's recent passing to breast cancer. She is prescribed Xanax to manage her physiological reactions and warned that she will get addicted to the medication. This allows her to mentally prepare for the inevitable withdrawals. The Xanax threads a safety net under Mama's shaky tightrope, but it is talk of moving to Perth that floats into our conversations at dinner that helps Mama see the ladder leading back to solid ground.

Halfway through the year, Papa lands a job as a telecommunication engineer for an oil company in Papua New Guinea after a decade working in intelligence. This is Australia prior to September 11th, and work at the spy base is winding down. As we pack life into dozens of cardboard boxes and move 414 kilometres south to Perth—the world's most isolated city where Papa will fly in and out to work—Mama's mental health improves. It physically removes her from the situation's toxicity and allows her to rebuild.

We adjust to the sunny city in our two-storey townhouse rental. Papa works month-on-month-off in the dangerous highland jungle. He returns home with stories of Indigenous tribes spearing people and two bodyguards accompanying him through gritty Port Moresby. Mama works reception at a retirement home. Sometimes her smile twinkles, but her once-glowing eyes are still occupied by a sad, faraway look. She triumphs through the withdrawals that come from weaning off Xanax. Then comes the next challenge: her family.

Mama's family are notorious for interpersonal conflict and no emotional intelligence. Her parents talk *at* you, not *with* you. It was common for my cold grandfather to strike his daughters with his belt buckle. When I am four or five, my grandfather smacks me for being my joyful and bouncy self. Mama is ropable. She instructs he never lay a hand on me again. He disputes her clear articulation of consent. Mama asserts that we will never be left alone with him, adamant to protect Emily and me from his harsh corporal punishment.

As children, Mama's three younger sisters were all sexually assaulted by outside individuals. Most tragic was the rape of one of the twins by her friend's older brother. After years of silence and substance abuse, Mama's sister finally disclosed what happened to the family. Instead of providing a safe and loving space for her to open into, my grandparents brushed it off and invalidated her trauma; thus denying her the first steps of healing. Mama emotionally distanced herself from her family after she married. Until she experienced a mentally healthy, supportive family she didn't understand there was anything unusual about her family's dynamics. When I hear of them denying a rape victim—*their own daughter*—a voice and place of protection, I too keep them beyond arm's reach.

As summer dries and crisps the trees, Mama and Papa buy a shabby 1960s house slouching on an overgrown block. It is a purchase based on land value and an eventual knock-down-rebuild. While nearby mansions trail towards the ocean, cockroaches crawl through our new home and rats run amok in the roof. Sometimes I laze in the musty scent of our wide breezeway, enchanted by miniature whirlwinds spontaneously spinning to life in the courtyard outside. The spiralling vortex of dust and leaves remind me of the way my head feels when I wake from night terrors that sometimes haunt my sleep. In the parasomnia episodes, my mouth tastes like salt, and I feel like I'm standing on a giant black canvas while someone scribbles circles around me with polychromatic crayons. Like the wild gyrations within and around me in my half-awake-half-asleep state, suddenly the vertical columns of air pirouetting out the window dissipate into invisible air currents that sweep through the rope swing dangling from a rotting tuart tree in our backyard.

I miss my friends from Geraldton and the clean taste of fresh country air. I don't like this snobby western suburb. When Papa is home, we climb onto the roof and watch the sunset over the shimmering Indian Ocean. I follow his calculated footsteps along a row of screws piercing the corrugated asbestos roof. Then we perch on the cement-filled chimney as golden streaks whisk the sky into an idealistic dream.

I continue weekly gymnastics and piano classes but replace dance with Kumon—a home-based, after-school learning program that enhances academic ability. As 1999 rolls into 2000, I receive distinctions in nationwide education competitions. I enjoy school for the learning, but by the end of the year I spend recess and lunch in the library alone. I am intelligent and eccentric. I've given up trying to befriend the cliquey group of girls who exclude me by running away yelling, "Loser, loner," as they shape their fingers in an L across their forehead, oftentimes using the wrong hand so the L points back at them: *low, lousy, lily-livered.*

In retrospect, the bullying is a blessing. It teaches me to unpick the subtleties of human behaviour; to understand what prompts exclusion and navigate ways to avoid it. Over time, it ignites a strong value within me to never allow those around me to feel unsafe, rejected or tormented. Over time, I become what psychologists call a high self-monitor. This enables me to regulate my behaviour and mould myself into different environments with ease. Nonetheless, these future learnings don't make the oppression easier in the moment. Emily starts high school and is suddenly too cool to hang out with me. Mama works overtime. Papa is playful but absent half the year. Crippled by loneliness, I fill the void by reading. Fictional worlds render mysteries where protagonists find justice and I connect with humanity through paper pages.

The density of school is brightened by quarterly holidays, where I pack life into a small blue suitcase and either venture to Baptist youth camp or meet Stacey in Guilderton for a week of mischievous play. Mapping soft dunes with our footprints, we imitate Indian war cries as thin air transports us into make-believe worlds where we spy on robbers speeding along the river in their motorized boats.

As wildflowers blossom with sweet, fruity smells, Emily performs in a school music concert that has us all to bed late. Papa is in Papua New Guinea, so I crawl into bed with Mama, enjoying the tangibility of human connection as we play footsies beneath the blankets. In the morning, Mama's radio alarm crackles with the solemn voice of a news reporter instead of cheesy music. I start chitchatting about the performance. Mama hushes me. Her eyes widen under a furrowed brow as the reporter announces that two planes have crashed into the World Trade Center, sending New York City's iconic twin towers crumbling to the ground.

In Australia, it is the morning after September 11 where a series of airline hijackings in America shake the world with fear. Later that day, more news emerges of other hijacked flights. The day subsequently becomes known as the deadliest terrorist attack to occur on American soil. In the years that follow, the word *terrorism* runs rampant with enhanced surveillance, airport security, and military deportation to the Middle East. At school, my white-cheeked teacher instructs us to write our thoughts of the event on a blank A4 piece of paper that I never see again. I imagine future generations reading our words. Is this the start of WWIII?

My ten-year-old utopian world bursts with a gripping fear of war exploding. Four hijacked planes cause thousands of deaths. In two weeks, we are flying to the UK. Growing up in privilege and peace, I learn much later of the Rwandan genocide, breakup of Yugoslav Federation, the African World Wars in Congo, and Civil Wars in Sierra Leone, Iraq, Algeria, and Burundi. The tiny slice of history I learn in school offers patriarchal views of imperialism that silence the oppressed and sustain institutionalised racism.

I learn the fractions and formulas of mathematics that threads the tapestry of our existence; the poetry of physics that connects everything and everyone. But I am not taught the beauty of connection, the power of communication, the gift of self-expression. I ponder how life would be different if our schools provided the tools to cultivate emotional intelligence. My generation knows a global epidemic of diminishing mental health. Our sheer IQ focus hinders the growth of socioemotional skills that empower individuals to navigate grief, distinguish/express healthy boundaries, and support loved ones disintegrating into the doom and gloom of dense emotional tangles.

I do not learn first aid, how to do my taxes, or what human rights are. As westerners we're taught to prioritise our individualism and hold our opinions as sacred as fact, yet I see a culture of disconnection with people shackled by fear of expressing their true feelings and needs. Our education system prepares us for a capitalistic society that commodifies humans. Somewhere, somehow, humanity is lost in institutionalised pragmatism.

Stomach acid burns my throat as we board our layover flight to Singapore. We rest in the clean, green city overnight as the pungent stench of bile pervades our hotel room with my anxiety of commercial air travel post 9/11.

In the UK, autumn welcomes us with crisp, mulchy winds and drizzly rains. Eventually my stomach stops lurching and the colour returns to my face as the novelty of being in the chilly, overcast country prevails. We explore medieval castles and quaint cobblestone towns with second and third cousins who embody the cheeky Sierra charm. When the bitter grey morning arrives for us to board a roaring jumbo jet to Hong Kong, a different energy is upon me. Fear no longer burdens me. I am confident. I feel ease.

Immersed in a peculiar, foreign-but-shouldn't-it-be-familiar feeling, I eye beggars stooped at screeching train stations jam-packed with people. I stop. I want to help. Then Mama points out their expensive shoes and explains that Hong Kong law requires beggars to have a begging license.

"How can beggars afford a license if they truly are in need?"

Mama looks at me with all-knowing eyes. "Exactly," she says.

A phoenix never really dies. It rebirths and rejuvenates as the cycle continues. Sometimes it's hard to remember that. Especially when you're on fire.

Back at school, the bullying magnifies as the year strings to an end. The kids feed off me like parasites constantly needing to boost their ego at the expense of my own. I do not disclose my agony to Mama and Papa. I am too ashamed. In retrospect, I wonder if my hesitation has roots in not wanting to cause Mama extra woe. I also see that my hyper-independence stems from my people-can't-hurt-me-if-I-don't-need-them belief created as a defence mechanism to the exclusion.

As summer barbeques and freshly mowed lawns permeate the air, I start percussion lessons with an ex-music student from my future high school. His deep-brown eyes are present with mine for the next two years as he teaches me classical percussion, marimba, and kit. As I tap out the rudimentary rhythms of jazz and rock, drum rolls and paradiddles give sound to my suffering and ignite purpose in my misery.

I dread the first day of Year 6. Dragging my feet into a classroom I know has no love for me, I grit my teeth and prepare myself for what will be the worst year yet. Puberty starts early for me, and my peers taunt my blemished skin. I wake early to smother my face with foundation. Smearing chemical-smelling paste onto my skin, I conceal my sadness with my acne. I anticipate every potential torment awaiting me then correlate a plan to avoid, manage, or backfire each preconceived scene.

As the year rolls on, the bullying becomes violent, with a group of guys chucking rocks, nuts, and balls at me with painful *thuds*. I start navigating different routes home from school to avoid being their prey. A burning knot cements in my stomach with every cruel word and hard rock thrown, but I discover hidden paths amid the weaving web of neighbourhood streets. This heightened spatial cognition comes in handy later in life. When Papa is home, he meets me on the edge of the school oval where we sword fight with fallen pine needles, laughing as we play. I relish our time together. I miss him when he goes.

The kids are cowards. They don't dare tease me on their own. When they do, I stand up for myself and voice their misdeeds. They freeze as their eyes dart from my piercing gaze. Then, when they are back in the pack, they chisel away at me again. I don't show fear. Perhaps that's why they provoke me. I am a target now, but this cultivates resilience. Unknowingly, they are teaching me to be strong, to be brave, to *feel* fear but *not* let it rule me.

I articulate my pain through music and journalling. Along with weekly percussion lessons, I pick up trumpet at school. Airy buzzes from sore lips soon tootle into royal tunes, sweeping my awareness into metallic melodies that wrap me in harmonic spells. Every day after school, I play trumpet for thirty minutes then practise percussion for an hour with the drum kit and massive percussion box that Mama's youngest sister lends me. Pressing pedals, slamming cymbals, and stroking the snare, I feel alive and connected to a creative force that expands beyond my ego. Each drag, flam, tap, and roll softens my agony. It taps out nasty words and threads a web of silky clarity. With eyes fixated on the dried-up grapevine outside the window, I enter a trance as bonks and booms echo in my mind with meticulous lucidity. I am certain that music saved me.

In 2002 I am in Year 6—my second-to-last year of primary school. One sunny afternoon, while the teacher is supervising students outside, I sit in the corner of the classroom journalling. A girl approaches and badgers me about what I'm writing. She has two troublesome brothers, and her parents are navigating a divorce. Her recent behaviour is more thorny than usual.

I ignore her and continue scribbling words. She demands I hand her my journal. I don't. I give an icy stare. This compels her to snatch it and run outside. Half a dozen kids in the classroom applaud. Body aflame with impassioned fury, I sprint after her to the bench of backpacks outside where I seize my journal and shove it in my bag. She lunges towards me. I hover my hands over the unzipped opening, but she grabs my wrists, twisting and crunching my bones as I lock her into a deathly glare. I yell for her to let go. She squeezes tighter. Wrists bulging, I let go of my zipper. She releases her grip. Violent red handprints scorch my skin as she dives into my bag, pulls out the paper pages mapping my inner terrain, and flicks through like they're slices of mouldy bread. My stomach buckles. I am slashed open, raw and red. When she's finished reading, she slams the notebook into my chest and saunters back into the classroom. For weeks, the kids jeer my own words against me.

Ideas innovate my mind of feigning sickness to avoid the toxicity of school. Sometimes I phone Mama at 8 a.m. already at work. I complain of an upset stomach as I intermittently pour water into the toilet in mighty splashes. Other times, I rub Mama's red lipstick into the birthmark on my right temple while she is in the shower. The small overgrowth of blood vessels naturally reddens when I am overtired or unwell. I then strategically place myself in her path with body language deliberately weakened. More often than not, my "illnesses" are believable. So much so, my report card reads: *Jess is a very capable student, but her many absences are beginning to reflect in her work.*

In an attempt to control my harrowing world, I monitor what I eat with the scrutiny of post 9/11 airport security. I skip breakfast, eat a small tub of yoghurt for lunch, and arrive home with stomach growling. I don't want to bring extra attention to myself by eating something too healthy, too unhealthy, too strange, etc. My peers take anything as fuel for their vicious fire. As daylight dwindles, I binge on fruit and junk food, unaware that high levels of fructose and sugar inflame my gut and impair my mood. Unknowingly, I make matters worse by adopting unhealthy habits.

Halloween rolls round with toffee apples, gingerbread cookies, and pumpkin pie infusing the schoolyard with the smell of cinnamon sticks, vanilla extract, orange peel, and clove. The spicy sweetness becomes haunting when I catch whispers of a plot to egg my house at night. At home, I peep my head outside every half hour and scan the street. Nothing. Midchew on a baked potato at a dinner, a *crack* on the driveway jolts me in my seat as I catch Papa's eye. The next *thud and bam* shake the windows. I feel like there is nothing protecting me; nothing between me and my perpetrators; like the eggs slam against me and drench me in sticky goo.

Mama and Emily look shocked and confused. Papa catches the sadness in my eyes I am trying to disguise. After another *clunk, clap,* and *crash* he leaps to his feet and paces to the door. I am on his tail. Outside, a dozen broken eggshells splatter across our driveway, accompanied by juvenile giggles shaking the bushes across the road. I am a raw egg smashed to pieces on the ground. My hard exterior is broken. My gooey insides burn and churn. The bullying has violated the inner world of my diary and the safe haven of my home. This doesn't just affect me now. It is impacting my family and my home. Tirelessly, I yearn to be loved and accepted for me.

That night, as I slide my fluffy blue journal into a dark corner of my cupboard, a realisation trickles over me with velvet waves. One day I will write a book to empower others. I will share my pain and the strength it gave to ignite hope and fortitude in others. With my newfound purpose, I become resilient to the rawness of life—for a few weeks. Meaning creates hope that lifts me from discomfort and fear into a courageous willingness to face each day.

With a replenished spirit, I embark on an end-of-year school trip to Wadjemup, known by the Whadjuk Noongar people as "place across the water where the spirits are". By colonial settler society it is called Rottnest Island. Ringed by white sandy beaches and secluded turquoise bays with small furry quokkas hopping and bounding through the trees, the seemingly idyllic car-free paradise was once a massive barbaric prison. Here, Aboriginal men were chained and beaten to death, condemned for laws subjected upon them by colonists; laws they didn't understand for the sovereignty of their own lore was denied in 1788 when Captain James Cook declared all First Nations peoples to be British subjects despite being instructed to treat Indigenous peoples with respect and establish partnerships. When compared with New Zealand, USA, and Canada, the United Nations found that our First Nations people in Australia are significantly more disempowered *because* they were never given a treaty. This is despite international law—both now and at the time of colonisation—recognising Indigenous peoples' rights to the land as well as every other Commonwealth nation having a treaty with the Crown, thus making the "fair" nation of Australia an anomaly. Of course, I didn't know this at the time. I didn't know that the largest known burial ground of Indigenous Australians was *unmarked* and resided under an old campground. I didn't know that prior to the colonisation of Walyalup (Fremantle) in 1829, Whadjuk people witnessed Wadjemup (Rottnest Island) as part of the mainland before the last ice age. This knowledge was passed down through oral stories for millennia—a tradition still present today. Australia's colonial history is blatant in white man's perception of Rottnest Island as a Utopian playground, while for Aboriginal people it is a rampaged sacred site of maltreatment and mourning. At the time, I did not know this because our white-washed version of history marginalises Indigenous worldviews, thus denying the cathartic understanding of truth-telling to foster genuine reconciliation.

That being said, a strange discomfort encapsulates me in my sleep. I feel pain on the fringe of my conscious mind that seems to extend beyond my subjective experience, but I have no words or knowledge to articulate the perplexing sting. The next day, I curl up on my top bunk in the girls' dormitory for an afternoon nap. One of the more gracious girls slinks in and informs me of a plan to lure me away from adult eyes and egg me in the basketball courts. When the bitch who read my diary invites me to go for a walk with her that evening, I feign interest then monitor her swift skips to inform the boys. This confirms the rumours are true. Instead of going with her, I approach a parent and tell them what is happening, wretched that doing so will inevitably magnetise more torment my way.

In the following days, my strength shatters, and I contemplate suicide. I think of jumping off the roof that Papa and I sometimes climb. That probably won't kill me though. I'll likely just break a bone. I think of running away. But where will I go? Finally, the solution comes in the clunky third drawer where a sharp kitchen knife glints with temptation of ending it all. The thought lingers for days before I unlock the front door after a distressing day to a bleak, dark, empty home. I need sympathy. I need solicitude. I need safety. I need support. Instead, I have malice and mistreatment by mindless menaces. Third drawer ajar, I press the knife against my heart. It pounds against the metal, knocking for me to feel something. *Ba bump. Thump thump.* Anything. Tears well, but I don't let them fall. My rib cage feels tight and constricted. I ponder how hard I must push for the pointed, metal blade to bleed me dry.

Goodbye, cruel world. Ten. Nine. Eight...

Keys clatter outside.

Seven...

The front door clicks.

I don't understand. Emily isn't due home for another half hour. I shove the silver steel knife back in the drawer and run to my room. Here, I wrap myself in the inky darkness of my feathered duvet and dissolve into complete surrender. It is the kind bound in despair, but also coiled in hope. To this day, I have no idea why my sister arrived home early. Perhaps it was a twist of divine intervention that bought me more time.

As I stride across the freshly mowed oval on my first day of Year 7, the stomach knot hampering me for three years loosens. I sense the school's social dynamics changing. The sun showers warmth. The air tastes crisper somehow. In class, a vivacious, blonde American with googly eyes is the focal point of everyone's awareness. She is observant, self-assured, and doesn't belittle others to make herself feel big. Though the girls swoon over her, she quickly fatigues with their cliquey drama and skips my way, where she cracks down on my negative self-talk. For so long, putting myself down has been a coping mechanism that stops others from throwing harsh words because I beat them to it. With her help, I see myself with fresh eyes. As my inner vista shifts, even the mean girls note my tall, slender physique and pretty face—though I still smear it with foundation.

At the start of the year, my future high school—boasting the state's largest and most successful specialist music program—accepts me into a small band of Year 7 students from surrounding schools. I am the cool chick swinging a bag of drumsticks and mallets that hold the beat for the rest of the band. From that first week of band practise, my fears of high school dissipate into the green room's cauldron of sweaty nerves steeping from twenty-five other eleven- and twelve-year-old's. Dara, a fast-developing clarinettist who is later sexually assaulted by the same man who violates me, subsequently tells me I have a mysterious air. The other kids allure towards me with a strange magnetism that is perplexing for me to swallow. My magnetic field is changing poles. No longer repelling, I draw people in.

Many of them are commencing high school with me the following year, and we start hanging out on weekends. One girl even convinces me to do a six-week modelling course with her. This shifts the way the kids treat me at school. Suddenly, my classmates rank me high in the picking of sports teams after years of scrunched-up faces when I am chosen last. Suddenly, they utter sincere apologies and start inviting me to their parties. Suddenly, the large proportion of kids attending high school with me the following year seek my friendship. I accept it with a forgiving yet discerning heart.

In the sweltering six-week summer holidays whizzing into Year 8, I start menstruating. Confidence born from will, I decide high school won't be like primary school. Present to my empowered heart and the resilience in my hazel eyes, I stride with a dignified stance. I am writing a new story.

"I can hear the birds again. I can feel the sun. I can think about a happy future."

- 2004 journal entry

Tugging my navy-blue skirt towards my knee, I sling my backpack over my shoulders and stroll into the maze of classrooms drenched with pungent pubescent hormones and floral deodorant spray. Two of my former bullies ask me to accompany them on our first day. I graciously agree, then wave down my bandmates amongst the dense, chattering buzz of several hundred voices congregated outside the canteen. Curious, innocent, and judgemental eyes assign faces into different levels of the social hierarchy that will mould, morph, and mangle over the next five years.

Then, a forty-something-year-old woman claps her hands, silencing the monotone ensemble of twelve-year-old's chatting like gossiping throngs. She welcomes us with the metaphor of big fish in a little pond becoming small fish in a larger pond.

"In five years," she says, "you'll look back on this moment and gasp at how fast high school flies by."

Consoling the map on my school diary, I trot to class with my Indian bandmate and Kim, her half-Vietnamese, half-Caucasian friend. Kim and I bond over us both entering the school on three scholarships for music, netball, and the accelerated learning program—resulting in the exact same timetable for the next three years. From there on, we are inseparable.

Kim's seamless face is beautifully sculpted with protruding almond eyes, a tiny button nose, and a well-defined cupid's bow. Brunette locks fall down her slender physique to her lower back. I relish her fiery, no-bullshit attitude and the cheeky expressions that dimple her cheeks when she says something darkly humorous or witty, which is often. I am astonished that she too was formerly bullied.

Kim and I are mirrors, yearning to excel with straight A grades while crushing on boys. Fate has flung us together, answering both our prayers for a loyal friend to unwaveringly stick feathers in our back through high school. Every recess I buy us a treat from the canteen. Every lunch we share her chicken and cucumber sandwich before roaming the school grounds. Liaising with musos, tomboys, mean girls, hipsters, class clowns, science nerds, artists, and skaters, we savour diversity in a dynamic array of friendships. Not attaching to one specific group is safer to avoid exclusion. It distances us from drama, allowing us to drift onto the next group when tension starts to boil. With retrospect I recognise a vast contrast in my social skills from Year 4 to Year 8. The bullying sensitised me to the subtleties of human interaction, allowing me to alter my behaviour in accordance to others temperaments and needs while creating safety for others experiencing social persecution.

As 2004 wilts then warms, we move to a townhouse rental in laid-back, coastal Scarborough while we demolish and rebuild a lavish new home. Our new neighbours yell and scream in a ramshackle house slouching in a barren yard. Their electricity is regularly cut off. Sometimes we find extension cords plugged into our power outlets after weekends away. One day my band friend Dara is over when a fight erupts in a frenzy of angry, grating words. They are alcoholics, I explain. Dara shakes her head and says it's something worse.

At the end of Year 8, my Year 9 friend Mariana approaches me after band practise with a confession. I breathe into my heart. I know what is coming but allow her the space to tell me she likes me as more than a friend.

"Thank you for your authenticity…I admire your guts to speak the truth," I say. Her tanned, freckled face looks hopeful behind short brunette curls.

"I don't feel that way about you, but I *really* value our friendship. I don't want to lose that."

Her chest collapses slightly.

I place my palms around her elbows and peer into her stunning green eyes. "Truly. You're a special friend to me. I'm just not into girls," I clarify.

She smiles graciously and thanks me for my honesty. It hurts now but bounds our connection with trust, truth, and tact. We go on to maintain a sentimental friendship with safety to disclose our deepest secrets. In the following years, Mariana is an important source of support and reliable information in my case against the man who is soon to steal Dara then Kim's virginity before narrowing in on me.

Midway through 2005, all Year 9, 10, and 11 music students merge into one giant choir in preparation for an International Tour through Austria and the UK. With a lower vocal range, Kim and I are placed in the alto section. At five foot six, I am placed in the back row. This makes it easy to duck down, squeeze under the tiered wooden stage, and crawl to the centre back where I knock loudly beneath the bass section's feet. Kim later informs me that four dozen eyes dart to the dusty platform. I hear the conductor yelling for the boys to pay attention as I slink back to Kim, stifling an entertained giggle. I like making her laugh. Her home life is dense and serrated with an absent father, spiteful stepdad, and distressed mother dependent on Kim to help care for her younger stepsiblings. She doesn't talk about it often, and I don't pry, but I know there is good reason we're inseparable at school yet never together on weekends. She is hurting. I am her safe haven.

Towards the end of the year we move into our grand, freshly built home surrounded by a garden of yellow sand. Mama and Papa decide we will paint the walls ourselves to lower costs—resulting in a bare, carpetless home intended for just a few months. Months trickle into years as September brings news that has us all feeling like the house's interior—shivery and dreary.

I find out on a hauntingly beautiful spring day that bursts with rich hues and sophisticated blooms. I am playing a sonorous four-mallet melody on the marimba I was gifted for my fourteenth birthday, six months earlier. Just as I get into a mellow groove resonating with earthy velvet tones, Mama requests a family chat at our large dining table. Something is bubbling. I've sensed it in my parents' hushed whispers. I squash my hands under my silky-smooth thighs as they disclose Papa has cancer. A rare type of non-Hodgkin's lymphoma. I later discover there is a 50 percent chance he will be alive in one year's time.

My world crumbles into Papa's downcast grey gaze. I keep my eyes dry. Strong. I must be strong. I must be responsible for my own emotions. Mama and Papa have enough to deal with. Trudging up to my dull, colourless room, I close the door and let the first warm tear fall. Salty drops drench me in despair. I don't cry. I weep. The pain comes in waves. I wonder if I'll cry myself dry. Sometimes my sobs stifle me, and a strange relief pierces into my gasps. *It's okay. Everything is going to be okay. Life never throws us curveballs that we can't overcome.* Then I think of life without Papa, and my feelings drown out my rational mind in rasping tremors that undulate with heartache and devastation.

When I'm done, I sponge my puffy eyes, waltz downstairs, squeeze Papa close, and tell him I love him.

Renewal is the result of every ruin.

My journals subsequently explode with poignant expression. I am growing with the pain, but my inner vista is thick and thorny when Grannie is diagnosed with lung cancer two weeks later. We are all jarred and jagged as life becomes a sequence of white-knuckle hospital visits, praying each Doctor bears good news.

Whilst Grannie has surgery to remove the cancerous tumours, Papa starts chemotherapy. Watching Grannie gasp and wheeze into an oxygen mask post-surgery, I wonder if there is a link between her and Papa's diagnosis. In traditional Chinese medicine, the lungs are associated with the manifestation of grief in one's body. Grannie has always suffered from weak lungs, stemming from her traumatic upbringing amid WWII. And yet the timing of it all feels uncanny.

Thankfully, Grannie makes a full recovery as Papa enters his second round of chemo. On a mellow, sun-drenched afternoon, Mama shaves Papa's hair beside the motionless rotary washing line. His short dark curls are thick and fluffy. He world is immobile, and we are stationary in this tranquil snippet of time. Papa smiles as Mama snaps a before and after photo with me by his side. Externally, his strength and stamina wither as the days warm, but Papa's inner light shines bright—unwavering, untainted, unafraid.

Mama, off medication for five years, is monitored closely by her doctor. With cultivated resilience she holds the family together. Papa does too. They are best friends. They've always told each other everything, but with his diagnosis there are truths Papa hides out of concern for how Mama will cope. From my perspective there are no cracks. In truth, Papa is close to death. One afternoon Mama picks Papa up from a session of chemotherapy. Papa is quiet. He retreats to the backyard then proceeds to smash a lump of concrete with a sledgehammer. He is there for hours. He's just discovered that a guy who started chemotherapy with him—same cancer, both in stage four, same treatment—has died after his first round. Papa pants and sweats and shatters the concrete to tiny pieces. His muscles burn. He is terrified. He stays silent about why until Emily's wedding two years later. There, he lets Mama pre-read his reception speech. Mama collapses in tears. Unbeknownst to any of us, as Papa shatters that course concrete slab into craggy fragments, he is grief-stricken that he may never be able to walk his daughters down the aisle.

Papa's illness changes their relationship. It isn't worse, just different. Up until that point, Papa was Mama's security blanket. Overnight, she is faced with the potentiality of bringing up her daughters alone. Mental closure is Mama's way of dealing with unpleasantries, uncertainty, things which she cannot control. Without shutting Papa out, she lessens her dependence and becomes more self-reliant. She describes the experience as character building and subsequently notes, "You either give up or you accept you can't change things and grow."

The summer holidays bridging 2005 into 2006 sprinkle hope that Papa's chemotherapy will work. In my dorm at Baptist youth camp, a bubbly blonde with heavy makeup unpacks bulky bags on my favourite far-corner top bunk. She sings hello and introduces herself as Polly Jane. We start chatting, and, well she doesn't stop. Initially, her incessant need to talk annoys me. After a few days, her vivacious, *ooh ahh wow* mannerisms become amusing. Her innocent heart oozes sunshine that soothes my pain.

Our twenty-something-year-old dorm leader, Amber, joins in on camp pranks and speaks to us as adults. She answers my questions about religion and spirituality with a realness that renders goose bumps of truth on my pale, privileged skin. I don't understand why there are so many religions in the world—each claiming the others are wrong, pitting people against each other. Through history, it seems that those in power have wheedled social control through religion to divide humanity with fear and incite terror. And yet, I feel a strong connection to God. My faith warms me. I want to understand God's truth, free from fluffy concepts that give more questions than answers. When I ask if she's encountered angels or demons, Amber ruminates for a moment, opens her mouth to say something, and then shuts it as she eyes me warily.

After a moment of contemplation she exhales and responds, "Yes. Angels, all the time. I feel their presence guiding me and protecting me in times of darkness. When I pray, I feel their light showering upon me."

With doting eyes, Amber glances from Polly Jane to me than back again as she adds, "I think people can be angels in our life too."

Amber then shares a story of a demonic entity entering her bedroom. Awakening to it standing over her as it reached out and scratched her, she trumpeted, "In the name of Jesus, go away!" This made it fled. The entity came from the spiritual realm, but it left physical scratches that abraded her arms for days. Later in life, I wondered if she was cryptically describing a drug addiction.

Between camp activities that stretch across twenty acres of beautiful native bushland, uncertainty constricts my lively nature with a heavy gloom. One afternoon, I disclose to my dorm the agony of not knowing whether chemotherapy will help Papa. The room is stock-still with compassionate listening. I feel a tiny spark of hope in my sharing. Amber asks for permission to pray for Papa. I agree. As she calls upon a higher power to heal Papa's cancer and bring him back to a state of optimum vitality, the energy in the dorm shifts. I feel an angelic spirit ooze through the ceiling then hold me in a loving embrace.

En route to lunch the next day, Amber halts by a massive gum tree and tells me she has a message from God.

I inhale a lemon scent and eye the tree's smooth pinkish-white bark.

"Jess, you're a fisher of people."

I have no idea what she's on about but there is urgency in her words.

She looks at a block of yellow-doored dorms. "Do you know what that means?"

I shake my head. "No..."

"James and John cast nets for fish. Your gift is collecting people who are lost and helping them see the light again. It's a rare and beautiful offering that will be with you for life."

A lone kid scurries to the dining hall that wafts with cheesy spaghetti bolognaise and lime jelly. I look into her sincere eyes as her words settle in my torso like clockwork pieces amalgamating and clicking a deeper purpose into motion.

As summer holidays roll to an end, Papa's fourth chemotherapy session leaves him gaunt, pale-skinned, and vomiting. He masks his inner turmoil with a smile. I often find him stirring milk into French press coffee as he reassures, "Today is a good day. Today I can drink coffee!"

On days he feels strong, we roll azure-blue paint onto bare concrete walls. One afternoon, alone in the bare, grey chamber that will eventually be a spare bedroom, I crouch over a paint tin and sniff in the acerbic plasticky fumes. I know it's bad for me. That's why I do it.

It's around this time I also engage in a detrimental eating cycle of starvation-binge. My primary school years revealed inklings of disordered eating, but I now weigh myself compulsively, Google tactics to hide the disorder, and stack magazines in two piles—one revealing how much weight I've lost, the other showing how far to go. Photoshopped images on the glossy pages taint my perception of what it means to be an empowered woman, coaxing me to starve myself on the damned quest to be "beautiful". With no knowledge of proper nutrition, I base my diet on how much food weighs. After a day of fasting my stomach growls, and I binge on fat and sugar because a caramel slice weighs less than a plate of vegetables. My track record is three days without eating. I drink minimal water because hydration adds numbers to the scales. By day three, my stomach convulses and shoots acid into my mouth, prompting me to inhale a bowl of cereal and devour two litres of water.

My moods are fluctuating oceanic tides with blood sugar peaking and plummeting like a roller coaster. I surge through rivers of glucose, spiral in whirlpools of insulin, then crash into a turmoil of neurotransmitters. My weight oscillates from 56kgs to 64kgs on a fortnightly basis. At dinner I "drink" water from a large, opaque cup. After cutting and chewing mouthfuls of food, I pretend to swallow then "sip some water". Instead of swallowing, I spit the sustenance into the cup. By the end of the meal, I've filled my massive blue cup with food that I subsequently hide under other garbage in the bin.

A self-destructive current seethes within. Yet simultaneously, an equally powerful cascade pours soothing self-responsibility into my being. Every day is a question of which current I empower by where I direct my energy. With retrospect I see my actions are an effort to gain control over a situation in which I feel powerless. Over time, I choose healthier habits and let the latter current flourish.

You are the architect of your life.
You create the foundations and choose its contents.

The 2006 school year begins with a brilliant, heady excitement electrifying all music students embarking on tour in June. Months waltz into weeks with agile swings from the conductor's baton as we perfect orchestral songs. Papa finishes his final round of chemotherapy and continues work in Papua New Guinea while we await the results.

Four days before departure, Mama decides to dig out my passport in preparation for the trip. Papa's diagnosis delayed our painting and carpeting of the house, which means our belongings still fill unopened cardboard boxes in the cobwebbed garage. Coated in dust, she searches all day. Sweating with stress, we search all night. The next day, I stay home from school and tear open boxes with Mama. Alas, there is no sign of my passports, citizenship, or birth certificate. Nothing to prove my identity.

The next day is an edgy whirlwind of faxing Papa in the remote highland jungle, scribbling signatures, and pacing between government offices. Being born abroad makes the issuing of an emergency passport arduous and clunky. But by sheer miracle we do it.

The day before tour departs, a knock at the door jolts Mama and me into a wide-eyed agility. As the postman hands us the magic parcel with my passport inside, my breath catches in my chest. Then relief drenches me. The international tour I've anticipated since I started drum lessons five years ago is finally a reality.

The next day, Perth's international terminal hums with 149 excited students huddled together in sleek, teal polo shirts. Kids snore on two long flights to Kuala Lumpur then Frankfurt. My eyes sting with fatigue. After snailing along the autobahn, we pull into Vienna. I've been awake for fifty-five hours.

Instead of sleeping in our dingy hostel dorm, I console a distraught Kim. Between stifled sobs, she stammers that her stepdad is a bad man. I do my best to be a safe space for her, but as midnight contorts into 2:00 a.m., she swallows the very words she needs to express, the ones that gnaw away at her like poison. She doesn't reveal what he did or does or threatens. All I know is my best friend obscures her trauma behind a deadlock with keys rusted from her silent, shaky tears. At 3:00 a.m., she lets out an anguished sigh and proclaims that we should rest. I tell her I love her, and though sleep deprivation tests us in those first few days, the City of Dreams immerses us in a musical reverie that threads our DNA into the same rhythmic beats.

Palaces and museums along Vienna's imperial Ringstrasse entertain us with an interactive display of the city's rich history. We collaborate with musicians from local schools, then sing and dance at a Heuriger where two live musicians serenade wooden tables in the rustic tavern girdled by grassy hills. Fresh wine, roast pork, and fried chicken infuse the air with mouth-watering aromas, and the buoyant resonance of guitar and accordion sweeps us into Salzburg.

My childhood dream of prancing through my favourite scene in *The Sound of Music* springs to life in the fairytale city burrowed between two mountains. We take a day trip to the Lake District, where Bavarian Alps soar behind the famous glass-panelled gazebo perched beside a shimmering lake. Later, we sing the "Song of Peace" with choirs from Austria, South Africa, Armenia, and Ukraine in a large university hall for the Cantus 2000 Music Festival. The song softens me, stirring hope for humanity as melodies meander through winding streets to picturesque squares adorned with naked stone statues and majestic fountains.

Forty minutes south of Salzburg, at the base of a German mountain, a granite tunnel leads to a polished brass-panelled elevator. In it we ascend to the mountain's peak where the retreat built for Hitler's fiftieth birthday—though he was afraid of heights—offers striking 360-degree views of snow-capped Alps and crisp, verdant valleys. The wind and jazz orchestras enrich crowds with music that crescendos like eagles on updrafts, inundating cultural barriers with the ancient language of song. Tour is a bizarre concoction of sleep-deprived adventure, zestful novelty, and the rehearsed familiarity of layered songs. I can't shake the feeling that Kim is hiding something terrible from me, but I don't know how to support her when she pushes me away. I try prying for more information of what her stepdad is doing, but she scowls at me and barks, "Anything I say can and will be used against me."

Kim's words echo between my ears as we hike a steep gravelly path to the world's largest ice cave. Fresh alpine air vitalizes craggy panoramic views. Upwards we pant and gasp. Our entrance into the frozen kingdom begins in a gaping limestone hollow unsuspectingly emerging from the mountainside. In it, a small dark hole is sectioned off by a door. With subzero breath, a sweeping gust of wind welcomes us into the spectacular cave system. I step inside. Kids howl into the glittering interior with thrilling animation. All I hear are my best friend's words resounding in the lamplit labyrinth with icy ambiguity. Her tears inundate me—though they've long dried since that first night. As I gaze upon massive, dangling icicles I see her pain. Once-flowing teardrops hang like daggers, stuck still in time. Outside, sunshine drizzles over forested ranges and sheer vertical drops. Kim's exterior is enlivening and warm with an assured stance and sizzling sass. Deep within, she is haunted by something chilling.

After touching down in tense London on the first anniversary of the London bombings, I link arms with Kim and tell her I love her. I am there if she wants to open up, but I won't keep bugging her for details she isn't ready to share. Giving her space to digest my words, I explore the city with a shy, Fijian double bass player who watches the world with profundity behind thick, dark curls. She has recently been outcast by her clique. I empathise with the lonely hollow of exclusion and dismiss her former friends' attempts to coax my amiability with their trivial drama. It isn't the first time this has happened.

Just weeks before tour, a fight between the popular girls results in one joining the hot ethnic group that I hang with at the time. Kim has past beef with the girl, but it's nothing to do with me, so I welcome her in—we've always had pleasant relations. The next day, the school's most *hideous* girl—in character, externally she is irresistible—comes to "warn" me about her old bestie with a malicious bitchfest. The interaction is comical because she expects me to yield to her desires and further marginalise her former friend. Instead, I look her dead in the eye and say, "What Sally says of Suzie says more about Sally than Suzie. I'll make my own judgements, thanks." Her jaw drops. She opens her mouth to say something, but no words come. Two weeks later, the girls are friends again. One continues nodding pleasant hellos in passing. The other diverts her gaze. Power lies in morals, not status. This is the golden nugget I learn. As red, double-decker sightseeing buses rev and screech past the murky Thames and commemorations crawl through the security-tight city, I keep my Fijian friend close and amp up my funny. I don't want anyone to feel the despair I knew in primary school. Over time, she becomes a loyal friend.

The next day, Kim slinks beside me on the bus to our performance with the world-renowned London Philharmonic Orchestra. Later, we laugh at the satirical comedy of *The Producers* on Drury Lane, where she glues herself to my hip once more—on the condition her half-confession from that first night is never spoken of again. I don't like her keeping me in the dark, but it's better than being kept at arm's length. En route to Hereford, we perform in medieval Dore Abbey. Magnificent acoustics sweep music into patterns of light that stream through stained-glass windows then strike pointed arches and fine wooden furnishings. I am captivated by the 900-year-old sandstone building. But Kim's unspoken words still loom in my periphery like the stony graveyard outside.

My worries wane in the gentle hands of Mrs Clementon, a maths teacher who is chaperoning us on tour. Sometimes she braids my hair between crumbling medieval castles and picturesque gothic towns. Sometimes she eats lunch beside me at our collaborating schools. There, she observes schoolboys ogling me and makes smoochy noises with her mouth. The attention is flattering—from both her and the boys. With retrospect, I see her flirtation is an omen. Eleven months later, Mrs Clementon defends a sexual predator against me in court.

*Destiny is always one step ahead,
guiding us where we're meant to be and to who we're meant to be with.*

Back in Perth's brisk winter, school is a pendulum of excelling and rebelling. Papa's chemotherapy seems to be working, and as spring flourishes with birdsong in budding trees, I grow a strange attraction to a boy I meet online.

One year earlier, my cousin Stacey introduces me to a joker named Reed who she connects with in a virtual chatroom. Reed is two years older and lives in Perth's forested hills. We occasionally chat on MSN, where he introduces me to two of his friends, Jarred and Cal. One of whom will take my virginity. The other, my heart. My intrigue is muted with half-assed interactions until Cal mentions that his younger sister's friend goes to my high school. It turns out we catch the bus together. She is the missing link verifying the guys are who they say they are.

From there on, I speed walk to the bus after school each day, as though it will get me home faster to chat with Cal. His endless puns delight me, and our conversation plunges to depths that renders an emotional warmth within my protective exterior. I disclose the torment of Papa's cancer. He divulges the pain of losing his mum to breast cancer as a child. Though we've not yet met, I feel a vicarious transmission of his feelings as though my brunette locks are antennas attuned to his inner world. He is funny and kind and a little shy. I am magnetised to him with passionate flames.

When Cal invites me to his birthday at the end of October, I face two hurdles. I've never drunk alcohol before and don't want to be intoxicated for the first time around strangers, and there is no way I'll be allowed to go to a *seventeen-year-old* boy's party who *I've met online* and lives *an hour away.*

I bound over the first barrier with Kim and a Year 11 boy we befriend on tour. The week before Cal's party, the three of us wag class and swig a bottle of smuggled rum beneath the empty auditorium's dusty wooden stage. We stifle giggles, and my worries burn with each swish of the smooth amber spirit. Cinnamon and vanilla undertones swirl in my stomach as I formulate a meticulous plan.

I tell my parents a friend from Baptist youth camps is having a sleepover party. Cal's younger sister agrees to play the part. As we cruise along the freeway, my mouth dries to an arid desert. In the driveway, my heart pumps so hard I wonder if Mama and Papa can hear it. We arrive fifteen minutes early. Cal's sister is not yet home from work. Sweat dots my palms as I knock on the door. Three guys appear at the window, then a brown-haired boy with ocean eyes swings it open and beams through crooked teeth. My body surges with electricity as we hug hello.

After ten minutes, Mama and Papa retire from awkwardly admiring a mythical forest painting in the lounge room and depart with me in tow. They aren't comfortable leaving me unsupervised in a house with rowdy boys. Driving back down the forested escarpment, I feel Cal's heart pumping in my veins. Vanessa Carlton's "A Thousand Miles" plays on the radio. Joy oscillates through my body in honeyed ripples because I have *finally* seen him. And him, me. We are star-crossed lovers, but our story has only just begun. We continue chatting daily, plunging headfirst into a burning romance that waxes and wanes for five years. First loves are the most intense, because our hearts haven't yet been broken open; therefore, our love is untainted and unafraid.

As the 2006 school year wraps up, I let music go in favour of pursuing other Tertiary Entrance Examination subjects. I love percussion, but I detest the heavy-eyed, early-morning choir rehearsals, so I scribble *English, Media, Chemistry, Human Biology, Math, and Geography* then continue daydreaming about Cal.

The next week Cal isn't online. Or the next. Or the day after that. Three weeks later he logs on. His username features another girl's name between big heart emojis. My heart shatters to shimmering, serrated shards that slashes my naivety and self-esteem. We weren't officially boyfriend and girlfriend. But he told me he loved me. A few months later, a MySpace thread reveals she has been unfaithful and their relationship is over. He subsequently edges my way. I have compassion for his splintered heart, yet I protect mine with a rigid shield. I am mosaicking myself back together. Cal penetrates the tile gaps and cracks the grout, stopping the paste from settling.

A few weeks later, Polly Jane and I stroll through a fluorescently lit shopping centre when Cal's pink-cheeked baby face appears amongst the buzzing chatter of shoppers with clanky trolleys. My heart skips a beat. He hugs me hello then we sit on a nearby bench. Polly Jane loiters awkwardly while his eyes lock on mine like magnets. The affliction and affection in his strangled expression conveys more than words ever could. Before parting ways, he whips a pen from his pocket and scribbles *I love you* on my hand. I resist scrubbing it off in the shower that night. I want the ink to sink into my skin and link me to him forever.

In some ways, it did.

Trigger Warning:

This chapter contains graphic scenes of rape and attempted suicide.

Help is available if you are struggling with depression or sexual assault. 1800RESPECT (1800737732) is Australia's sexual assault and domestic violence counselling line. Lifeline 13 11 14 is Australia's crisis support and suicide prevention hotline. Both are open 24 hours. You're not alone.

U.K.:
- Samaritans:
116 123
(https://www.samaritans.org/)

- The National Domestic Abuse Helpline
0808 2000 247
(https://www.nationaldahelpline.org.uk/)

- Rape Crisis:
0808 802 9999
(https://rapecrisis.org.uk/)

U.S.A:
- National Suicide Prevention Lifeline:
1-800-273-8255
(https://suicidepreventionlifeline.org/)

- National Domestic Violence Hotline:
1-800-799-7233
(https://www.thehotline.org/)

- National Sexual Assault Hotline:
1-800-656-4673
(https://www.rainn.org/)

Canada:
- Talk Suicide Canada:
1-833-456-4566
(https://talksuicide.ca/)

- For Quebec:
1-866-277-3553
(https://suicide.ca)

- Salal Sexual Violence Support Centre
  1-877-392-7583 (national toll-free 24-hour)
  (604)-245-2425 (text)
  (https://www.salalsvsc.ca/24-hour-crisis-and-information-line/)

Europe:
- European Victim Support Line:
  116 006
  (https://ec.europa.eu/info/policies/justice-and-fundamental-rights/criminal-justice/victims-rights-and-compensation/victims-rights/european-victim-support-line_en)

India:
- Sneha Foundation:
  +91-44-24640050, +91-44-24640060
  (http://www.snehaindia.org/)

- Sakshi Violence Intervention Centre:
  0124-2562336, 0124-4221550
  (http://sakshingo.org/)

- The Survivors Trust:
  +91 98190 86444
  (https://www.survivorstoday.org/)

Chapter II
DEATH

Breath. Death.

Womb. Tomb.

How thin is the veil?

Can you see us on the other side?

Disintegrate.

Reintegrate.

Have you found your peace?

Can you hear our cries?

The brightest light

in the darkest night.

This duality,

unifies.

March 2007, three months later

The girl in the mirror scrutinizes my slender body with inquisitive hazel eyes. Thick liquid eyeliner accentuates her desire for unattainable ideals sprawling like weeds in her once guileless mind. Eyeing the contours of my tiny fifteen-year-old waist, she grimaces as my body curves like the bottom of an hourglass slowly filling with sand. Flicking a long brunette strand over my freckled shoulder, I lean towards her mirrored eyes. I look not at her. I peer *inside* her. She is timid and uncertain, yet a slight postural adjustment portrays the leisurely confidence and sun-kissed grace of a fearless lioness.

I revel in the introspective green deepening in her irises like the canopy of an old-growth forest transcending time. There's no sham. There's nowhere to hide. The answers to questions I have not yet asked glisten in the unwavering contact we hold. Innocent yet unflinching, the girl in the mirror enquires with just her eyes: Are you my combatant or companion? Who will you become?

A buzz from my phone pulls me from my trance. *On my way*, the message reads. My heart hammers in my chest.

"This is it, Jess. If you do this, things will never be the same... Are you sure you're ready?"

I stare at my azure-blue bedroom wall. Inside the double-bricked wall shielding me from the world, a cavity of empty space consumes my conversation. Every fibre in my being oscillates with anticipation of losing my virginity to Jarred, the boy I've chatted with for years but not yet met. A few months earlier, I kissed a boy for the first time at my Bulgarian friend's birthday party. Despite this, my best friend, mother, and crush all dub me a "slut" on different occasions. Kim and Cal were drunk. Their words were slurred. Mama seethed in reactivity to a mother-daughter squabble. Sometimes she is fiery. I bite back. They don't understand the repercussions. They don't know I've devoured the scandals they hurled. They don't know it stings and scorches, slashes and stirs. My light-hearted exterior camouflages my delicate fragility. In hindsight, the detriment of being draped in an inaccurate identity is clear. I wish I could console my fifteen-year-old self that hurt people hurt people and their maliciousness was never my burden to carry.

Cal and I are in a waning phase. His nastiness prompts me to engage with

Jarred's flirtation on MSN. My resentment at Mama compels me to rebel against my chaste Christian upbringing. There are two parts to my personality—one seeking new thrills, the other grounded in security. If I don't jump in and trailblaze a situation, my caution stifles me. When I read the words, *I could drive to your house now. The passenger seat in my car can tilt right down*, I become aroused and agree to sneak out once my parents are asleep.

In my darkened room I wait for the stair light's click and count the minutes following their trudging footsteps. Then something drips between my legs. Scarlet blood oozes on my black lace panties. *I have bad news*, I type using a T9 predictive keyboard. *I've just got my period. It's light though.* A few texts attest he doesn't mind. Sometime after 11:00 p.m., he buzzes *I'm here*.

Delicately and deliberately, I tiptoe down the stairs and slink out the laundry's sliding door. The air is crisp on my freshly shaven legs as I approach his white Commodore parked down the street.

"Hello," I coo, relaxing into the seat that will carry me into adulthood.

He is tanned with blond highlights and a down-to-earth demeanour. "You're prettier than I thought," he endears with twinkling eyes.

Butterflies flutter in my stomach. I smile between closed lips. I am present to the air of mystery I create with my silence as he drives to the ocean. Boats draw lines on the horizon, illuminating the depths I am about to dive.

In a darkened corner of the large, empty carpark, silence eddies around us as waves kiss the shore. I give a nervous giggle. His marble-grey eyes wait for my look of invitation. Then he leans forward and kisses me. Static cascades through my veins as he draws back, savouring the moment by letting his excitement build. My back arches with raw intensity as he strokes my cheek, then manoeuvres himself across the car on top of me.

Maintaining eye contact—tender yet firm—I ease into the dance of our clothed bodies familiarising. My mental chatter dissipates as he caresses my curves as though spinning silk from the waxing moon's tiny sliver of light. Intoxicated with the tactile sensation of his hands roving my body, I run my fingers down his spine and pull him close. Slowly, slowly, entering me gently, he stops upon my instruction and holds me with care. Through unwavering eye contact he gauges a comfortable tempo. Tasting my breath through quiet moans, he moves our bodies into a silhouetted rhythm that rises and falls like ocean waves. It feels like a scene from a movie: the car bounces vigorously as salty zephyrs breeze through the window, which fogs with our unified breath. When it is over, Jarred kisses me good night and asks to see me again. It is the start of a connection that remains deep, intimate, and kind for years to come.

Legs trembling, I squelch barefoot across my neighbour's dewy lawn. My awareness sharpens with invigorating precision as cool liquid beads and fine bushy blades render a varied yet pleasant texture on my feet. I glide through the laundry door like I am levitating. Then I creep upstairs to my bedroom. With a long exhale, I realise that life will never be the same.

*Some things speak for themselves,
others are never spoken of.*

I wake for school, wondering if it is all a dream. Incoming texts confirm it's real with Jarred checking in and feeding me flattering words. I disclose the night to Kim beside our shared locker. Her slack jaw becomes raised eyebrows then multiple head nods as she probes me with questions until the morning bell dings.

Six days later, Kim loses her virginity. Like me, she sleeps with someone she met online. Unlike me, she cannot verify he is who he says he is through a real-life mutual friend. With the turn of the 21st century, social media becomes a highlight reel with dopamine rushes accompanying every virtual like. In the years preceding the rise of Facebook, MySpace is the chosen platform where we acquire friends and followers online. At the time, I frequently accept friend requests from people I do not know. Cyberspace popularity depends on the quantity of people commenting on photos, and I—like many youngsters—am careless with whom I allow to access my images and personal information.

By our steel-grey locker, I press Kim for details as she talks of a guy called Luke finding her MySpace profile. I recognize the name from an account I scrutinized a few weeks earlier.

"Is that the topless guy with his head cropped out of the photo?"

"Yeah, the sexy one," she squeals. "You know him?"

"Yeah..." I ruminate. "Well, no, I don't. We chatted on MSN one time. Then he started a group convo with his friend... What was his name... Cult? *Colt?*"

"Colton," Kim verifies. "That's him! That's who I lost my virginity to."

I twinkle a smile then continue recollecting. "He was super flirty in the group convo...Colton. We chatted for a few weeks or so. Then I got bored."

"*I'm* not bored of him." Kim flashes a cheeky grin.

I waggle my eyebrows at her. Then a thought furrows my brow. "What happened to Luke? I said hello a few weeks ago, but his profile suddenly disappeared. On MSN and MySpace. I think he blocked me."

"That happened to me too!" Kim exclaims.

In the back of my mind, an alarm bell sways. I don't think "Luke" is who he says he is. His cropped-out face, no other photos, and the lack of comments indicating close friends stiffens me with suspicion. My stomach tightens. My chest weighs heavy. Kim's identical description of how she met the two men concerns me. Intuitively, I know "Luke" is Colton. But there's no time to flag it with Kim gasping to tell me more.

"So...how was it?" I ask.

"It was...interesting..." Kim flicks a long chestnut lock over her shoulder then discloses that Colton, twenty-three, lives with his mother a short walk from school. Early that morning, before 9 a.m., Kim walked to Colton's house and lost her virginity. Somewhere in his couch.

I search for emotions in her features as she confides. I can't help but think her actions are a reaction to mine six days prior. Would she have lost her virginity to an online stranger if I'd not done the same? I always thought that she'd lose her virginity first. We both did. She is more confident and experienced with guys. As she shares the finer details, my danger instinct melts into curiosity. *Did it hurt? Did you use a condom? Please tell me you used a condom! How do you feel now?* Our rebellious secrecy is exhilarating as we step into unfamiliar adult terrain brimming with novelty that mutes my apprehensions of his intention and age.

It will be years until our minds are mature enough to process the complex emotions of giving ourselves to another. It takes me longer to distinguish the conundrum of society commodifying women's sexuality yet also condemning us should we savour pleasure. We're expected to partake and not partake. It's impossible to fit inside these juxtaposing expectations.

I wish I'd known more than my school's limited education of sex being a mere physical act and my strict, self-denying upbringing forbidding any inclination of curiosity or desire. Despite multiple waves of women's liberation movements—affecting women's suffrage, access to education, equitable pay, and increasing our rights to property and our own bodies—I wish that society recognised it is *still* backwards when it comes to a woman's sexual expression. We are expected to satisfy men's needs yet are slut-shamed if we enjoy it. I wish I'd understood the psychosocial consequences of societies discursive drivers that stereotype men as emotionally devoid boys wanting no-strings encounters while portraying women as exploited romantics with secondary needs. By shaming women who seek equal intimate participation, the outdated slut versus stud double standard perpetuates a misogynistic, patriarchal worldview. It's time to shatter these oppressive norms and revere the myriad feminine expressions.

Kids throw damp paper balls and "surf" the school bus's sharp turns. My phone vibrates. I glance down and smile. The other night I met with Jarred again, but it is a sweet message from Cal that warms my chest. I've been radio silent for weeks. He tells me he misses me. Midway through a daydream of his heart-shaped lips, Mariana's honey eyes find mine. As she squeezes through the rowdy horde, I shuffle back to make room beside me. Sometimes I think she still harbours feelings for me, but she has been respectful and contained since our conversation two years ago.

As Mariana grips a handrail above our heads, my phone buzzes again. The screen flashes with Colton's name. Lately Kim's been bubbling with the idea of a threesome. Deep down I know the proposition stems from him. I feign intrigue, but I'm not sold. This prompts Kim to suggest that I start chatting with Colton again to "feel into it". Without conscious reasoning, I ask Marianna if she knows him.

"Why?" She inspects me with piercing eyes.

The bus squeals to a stop. Excited chatter blurs into a police siren.

"Just curious," I reassure. Without mentioning Kim's name, I divulge that he added me online.

Once Marianna concludes I don't have an ulterior motive for asking, she confides that Colton chats up her friends. She also notes he texts with a freakish speed.

"Oh my gosh, he does too!" I agree. "He just bought me fifty bucks phone credit 'cause I ran out and stopped replying. *Every* message has a sexual innuendo..."

"That sounds like him." Marianna presses her lips together and glances out the graffitied window. "Have you met up with him?"

"Nah." I scrunch my nose at a curious whiff of sweat, fart, and hair spray.

"Have you?" I ask, veering the conversation away from me. A strange fusion of curiosity and caution itch down my spine and swirl in my torso.

Mariana tugs at her earlobe then rakes her fingers through her curls. "No...but a good friend of mine has. They fuck. *A lot.*"

I am about to prod for more information, but she interjects, "I'm *not* telling you who."

"That's okay." I smile and straighten my stance to mirror hers. I think I know which friend that is, anyway.

Her chest swells and then shrinks with one rapid breath. She scans the kids nearby then she leans in and whispers, "He's really close with Mrs Clementon."

I blink under a creased brow. "*Mrs Clementon?*"

Mariana nods.

"Mrs Clementon *who came on tour?*"

She chews her mouth ever so slightly then places a *shhh* finger upon her pursed lips.

*Sometimes our split-second decisions
will haunt us for the rest of our lives.*

Outside my neighbour's house, concealed from all windows in my home, I open Colton's passenger door. He is a less attractive Justin Timberlake lookalike. In those first ten seconds, my body's primitive wisdom gives a visceral feeling that something is wrong. He is older than I thought. He told me he's twenty-two. Yet Kim professes he's twenty-three. Thin slices of information aren't adding up, but my best friend vouches for him, and this fogs my intuition. Settling into the passenger seat, I decide against their proposition.

Three streets from my home, he talks up his day job managing events at Challenge Stadium, a local sports and entertainment venue. As he attacks the "bucketloads of offering money" collected by a Christian worship band, my own voice bellows inside my head:

Alarm bells.

My intuition often speaks in inklings and insights. This is the first time it's used literal words. As we wind down a hill, I gaze past his silhouetted profile to the vegetated golf course out the window. He's hiding something. It's as transparent as the glossy glass. But though I know that he's concealing something, I don't yet know *what*.

I mask the confusion storming my mind with a bright-eyed smile. He parks in a driveway nestled behind two brick houses and instructs me to be silent because his mother is sleeping. Inside the garage converted into his den is a desktop computer and the couch where Kim lost her virginity. He sits in the ergonomic chair and pats his thigh. I hesitate. He taps his leg again. I perch upon his lap. He probes me with questions of my previous sexual experiences. Then he clicks open a file containing hundreds of photos from high school balls—Australia's version of prom. Each photo depicts the innocent bloom of radiant teen girls yet to become women. Many schools hold their balls at Challenge Stadium, but an eerie force edges into my periphery. How and why does he have access to these photos on his home computer? He isn't a photographer. And what's his intention with showing me? Is it to boost his ego? Or is he trying to ruffle feelings of insecurity in my supple skin to then swoop in and stroke compliments into the creases?

I note the girls are attractive, veiling my speculation with a graceful air. Then we creep into the house with his mother's soft snuffles. Halfway along the hallway is an enormous framed headshot of young Colton sporting my school uniform. I quiz him about it behind his closed bedroom door. He explains he was once the Head Boy. Mrs Clementon was his year coordinator.

"What was that like?" I ask.

He doesn't respond. Instead, he turns to me and pushes me onto the bed. His eyes are dull and filmy. I'll never forget his vacant expression. He looks possessed. On the duvet, he admits his unrequited love for the Head Girl. I have no chance to inquire further. His lips are on mine.

Colton admits he is sleeping with other young teens. I peer into his cloudy eyes, trying to pierce through the mask. He tells me I'm not like the others as he tucks a loose strand of hair behind my ear. Maybe it's another line. Or maybe he isn't used to someone relentlessly searching for a spark of his true identity. It isn't my intention to sleep with him, but it feels expected, so I do. I can't legally consent by age, but he's groomed me with honeyed words that depict a norm of young girls sleeping with him, sometimes even giving him their virginity.

Lying in bed after, he says I'm a natural. The statement both endears and confuses me. It sounds like sex is a performance and not something we do to connect. I wish I could pause that moment and tell my starry-eyed self that sex is not *something you do*, it's *somewhere you go*. I wish I could hold that girl tight and articulate her power. I wish I could wrap her in velvet and adorn her with a crown. For in that moment a warped pattern clicks into motion that taints my perception of intimacy. With Jarred I feel connected in a bond that remains for years. With Colton, I am infiltrated by a new norm.

Colton fondles my skin of goose bumps and ivory, then confesses that the others don't always know if they want it. My stomach knots. Before dropping me home, he touches on age. Kim is sixteen and legally able to consent. I am fifteen and thus Colton orders I delete all incoming and outgoing texts as soon as they are sent/received. I agree but disobey. I enjoy the attention. I want to keep his bouquet of praise. This becomes a godsend in my prosecution against him as his digital grooming becomes evidence in court.

"I've got to tell you something," Kim whispers as she eyes a kid ambling by.

"Ooo, tell me!" I chirp.

She glances behind my head then lands her gaze on mine. "Later."

At recess I can't find her, so I stroll to the music department to give my Fijian friend a long letter and giggle at our inside jokes. Kim's darting eyes and furrowed brow permeate my mind in third period. When the siren rings, I skip to our locker. She is there fidgeting with her physics book. With a little persistence, Kim confides that she met with Colton again using the cover of "studying in the library after school". Then she divulges his fetish for schoolgirls.

"Oh. Yeah, that makes sense," I mutter. "How'd you figure that?"

She bites the inside of her lip. "He told me."

I look at my shoes—once white, now stained. She has more to say. I feel her unspoken words press against my ribs like a corset.

In a raspy whisper, Kim continues, "He wanted to fuck me in my school uniform. So, we did..."

In the periphery of my conscious mind, something shimmers in the murky pool connecting him with Mrs Clementon. I am pulled in two directions—highly impressionable and wanting to please while the muffled chimes of alarm bells resume.

Pain is our greatest pathway to growth.

Colton's compliments come in frequent *dings*. A few days later, I agree to meet him again. If all those other girls are sleeping with him, it must be normal—right?

This time, his mother is on night shift, and we waltz straight into his bedroom. Lying above the duvet, we chat for a bit. Then he whips out his phone and flicks through an album with dozens, maybe even hundreds, of sexualized photos and videos of young girls. Some are of him having intercourse with them. Most are stark-naked girls in provocative poses. I recognize Kim and Mariana's friend amid countless faces and bodies. Some look younger than me, others slightly older. None appear to be older than seventeen.

I wonder his reason for showing me. He trusts me enough to open up to, but why? People often tell me their darkest secrets, knowing that I'll carry them to my grave. It's what makes Kim's untold truth about her stepdad so troubling. It must be bad if she can't confide in her own best friend.

My mind ticks double time as I guess his motives. Is this a man confessing his sins for some kind of redemption, or is he coaxing me to join the album? Does he even know why? My thoughts are interrupted as he peers into my eyes and tells me he's not shown the photos to anyone before. Something in his gaze compels me to believe him. I sense guilt. Maybe even shame, loneliness, and sorrow. I feel for him. But I also discern danger.

Suddenly the fumes from his deodorant spray fester, and the bells dinging in my mind's periphery crescendo until they are all I can hear. Intuition shatters the illusionary veil. Finally. He is a predator. There is digital evidence on his phone. I feel perplexed, disgusted, helpless, and aghast. The emotions convolute and heave. The concoction is heavy, course, slimy, and thorny with every rough, weighted, greasy prickle leading to the same conclusion: Get out now. But how?

Colton turns his phone on me and, without consent, films my naked body. Face to thighs, the hairs on my skin rise. No words come. I am in survival mode. I wish I understood the instinctual physiological response occurring in my body in that moment to ensure my survival. I knew of fight-or-flight. I didn't know about freeze and fawn—responses more common in women. The problem with mainstream psychology's long-standing fixation on white, male, middle-class perspectives is its limitation in understanding different worldviews. For example, a pirate appears in a narrow alleyway with a knife drawn. Is the pirate larger than you? Yes = flight. No = fight. Is the pirate seducible by you? Yes = fawn. No = freeze. Where freeze shuts the voice, fawn opens the voice up but does so without conscious thought. From an evolutionary stance, freeze allows us to escape a predator's attention by making us invisible through immobilisation. In fawn—also known as tend and befriend—placating, negotiating, bribing, or pleasing may de-escalate dangerous scenarios with amiability. I can't help but wonder if things might have played out differently had I learned this in school and been able to transcend my freeze then fawn responses by understanding that I was in them.

Colton sees me contract. He stops filming and tells me he'll delete the video. After what I've just seen that seems unlikely. His static fingers reveal the lie. I am consoling myself with internal dialogue when he tells me he wants to try something new. My heart pounds. Shivers crawl down my spine. He ties me to his bed and fastens a blindfold over my eyes. The alarm bells swaying in the back of my mind for weeks now boom with fury.

"I want to open you up," he blurts.

A coarse cotton fabric rubs against my vulva then enters me. He is fingering me with a towel. Why? I do not know. Tonic immobility temporarily paralyses me—I am mute, numb, and frozen. His penetrating silence is focused. I sense him filming me. Police evidence later reveals my inkling to be true. I squirm at the fabric's friction. Then the stubble from his facial hair scratches against my inner thigh and his tongue slops over my genitals.

I wish I'd known that by freezing in that moment—despite being underage, tied up, blindfolded, and not giving consent to be touched or videoed—my body both ensured my survival and betrayed me by doing so. I wish psychology's pale, male, stale pivot didn't limit our understanding of the freeze and fawn responses that are more prominent in women. I wish I'd known that the rights to my body are my own. That consent is situation dependent and can be retracted or changed at any time. My previous engagement was not a continuation of consent. If you and I are in a boxing match yesterday, it doesn't give me the right to punch you on the street today or whenever I choose.

My gut twists as Colton retracts his tongue then shoves his penis inside me. I can't see. I can't look into his eyes. For connection. For answers. I can't see if he's wearing a condom. I can't see if he's filming. The thought of becoming another file in his album of objectified girls impels my inner strength to mutter "No".

It takes all of me simply to vocalise the two-letter word.

But he continues.

Maybe I was muffled the first time. I utter "no" again. This time I'm certain he hears me.

He keeps going.

I repeat myself again, slightly clearer, slightly louder.

Still, he ignores me.

Silent tears stream beneath the blindfold in warm trickles. In. Out. Again. And again. Unrequited arousal. I am no longer a human with valid thoughts or needs. I am an object for his lust.

I am long silent when he asks if I want him to stop. I say nothing. An involuntary freeze cages me in a neurobiological protective mechanism meant to detach me from the trauma. I have lost faith that my voice holds any power, forfeited confidence that men will respect my boundaries, yielded trust of the world and the people in it. In this moment a pattern emerges of actively giving away my sex because I don't believe my "no" will be heard. Saying "yes" becomes a way of recreating my trauma with the illusion that I'm in control. My perception of sex is tainted. A portal to deeper connection where safety is the foundation for pleasure is erased. I am degraded to an object of man's desire. I shut down my sharp intellect, brimming creativity, and soft emotions in emphasis of my physicality. I create a story that sex is all I'm valued for. A repercussion that haunts me for years to come.

When Colton finally pulls out his dick, the blindfold is damp with my tears. My legs tremble. He rips the fabric from my eyes, unties me, then chides, "You just need to tell me if you want me to stop!"

My lips quiver as he pulls me beside him and wraps me in his arms. I am confused. He exploited me. Yet now he acts like he cares. I want away. I want to go home. But how? I picture myself jogging through brisk midnight streets in a singlet and skirt when my fawn instinct kicks in. I don't know what his next actions will be. To subdue potential aggression, I need to appease. Acting small and submissive fools him into thinking he's fooled me. In the moment it results in him driving me to the safety of my home. In hindsight the long-standing impacts are consequential. From there on, I diminish my intellect to a ditzy persona. Dumbing myself down makes me feel safe, for people reveal more about their unspoken intentions when they think I notice less. It allows me to be three steps ahead of their game.

At home I crawl under the covers with mixed emotions. In the days that follow, I draw away from Colton and stop communicating. At the time I don't label it as rape. I think that rape is something strangers do in dark alleys before murdering their victims. I wish I knew that most cases of sexual violence occur from perpetrators the victim already knows. Despite not understanding the severity of the situation, for both myself and other victims, I recognise a hungry ghost looming inside him. Why else would he prey on young girls?

The wound is deep and tender to touch. I know not the cause or the cure. I agreed to sneak out and meet him. Thus, because I don't yet understand the power differentials in our dynamic, his commodification of young girls' virginity, the mechanisms of consent, or my body's innate responses to threat, I overlook his crafty usage of social media, the pornographic files of visual media, and his blatant disregard of my "no".

I think what happened is my fault.

❦

The school bus trundles up a tree-lined hill to a waterpark in Kalamunda. Perched beside Kim, I finally find words to articulate the question pealing in my mind all week. "Don't you think that Colton's schoolgirl obsession is a little creepy?"

Her body goes limp. "I guess so. I've never really thought about it."

Kim's voice is deep, a semi-octave lower than most girls. Usually, it anchors me in the present moment. Today I find it unnerving. I straighten my spine and roll out my shoulders to open my heart. Kim easily recedes if she thinks she's being attacked. I don't want her to think I'm chastising her, but I need to stay strong—in head and heart—to navigate this conversation.

"I mean, why wouldn't he go after girls his own age?" I quiz.

Kim drums her long, delicate fingernails on the window. Then she gives a mirthless laugh.

I cock my head to the side, but before another word escapes me Kim requests that we not talk about it while nearby ears are burning.

At the waterpark, I sit on a bench and watch kids squeal down a twisting slide. My body is covered by my white polo shirt and navy-blue pants. In mid-Autumn warmth, I still don't feel like I'm concealing enough skin.

I'm wondering if this dismal fog will ever lift from my head when Dara strolls past with a group of arty intellectuals. I give a small wave then she doubles back and trudges over to me alone. After a bit of chitchat, I ask if she knows Colton. It's an impulsive question. The kind that my logical mind can't explain, but the depths of my soul knows is right.

She admits she lost her virginity to him when she was fourteen. She verifies that "Luke" doesn't exist. "Luke" is Colton's way of grooming girls with less trace online.

"He's fucked!" she fumes. "He did to me what he did to you."

The air feels thick and heavy as I soak in her words. How many girls has he exploited? Do we all carry a similar story?

The smell of chlorine pervades my nasal cavity as water splatters onto the concrete path. Cheerful kids continue gliding. Dizzy with excitement, they are oblivious that they could be his next victims. The weight of that is too much for me to carry alone. Yet I hold it. Composed on the outside, my shoulders crumble and my rib cage breaks.

We develop wisdom from the wounds.

The home phone rings for a microsecond before I grab it and tiptoe from the dark study to my bedroom.

"Kim?"

"Yeah, it is I," she whispers.

We're out of mobile credit, so she calls my home line for a midnight chat. Amid our hushed chatter about school and boys, I confess I've sent a topless photo to Cal. Sometime later, I sense someone is eavesdropping. I verbalize this to Kim then slink downstairs to investigate.

At the base of the stairs, I open the glass-panelled living room door. I feel my father's presence before he emerges from a dark corner with phone in hand. His eyes narrow in on me. I freeze.

Through curled lips, he growls with all the calm he can muster, "Say good night to Kim, and get your phone!"

In hindsight, I understand he is detonating with anger. What he overheard would infuriate any father concerned for his daughter's safety and wellbeing.

But like the dark room where he stands, the severity of the situation is yet to be illuminated.

I gulp and unmute the phone. "Kim, I've gotta go..."

"Okay—"

Click.

It's the last she hears from me for a month.

Desperate to delete all evidence of what I've been up to the past few weeks, I sprint upstairs and lock myself in my bathroom. The tiles freeze my feet. I erase the topless photo and then my sent messages one by one. I'm starting on my received messages when my parents pound on the door in tempo with my hammering heart.

"Jessica! Open the door," my father's voice berates.

I ignore him, fingers cramping as I delete more messages.

He continues banging. "Right *now*, or you'll be grounded for a *year*!"

"Oh-*kayyyy*." I mouth a quiet *Shit* to myself in the mirror. There's no way I can erase all the texts.

Head slumped to my shoulders, I open the door. Papa snatches my phone. After a gruff scolding, they ground me for two months and lock my phone in the safe. Then I am alone in my room. Under my duvet, the untold truth hacks and throbs. It consumes me like venom. Colton is exploiting young girls. Why am I the one being punished?

Two days later, Mama drives me home from a doctor's appointment along a tree-lined avenue towards the ocean. She raves about my straight A Term 1 report. Bags sag under my rolling eyes. What does it matter when I'm confined to my bedroom's four walls?

My right triceps shoot with mild pain from the cervical cancer vaccine. I wonder if there's a clinical remedy for the happiness and vitality gushing out of me like a ceiling leak in a wild rainstorm. Impulsively, I ask Mama if we can go somewhere to talk. Her chatter hushes as she indicates left then ascends a spiralling road to Reabold Hill—metro Perth's highest peak.

In the carpark Mama turns off the ignition. Without background music and forward motion, the situation densifies. I am present to all the confusion and pain festering inside me, like the simple gesture of rotating keys to turn off the ignition twists a tap and suddenly all my bound-up emotions have a spigot to release.

"What's going on?" Her question is followed by a silence that permeates the shimmering ocean vista stretching beyond hundreds of hectares of dry bushland.

When needed, Mama embodies an attentive presence with immediacy and ease.

I open my mouth. No words come.

She rubs my arm. The love in her touch is palpable. "It's okay, Jess. I'm here."

Distant birds screech and squawk. I draw a sharp inhale. It's not okay. I don't know if it will ever be okay again.

"I know someone who should be charged." My voice is an octave lower than its usual singsong quality.

Mama's façade is calm, but I glimpse her hands tightening into fists. She is being strong for me. As I disclose Colton's online personas, the photos he showed me, and his association with school balls, clouds mist the horizon into a foggy abyss. It sifts sunshine into intermittent patches of darkness and light.

"Did he touch you?" Mama asks.

I weigh my next words with caution. The premarital sexual condemnation I feel from my Christian upbringing's suppressive norms eclipse me. I am certain I will carry all sexual engagement to my grave.

"Jess, you're safe with me. But if he touched you, I need to know."

I am suffocating with shame. I cannot speak. It takes every ounce of courage inside me to nod yes.

"Did he place his hands inside your clothes?"

I lower my head. My skull pounds like thousands of thoughts are squirming and somersaulting into my stomach. "Yes."

I gasp for a slow inhale, but icy, spiderlike fingers press into my spine like Colton's hands. Days have passed, but I still feel his hold.

Out. I need out. I need space to breathe. My vision tightens to a fish-eyed lens as hyperventilation becomes me. Mama is rattled, but she maintains composure and guides my breathing back to a healthy rhythm. When my respiration is steady, she descends the summit where half the truth was unveiled. Back on lower ground, both our perspectives have widened.

At home, Mama requests Papa to the dining room table where they pry me for more details. I am compressed by forces from every angle. The assault from Colton. My parents' interrogation. My compounding agony. My motive to protect Kim. The pressure bursts out of me in warm, streaming tears as I reluctantly disclose more—still excluding the sex for I am imprisoned by fear of being chastised. My parents immediately call the police, adamant "to keep other children safe from this paedophile." It's the first time I've associated Colton with that word, and it shines a little clarity on the puzzle that's been stabbing me with barbed shards. To be word perfect, I now identify Colton as an ephebophile—an adult who is sexually attracted to adolescents.

As night drenches day in darkness, the police come and take my phone, MSN, and MySpace passwords. School holidays begin. The investigation starts. The upside of internet predators? Once something exists online, a digital web forms from their sticky trail of bunched-up 1s and 0s. The texts I didn't have time to delete become evidence for my case. This makes prosecution tangible.

Mama pushes for a medical examination to prove that my hymen is broken and thus assault occurred. The notion puts my nervous system into distressed overdrive. It is intrusive and disturbing. I am grateful that the police knock the idea back on the basis of childhood gymnastics and unnecessary additional trauma.

It is paramount for me to testify what happened as soon as possible. In the meantime, the police prohibit my access to the outside world so Colton is leaked no warnings. Because I am underage, I don't have to step foot in a courtroom. I attend an open camera session instead. No public. No jury. No press. This video recording of the three-hour police interview acts as my testimony in court. It is scheduled at 10 a.m. on April 20—the morning of my "sweet" sixteenth birthday.

"The truth is...
The last few weeks things changed. I stopped caring. Thinking. Feeling. The consequences of that have hit me now. I guess I had to hit rock bottom before things could get better.
The bad news? I hit rock bottom. Badly.
The good news? Things can only get better."

- 17 April 2007 journal entry

"I'm scared.
I'm scared of what I think.
I'm scared of what I feel.
I'm scared of what I did.
Of who I am.
I'm scared that things won't get better from now on."

- 18 April 2007 journal entry

Blood swirls in the porcelain toilet bowl as I cough and retch viscous chunks. My throat flares. My head pounds. Snot and bile drip into the vile stew. White pus oozes from my tonsils so swollen they are millimetres from touching. A red rash sears from hips to legs. It is the morning of my not-so-sweet sixteenth birthday.

I look at the deathlike pallor of my reflection. What the hell am I going to say? And how am I going to say it? I am literally unable to speak with my bleeding, burning, choking throat. Will I be chastised if I relay the truth, the whole truth, and nothing but the truth? No matter what I say, somebody gets hurt. I ponder disclosing the full story, but it drowns me in fear. I've been grounded for two months for sending a topless photo. How will I be punished if they find out I'm not a virgin?

My belly lurches at the stomach-acid odour of what I cannot digest as Mama knocks on my door.

"Jess, we've got to go."

I open my mouth to reply. It scorches just to swallow. How am I going to sit through a three-hour interview when each breath feels like a scalding wind? Through the pain of each syllable, I plead not to go.

Mama wraps me in her arms and utters, "It's better to get it over and done with."

At the station, a female officer takes one look at me and postpones my testimony. Temporary relief inundates me. I slide towards the door, but she requests a private word before we go, looking to Mama and Papa for permission. They nod. She leads me to a balcony protected by nature's leafy arms.

"I know this is hard for you," she comforts. "It shows in the state of your body right now. I hope you get well soon and can enjoy your birthday."

I divert my gaze from the slow dance of green foliage, watching as she mulls over her next words.

"This case is important. There may be others like you who haven't got the courage to come forward. You're protecting them. And others he could harm." She swallows what I glimpse as sadness, maybe even pain, then looks at me with empathic eyes. "I'm sorry this has happened. We want to convict him. We really do. *As soon as possible...* In the meantime, it's important you look after yourself and keep yourself safe. You're a pretty girl, but you're also very bright. You need not hide your intelligence."

A wave of anger surges. *Protect others? It's already happening to others! And what's this dig about concealing my smarts?* My death stare conveys what I physically cannot say.

At home, my pain intensifies as the day rolls on. Mama takes me to our local GP, who extracts blood to test for glandular fever. I'm getting used to adults pricking and prodding and probing, but familiarity doesn't make it easier to endure. I'm growing resilient, at the expense of becoming numb. The scrawny doctor writes in his notebook and prescribes stronger meds. He lacks the emotional and somatic intelligence that the venom of my suppressed truth magnifying inside me is what causes me pain.

Just after midnight, I hack and purge over the toilet. I am drowning with sweat. At this point Mama drives me to the hospital's emergency department, where I slouch on a beat-up plastic chair for three hours. It is Saturday night. It is busy. I stare at my hands, white fists clenched. Antiseptic, cleaning products, body odour, and booze pervade the air-conditioned room with pain and despair. The vending machine clinks and clanks. Soft drink cans pop and fizz. I suffocate in an endless storm of wheezes, yells, whimpers, and groans. It is 4:30 a.m. when I am admitted. With tonsils now touching, breathing is problematic.

"On a scale of one to ten, how much pain are you in?" a doctor asks.

I lift all fingers and thumbs. The tightening of blood pressure cuffs is floppy compared to my internal tension. A needle pricks. The cool rush of a saline-based electrolyte solution rehydrates me, with painkillers reducing my affliction. Around midmorning, results from the GP come back negative for glandular fever. I have acute tonsillitis.

The beauty of western medicine is the quick fix when you need it. Though doctors don't address the emotional roots of my pain, two full doses of antibiotics reduce the swelling, which allows me to swallow, breathe properly, and eat again. That afternoon, a nurse with sincere eyes moves me to her sterile, windowless ward. Behind the listless curtain encapsulating me in my own bubble, I drift in and out of consciousness as I drench my bedsheets with hot rivers of sweat. Beeping monitors and the quiet hum from a neighbouring patient's TV sail in and out of my awareness as I stare at the plain-white ceiling and nibble processed food. Will this agony ever end?

Pain can be crippling,
but it allows us to transform.

One week later, I lie on the top bunk in the kids' room of my grandparents' serene wooden home. Melodic wind chimes serenade me into stillness and rejuvenate my entire being. My soul finds sanctuary. My mind eases. Finally. After contemplating if they should cancel their prebooked trip to Melbourne or bring me with them, my parents send me to Guilderton and venture interstate alone. It is the first week of Term 2. I crave the stimulation of learning and the comfort of friends, but I am still forbidden access to the outside world until after I give my testimony.

It's been three weeks since my late-night phone chat with Kim. It's been three weeks of anguish and isolation. The detriment of feeling alone and punished when I most need connection and support becomes apparent in subsequent years. I later realise that my default pattern in the face of challenge is to withdraw from the world and encapsulate myself in an impenetrable bubble. It is the process conditioned upon me in my darkest hour. I am forced to find sanctuary inside my own bones.

I delve into study to distract myself from the pain as rain strums against the metal roof and trickles onto tall sunflowers. Somewhere in the pitter-patter is a murmur inviting me to take the reins of truth and empowerment. All I feel is a hammering shame. Grannie and Grandad feed me garden-grown vegetables that I digest with antibiotics and painkillers. They are the first adults not to bombard me with questions about what happened. They simply let me be. The safe space to process what happened is monumental. Though life will never be the same, it allows the first rays of healing to warm my icy insides.

As birds flutter into fluffy calligraphy clouds that draft my blurry destiny, I watch the river flow towards the ocean and ponder water's prophetic nature. Did the ocean see this coming? What does it whisper in the murmuring salty breeze?

Two female police officers settle across the table in the interview room fitted with microphones and cameras. They offer me water before pressing record and asking the necessary questions. For three long, hard, dry, bristly hours, we unpack the experience. I unveil what was said, what was done, what I wore, what I saw, what I smelt, what I felt—everything. Everything but the sex. I'm not ready to tell the truth, the whole truth, and nothing but the truth, so help me God. I am still holding on to shame, still blaming myself, still fearful of how the case will impact Kim.

At the end of the testimony, they ask, "Is there anything else you should tell us?"

Yes. He had sex with me when I said "No". I only met up with him because Kim did, and she only did because of what I did six days earlier. Yes, but it all points to me, so....

"No."

Grey clouds diffuse the sky into a gloomy gravitas on my first day back at school.

Trudging to Kim's and my shared locker, I dodge a large murky puddle. A chilly gust tousles my hair into artist swirls as I peer at my reflection in the mud. I glimpse an unfamiliar expression. It is a medley of protective sharpness, stoicism, and the soft promise of growth. I tear away my gaze. Goose bumps prick my skin. I don't know if they're afflicted from the weather or my emotions.

Kim spots me and gapes like I'm a ghost. It makes sense. I feel dead inside. Eyes welling with tears, she runs over with a tender embrace. Droplets of discombobulation and despair, then remorse and relief slide down her perfectly sculpted cheeks as I fill her in on the police testimony, emergency ward, and solitary confinement that shackled my life the past four weeks.

Her body quivers as she holds me close and sobs. Shives spike my spine, but my eyes remain dry. I have no more tears left to cry.

♥

Kim refuses to attest her own case—she doesn't want to "get into shit" with her mum and stepdad—but agrees to testify mine. Because of the nature of the case, the testimony of the first person in whom I confided is considered evidence in court. Her word becomes his inadvertent fingerprints on my body. While Kim's testimony is scheduled, Colton is arrested in a surprise home apprehend. As his phone and computer are seized, he screams, "I'm fucked, I'm fucked!" Meanwhile, his distraught mother weeps.

The police keep us informed as the investigation progresses. They find the video of my naked body being scanned. Then they mention another video that appears to be me and question if he had sex with me. My heart drops past my stomach to the pits of hell. I was right. He did film me blindfolded. Papa examines my deadpan expression. I look the officer directly in the eye—remembering what I've read about body language and microexpressions that give away deceit—and reply, "No." I don't want to repeat the month I've just endured. I don't want more solitary confinement, police probing, or condemnation from my parents. Despite the vast evidence he's engaged with other underage girls, without them coming forward, there's no way of linking faces and bodies to names.

Colton gets a lawyer. Trial begins. Kim's video testimony is shown with mine in court. Mrs Clementon acts as a character reference for him in court. He doesn't change. Mariana's friend continues fucking him.

Colton pleads guilty before a judge and jury and is convicted with four counts of sexual assault. Instead of jail, he gets eighteen months' probation. If he breaks any law during that time, he goes straight to jail for two years. Do not pass Go. Do not collect $200. His name is added to the child sex offenders' list, but he is still closely affiliated with school balls. The news burns. It stabs and stings like a crazed rabies-infected dog on a biting rampage. Will he continue exploiting wide-eyed girls, sitting them on his lap as he flicks through photos of *me* and *my friends* with his veiny penis erect?

Long after the gavel hammers in court, my world remains in slashed shards. Confusion clouds me in a billowing haze. I wonder what he does with the pornographic visuals. Does he upload them to sell online? Why collect them to begin with? Are they trophies of young virgins he's deflowered? Why did he plead guilty? Was it to lower his sentence, or does he genuinely feel remorse? For years I question if he's changed. Does he assimilate a lesson and become a better person?

Eventually I decide it isn't for me to know. His evolution, or lack thereof, is out of my control. It's not my responsibility. But my growth is. All I can do is slowly unstack the stories I tell myself that jade my perception of the world. I am worthy. I am safe. I am protected. Genuine, loving men do exist—real men who respect me and my boundaries. My voice has power. I will be heard.

Can you feel it dripping through the syllables that string these sentences together?

Healing isn't easy.
But it beats the alternative—staying shackled in fear.

Stretching my feet into the chilly corners of the bottom bunk, I turn my music up. After my first nightmare of Colton raging through my bedroom, I start sleeping in the spare bedroom. If I change my location, maybe my situation will change.

Post trial, Mama and Papa extend my two-month grounding—which prohibits access to the computer or phone—by three weeks, arguing that it began after my hospitalization. I sizzle beneath my calm façade. It doesn't teach me to change my ways. It triggers me to emotionally withdraw and suppress my vulnerability for fear of further punishment while acting the part they want me to play. It is the beginning of me plastering on masks.

Bitter rains hammer against the window. I pretend the precipitation caused my wet pillow. That morning, I sat opposite my soft-eyed counsellor and lied that I am okay. I detest the perpetual onslaught of adult strangers into my ragged and jagged terrain. I need compassion, support, and understanding from friends, but that privilege is stripped. So, I stack the bricks higher.

From songs on shuffle, "Otherside" and "Heart-Shaped Box" cascade with raw emotion. Cocooned by darkness, I stay up with the night. The music stirs my stagnated pain and smooths my turmoil into hope for better days. I seethe. Then I soothe. It is the release I need. My heartstrings are pulled and plucked and stretched and strummed. I remember what it feels like to feel in the ephemeral eternity etched into the songs.

Tilting my head back into the water, I disguise my tears as warm drops. I sit on the shower floor, lady parts pulsating, fingers still wet. With the benefit of hindsight, I understand that I cry after self-pleasuring because toxic beliefs cement me in shame that separates sex from love. Lathering soap onto my body, I scrub every inch of my skin. Steam fogs the mirror. My fingers wrinkle and prune. I emerge from the shower smelling of fresh citrus and mild lavender.

In my head, I am still dirty.

The man on stage preaches about Jesus while I luxuriate into the velvet cinema-style seat. Friday night youth group is the only form of socialising I'm allowed during my grounding. Bubbly Polly Jane usually meets me inside the massive warehouse converted into a nondenominational church. Tonight she is absent. In our letter book we take turns to fill, I admit that I've been prescribed my first round of SSRI antidepressants—a small white pill to swallow my pain and sweep my unresolved trauma under a pharmaceutical band-aid. Around this time, Mama is re-prescribed antidepressants because of another hostile work environment. We later connect the anxiety and lack of control she feels to what is transpiring in my world. With retrospect, Mama recognises that her unknown gluten intolerance is an invisible barrier to her wellbeing with gut microbiome connected to emotional health. She is under huge emotional strain with nothing left in her reserves. Stomach aches are stress internalised.

My gaze drifts between the two large projector screens on either side of the stage. Between the preacher's wise words, I daydream about Cal. What is he doing? Does he wonder why I suddenly disappeared? Sometimes we pass messages to each other through Kim, but I don't feel galaxies exploding within me like I do when we chat privately or are physically close.

The band plays Christian worship songs as lasers flash across the stage, cutting up my reverie. Kids sing and dance to the music. I lip-sync under my breath.

Behind the smiley Mauritian youth leader beside me, a brunette girl peers my way. At the end of the night, he introduces her as Courtney.

"Hey dardy," she blusters.

I smile coyly. "Hello."

She is well-groomed in jeans and a hoodie, but her mannerisms are rough. I am simultaneously intimidated and enthralled. I've been so restrained lately it's refreshing to meet someone unpolished and raw. As we hug hello, I whiff hard liquor on her breath. I don't know we are fumbling the same sexually traumatised path. I don't know she is addicted to heroin. All I see is a radiant smile that makes her tanned face glow; the façade that conceals her inner agony.

It takes courage to shine hope on our darkest parts.

In the granny flat behind her parents' home, Courtney peers behind the curtains to check the house lights are off before pulling out a large bottle of vodka. She takes a few swigs. I take two. Then she flips through photos of her alcoholic boyfriend and praises him.

A few weeks earlier, he verbally abused her outside the church. She too is forced there as punishment for drink-driving. His fists clenched when she refused to ditch youth group and get in his car. As he spat on the ground and called her nasty words, I stepped forward with fiery protection. She wasn't sticking up for herself. But I would. A youth leader intercepted the commotion and ushered us inside. He tried to follow. Eventually he was sent away on the basis of age and intoxication.

"Courtney, I love ya, girl," I profess, purposely stealing her attention. "Thanks for visiting me in hospital the other week when I had my tonsils removed. It meant a lot to see you."

She cracks a grin and combs her fingers through wavy strands. "You too, dards. Love ya, babe."

After a few face-scrunching sips, I glimpse a blotchy home tattoo on her ring finger.

"What—what is that? Are they *someone's initials?*"

Courtney penetrates me with a fierce green gaze. I meet it with love, relishing that it softens her. She tells me about an older man with whom she regularly injects heroin. Externally, I remain nonjudgemental, knowing that doing otherwise will cause her to shut down. Internally, I am stunned. I wonder if there's a reason for her addictive, self-destructive tendencies.

Halfway through the bottle, I disclose the assault to Courtney. She sets the vodka aside. She is present and silent in her listening. When I am done, she takes a swig from the bottle then starts talking in a low, clear tone. As I suspected, we share a similar story. Tears well from haunted eyes as she recounts her sister's boyfriend entering her room late at night and touching her inappropriately. She was fourteen when the assaults escalated to rapes. I ask if her sister knows.

"Yes, but she doesn't believe me..." Courtney laments. "She called me a stinking liar! And she—she's still with the filthy bastard."

In that moment, I understand Courtney's saboteur escapism; her risky behaviours; the re-traumatisation of being silenced. I see her pain, and it encapsulates me with barbed sorrow and scorching rage.

A few hours later, the room spins. My eyes are heavy from liquor. Yet so clearly, I see the toxic roots that connect us and distort our perception of intimacy. I understand we are stuck in a vicious self-destructive cycle that drills the delusion deeper that our voices are undeserving of being heard. Venomous beliefs splinter our self-worth to inadequate specks.

I cannot see the flicker of an empowered path that beckons us to transcend our savage deterioration. I am drenched with darkness. It is dense and disorientating.

♦

Around this time someone dear to me confides of an older man using a catfish profile to coerce her to meet. He had anal sex with her. Despite her not wanting to. Despite her being a virgin. Despite her being fifteen and him over forty. I drown in sorrow. Fury slashes me with searing embers. I am fragile and powerless in a world brimming with danger, nauseated and betrayed by society. Once again, guilt and despair consume me because I perceive my interactions with Jarred as sparking a dangerous chain reaction of toppling dominos that cut and crush those I love. In hindsight, I discern the grown men grooming underage girls with fake internet profiles are to blame. Not me.

I now see sexual assault for what it is—a violating fire that destroys us from the inside. The starry-eyed part of us that trusts in love and believes in the emotional sacredness of sex burns to oblivion. When the fierce flames extinguish, three smoky paths twist and trail from the burn, prohibiting us from seeing ourselves and the world in its true light. We are stuck in a downward spiral.

Courtney and I walk the first path. We appease men and give ourselves to anyone willing. To ourselves, we muster, "One man didn't listen to my no, why will the rest?" We believe that men only value us for sex and become slaves to others' gratification.

Pilgrims of the second path tiptoe the opposite way. They freeze and shy away from lovemaking completely. To themselves, they whisper, "Intimacy is not safe" and forgo connections that can be devotional, reverent, and nurturing.

The third path dissociates from the pain by deviating from men and finding solace in women. Inwardly these women scream, "All men are scum!" because the folly of one man taints their perception of an entire gender.

My expression is not that every women-loving woman has been assaulted or mistreated by men. Love is love. That part is simple. Nor is my expression that women who feel liberated through sexual exploration with multiple partners have issues. That's not for me to judge. Or you. My expression is that long after the tears dry, we are torn to tatters with the trauma that transmutes into our tissues.

It takes courage to face each day and seek beauty in a world that is scorched and broken. Physiologically speaking, emotions have a ninety-second lifespan in our body. It is these stories we tell ourselves after that perpetuate the fierce inferno and become our ruin.

Creating stories of "My only value is sex" or "Intimacy is not safe" or "All men are scum" is our way of rationalising what never should have happened to begin with. It is a thought that influences our behaviour, and thus shapes our reality. By accepting these stories as truth, we become victims. Not because of the experience. We are victims of the assigned meaning.

It takes me years to discover an alternative way. A path to liberation, where my wounds become wings. It does not appear amid the smoky trails because it transcends the stories completely. In being aware there are warped beliefs jading our existence, we have the choice to change. We are caged birds. The cage is the story. Without it, we are free to fly.

With hindsight I see the link between trauma festering in my body and my sixteenth birthday hospitalization. I didn't want to talk about what happened. I was terrified of speaking my truth. I lost belief in the power of my words. On a physiological level, my bleeding, pus-saturated, swollen tonsils blocked my ability to communicate. Doctors surgically removed my infected lymph nodes, but the only way to abolish a story is to first uncover it so we can consciously let it go.

Only then can we form new beliefs. Ones that unshackle us and give us feathers to fly. It is here we transcend the victim mentality and embody the warrior's spirit. You are your own knight in shining armour. Your spirit may be seared with scars, but it is in this suffering the strength of your soul ignites.

It is in the ashes we rise.

Inside the small stone church, I clutch a velvety bouquet and hide my secrets behind a smile. In my royal-purple bridesmaid dress, I feel like the black sheep in my family as Emily glides down the aisle on Papa's arm. Like our parents, grandparents, and great-grandparents, Emily saves sex until marriage. She holds herself with a dignified poise, and the shy sincerity of the newlyweds gives me hope that I too will find love—deep and true.

My desire transpires in Cal and me reconnecting. As spring blossoms with the fragrant promise of new growth, he invites me to his eighteenth birthday. It's a whole-body yes. I feel it with every cell and fibre. Him and I have unfinished business.

Destiny interlaces us in an invisible web.
I feel your presence in the silky silver threads.

Welcome to Perth Hills, the sign reads as my friend's dad steers us up the highway. I tell Mama I'm sleeping at my friends. My friend tells her dad the truth—we are going to Cal's party—and he drives us there, knowing that his trust breeds an honourable candour.

At the recreation centre encircled by rustling trees, Cal embraces me.

"You're even more beautiful than I remember," he whispers.

My cheeks warm. His words caress my bones.

Then a loud *shatter* has him bounding.

I quench my anxiety with a sugary vodka premix. Clutching the icy bottle, I sing chirpy hellos to Reed and Cal's friends. Aussie hip-hop shakes the room. In my periphery is a group of girls dancing. I glimpse the long, tanned legs of the bleached-blonde babe I will later know as Laula. Just as I'm wondering if I should join them, a short, freckled ginger skips over and introduces herself as Eve. She oozes a genuine warmth that eases me into the party.

After downing a few vodkas, Eve and I bolt across the dewy oval, barefoot in giggles to climb a cricket net. Reed flies after us and yells at us to get down. We do as he says and skip towards the party with arms linked. I like Eve and Reed. They feel familiar. Before we reach the hall, stomach acid pervades my taste buds, and I stumble to my knees. Eve holds my hair back as my stomach lurches with liquid confidence surfacing in fluorescent tsunamis. Someone drives me up the road to Cal's with Eve, who leaves the party early to nurse me. It is the beginning of a friendship that is tender-hearted and tragic. For us both.

Some dude is passed out in Cal's bed when he gets home, so we canoodle in a tent outside. With limbs entwined, he presses his lips on mine. Tingles shoot through my body like two currents sharing the same circuit are connecting. I trace my fingers around the contours of his body, then rest my hand on his pounding heart.

"Why's it beating so fast?" I slur.

"Because I'm in love," he swoons with surprising clarity.

I melt. Cal is the one exception to my intimate interactions being hollow. He knew me before the assault. He tears down my barriers, sees through my masks, and loves me at my most vulnerable layer. Partly because I let him. Partly because he can. He's met himself there.

The following weekend I find a way up the hill again. This time I refrain from drinking and inform Cal I won't sleep with him unless he is sober. He sidelines his beer and devours me with kisses that soften my serrated insides. Intoxicated by every atom in his anatomy, we become a beautiful dream that interlaces with a devastating nightmare.

eve is not naïve> *jess! you haven't been online in forever???*
jesssska> *i've been studyingggg for exams*
eve is not naïve> *oh. good luck!*
jesssska> *thanks, babe! all done now. got my report card today :)*
eve is not naïve> *how'd you go!?*
jesssska> *straight A grades! except for chemistry...*

It turns out there are other elements in the equation. In a lengthy two-hour conversation, Eve discloses her feelings for Cal. I sensed this from her keen interest in our dynamic. A prickly blend of empathy and guilt stirs—she nursed me so lovingly before Cal and I shared our first kiss. A kiss that was years in the making after hundreds of online chats but just two in person meets. Our connection must pain her. Then she reveals he slept with another girl while I was studying. Even with retrospect I don't know if her intentions are friendly or malicious. My heart sinks to the ocean floor's benthic depths. I let my walls crumble, and he's tossed a brick at my unguarded heart.

Angry flames roar and our first fight sizzles. As 2007 ends, silence eddies into the space between us and he starts seeing another girl. Days before he asks Felicity to be his girlfriend, he texts me his true feelings. *I'll always have feelings for you, Jess. I want something serious with you. Not just some girl I go out with, then it goes to shit. But*

I don't want you to wait around for me. You're beautiful. Go make someone happy.

Gentle, undulating waves roll me into the new year at the same beach I lost my virginity at nine months earlier. I trail my fingers through the satiny currents, wishing I could let Cal dissolve into the sweeping flow. A silver path of midnight moonlight oscillates into the horizon. It glistens and glows and listens and flows, beckoning me to walk it. I am the moon that hides its dark side, the part that pulls the entire ocean from shore to shore.

Liquor on her lips, Courtney stumbles in the shallows. She doesn't want to look at the dark undercurrents, and she can't fathom pushing through the surface waves. Hindered by inertia, she is a rag doll in the unending surf. When she garbles that she's been smoking "rock", I tilt my head. *Do you mean a small pebble? What do you mean it's a crystal that keeps you up all night?*

"My sister gave me my first high," Courtney laments. "She's regretted it ever since."

On the fifth floor of a dank hotel, we get higher than the city skyline. In the stark artificial light, Courtney's eyes brim with the consideration she was neglected. We both glance at my friend applying a temporary tattoo of the Australian flag on her arm. Courtney reiterates that partaking is our choice, and if we do want to, she will only allow a "tiny taste".

From the streets, people yell, "Aussie, Aussie, Aussie! Oi, Oi, Oi!"

I nod. I'm curious to the physiological and psychological effects of the drug. I will try it just once and never touch it again. Courtney's boyfriend heats a clear chunky crystal of methamphetamine in a light bulb, then instructs us to inhale sharply through the body of a pen. Six eyes are on me as I gulp the swirling white smoke, hold it in, then exhale.

As euphoria ripples into a rapid flight of ideas, Courtney sends my friend and me high into the dusky city. Striding through the drunken maze of teens crowding the river's foreshore, I spot Dara and waltz over. She looks bummed, so I mute my relentless urge to chatter. This gives her the space to disclose. Colton is threatening to have her excluded from our upcoming ball if she doesn't comply with his demands. Logically I know I should be angry that a sex offender is *still* involved in the organisation of school activities and that he hasn't changed his ways. But the illicit substance billows in my bones. It makes me feel untouchable. For a moment

I contemplate how easy the drug could numb me from my grating reality. Then I centre myself in my promise that this won't be reoccurring.

My high nosedives as Australia Day fireworks explode in chemical colours. Waves of residual stimulation roll through me as the prismatic aerial display blasts in whizzing whistles and hollow booms. Up and out, sulphur-smelling paper wicks sizzle and soar. But the outcome is inevitable. Climatic flashes always extinguish in ebonized embers.

🍎

We face our reflection in the mirror, but sometimes the picture projected onto others is a little harder to swallow.

Holding my breath, I spray fake tan onto my skin in my bathroom. Once the fumes dry as honeyed caramel on my body, I lather my face with makeup. Permanent dark circles cling to my eyes—the only outside evidence of the baggage I carry within me. I try reviving them by going to bed earlier, but it's the kind of tired that sleep can't solve.

My phone buzzes with a text from Charlie, the rosebud-lipped, dimple-chinned sweetheart who is friends with Cal, Eve, and Reed. What starts as befriending David's mates to weave myself into his world quickly becomes long-lasting, genuine bonds.

Hey baby, are you still coming up tonight?

I look at the time. Ten minutes until my first bus.

Yes, beautiful. See you in two hours ;)

In a frenzied rush, I straighten crinkled strands of my newly bleached blonde hair. I think that armouring myself in protective layers of an artificial mask will stop the world from hurting me. I see now that vulnerability is not a weakness. With great sensitivity comes great strength. The ability to drop your armour and be authentic is more courageous than rushing headfirst into battle.

On the two buses and two trains to Charlie's house, I smile at how close we've grown since Cal introduced us in an MSN chat a few weeks back. When Charlie confides she lost her mum to breast cancer two weeks before her thirteenth birthday, I understand her and Cal's tender bond. Her protruding brown eyes emanate a softness and resilience that only hardship can bestow. She empathises with others' pain for she has endured her own.

At a bus stop girdled by trees, Charlie welcomes me with a smile. Crickets click as we stride to her musty, cluttered home and she offers me a Vodka Cruiser. We down a couple, then Reed picks us up to go to a party. We've been chatting frequently since he admitted he doesn't like Felicity because "she has Cal by the balls". Our friendship strengthens when I discern that he doesn't have an ulterior motive with me. We speak with depth behind our words, and his baby-blue eyes sparkle whenever he says something comical, which is often.

At the party, Cal's eyes flash with remorse. I can't bear to look at him too deeply or for too long. Static connects us with untouched passion. It teases to release like stretchy thread pulled to full resistance by a single strand. Bound by invisible strings, I feel his heart pumping in my veins. But he is with another girl, and heartache debilitates me with stinging self-doubt.

🍎

I want to dislike Felicity, with her upturned nose and greasy dark hair, but when I finally meet her, I cannot genuinely look at her with spite. At the end of summer, I use "youth group and a sleepover" as a cover to gate-crash her ball afterparty after busing across the midnight city with a friend. Beneath my jealousy, I understand what Cal sees. Her striking blue eyes emanate a sincerity and strength that can slice a man open or beckon him into an intoxicating devotion.

Minutes after meeting Felicity, I dawdle onto the driveway facing a massive skatepark and spot Laula. She's recently befriended me on MySpace under her username: watupdetroit.

Without hesitation, I waltz over and ask, *"Are you wat up detroit?"*

The six-foot-tall, bronzed blonde grins. "Yeah! Are you *jesssska?*"

"Yes." I beam as we hug, unknowingly binding a forever friendship that is nourishing, hilarious, deep, and telepathic.

🍎

"I'm scared Colton will be at our ball...angry and waiting for me," I admit with a heavy stomach as my friend's eyes bulge from her head.

Kim is busy kissing her Maori boyfriend, so I strolled to the music department to find my demure Fijian friend from tour. She is the only person I confide my inner undercurrents. Unlike Kim, she holds me through my fears and doesn't invalidate my emotions. I ruminate on what I'll do if he appears behind one of the long, dark curtains at our *Casino Royale*-themed ball. Is he waiting for me to be in the wrong place at the right time?

En route to Challenge Stadium in a hired limousine, Kim's boyfriend pulls out a massive flask of cheap whiskey. The sweet woody liquid is easy to swallow. Each dry, astringent drop drowns my trepidation. The smell gently oozes in the sweat collecting under my silky turquoise dress, streaking my bronzed, borderline-orange tan as '90s pop booms. I am no longer the naïve brunette he knew. Will he even recognize me with my new mask?

*Rawness looks good no matter what form it takes
for it oozes an untamed heart.*

Goodbye cruel world. K. Thx. Bye.

I rub my eyes and reread Jarred's text. It is 1:37 a.m. I've twisted my sheets into a tangled mess as my ruminations churn. I keep picturing underage girls ensnared on Colton's lap while he flicks my ball photos into their naive eyes.

Jarred's message drowns me with fear, yet it frees me from my own woes. He doesn't answer my calls, so I message some loving words. Then I finally succumb to sleep. In the morning, I check in again. Eventually he replies. Family and friends stopped him from actioning the irreversible tragedy that is suicide. He is tender nonetheless. From thereon I check in every few days. Sometimes he doesn't have words for the concoction of emotions fusing into a chunky bundle. But knowing I'm there helps.

A few weeks later—a year after he took my virginity—he invites me to a luxury hotel above the city's only casino. The gesture isn't as romantic as it seems. He'd booked it for his ex-girlfriend who bailed last minute, leaving him with an expensive room, and a reason to party. I tell Mama and Papa I'm walking to a friend's house for a sleepover, then perch on the cement steps of my old primary school. Jarred isn't available to collect me for another two hours, but I must leave home in daylight to dissipate parental concern. Mosquitoes feast. Darkness swallows the sky. Jarred arrives with drum and bass blasting. With legs itching from stinging red bites, I slide into the backseat and introduce myself to his friend. The car screeches around city corners as heavy basslines rumble over fast, broken beats.

In the hotel with my friend we collect en route, Jarred pulls me into his arms and kisses me. Then he offers us ecstasy. My friend and I split a pill. My motive is the same as Courtney's "rock": try it early, kill the curious cat. Euphoria pulses through my veins with promise of a fun night. Until Jarred swallows three pills in one giant gulp.

His friend fires up. "What the hell are you doin', man? Are you insane?"

The confrontation prompts Jarred to down another three pills, bolt out the door, and drive across the city to find his ex-girlfriend.

He is gone for hours. My mate climbs the walls. Literally. His friend jibber-jabbers. I sit cross-legged on the floor, trying to read through a ten-page narrative for an upcoming essay. The words convolute into an indigestible jumble, so I too clamber and chatter until Jarred returns at 1 a.m., wide-eyed and silent.

His mate scolds him for driving high. Jarred steps towards the door. Before he can run off again, I throw myself on him in an affectionate hug. He is rigid in my arms. Then he slackens and feels mushy. We are all rattled by him running out. But he doesn't need a lecture. He needs love.

"Next time, call me. Even if you don't want to talk, just call me, and know I'm here."

He examines me with doting eyes. Then he smiles for the first time all night. "You're so good to me."

Our friends fall asleep entangled, as do Jarred and I. It is a restless slumber. I toss unobtrusively all night. Mental clutter clogs the space between us. It mattes my mind. With morning's first rays, I awake to Jarred's attention anchored on me. His eyes aren't wandering for some sort of urgent truth. His mind is still. Finally, I peer into his marble-grey pools. Fragile and washed out, yet resilient and growing, he lets me climb inside. Then he tucks a strand of hair behind my ear and kisses me. His appreciation is toasty as I snuggle into his muscular arms and we slip back into slumber.

When I awake again, Jarred slouches in front of the TV watching cartoons, bong in hand. Smoke eddies into midmorning light streaming through the window. In his illuminated giggles, I see how life is simultaneously tragic and magic. I recognise his pain of not knowing who will help him and who will hurt him. Maybe I can rekindle his trust in the world by being a luminous example.

*

The veil is thin today.
I still feel you.

May God have mercy on your soul, the epitaph reads. I look from Courtney to the tombstone she adorns with wilting flowers blown into a woven wire fence from nearby gravestones. She doesn't know who John is or why he died in 1905, but she feels an intense and curious connection. Sometimes she passes out by his grave late at night, adamant that he communicates with her through her dreams.

She is swinging on a pendulum between utter destruction and the inception of healing. She says she feels a higher power directing her to leave her brutish boyfriend, but she can't seem to jump off the weighted rod before it swings back into his savage arms. I eye the graveyard's stony reminder of life's inevitable end. How thin is the veil between death and breath? Does Courtney's connection with John border on psychosis?

Kids gulp water from the fountain as the morning siren rings. I line up behind them with a quiet smile. Cal messaged out of the blue to ask how I'm doing.

Suddenly icy shivers crawl down my spine. I turn around to Mrs Clementon sneering as she passes. I maintain a straight demeanour, but her eyes pierce my skin with venom. It is the third time this fortnight she's drilled malice into my bones.

That afternoon I attend a private lunch the principal puts on for a dozen high-achieving Year 12 students. It's not the cucumber sandwich I digest as I shake hands with the man. It's bewilderment whether he knows Mrs Clementon defended a sexual predator in court, a man who assaulted at least half a dozen other students. It is in this moment my academic inspirations crumble. I abandon trust in authority. I stop giving a fuck.

"Jessica! Come downstairs, please. It's time for a family conversation."

Atop the dining room table, a large yellow envelope stations beside my chair. Papa orders me to open it and read the contents out loud. I roll my eyes. I cross my arms. Papa repeats his command. Reluctantly I peer inside to find a private MSN conversation between me and a boy. Not only has Papa snooped through my private chat logs, he's printed one onto seven smooth, white pages, and now demands I read it aloud.

My entire body inflames. Yet again, my privacy is purposely violated with Papa's determination to needle the truth from the hay I've stacked before my cave. I look to Mama for sympathy. She sits silent and diverts her gaze. Papa threatens to ground me for the next year if I don't obey. Simmering with rage, I read until the nugget emerges. *I've been with 6 people.*

I try to twist my words, saying I've kissed six people, but I am hemmed and halved by their irate eyes. Mama and Papa are present parents. They just want what's best for me and expect me to uphold their rules while living under their roof. I understand this in hindsight, but the needle still stabs me with shame as they dig their fingers into my wounds in a gory showdown.

I resent them for squishing my freedom and stamping out my sexuality with their conservative stance. It pushes parts of me that want to be expressed into my shadow self—innate aspects of me that I deny because they are condemned and rejected. In retrospect, I see they are simply trying to guide me to be a young woman with good morals. They raise me to believe that sex is contained for marriage, but there is never an opportunity for me to voice legitimate questions or concerns. It's their way or the highway. I've known this for years.

In Year 9, schoolyard talk aroused my curiosity about what "head" and "hand" were. I didn't trust my parents could hold a safe conversation, so I Googled it and came face to face with graphic porn. Pop-ups later alerted them to my search. In a shocking confrontation, Mama threatened to watch the videos beside me if I dared look again. Their fierce reactions bound sexuality with shame. But repressing primal impulses doesn't make them go away. It simply gives the unconscious more power and makes us less integrated humans. This—along with my primary school exclusion and perpetual adult probing post-assault—compels me to hide myself behind a mask. It is unsafe to be me untethered.

I tug at the cotton blue tablecloth and seal my lips shut. When they realise that I won't reveal the finer details, they send me to my room. There, eighteen months of repressed emotions fizz and foam. No more can I push out, push away, push down. Chaos ferments.

The conversation is not over. It is paused until after my final university-determining exams. As twelve years of schooling trickles to an end and my peers gear up to party, I dread the study period closing. My parents confrontation lingers like toxic smoke on the horizon. What's the point of pushing forth if they strip my freedom from me again? What's the point of living?

A few days later, I am admitted into a private psychiatric hospital nestled inside high brick walls. Mama and Papa love me, but they're lost for approaches to protect me. Their misguided method pushes me into a dense hollow where I no longer want to live. City traffic hums into tall, leafy trees as Mama stops the car beside a three-tiered stone fountain inside Perth Clinic's circular driveway.

"Go to reception," she instructs. "I'll meet you there once I park."

I peer up at the two-storey brown-bricked building welcoming me like a homey boarding school. It's not the stark white walls I imagined. The smiley-eyed receptionist hands me a thick, heavy folder. It contains everything I'll need for the next two weeks.

Fresh, seasoned vegetables waft in decadent aromas as Mama walks with me to my room. Sunlight streams onto a single bed where I skim-read the folder's introductory pages. Mama kisses me on the forehead and makes plans to visit the following day. A little while later, a nurse knocks on my door and requests I accompany her to the ward station up the hall. There, she hands me my antidepressant in a small plastic container. I gulp it down and step away. She stops me, instructing I open my mouth and lift my tongue. Then she directs me to a spacious dining hall for dinner.

⁂

My hands are clammy as I line up for food. I examine the sea of faces. Some smile. Some frown. Others catch my eye. I am definitely the youngest. The bald head chef serves me mashed potato and sautéed vegetables with a wide beam. Further along the queue, a patient asks him the title of his cookbook.

"*Healthy Food, Healthy Mind,*" he replies.

I soon discern that a hospital's care for health is revealed in the quality of their food. There's no white bread or processed deli meat here.

The next morning, I sleep through breakfast and my first ninety-minute group therapy session. The nurse on duty tells me it's important I attend all three daily sessions because it's an integral part of my treatment regime. I nod and ask if I can eat lunch in my room. She explains we're encouraged to eat with others because it endorses connection which heightens solidarity for healing.

My apprehension of sitting alone dissipates with an athletic twenty-something-year-old blond introducing himself as Konrad. He is handsome, with a warm air, brawny arms, and a gentle smile. Two days earlier, he checked himself into the clinic for alcoholism. Every morning, he asks if I've slept well and listens intently to my reply. Between group therapy, he insists on teaching me self-defence in the shaded grass park across the road.

"You're a pretty girl. You might need this one day."

With a determined look, he protects his face with boxing gloves as I throw punches. I don't want to tell him it's too late.

While Konrad attends therapy tailored for substance abuse, my sessions focus on managing depression and anxiety. I develop new understandings around coping strategies, the power of social networks and effective communication. I remain guarded as nine others shed skin in vulnerable layers. The capacity for me to heal is potent, but I am reluctant to first strip my armour.

⁂

Inhale. Exhale.
Be still. Breathe.

A meditation tape guides us into deeper presence with our breath as we close our eyes. The last group session combines all treatment programs for ninety minutes of mindfulness and relaxation. I internally scoff, unaware it will later become a potent part of my healing journey. At the end, an athletic blonde sporting bright yoga tights proclaims she tapped into an inner stillness she hadn't previously fathomed. Cate is in her early twenties, tackling an amphetamine addiction.

One sunny lunchtime, in the outside courtyard, Konrad quizzes Cate, "How d'ya think you'll go once you're outta here?"

"I dunno." Her chest sinks as she exhales. Cate naps for hours after the group sessions, but she is adamant to get clean, and stay clean. "I'm so tired. It's like my body is finally catching up from being so speedy for so long..."

"How did it start?" Konrad asks.

"Dexies," she confides. Even in the shade, her hair is golden like the sun. "My doctor must have known. I was in there *every week* getting another script."

"But he was making money with each visit?"

"Exactly."

As they talk of the temptations in "the real world", I gaze at the passionfruit vines draping over brown-bricked walls. Are there fruits growing over the walls I stack inside me? Is anything flowering within?

I drift back into the conversation as Cate comments on her weight gain. She pulls out her phone and shows us a stick-thin photo, asserting she will get back there, drug-free. Their authenticity makes the world feel more real. Colours are deeper. Even the air tastes crisper.

Suddenly Konrad turns to me with steady eyes and presses, "Promise me you won't ever do drugs."

Cate leans in. "That's a big ask! And how do you know she hasn't already dabbled?"

I swallow my thoughts of Courtney and Jarred and maintain a refrained expression.

Konrad scratches his head. "Fair call. Okay, how 'bout this...promise me you won't ever *lose yourself* to drugs. It's not worth it."

A poignant silence follows as I nod.

"You're a smart girl, and you're young. It sounds cliché...but the world is literally at your feet."

I look from Konrad to Cate. She nods to herself slowly. Then I settle my gaze on

Konrad. Don't ever *lose myself* to drugs. It's a reasonable ask. Peering into his eyes, I hold out my pinkie to seal the promise. Konrad wears an earnest expression. It's one I will never fully understand, but it lingers in the back of my mind for decades.

Scanning the lively dining room of patients chattering over food, I ask Cate if she's seen Konrad. She shrugs. The cook, who is usually charmed into separating six yolks from egg whites for Konrad's high-protein diet, hasn't spotted the sexy boxer either.

At lunch, Konrad is still MIA. Admission is at our liberty. We can leave anytime. My heart drops when he is still absent at our last session. The clinic gives us the tools to enrich our lives, but it's up to us to utilise them.

That afternoon, Laula visits. We aren't that close, but she drives 45 kilometres in peak hour traffic to be present with me in my darkest hours. She doesn't pry me with questions of why I'm there. She's there to support, not snoop, and from thereon we grow closer.

The next day, Konrad returns with downcast eyes. He confesses he checked himself out of the clinic and blacked out after his third vodka bottle. His determination moves me. He knows alcohol is his kryptonite, yet here he is starting again at ground zero.

As my two weeks stretch to an end, I bid farewell to Konrad and Cate. They aren't ready to face the traps and snares beyond the white, wrought-iron gate that is locked each night. Konrad and I stay in correspondence for a few years after. The last I hear, he is fifteen months clean, after another relapse. *Sobriety is a gift*, he says. *I grow stronger each day.*

"No one tells you that entering university from school is the hardest path." The vice principal gives a compassionate look and continues. "All these exams stress students out. But there are other ways. You can do a bridging course or take a few years off and do an aptitude test when you're ready."

I examine the middle-aged lady with kind eyes, wondering why this information isn't more readily shared. Finally, I am being spoken to as an adult, but it takes a breaking point to get here. I'm dismayed at all the schooling I've missed at such a pivotal time. I feel like I've squandered twelve years of distinguished education. I decide not to partake in my final exams. Instead, I take a gap year that stretches into eleven.

At graduation, the gravity of everything that's happened dissipates into nostalgia. Our yearbook awards Kim and me "the best friends", but when school finishes, we drift in different directions. My parents let the unfinished confrontation rest, but keep a sharp eye as I pass my driving test and spend more time in the hot, dry hills. Far away from the pain. Far away from the past. Closer to Charlie, Laula, and Reed.

As 2008 thins to an end, I catch whispers that Cal and Felicity's relationship is rocky. Despite this, I decide to let him go. He is like a cigarette. Though I crave him, I refrain from indulging in him because holding on is bad for my health. At the end of December, Reed invites me to a party at the recreation centre where Cal had his eighteenth. I'm apprehensive about going. Seeing Cal will spark up my feelings. I decide to go only upon hearing that he is away for work.

Charlie and I arrive as dusk melts trees into long shadows on the crunchy ground. I instantly feel Cal's presence. It's strange because he's meant to be in the Pilbara. A moment later, he appears and walks towards me. I blink as my eyes adjust. My body stiffens. Then it softens. Then I become a strange dense goo. Our interactions have been scarce and guarded all year. Occasionally we engage in small talk, but it is always monitored by Felicity, who watches unblinkingly beneath thick, sculpted eyebrows. If our interactions are a second too long or a smidgin too friendly, her eyes freeze to glaciers that shoot ice shards into my spine.

"Cal? Aren't you meant to be up north?"

He shifts his gaze from his shoes to my eyes. "Yeah. I missed my flight..."

The way his blue-green eyes ever so slightly widen then soften tells me he still loves me. He misses me. An unexpected warmth floods my chest. Our heartstrings still strum a familiar song, faded but impassioned.

A horde of people interrupt the moment. They tell us the cops are en route. In the migration of people moving to a new party location, Cal hops in my car. A wave of bewilderment breezes through me, mixed with a strangely detached sensation. We've danced around each other all year, rocking and sidestepping but never daring to tango.

Charlie directs me through winding, tree-lined roads, as Yellowcard's "Empty Apartment" glides through the speakers. The lyrics awaken what I've yearned to convey for months. I wonder if he knows this as he studies me through the rearview mirror. Charlie initiates small talk, revealing he isn't happy with Felicity anymore.

He hasn't been for months.

"I miss you guys," he exclaims.

My breath hitches.

There's an urgency in his voice as he expresses sadness that he's been "pussy-whipped" away from friendships he holds dear. Cal isn't one to throw meaningless words. He's the quiet guy with funny one-liners. When he says something, he means it.

I am light-headed with appreciation, but I continue driving to the party where Felicity awaits. It is the honourable thing to do. As I pull up, Charlie and Cal decide we should ditch it and hang out like the old days. I'm hesitant—still wanting to let him go, not wanting to pull him away from Felicity—but I agree.

Felicity appears on the driveway as I reverse onto the road. Cal ducks out of her sight. Charlie yells to keep driving. I do.

In fear the others will come knocking on Charlie's door, we walk to the nearby school oval with a cask of wine. It is half empty amid a game of truth or dare when Cal confesses, "I never got over you."

Deep down, I already know. His feet point to me whenever we're in the same room, indicating the direction he wants to walk. I've seen the way he looks at me when he thinks no one is watching. I pretend not to see; I pretend I don't care, but I still feel him and I know he feels me too.

He is dewy-eyed, awaiting my response. Something endearing arises inside me. Something I want to discover in totality. I could cut him down and slash him open. Make him feel the way I felt when he started dating Felicity. But I look beyond the boy who ran away out of fear and see three years of history with the sweetheart who has shared so many secrets and laughs. I see him in his entirety, and it softens me. Him, as a young boy, losing his mum to cancer. The way that translates to his fear of losing those he loves. I see his shadow and his light. He's human. And terrified.

My voice breaks into the penetrating silence. "I never got over you either."

"Awwww, you two!" Charlie bubbles.

A buzz from Cal's phone interrupts the moment. Forty missed calls from Felicity become fifty. Then sixty. Then one hundred. Her name flashes with incessant desperation to stay current in his life. It's crazy. If he caught that flight, none of this would be happening.

Eventually the three of us stumble back to Charlie's and snuggle in her four-poster bed. As Charlie's deep breathing jumbles with the odd snore, Cal's lips find home on mine. A billion fireworks explode in my bones. He pulls me out of her bedroom to the laundry, then I pull him back to the oval where we make love beneath a billion twinkling stars. Our bodies express what no combination of twenty-six letters can convey. Magnetised in, I give myself to him. Again. And again. And again. Taking all of me, he savours every moment. Every inch of skin, ever untamed gasp, every subtle emotion. Finally, we are one. After prancing back to Charlie's mouldy home, we fall asleep in a convolution of relieved limbs.

Morning comes with a loud knock at the door. It's Reed. He looks from my messy hair to Cal's discreet smile and warns that Felicity has been up all night. When Cal returns to his sleepless girlfriend, she throws a shoe at his head. There is yelling and screaming. Their relationship ends. A bizarre concoction of elation and shame swirl inside me. I have knowingly slept with another woman's man. But it's Cal. We are in love.

We both deny what happened when questioned but hang out in the weeks that follow. Months later, I admit the truth to Felicity. The lie burdens me. I need to be accountable for my actions. Over time, she finds space in her massive heart to forgive me. On the surface, I've gotten my way. But karma looms in fierce undercurrents billowing on the horizon.

🜚

> *We cannot be responsible for the actions of others.*
> *We are always responsible for our own.*

In 2009's first pages, Cal's eyes electrify me like lightning striking velvet tides. As we duck our heads under water and make out in a friend's chlorinated pool, I am illusioned into thinking I've found my other half. My eyes are red-rimmed from the chemicals. I have yet to see that relationships only work when two people come together already whole humans.

In the first week of the new year, we celebrate Eve's eighteenth birthday on a large bush block swaying with eucalyptus trees. I know Eve still harbours feelings for Cal. It is salient in her subtle lip bites, increased eye contact, and incessant fidgets whenever Cal and I are near. I do not see her as a threat. I brush it off as insignificant.

Intoxicated with vodka and desire, Cal and I stretch out on a warm asphalt road lit by a smiling lunar crescent moon. In the cool midnight sky, Sirius and Orion watch as three fragments of space rock flash across the Milky Way. I wish on those shooting stars. But I do not wish for Cal. Through my infatuation, I trust we will be together if it is fated. He is my sun, my moon, and the constellations above. And yet, on those incandescent combustions, I wish for life to unfold as it must.

The stars momentarily pass in a remarkable stream of light. Burning out, collapsing, shining long after they faded. It's a curious habit to wish as luminous serenades disintegrate into dense black holes. Maybe the events that followed were always intended in the divine design.

"You think you're so much better than everyone else because you live in City Beach!"

Midsummer humidity weighs upon me in a sticky haze. I catch Courtney's eyes with mine, silently pleading for her to calm as I step forward with my palms outstretched. One moment we're hugging and laughing in her sister's polished kitchen. The next, she's throwing spiteful words.

"Courtney...I don't think that. *You know I don't.* If I did, why would I always come see you?"

My throat burns with vodka. Suddenly, my premix bottle feels rigid in my hand. "I love you, babe. You've been there for me through my *hardest days*."

She flicks her hand like she's shooing a fly, then juts out her chin. "Fuck off. Go back to City Beach!"

Her sister beckons her to the lounge room. I pace the white-tiled kitchen. They've been smoking crystal meth, but surely there's a deeper trigger for her fumes. Maybe I shouldn't have been so vocal about my promise to Konrad. Is there anything I can say to convey my love through her illusion? Just as I'm wondering if I should risk driving to Polly Jane's house nearby, the front door slams. They've gone to get more drugs. They aren't returning.

My certainty that we'll amend the prickly feelings squanders to a nightmare that continues with eyes open wide. As our connection crumbles with unspoken resolution, I remain grateful of her friendship through my soul's darkest nights.

"*I love you,*" he proclaims.

I clasp his face and draw him closer.

I love you; I reply with my eyes. It feels too vulnerable to actually say it.

"I love you. I love you. I love you," Cal repeats, stealing my breath as he peers into my soul.

Morning light trickles through the trees, striking our naked bodies squished in the passenger seat of my Celica parked in his driveway. I don't know why we're sleeping in my cold car instead of his warm home. The rest of the world is an unimportant blur dissipating beyond the trees. All that matters is his touch, his gaze, another dose of his love.

His lips linger near mine, tantalising me with anticipation. I kiss him with fierce passion. Pull back to make him miss it. Then lean in for another.

Deciduous leaves fall with autumn's crisp exhale as I breathe in the nutty aroma of coffee and sponge crumbs off a table. My black-haired manager steams milk with a high-pitched screech. I wonder if I can be toned like her if I train with our burly Italian boss who sells steroids in the back storeroom.

Midmorning, I am trounced by a cutting pain in my lower abdomen. I brush it off as a cramp. It sharpens like a whetstone as the lunch rush peaks then falls. Each jolt is a dozen daggers slicing my intestines into mattered flesh. My manager refuses to let me leave but sends the other barista home early. I wonder if she's power-tripping or if she genuinely thinks I'm crying wolf.

That night, I gulp painkillers as I toss in nauseated disarray. In the morning, my sister Emily finds me collapsed on the stairs. For the fourth time in two years, I am hospitalized. This time, I arrive with ambulance sirens wailing. My diagnosis is immediate: acute appendicitis. Emergency surgery removes the small swollen sac and abolishes my physical pain with three small scars. But something brews beneath the surface. Something I cannot digest. I don't want to face my low self-esteem, nasty self-talk, or inability to hold boundaries. I don't want to admit that my attachment to Cal steals my fiery independence. I don't want to look at my shit. So, the toxicity festers into my physical being where I cannot run from the pain.

Empowerment begins the moment we bring sovereignty back inside our skin.

At work, I return to a sheepish-looking manager who gives no apology. The part of me that prides my diligence takes initiative to show I work harder than her. After three months, my boss commemorates my strong work ethic and promotes me to shift supervisor. In the dimly lit storeroom, he slides me an extra thirty dollars cash each week. It's enough for a bottle of vodka that I guzzle without food or adequate hydration. The white spirit allows me to bypass my emotions, postponing what I eventually learn: You've got to feel it to heal it. It must be realised to be released.

Sometimes enough alcohol brings me to a place of no thought. I like it there. It's peaceful. Day to day, my head bursts with messy thoughts and tangled emotions.

I'll do anything to bypass them. Drinking delivers me to the destination that I eventually learn to enter through meditation. This makes it sustainable. In the meantime, what's missing is my desire to venture deep within myself and disrupt the vicious cycle by first finding my centre.

I often awake to a spinning world after big nights out. The edges blur. Life isn't so jagged. Draft texts in my phone addressed to no one reveal the uncensored flow of my subconscious mind.

Remember, this barrier isn't keeping others out. It's keeping you in.

The heart doesn't stay the same size. It expands.

I should have read your eyes instead of listened to your words.

The homeless aren't the only ones begging for change.

There is a wisdom inside me that bursts with fervour and searches for release. I start articulating my pain on a Tumblr blog, *Risk Everything Fear Nothing*, where I make public my search for meaning. The rawness in my posts attracts readers far and wide. Weaving beauty into the breakdown empowers others to have a breakthrough. It's cathartic for me too. Finally, I have a safe space to share my depths and let the world see me.

Over time, I learn to befriend all aspects of me and hold safety for their expression. This means that my darkness is no longer pushed aside and suppressed, causing it to leak in subtle yet unruly ways. It is through a Jungian psychoanalytical process called Active Imagination that I eventually forge an alchemical bridge between my conscious and unconscious mind. It is not a method that will work for everyone, nor should it be explored without adequate understanding. It works for me, but first comes a strangling spiral of smothering my emotions while playing with fire.

Music pumps from the house party where Charlie mingles with random dudes. Girls in short skirts and heels stumble in giggling huddles. I take a swig of vodka and skip outside to find Laula as my pleasant buzz plummets to woozy.

In the courtyard, a girl inspects me with a piercing stare before beelining towards me with lips curled.

"No offence, but your shorts are really slutty," she jeers.

"Huh?"

I examine my denim shorts and UGG boots as she walks away. It's a mellow autumn night. I'm comfy. My expression storms with the slow uncoiling of rage that once again the word "slut" is brazenly thrown. Something snaps inside me. I am consumed by fury. Not by the stranger's sneer, but the surfacing memories of loved ones throwing barbed words.

In my periphery, I spot Charlie. I shoot her a warning look as I march to the girl, pour my vodka in her hair, and waltz out the gate.

Outside, Laula sits in her car kissing a random dude through the window. I slide into the backseat and duck down.

"Babe, we've gotta go."

The girl flounces out, followed by Charlie. Laula start the engine. Charlie jumps in.

As we venture up the hill, I ask Laula to drop me at Cal's.

"Does he know you're coming?" With lightning eyes, she watches me through the rearview mirror.

"Yeah," I lie.

The lights are off at Cal's. He's still at the pub. I slink around the back and stagger through the unlocked laundry door, as I've done with him many times before. Before even considering that my presence won't be welcome, I pass out in his bed. All logic drips down a delusional drain. When we possess people, we possess ourselves with the spell of attachment that always ends in heartache.

I wake to the stark light from his bedroom globe. Cal stands at the door blinking. Eve pokes her head in from under his arm. Her jaw drops then she storms off with Cal at her tail. I shrug it off and close my eyes, expecting him to crawl up beside me. A moment passes. I'm still alone. Down the hall I wobble. Cal feigns sleep on the couch with Eve on his lap wrapped around him.

I glance from him to her, then back again.

"What the fuck?"

Eve senses tension and skulks to his sister's room. I feel my presence striking the pit of Cal's nerves, but I'm fanatic. I've pushed the subtleties into an inky abyss, but now the truth beckons.

Eve recently divulged that she lost her virginity to Cal before Felicity was in the equation. It was a foggy, drunken night. He left her straight after.

I sense the fear ruling his defence mechanisms to protect his tender heart. The faraway look in his eyes when he thinks no one is watching. The way he holds me as though each time might be the last. Is his "leave them before they leave me" attitude hiding the risk of losing another loved one? Is it a way to fill a childhood void?

Rather than bite my tongue or find a tactful expression, I blurt, "You crave female attention to make up for the mum you never had."

His eyes lash me first.

Then his hands.

It's his words that strike the hardest.

"I initiated *every* time with her."

I am hot and tangled on the coffee table where he pushed me.

Every time? It's happened more than once?

"What the fuck, Cal? You *told* me you *love* me!"

Cal ignores me and covers his head with a blanket.

I continue badgering him.

Eventually he pulls the fabric off his face, gives me a look of thunder, and barks, "I changed my mind."

Cal passes out, leaving me to collapse in a trembling mess on the cold tiles. His black border collie cross Labrador licks my legs as I weep silent cascades.

In the afternoon, after ignoring me all morning, Cal drives me to my car the next suburb over. He is seething in quiet resentment at me rocking up unannounced and talking about his mum. Valid. I am drowning in a savage fire of sorrow and confusion. Deep down, I always knew our connection wasn't conducive for growth. Knowing that doesn't make it easier to let him go.

The week before my eighteenth birthday, the bottom of the abyss appears in a painful *thump*. Cal and I are on talking terms again, but a friend discloses that he's still sleeping with Eve. I call him. Scream. Then, in a calm tone that chills the hairs on my body, I instruct him to look behind some of my writing he framed in his room. Behind my scribbled words is a letter I recently hid. The prose is raw and unrestrained. It will stay between Cal and me, except the close.

Let me go, let me live, let me smile on my own. Knowing there's a finish to our fairy tale is better than dreaming of a middle that's really an end.

I speak to Eve next. I am gentle. I wish I didn't feel her agony tremble inside my bones, but I do. She is my friend. Cal's heart isn't in it with her. We all know it. It's hard to discern what pain is mine and what is hers as she confides the final sliver.

"I'm pregnant..."

Tears scald my cheeks.

"It's his."

She's been yearning to tell me by letter, but writing it down is too agonising. It's too real. The truth twists in my stomach as I digest the final fragment. When she aborts their baby, I think a part of her dies too. The once-solid puzzle disintegrates before her eyes. Before all our eyes.

With space for new pieces, the puzzle changes. Autumn marches into May. Trees shed their leaves. Sometimes I gaze at the pirouetted swirl of two leaves falling. The silent descent is choreographed from the highest boughs. Dancing in circles, the leaves twist and turn in a graceful return to the earth from which they came. Cal and I were two leaves caught in a breeze. Swept up, we were lost in an earthbound dance.

Disintegrating to reform is horrifying at the start. But we must let go. We must dissolve to evolve as we go our separate ways.

🍂

Autumn reminds us to let dead things go
Winter contemplates what seeds to sew
Spring promises that new opportunities grow
Summer is inevitable, so go with the flow

The nightclub booms with remixed corny pop. In a giant cage, Laula's swaying hips are cut up by a strobe. We often meet at the old Leederville Hotel on Wednesday nights when patrons become every definition of the nickname "Seedy Leedy". The floors are sticky. Smoke machines cloud into rainbow lights. As I stride towards the dance floor, a gawky dude intercepts me.

"Hey there. Let me get your opinion on something."

He doesn't wait for my consent.

"I'm trying to give my friend some advice, but we're just a bunch of guys and not qualified to comment on these matters…"

It takes every ounce of self-control to stifle laughter.

His words are direct from a famous pick-up artist memoir, *The Game*. I read it two years ago. Before he blabs on with a made-up story and pretends to care about my insights on relationships as a way of sparking conversation, I give him a piercing gaze and interject.

"I like Neil Strauss's books too. But c'mon, mate, you can do better than the Jealous Girlfriend Opener."

The guy gapes as I skip off to Laula. When I glance back, he's at the bar recounting the story to his friends. One of them catches my eye and grins. I shake my head and smirk. Portraying a false persona to attract women is appalling, but I like getting inside players' heads. It puts me three steps ahead of their games.

🍂

Perched on the rocky groyne, I gaze into the dark abyss where stars hover above the horizon. Crashing waves mist me with cool spray. I lick my salty lips, wondering if anyone is doing what I'm doing—drifting and dreaming, sifting for meaning. The ocean's silken kisses connect me to a distant stranger's breath, and I don't feel so alone sitting on their horizon. Maybe someday we'll be friends. The thought of venturing to mysterious lands inspires me to get a second job at Burswood Entertainment complex. Crowds get rowdy as Pink, Beyoncé, Metallica, Foo Fighters, Lady Gaga, Britney Spears, and Rihanna sing their best. The music renders a cathartic release.

When the songs of the sea can't soothe my soul, the lullabies of the land calm my storm. On the city's eastern edge, urban sprawl merges with forested hills at the Kalamunda Zig Zag, a lookout over Perth. One hundred years ago, a train line zigzagged up the escarpment that is too steep to navigate in a single straight line. Now the snaking, narrow switchback road is a place for underage pregnancy and reckless adolescent hooning. Driving there is a weekly ritual. It's where I find peace. From the Zig Zag's vantage point, city lights stretch before me like a sea of stars reminding me that I'm not the only one awake with the night.

Transient turquoise tides kiss the shore with wild resolve.
Tempestuous or tranquil, ride the wave.

With the first blossoms of spring, I'm offered a management position at a café in Perth's most pretentious suburb. It's great for my resume, but women sneering through Botox isn't really my vibe. It looks like they'd rather drink cat piss than place their manicured hands on the same surfaces as us peasants. They probably have butlers named Martin in intercontinental mansions. Despite having it all, they lack the sweetness of humanity and the warmth of manners.

Life is a cycle of work, party, minimal sleep, repeat. Forty-hour work weeks swing into a silver platter of weekend parties. I fast all day then splurge on sugar and junk food. I am sprinting at irrational speeds.

Overloading myself prohibits the space to feel the heartache I've been avoiding and process the pain of losing Cal. Not showing who I really am emphasises my childhood wounds of feeling like I don't belong. Though it is the answer, I can't bear to tear down my walls and articulate that I'm not okay because I fear people knowing how I truly feel and casting me aside. It seems easier to risk being rejected for something I'm not—ditzy, plastic, and reckless—than be spurned in my vulnerability of being sensitive, insightful, and bright.

Sex gets me out of my mind and into my body. I am a junkie looking for love in others but not willing to show my own heart. I'm fucking the pain away. Sometimes I glimpse my soul in my mirrored reflection. It penetrates me like the moon's silver path on an unruffled body of water. But like water, I fall through the fingers of those who try to hold me, love me, see the real me.

On days I don't distract myself with work or partying or engulfing myself in other people's problems to distract myself from my own, I cocoon myself in bedsheets. Beneath the covers, I let my emotions rise. I think of death often. Of nothingness. No longer existing. Being in a still, dark environment reminds me of the end I crave. I think about Cal. Is it really over? Over time the pain heals, but first it is debilitating. I no longer hang out with his inner circle when he's around, but Reed phones me most nights, and I often pick him up from the airport returning from the mines.

One evening, Reed and I watch *Twilight* as we swig straight American Honey. I promise not to tell anyone I've roped him into watching the vampire fantasy, so if he asks, we're watching *The Matrix*. As Bella, I mean Neo, searches for truth, I am cajoled with the thought of seducing Reed. Partly as vengeance on Cal. Partly because our friendship is effortless and safe and I confuse it for being more because I am so lost. I proposition him as the credits roll. Held captive by my eyes, he exhales. After a reflective pause he voices the stupidity in the idea. He is Cal's best friend. I am Cal's ex-lover. It's the taunting romance of a reality never meant to be.

In the morning, our heads pound with parched pressure as logic disintegrates into hangover's perpetual spin. Our bodies succumb to temptation. We convince ourselves it'll all be okay. When Reed flies back to work, confusion hazes me. We added sex to an equation where it should never exist.

On his next stint home, we go to the "Seedy Leedy" with Charlie. Someone he recently met and likes will also be at the club. On the upstairs R'n'B dance floor, a lanky girl with strawberry-blonde hair rubs her ass against his legs. He goes home with her. Fury sweeps through me like a wildfire. My emotions are no one's responsibility or fault but my own, but I lack the emotional intelligence to distinguish that my feelings are the tip of the iceberg with unhealed trauma looming beneath. I wish I had the tool belt to distinguish and accept my emotions rather than diminishing them to tiny, suppressed shards. To see that my attraction to Reed isn't romantic or sexual in truth. We share an emotional and intellectual bond. With him I don't wear a mask. It's this uninhibited expression of me—the way that I feel when I am with him—that is the real attractor.

In the morning, he knocks on my door. It is a warm, blue-skied day.

"Let's walk and talk," I insist.

He nods.

We stroll to the beach and share our thoughts and feelings like adults. We both talk. We both listen. He has genuine feelings for this girl. To him it isn't just another hookup.

"In another life, we'd be perfect for each other, Jess. It's just not this one."

Beneath his thick almost-monobrow, a shooting star falls in his baby-blue eyes. The ocean is a seamless sapphire shimmering with all the answers. Suddenly I feel distant from the situation and present to the crunchy texture of sand gritting my legs on the low stone wall. I feel déjà vu. It is the first time I ponder the possibility of our souls living multiple lives. Maybe we were friends in a past life and lovers in the next. Or maybe its certain memory lapses coiling into the intuitive knowing that my closest friend is about to become someone I once knew.

Within weeks, our friendship ends, sparked by his new partner's disapproval of us remaining close. Losing Reed isn't just losing a friend. It's losing the part of me that is real; my essence; me.

A few months later, we bump into each other at a party. At first, I avoid him. He chose life without me. I will do the same. Eventually, he sits beside me.

"I miss ya, Jess. Truly, I do. But every time your name is mentioned in my relationship, it starts a fight that lasts for days. I wish we could go back to those days, but...I'm in love."

I look at my old friend with compassionate eyes. Sacrifice occurs when we choose one thing over the other. It's an inevitability of life. The ones we lose are never lost, for our hearts are built from those we love. His place forever remains, as a memory spot, a learning spot, a forgiveness spot. I wish him all the best. In love, and in life.

Life goes on. It always does. We can stay up all night, letting our minds devour us from within. Or we can accept what we cannot change and rest up for a better tomorrow. It feels like the world stops spinning, but Earth keeps rotating at one thousand miles per hour. The sun still rises on the eastern horizon. Every single day.

Externally, spring wildflowers blossom. Internally, weeds dilapidate my inner terrain. My façade is heavy, uncomfortable, and straining. An endless hollow devours me from within. I've lost something precious but forgotten what it is. I pine for people I've never even met. I'm homesick for places I don't yet know exist.

Dark thoughts wheedle me in a gyrating murk. It's game over. I've been fooling the world I'm okay, but I can no longer deceive my mirrored reflection. Stuck in stalemate, I'm unable to move forward, unable to back down, unable to rid the darkness from me. My unhealed emotions surface matted, raw, and violent. I don't know how to contain them, and I don't know how to release.

Mama has swine flu. She is feverish and achy. After three days of constant vomiting, Mama abruptly ceases her antidepressants. They aren't staying down anyway. The cold turkey intensifies her volatility and fatigue. We are often snarky with each other. She wants to protect me. I want freedom. I am now eighteen. They cannot legally enforce me to do anything, but I am a train derailing with flammable sparks. They are lost with how to shield me; bewildered with whether to give me space or create more rules.

On Thursday November 5, 2009, I cake on my makeup to meet some friends at a pub in the hills. Since childhood, Thursday is my day to cook dinner for the family. Amid the whirlwind of heavy tides crashing against my skull, the responsibility slips.

I pace towards the door as Mama hisses, "You're not going anywhere until you cook dinner!"

It is 8:00 p.m. She's been seething in silent rage, surrounded by a floor of snotty tissues.

I roll my eyes.

"I'm leaving."

She can't eat right now anyway. And I'm running late.

She looks up from the TV with fire in her eyes.

"Go then! And don't come back."

I examine the scene. The TV blasts. The woman who birthed me is scowling. She won't even look at me as she shoos me away like I'm worthless. It seems my mere existence infuriates her. I feel empty and alone.

"Fine. I'll go..."

...and never come back. Be careful what you wish for.

I leave in a huff and slam the door. Then, I creep back to my bedroom, grab my journals to protect them from prying eyes, and scribble a note.

I love you, but by the time you read this, it will be too late.

Across the city I speed, to the heritage-listed pub supposedly home to several ghosts. I parade into the beer garden, pretending that everything is fine. Under my mask, I am lost for moves. Who can I trust? Who can I let in? I've pushed my true essence down for so long, the real me drifts through the hotel's draughty corridors with the other ghosts.

In the sea of faces, I feel Cal's eyes on me as I charm the crowd. In a quiet corner, my façade falls when he asks how I am. His eyes are nostalgic and remorseful. With him, my energy doesn't lie. When I confide what happened, he offers his home for the night.

As the last song plays, I slink away to the Zig Zag. I can't bring myself to drive to Cal's. I can't bear another fake smile. He's trying to be there for me, but what's his agenda? It's too little, too late. I speed down the winding narrow road like a maniac. My veins clog with stagnated life force, dwindling and dimming with each shallow breath. At my favourite lookout, city lights shimmer beneath twinkling stars. All I see is darkness.

Punk-pop bawls through the speakers and muffles my wails. I can't do this anymore. I can't keep living this half-life. On the passenger seat are three packets of antidepressants and codeine-containing flu tablets that I've grabbed in my quick pack. Two songs pass. The pills beckon. They call for me to end it all. To sleep and never wake.

I push two dozen into my open palm. Tasting salty tears, I swallow them one by one. Lost in the magnitude of my depression, lost in the aimless darkness, lost in my own loneliness, I am coaxed by the disease state of my unconscious mind as I willingly devour death.

I wish I'd known that suicide doesn't stop the pain. It simply transfers it to those we love most. I wish I'd known that I can transfigure my agony into wisdom, compassion, and love. All I have to do is face it. Allow it to roll through me and transmute each wave. By experiencing what I fear to feel, a natural alchemy transforms every microgram of anguish into profundity and strength.

Ten minutes pass. My stomach rumbles. Dozens of pharmaceuticals stew. McDonald's drive-through delivers a gluttonous slab of animal-cruel beef and sodium-packed fries. It's the last time I ever eat there. I've taken one bite into the thick, fatty burger when a call from Cal dings.

Are you still coming over?

It is 1:30 a.m. The pills don't seem to be doing anything. It's better to sleep in a bed than squish up in my car.

I'll be there in 20.

My body weakens as I drive up the steep escarpment. Drowsiness tugs at my eyelids.

I don't tell Cal what I've done. I don't know how. I don't think he'll care. I don't yet understand the healing powers of vulnerability. I think that I'm protecting my heart from the world with carefully constructed walls. I'm not. I'm stopping love from entering.

We sleep together that night. For the very last time. As our bodies reacquaint, the first blackout comes. In an instant, reality flicks into nothingness. I find the alluring void I've contemplated for so long.

Cal's hands roving my body signify I'm back in the pitch-black room. He kisses my neck. Breathes in my ear. Then I lose consciousness again.

Back into my body.

Back into the abyss.

Again.

And again.

Until Cal holds me tight.

Even then my pain doesn't mitigate. I am empty inside. My body caves from the downfall of my mind, but my spirit holds on. Even on my deathbed, I can't voice the severity of what is happening. Even on my deathbed, I keep gripping my mask.

A rooster's crow wakes us at the crack of dawn. I mumble an awkward hello to Cal's sister and her partner as I walk to my car. Then I leave. I never return. The blackouts continue as I navigate peak-hour traffic from the eastern hills to the western suburbs.

I'm there.

Then I'm not.

Car horns jolt me back into my body as lights turn green and I falter in roundabouts' clear passage. I don't know how I manage the drive without a fatality—there must be an angel watching over me.

At work, a store assessment with the state manager awaits. Worried faces send me home the second time my eyes roll into the back of my head. I don't go home. Home isn't a nurturing place to be. I drive to the ocean instead.

Drawn to the hypnotic breath of ocean waves, I lie my tired body on the cool November sand. With a hollow heart, I bid my world goodbye.

Slipping into the void, I black out one last time.

Chapter III
AWAKENING

Reach and retreat;
teach and repeat.

The ocean caresses the land;
the motion undresses the sand;
the potion blesses our hands;
contractions allow us to expand.

Friday 6th November 2009

I awake to seagulls screaming in desolate shrieks and hungry howls. Beyond my throbbing head, a cathartic stillness floats on the fringe of my conscious mind. I want to get back there. I want to be encapsulated in its tranquil bubble. I want to taste that all-encompassing freedom unshackling me from worldly pain.

I open my eyes to a shrivelled plastic bottle. Wondering if it is safe to drink, I swig a warm mouthful. Sand crusts my tongue to sandpaper. I spit it out and sit up. Crunchy patterns etch my skin as wild tales from beyond the horizon fan my sun-scorched shoulders. I am lying on a billion hourglasses shattered and spilled before their time is up.

For fifteen hours I have floated between life and death, dreaming and awake. Like sea foam floating on shallow shores, the void beckons to swallow me with another blackout again. I gaze into the salty abyss. A wave crashes. On the soft sandy shore, it leaves frothy white spume beyond the reach of turquoise tides pulling the entire ocean back into itself again.

With the plummeting breaker comes the piercing realisation:

My suicide attempt was unsuccessful.

I am awake. I am alive.

In the distance, people chatter and stroll. I roll onto my back. Waking up wasn't part of my plan. Now what am I going to do?

My thoughts are poison.
Stillness is the potion.
Depression is a dark ocean.
I am learning how to swim.

With each inhale and exhale of the ocean's reach and retreat, I feel my heart pounding inside my chest. Just as yours does now. There's a reason you're still here. You may not yet understand it, but one day soon, the fog will fade and all will become clear. Trust in that. Believe in the strength of your own spirit. The deeper we dive, the higher we fly.

In those first few moments of opening my eyes, I accept my fate. I don't understand it. But I accept it. The shadow from my water bottle tells me it is midafternoon. I'm scheduled on the bar for a P!nk concert that night, so I sneak home to shower while Mama is out. In the safety of my white-and-blue-tiled bathroom, my eyes flood. The cool cascades extinguish the heat of my agony. Finding shelter in my own shudders, I weep. It's the kind of release that needs a moment to be felt and heard.

I weep because I don't want to wake up, but I do. I weep because I've been selfish in my attempt. I weep because I've been given a second chance and that's a miracle that I'm finding difficult to relish with gratitude. Steam fogs the mirror as I surrender into my suffering. I wipe away the misty veil then mask my misery with foundation. In my reflection, a slither of the real me shines in my hazel eyes: soft and strong, yet lost and lonely.

"You can do this, Jess," I assure, giving myself a pep talk that my friends savour. "You're going to do this. Everything will be okay."

People are already queuing outside the stadium when I arrive. I march inside as though I haven't just danced with death. Pouring alcohol into disposable plastic cups, I tune into the music and let it permeate my pain. Pink's distinct, raspy voice and down-to-earth stage presence evokes an adoration within me as I awe at her daring aerial performances. Maybe I can learn to fly above it all.

Towards the end of shift, I am requested at the office.

Shit, Mama's found my note.

There, she paces and twists her golden ring. The lead medic arrives with a large first-aid kit and does some routine checks. My blood sugar levels are dangerously low. He asks what I've eaten.

"Not much."

With caring eyes, the man notes that diet influences our mood and requests I eat something substantial.

I'm free to go when he concludes that I'm physically okay. Mama summons me home. I refuse. Her antidepressant withdrawals are fierce. We're both tense and unstable. I resent her for lashing out at me. I'm mortified that she's called my work. I see it as a repeated infiltration into the sanctity of my inner world. It compels me to stack my walls higher.

In refusing to take responsibility for the symbiotic relationship between how I feel and the thoughts I choose, each day becomes a roll of the dice. I think outside influences are the master of my destiny. But it is my own hand manipulating the numbered cube.

The nightclub strobe reduces Charlie's movements to intermittent pictures shown in slow motion, highlighting cheekbones and cleavage in the stumbling sea. Crisp beer rivulets down my legs. Blasting dance-pop silences my inner voice. I dangle my arms above my head, glimpsing *Risk Everything Fear Nothing* written in elegant curves on my left triceps. The name of my blog has become my tattooed mantra.

Since waking on the beach, I sedate my mental chatter with nightclubs and alcohol, trying to make my way back to the stillness I found. In moments of clarity, I know it's not the right path. But more often than not I fool myself into believing that suppressing my emotions is easier than acknowledging them. I'm fumbling around in the darkness, stumbling to a crooked rhythm, mumbling lyrics that aren't my song to sing.

Somewhere in our merry whirl, we chatter with a talented cricket player and his friend. As the clock dings midnight, we hop in a car with them to the friend's house. I snuggle the cricket player on the floor. Charlie canoodles his friend in bed.

At the crack of dawn, the four of us wake to get dropped at our respective cars and start work. As the friend reverses out the driveway, his electric-blue eyes fixate not on me but *in* me. The interaction is brief, but the intensity thrills me. I've been caught off-guard. Somehow, he's found his way past the rocky ramparts barricading me from the world. Our hearts hum a familiar song. I feel it all around me.

The exchange lingers in my mind for weeks until we next cross paths. Again, his eyes pierce through my mask and swim in my deepest layer. He reminds me his name is Jonny and puts his number in my phone. From there on, small talk electrifies me with dinging texts and flirtatious banter.

Curiosity is the first step to awakening;
opening to the idea that there is more.

As the earthy scent of summer solstice hangs heavy in anticipation of a sticky day, Charlie and I venture to a southern coastal town for a girls' weekend. I work all day at the café, then cruise the forested highway to rendezvous. Music booms as urban sprawl dissipates into brown crunchy trees. In the space between songs, the wisdom of the world seeps through the windshield and enchants me. Observing the different shapes, sizes, and stages of life, I see the trees as people. Some extend roots deep into the earth, allowing branches to nearly seize heaven. Some retain more water. They are boiled broccoli amongst the convolution of earthy colours flashing past my windshield. It is their photosynthesised union of purpose that amazes me. I can't help but ponder what humanity could achieve if united in the vision of making our world a better place.

The girls are tipsy at a winery when I arrive. I pick them up and drive to our weekend rental. All but Charlie crash from vodka and wine. Sensing my sadness, she stays up with me all night with her unwavering empathetic gaze.

Wide-eyed and searching, I confess my attempted suicide and my heartache of losing Cal. I divulge the pain inside me that patiently awaits the day I have the fortitude to face it. I can't focus on her eyes, but I see the concern in them. It is the first time I truly verbalize my grief. The simplicity of her listening is healing. Sometimes I think Charlie is the only one who understands me. I feel safe because I am seen, or maybe I am seen because I feel safe.

New Year's rolls around with a smorgasbord of parties from all corners of the purring city. I refrain from drinking to relish the flavours of them all. Just before sunset, my phone buzzes with Jonny's name. Between euphoric laughs, he slurs that he's been kicked out of a coastal bar. I agree to backtrack from the foothills to bring him on my adventure.

In the car, I chuckle at his tipsy mutters. He ups my music to maximum volume. I lower it using the steering wheel control buttons. He scratches his head. The cycle continues.

At a fluorescent-themed hill's party, he drools at sausage rolls crisping in the oven. The mum of the house asks if we are together.

"No." I giggle, as Jonny claps his hands to make the savoury treats cook faster. "We're not together, just best friends."

"Be careful that best friends don't break your heart," she warns.

We both laugh as he attempts to chow down a frozen sausage roll.

At 11:50 p.m., Jonny reminds me I want to be overlooking the city at the Zig Zag for midnight. I'm surprised he remembers and moved that he supports my intention. Led by a force that turns every traffic light green, we pull into the bottom of the winding road at exactly 12 a.m.

My foot is still on the brake when he grabs my face and presses his full lips on mine, kissing away our prior utters of being "best friends".

❦

January is steamy with budding romance. We spend the first week of the year together, then he embarks on a three-week cruise through Polynesia. We both imply from the start that neither of us are looking for anything serious. We're both untying strings strangling us from old loves. We're both hurting. We're both healing. Nonetheless, I play our sunshine days on repeat, daydreaming of his sapphire eyes piercing through my veil as he whispers, "I don't know which eye to look into, they're both so pretty."

When he returns, our dynamic is different. The exhilarating passion of possibility peaks then plateaus as the daily grind grimes my daydreams. Our orbits collide most weeks at "Seedy Leedy" and other clubs. Sometimes our nights end wrapped in each other's arms. Sometimes they don't. When he comes to mine, he glues himself to my bedroom wall, where I've stuck poetry and prose, the bleeding of my soul. His captivation to my writing is a huge part of my attraction to him. And him, me. My walls are high, but he revels in the parts of me I etch onto the barricades, the tiny slithers I let the world see.

❦

At the end of summer, I drop ecstasy at a mainstream music festival and fly on artificial euphoria. While recreational drug use becomes a norm for some friends, my promise to Konrad lingers in the periphery of my awareness. For all my maladaptive behaviour, I know that substance abuse isn't the way to deal with my pain. I dabble out of curiosity. It isn't a regular practise.

Post suicide attempt, I hold a rawer intensity of emotions that need release. I find it in cold sweat dripping from my torso as I ride clammy waves. Music booms against my brain. My heartbeat pulses in my fingers. It beckons me to feel something. Anything. Unanswered questions tingle on the tip of my tongue, but to taste them I must turn the telescope around and look within.

The highs reel in waves that crash into a gloomy morning. It is a false awakening, a rapture I cannot capture, because the euphoria has external roots and that makes it unsustainable. Dehydrated and depleted, I'm sick of swimming survival stroke and skimming the depths of my emotions. I fear introspection because it requires me to peel back my mask where my un-cried tears gnaw at me like poison. As my comedown nosedives into its fourth day, I gasp for air in the stormy undercurrents of my inner terrain.

By this stage I'm back home after spending some time in the hills with a friend, his mum, and her live-in boyfriend and girlfriend. Mama's cold turkey withdrawals have passed. She's also cut gluten from her diet in recognition of her intolerance. Doctors subsequently admit that Mama was stressed, not depressed. Huge emotional strain meant her body wasn't coping. This compounded with gluten inhibiting adequate nutrition rendered her depleted. Mama now understands the link between gut health and emotional wellbeing. For decades her body communicated through regular stomach migraines. Finally, she's listening.

When I tell Mama I feel suicidal, she ushers me back inside Perth Clinic's white wrought-iron gate. There, my psychiatrist switches my antidepressants from SSRI—preventing the reuptake of just serotonin—to SNRI—preventing the reuptake of serotonin and norepinephrine. I am told medications sometimes stop working because one's brain chemistry develops tolerance. With seasoned wisdom, it concerns me that doctors never tested my neurotransmitter levels and understand which antidepressants would work with my brain chemistry. I'm not convinced that pharma giants want us to heal when they generate billions through the marketization of healthcare that keeps us locked in prescription band-aids. In a capitalist world, wealth is valued over health. The implications for this are far-reaching.

While I no longer agree with the widespread prescription of antidepressants without considering long-term lifestyle change programmes and other wellness modalities, at the time I believe they are my happy pills. This disempowers my ability to fuel a joyous fire within. My locus of control is external. The medication doesn't allow me to get to the roots of my trauma, because it doesn't allow me to feel. It is a procrastination. Not a cure. But it also buys me time. Time to stabilise the highs and lows. Time to cultivate strength. Time to integrate healthy habits.

🌰

Let your emotions swirl like ocean currents,
deep and strong.

My new psychiatrist, Dr Sumptio, is a warm man with bouncy titters and great humour. As an outpatient, I continue seeing him in his office beside the hospital. I am enthralled by his bookshelf. It reveals an interest in meditation and Eastern philosophy. Dr Sumptio explains that immigrating from Sri Lanka rendered an integration of western and eastern worldviews. This intrigues me. It cultivates respect for the man so passionate about understanding me. From a black leather couch, I read him prose expressing my feelings about depression: the diminishing of spirit, the slow erosion of self, the doorway to hell that seems to invite me, and only me, inside.

Shortly after my discharge from the clinic, another mainstream music festival inspires my friends to source some LSD and trip for the first time. A tiny square tab appears in my hand. I don't take it. I don't want my first psychedelic journey to be crammed inside unfamiliar crowds. I giggle at my friends' enthrallment with strange bodily sensations as they describe trees pulsating with vibrant patterns that merge with the clouds. As dusk steals the day, my friends leave. They can't handle the world's weird warping.

Solo and sober, I bump into Jarred, and we float towards the main stage. He zips. I coast. I am content when different desires pull us different ways.

Gazing into the intoxicated crowd, I observe my surroundings with eagle eyes. Unattached yet so involved, I revere in unpacking the nuances within interactions because I see simplicity beneath complex emotions. We are all human. All we really want is to be understood, loved, and seen.

In the sea of swaying bodies, a slender girl with enormous blue eyes rests her gaze on mine. I recognize her seductive pout from the grapevine and prance over to introduce myself. Somewhere between the unce unce unce, she turns to me and asks, "Are you friends with Ruby Brown?"

"Nah, but I've heard of her. Why's that?"

"Be careful around Ruby. She's toxic."

It isn't the first time I've been cautioned of Ruby. Another friend has spoken similar words. Beneath my listening, curiosity simmers. We all have a past. Perhaps our pain is kindred.

The LSD burns in my wallet for a month before I feel called to take it on a warm early-autumn evening. I slide the small paper square under my tongue as I fill my car with petrol, arriving at the Zig Zag just before it kicks in.

The switchback road welcomes me with glistening skyline views. I park at a lower lookout near a sharp bend. Then I walk. Trailing around an old stone quarry, I follow my feet into what feels like Ancient Egypt. The full moon illuminates my narrow path. Stars shimmer intensely and intently. I stop often to contemplate the secrets of their twinkling beam as déjà vu ripples through my fingers and tunnel vision bursts into the Milky Way.

Clambering atop a dizzy ledge, I brush orange dust into the jagged rockpile below. Then an old friend buzzes. I invite him to join me. He arrives sporting a large hoodie and his handsome, dimpled grin. With intermittent giggles, I guide him along the steep circular trail to the dangerous cliff face where I wonder if I'll fall or fly. Kalamunda Zig Zag has a special place in my heart. Here, I tried to end my life. Here, I'm shown a new one.

In hindsight, it's a miracle that my friend called when he did. It's not safe to climb high cliffs on LSD alone at night. He likely saved my life. Back at his place, I examine my reflection in his sliding wardrobe doors. My skin squirms. My pupils dilate. I am melting and morphing. Something shifts inside me as my consciousness expands into realms that cannot be retracted. Later, my friend reads me a zesty letter addressed to his future self. His fleshy vulnerability inspires me to write my own and bury it in a time capsule at the quarry we just explored.

On the eve of my nineteenth birthday, I march to the top of the quarry with a metallic coffee cylinder filled with letters and sentimental trinkets. I dig a hole. I drop my time capsule. I fill it. As the earth bounds me in time, I am enthralled by the idea of surrendering to the elements parts that no longer serve my highest good.

A few weeks later, I tuck another letter inside a glass bottle. Wind lashes my eyes as a high school friend battles the salty gales beside me. We sometimes meet here late at night and talk atop the sloped wooden roof of the picnic table pavilion. I revere his philosophical mind that navigates the universe's labyrinth of mysteries. He likes my fearlessness of plunging deep—not yet into my inner terrain but the innate truth, love, and suffering of mankind.

I plead for him to throw the bottle so it won't shatter on the rocks with my poor aim. In a serious tone that deafens his usual joking manner, he refuses. It's my message, he says. I must be the one to set it free. Flinging the bottle into the ocean, I exhale.

The water washes my words away. It carries me out to sea.

Torrential rain floods the city as lightning electrifies the sky. Driving up the hill to Charlie's feels like a death wish as violent winds and cascading water storm against my car. I can barely see through the windscreen wipers hurling at full speed. Between the rubber blades' frenzied motion, I think of Cal. We haven't spoken in months. The more I kiss Jonny, the less he flashes to mind.

The power cuts out at Charlie's, so we light candles and open a cheap cask of wine. A few swigs in, Cal messages out of the blue and voyages through the superstorm to hang out. It's uncanny that I can still feel when he thinks of me.

A few months ago, I wrote an unsent letter to Cal expressing my feelings towards our five-year roller-coaster romance. For some reason I brought it with me that night. As Charlie hobbles to bed, using the empty wine cask as a pillow, I pull out the letter for Cal to read. Thunder growls. Hail snaps small branches. I excuse myself to the cluttered kitchen, giving him privacy to absorb our loose ends tied in a bittersweet bow of words.

When I return, Cal is dewy-eyed. He leans forward to hug me. An intense flurry releases with the rain. After sharing one last kiss, we succumb to slumber in bed with Charlie. His arm is heavy on my torso as he holds me close. We are both free to move on with our lives. Holding on will be a burden. It's uncomfortable. But it's over.

There is nothing left to say.

Every song ends, but we still savour the lyrics.

My reoccurring themes in 2010 are letting go, completing unfinished business, and allowing life to unravel. As autumn frosts into a drizzly winter, I am clubbing with a friend at a venue with dozens of helium balloons. We attach two to our wrists with string. As the bright buoyant bags swim across the ceiling, we use them to find each other while chattering and bouncing on the dance floor.

Later, we stroll back to my car under a midnight moon. I impulsively untie the string from my wrist. From the empty street I watch the balloon levitate and shrink. My friend's brows twist as she shoots me a blank look.

"Babe, *why* did you do that? We held on sooooo tight all night, fighting all those *dickheads* trying to steal it!"

I maintain my gaze.

"If it's meant for me, it will come back. If not, it's time to let go."

The balloon is a metaphor for many things. Seemingly colourful and expansive, it is empty inside. Always above me, the balloon is held down. It doesn't want attachment via a mere string. It wants freedom. I do too. Even if it does come back, it won't ever be the same. No one will notice an airless bit of rubber screaming for attention on the ground. Like water spilling from a bottle, it can never be gathered back together again. It must release in messy chaos so there is space for something new.

Perched on the rocky groyne where I threw my bottled message, I watch the silhouetted figure approach. A cool, salty breeze caresses my cheeks. My hands are toasty in my jacket pockets. Massive floodlights illuminate Jonny's smile and accentuate his buff thighs. Behind him is the carpark where I lost my virginity and the patch of sand where I woke from my unsuccessful suicide. I often come here late at night. There is solace in contemplating the illuminated voyage of ships into distant lands.

Jonny kisses me on the cheek as we embrace. It's been a while since we've caught up outside of the club scene, but it's a lonely night, and he is lost in the maze of his mind. As waves rush into rock crevices in soothing swirls, I confide my desire to leave Perth. Jonny nods. Slowly. His riveting focus in my peripheral arouses a newfound freedom. Nothing is certain, and that makes anything possible.

The next day, a single-engine plane buzzes and whirs Papa and me through the clouds. The panoramic coast widens in a sparkly expanse as sky dive instructors tighten straps and double-check clips. Papa places two fingers on my neck. My pulse beats in a slow rhythm. A dazed look sweeps across his face. He admits his heart is racing. As the door opens to the engine's fierce roar, I cross my arms over my chest.

Three, two, one.

Go.

I'm in the clouds. Swooping through, I gasp for breath in the oxygen-scarce air. Winds of freedom lash my cheeks. This is the taste I've been craving. The instructor yells something, but I've lost hearing in my left ear. Then he unfurls the yellow parachute, and the adrenaline-pumping free fall jerks to an end. The harness cuts into my groin. My eyes burn in the frigid breeze. Below the baby-blue sky, the turquoise coast bestows a stunning view as cars crawl along the virescent countryside.

It's ironic: falling in love again is terrifying, yet I have no fear in jumping out of a plane. Risk is thrilling. I feel like I'm truly living because I'm transcending fear and exploring the edges of my comfort zone. This is true physically. But it's not emotional. I'm still so resistant to being vulnerable and opening up to how I really feel. I still shackle my depths in a cage under lock and key.

In the weeks that follow, I detach and draw away from Jonny. We've always played a game of hot-cold push-pull. It's an underlying power play, and whoever reaches out is losing. Yet, beneath the façade of not caring, there are bits of me in him and him in me. I exhale him out, only to inhale him back in. No matter how far the riptide carries us, we breathe the same air.

🌱

Pressurised vapour from the steam wand gushes into a warm fog around me. As I count the seconds it takes hot water to pour through coffee grounds, my mind works double time. Before I know it, the water stops, I've lost count, and a thought echoes.

There's more to life. You know there is, Jess. It's time to seize it.

I snap back to my barista duties as the steam vanishes into an elusive aroma of sweet, nutty coffee. I don't want to be steam. I don't want to dissipate into nothing. I don't want to die without giving life my all.

Strolling to my car that afternoon, I pass a travel agent and enquire about flights to Europe. Two weeks later, I've booked two back-to-back Contiki Tours, leaving in five weeks' time.

🌱

Don't give up on your dream now.
We all have restless nights.

Before leaving for Europe, I see Dr Sumptio again. Between two jobs and preparing to go away, I haven't renewed my prescription. I'm on day three without medication. Cold turkey lours me in grey. As I scan the busy street for parking, an internal battle wages between hating life and healing.

"I detest this place," I spit to myself, seething in anticipation of the receptionists looking down their pointed noses at me when I walk in late.

Deep exhale.

"Suck it up, princess. There ain't no getting better till you help yourself."

The power in my own voice is sobering. Our first thought is our conditioned way of thinking. Our second thought is an opportunity to rewire those patterns. It is Dr Sumptio who teaches me this. Slowly, I integrate the notion into daily life.

In his office, Dr Sumptio examines me.

"You sound flat today. Not how you usually are when we talk."

"Yeah, I actually just came to get a new prescription because the other one ran out..." I divert my gaze to a book about Buddhism.

He blinks twice and tilts his head. "So, you've been off your meds?"

"Yes, but I've been doing okay. I mean, I've been feeling sad, but I've been feeling happy too... You know how life goes."

"And there's been no bad thoughts?"

"There's been a few off days, but I'm learning. I know even though there may be no trigger or reason, it will pass. I sleep it off...or call a friend. But I know I need to go back on them before I go away, you know, in case something happens."

"Yes. Even though you could be in a good place with good people, you might not be having a good time, and we don't want that to happen."

He pauses for an exhale and catches my gaze.

"It's very dangerous to stop taking your medication so abruptly, Jessica, because we've established that you need to be medicated for life." I nod. Then the *"for life"* part lands. I blink.

"Did you get any withdrawals?"

"Just the usual dreams..."

Sometimes I cease medication for a few days, curious to what will happen. On day one I am flooded with raw emotion. On day two, my creativity peaks as I tap into the cascade and give words to my pain. Interestingly, my dreams then become lucid. I'm aware that I'm dreaming, and I teach myself to fly. At first, I flap my arms through the gridlike streets of Perth. Overtime, I navigate the oceans to different continents and attempt to break through the stratosphere en route to the moon.

Dr Sumptio calls me out on my belief that there are no triggers for my depression. He says it is important to get to the roots of my havoc so I can remove the weeds.

"The worst is over now," he assures. "There are triggers in life that can take you back to those days. You should remove yourself from them." Sometimes I feel stupid for talking about my futile problems while children are starving in Africa. Then I discern that silence won't feed the hungry. I can't help others unless I help myself first.

Dr Sumptio often asks me to share my writing. I read something particularly poignant that day.

After a reflective pause he asks, "So, when's the book coming out?"

"Never," I mumble dryly.

"No, Jessica, remember what we talked about. You must never give up on your writing."

His chocolate eyes glimmer with sincerity. They are some of the last words we ever share.

As the plane descends through a heavy convolution of grey clouds, electricity zaps through my fatigue. The London Eye spins beside the murky Thames. Big Ben overlooks cathedrals embellishing the sprawling city.

I wheel my suitcase onto the Underground, meet my predominantly Australian tour in a funky hotel basement, then we cram into a bus that will carry us across ten countries in eighteen days. An Australian dude in his late twenties introduces himself as Richie, our tour leader, and invites us to the front of the bus to introduce ourselves one by one. Along with name and occupation, we play the "traffic light" game, stating if our relationship status is "green" single, orange "it's complicated", or red "taken".

The week before leaving, I am fired from the café for not toasting a sandwich. I didn't take the order or make the sandwich, but I'm the manager on duty who deals with the angry lady slamming the sandwich on the counter midway through serving another customer. The woman's power trip and executive-manager-of-a-store status threatens the café owner, who fires me two days later without warning. I later win an Ombudsman case for unfair dismissal.

The story has the bus guffawing with laughter, and I become the butt of every sexist, woman-fucking-up-a-sandwich joke as I enter a paradigm of drunk, hungover, commercialised tourism with forty-eight strangers.

High trees catch a lot of wind.
- Dutch proverb

Dover's iconic white cliffs shrink to tiny ivory speckles on a shivery, goose-bump-inducing ferry to France. British accents diffuse into sophisticated French dialogue as we disembark in Calais then venture through lush Belgium meadows into Amsterdam.

Upon arrival, I message a Perth friend living in the Dutch capital on the hostel computer to organise a catchup. He is elsewhere in Europe, so I explore Amsterdam's narrow roads clinking with bicycles and crisscross the maze of canals dotted with picturesque houseboats with others. Quaint gable houses perch at crooked angles. Ornate bridges illuminate iconic waterways. Whiffs of marijuana sail through the late-summer air.

As my new friends buy joints from a cute underground coffee shop, I get a special brownie for later. Then Richie leads us through the Red Light District where hundreds of young women dressed in lingerie blink and yawn through full-length, glass-panelled, red-lit windows. Some apply fresh lipstick. Most move their bodies provocatively. Others disengage and text on their phones.

I feel a bizarre fusion of sorrow and intrigue. I feel for women succumbing to objectification to make ends meet in a patriarchal world. Yet, the legalization of the world's oldest occupation reduces sexual assault and violent crime. Sex workers are less vulnerable to abuse, exploitation, and trafficking with unions and police protection. Richie talks of the contrast to conservative Japan. Sexuality is suppressed, yet graphic and animalistic porn is normalised. He links this to primal human impulses being subdued and thus unnamed, resulting in a cultural shadow of savage domination.

Before cramming into cinema-style seats on tiered rows at a live sex show, I chew down the brownie. It helps me relax into the absurdity of watching couples have sex on a rotating bed. An attractive waitress offers complimentary champagne. The bubbles fizz. I tire at the lack of passion onstage. Then a jacked man saunters on and requests an audience volunteer. My hand shoots up. Maybe this will enliven me.

All eyes are on me as he sits me on a wooden chair and my hands dangle like weights. His hips don't lie as he twists his body around me and removes his clothes. Every item but the hat. The hat remains. The crowd cheers, but his regimented sexuality doesn't turn me on. At the end of the song, he flaunts his booty to the audience while whispering an invitation for post-show drinks. In the upstairs bar, Richie thwarts our meet. He says the dude is notorious for not treating girls right.

His concern evokes adoration that I hide behind coy glances from my squished backseat. In Edam we cycle past clog museums, traditional Dutch windmills, and hand-operated drawbridges. I catch glimpses of cultural liberalism steeping in medieval architecture. I want to delve deeper, but there is no time, and I feel cheated.

Techno echoes with memories of crisp German beer as we stroll along the Berlin Wall remains in impassioned silence. The hairs on my arms tingle at colourful murals depicting the giant, fortified barricade separating Western Europe from the Eastern Bloc. It seems to stretch forever as Richie talks of divided neighbourhoods, separated families, and communist soldiers armed to shoot and kill after an erected-overnight, barbed wire fence evolved to a no-mans-land of attack dogs and explosives prohibiting free movement.

Beside a mural of multicultural crowds tearing down the wall from both sides are the words: *He who wants the world to remain as it is doesn't want it to remain at all.* The notion strikes me. For three decades the Iron Curtain divided and conquered. Now, it is a symbol of German reunification.

Prague is a quirky cobblestoned labyrinth embellished with Czech marionettes, cheap craft beer, and Bohemian art. Street musicians create sonic portals into different eras of time. The language is a rhythmic dance inflected with too many consonants. I like it. Its fusional nature and rich morphology stir my emotional terrain.

I'm still not consciously sitting with my feelings, but there's a fluidity arising. Sometimes I wake from nights out with black Biro scribbled all over my arms. Travelling without a phone means I'm without unsent draft messages addressed to my future self. The emotion inside me wants to release. It wants me to arrange it into something I can work with, work out, work through. Like the flexible word order I hear around me, I'm becoming malleable to another way of being.

On our second night in the picturesque city, I rest while the others prepare to party. I need a break. I need a sober night.

As the taxis arrive, I am overcome by a sudden impulse to jump in the backseat with heels in hand. I can't explain the somatic knowing of instinct. I just trust it.

Shots of absinthe welcome us to a dim, draughty bar. I drown two then sway into the sunny courtyard for fresh air. In the line, a familiar face catches my eye. I blink twice and rub my eyes. It's my Perth friend living in Amsterdam. Turns out he's taken a last-minute trip to Prague, and somehow we're at the same pub. For all my love of logic, I treasure the unravelling mystery of intuition.

The pub crawl continues with staggering antics. Old-world magic sweeps through a 14th century bathhouse converted into a five-story nightclub. It wraps around a six-hundred-year-old clock depicting celestial movements and glides over grotesque stone gargoyles perched on Medieval cathedrals. Eight centuries of history spellbinds us with dropped jaws. It is revitalizing and moving.

History is constantly teaching, but it does not find many pupils.
- **Austrian proverb**

Octoberfest is a few weeks away when we pull into Munich, but that doesn't stop us from devouring Bavarian beer and annihilating giant pretzels. In a large timbre-floored hall, sexy maids balance four one-litre pints in each hand. Though the scene is chirpy, I crave solitude after a crowded week and slink away. On a lonely gravel path, my crunchy footsteps calm me.

Earlier that day, on a long head-throbbing bus ride, Richie chattered about the Baroque period. Snores erupted around me. I absorbed his words. He talked of his desire to run tours through South America and veer off the beaten track. As stars shimmer through the silhouetted canopy, I decide I want to be a traveller too. I don't want to be a tourist. I want to let different tastes and textures seep into my skin and inspirit me.

Munich is a short stay with long travel days on either side. I relish the mountainous scenes whooshing past the window as I write on postcards and muse on the patterns of history repeating, of different civilizations marking their legacy by pointing at common ground and claiming it as their own. I feel small by the notion yet empowered that I can be part of social change.

Dreamy green hills roll into Hopfgarten, a quaint village in Austria's idyllic Tyrol that is nestled within snow-capped Alps. Embracing another solo walk, I relish the serenity of rustling pine trees. I want to connect with locals. I want to listen to their stories.

The shops are closed for afternoon siesta, and the dusty streets are empty. What do travellers do without a structured itinerary? Do they surrender into the unknown?

The next day, the entire bus goes white-water rafting. Like freezing rapids blasting through the valley, I want to be like water. Carving my path yet adaptable to change.

᛫

Back on land, we meander past medieval towns into the fairytale lagoon of Venice. The impermanence of my own existence becomes blatant in the city that is sinking. Flood water seeps into porous bricks. Low tides rot the cities foundations as air permeates pilings drilled into mudbanks. Fuelled by greasy pizza and fruity gelato, we trot along winding stone streets and ornate bridges. Canals shimmer. Some reek of rotten fish and algae.

Locals sing from traditional wooden gondolas as though the city is eternal. Life is meant to enjoy now in the metropolis masterpiece of mazes and mirages.

In our mosquito-strewn campsite, raw sewage fuses with the fresh salty breeze. Music booms from the bar where girls get free shots if they flash their boobs. Clutching a cobalt masquerade mask, I skip back to my dorm for a quiet moment.

A loud bang cuts through the air followed by drunken laughter. In a nearby dorm, our bus driver collapses beside her own vomit. I'm the youngest on tour, but I rarely feel it. I fetch her water. Then I spot my dorm mate fumbling by a lonely stone bench.

I foresee her head hitting the concrete and sprint over. She thinks it's a game and bolts through the sticky campsite. Eventually I catch her, and sad truths pour—words of love, words of loss, words of longing. Spoon-feeding her the very wisdom I need to swallow, I balance her wobbly body on mine and point at a muscular man passed out face-down on the grass.

"See, you're okay, babe. You're not as drunk as *that guy*..."

As the words escape me, I realise the guy is our friend.

Suddenly I have another slurring adult to nurse.

As we roam Rome, I notice the colloquialisms of wanting to "tick __insert country__ off my list" or "do __insert country__ next." My body recoils for it reduces countries to a to-do list, rather than people and places with which we connect. Travelling isn't something we do. It's something we experience with all senses engaged.

In the Eternal City, lavish architecture exhibits every period of history. It is hot and holy. Locals communicate with exaggerated motions as they park mopeds beside cast-iron drinking fountains and fill plastic bottles with ice-cold water. The gushing founts—a legacy from ancient Rome—subdue the screech and vroom of traffic as I sweat salty cascades, ponder the Vatican's secret archives, and sink my teeth into thick, crusty pizza.

Constant movement fuses into a strange blend of lively fatigue as we drink cheap liquor from giant fishbowls in Florence. A treasure trove of structural masterpieces, prolific art, and famous sculptures bejewel narrow cobbled roads. I yearn to explore the birthplace of the Renaissance beyond the giddy string of bars. I want to devour the city that enlightened Europe from Medieval misery. I want to savour the flavours of Leonardo da Vinci and Michelangelo. But all I taste is bitter alcohol and burning bile as I wake with more inky musings.

Little by little, the bird builds its nest.
- French proverb

As rustic Italian countryside blends into stunning Swiss Alps, I see that when I am present with the world, the world is present with me. Perched at the front of the bus, Richie explains that Switzerland is wired with dynamite to activate valley-sweeping landslides in the event of foreign invasion. As usual, I'm the only one imbibing his words. I relish the small country's politically neutral stance—uninvolved in war for two hundred years, yet armed for self-defence if necessary.

The glacier-encrusted landscape is even more majestic knowing that nuclear-proof warehouses, hospitals, and artillery are hidden in the glistening mountains.

Bare, icy summits loom over flowering meadows alongside the unspoilt village of Lauterbrunnen perched in a trough valley. We bunk up at a chalet nestled beside a thundering waterfall, then ride an electric train through a seven-kilometre mountain tunnel from the world's highest station.

At Jungfrau Mountain's peak, fluffy clouds whisk into blinding-white snow. I crunch it into balls and hurl them at my friends. Then soft ivory flakes fall. I catch the crystalline feathers like they are gold. Each unique formation holds its shape before melting into cool pools that fuel introspection. We can't hold on to moments forever, but we can enjoy the journey.

Another long drive steers us through gorgeous Burgundy countryside dotted with ripe vineyards and simple stone hamlets. I snap selfies beside friends snoring off hangovers as Richie narrates Caesar's conquest, Charlemagne's rule, Joan of Arc's courage, and the guillotining of Marie Antoinette and Louis XIV that sparked the French Revolution. As I daydream upon cottages, chateaus, and steeple-topped churches, we trail into Paris. Lamplit bridges arch over the Seine, inviting us deeper into the City of Lights where champagne is popped and we sing "Salut" over a dish of garlic snails. The cityscape shimmers like a sequin-fringed leotard.

Three weeks slumped on the bus, staying up late, and drinking to excess trounces me. While the others jampack their exploration of the seductive city into just one day, I sleep. In doing so, I commit to returning to relish the city slowly.

With fresh eyes, I catch the metro across the city to our farewell dinner. Locals sporting jeans and heels carry brown grocery bags. Effortlessly, the word casual translates to poise.

At dinner, Richie advises attempting French, even if we fail. It expresses respect and evades the cultural clash of assuming locals will speak English. Between decadent dishes, I try chatting to our waiter in French. Alas, a kerfuffle of Italian rolls off my tongue. Rookie mistake. He laughs it off with our appetizer of warm, freshly baked bread. As my main slides into my stomach like velvet butter, he shrugs. Then I spill the dessert wine I'm meant to savour. He looks down his nose, drapes an oversized white napkin over my lap, and declares, "You baby. You need bib."

A drop of wisdom is better than a sea of gold.
- Greek epigram

Back in London, our tour whirls full circle, and bittersweet goodbyes usher us different ways. I catch a flight to Athens, where a smorgasbord of salty Greek tapas relish my taste buds, and I meet my new tour group gushing about cruising crystal Mediterranean seas. Azure currents sway us as we devour four-course buffets, let the sun kiss our skin brown, and explore popular port cities in just four hours. Once again, I'm given a whiff of the menu that I wish to savour in entirety.

Wind gusts through Mykonos's maze of winding whitewashed lanes designed to confuse pirates so villagers could escape with ease. In Kuşadasi, hungry Turkish eyes penetrate me like a walking dollar sign as catcalls pierce my ears. I feel sticky and prickly in bustling bazaars. I'm just another sale from the cruise ship crowd. I'm not seen for me, and I'm not seeing authentic Turkey.

Patmos's rugged hills provide the quiet I crave. From the crisp cave where the prophetic Book of Revelation was scribed, I gaze upon pebble beaches and pine forests, pondering the cryptic symbology of the Bible's final book that is also classified as apocalyptic literature. My introspection ceases with swarms of G-string bikinis on Crete's crowded beaches.

Santorini strikes me with glistening blue-domed houses trickling down soaring cliffs. There, the novelty of hiking an active volcano, swimming in warm thermal waters, and emerging with a sulphur smell as the horizon orchestrates a world-renowned sunset bring the cruise to a picturesque end.

Back in Athens, I perch on thousand-year-old ruins and reflect how the trip changed me. The questions I left with are answered with more questions—queries of where I belong and what comes next. The more I know, the less I know. My awareness is expanding.

Far from home, searching for home, I feel at home. This invigorates me. Homesick for wanderlust, I don't know where I belong. Strange stirrings free me from stagnation as notions caress my subconscious mind. They lure me in, only to float away as my fingers reach out to catch them. Unable to construct my thoughts into words, gaps fill the space inside me. Maybe I'm not the person everyone thinks I am. But then again, who is?

Three weeks later, it is October in sunny Perth. I've started bartending in a windowless tavern that slouches with memories of its glory days. It is a busy Friday afternoon. At 5:15 p.m., a pretty girl skips through the door with a small suitcase in tow. All three men waiting for beer swivel around and drool at her curvy figure. Two others stop playing pool to whistle as she passes.

"Hi, boys," she purrs in a thick British accent.

At the bar, she flicks a long brunette lock over her shoulder. It looks like she's glued rock candy on her fingernails and pressed her face into a cake.

"Hi, darl. I'm Emma, your skimpy this afternoon."

A skimpy is a woman who serves alcohol in a bikini or lingerie. They are part interactive entertainer—charming people with friendly chatter and party tricks—and part regular bartender. It is a tradition unique to Western Australia with its mammoth mining industry, where men sometimes work weeks without interacting with women. In the former wild-west gold mine boom, slack legislation enabled lewd behaviour. Now, the industry is an offshoot of the decades-long staple in working-class pubs with strict legislation for underwear length and appropriate conduct.

A man queues up for a drink. I nod at him, then motion to the two others waiting before him. He's third in line.

"Emma, do you start at 5 or 5:30?" I quiz.

She looks up from her phone. "Oh, traffic was hectic, darl. I was meant to start at 5:00 p.m. Is there somewhere I can get changed...or...unchanged."

We both giggle.

"There's a bathroom by the door," I answer, pouring a pint with one hand and pointing to the only source of natural light streaming into the ramshackle tavern with the other.

Back across the room she struts, without apology for being late. Some men continue yelling at dogs racing on small TVs. Most watch her pass. I wonder if all skimpies are so blasé to the attention or if they revel it.

She returns in silky red lingerie, a black garter, and fishnet stockings. Three crusty faces appear at the bar, suddenly thirsty. Rather than serve them, she slams down two empty beer jugs adorned with sparkly acrylic stickers.

"These are my tip jars. If you want to see my tits, you've got to show me your tips," she informs with a wink, tracing her candy fingers around the contours of her body.

I show her where the glasses, beer bottles, and spirits are, holding my breath as I direct. She reeks of perfume. The fumes remind me of the play fights Papa and I used to have in lavish cosmetic stores, spraying each other with expensive tester bottles as we laughed and ducked behind counters. Emerging smelling like black cherry and crème de musk, he always ended up worse.

A young Irish guy orders a pint. She holds the glass upright under the tap as it fills with froth.

"Do you have a spoon?" he jokes.

I snatch it away, grab a new glass, and repour it.

An hour into her shift, she waltzes out to the patrons' side of the bar, rattles her tip jugs, and yells, "It's change-for-change time, boys. If you want to see me in less clothes, show me your tips!"

A wrinkled man with sleepy eyes calls to me, "A middy of Carlton Draught, please."

I nod and continue pouring the two orders before him while Emma prances back behind the bar. He barks his order at her. She rolls her eyes at him as another man slides a ten-dollar note into her knickers.

"Hey, skimpy. What was your name—Emma? Could you help me serve, please?"

"Sure, darl," she agrees, then leans across the bar to shake her boobs at another patron who passes her five dollars.

The Carlton Draught man looks at me with compassionate eyes as I place his drink before him and Emma swanks back to the patrons' side with her bag in tow. I eye the empty beers piling along the bar as she slinks into the bathroom.

"You're next, then you, then you." I gesture to three nearby men, trying to conceal my annoyance with a smile.

She returns in a black G-string bikini that barely covers her nipples. I later learn what she's wearing is illegal—legislation depicts that seventy-five percent of a woman's butt and boobs must be covered.

"Here." The sleepy-eyed man motions to my tip jar where he places a small ball of foil. "This is for you. You'll need it later."

I lean towards the pint glass filled with coins and inhale a whiff of marijuana.

"Oh, I don't smoke..." I start, but the man has strolled away.

That night I sit on my parents' roof and puff the joint as distant waves rumble on the wind. In open conversation with the stars, I wonder if all skimpies are crass and unreliable. From there on I pour my mad-as-a-hatter-yet-borderline-genius friend's beer as soon as he walks through the door, and he tips me tiny marijuana nuggets for my quick service.

Developing depth is the virtue of pain.

Smoking weed begins as a healthy release after long shifts. Creative ideas whirl me in their flourish, and a reflective mood enables me to peer into my past and acknowledge what I've been avoiding. Sometimes I scribble my thoughts on paper with a stinging poignancy that reduces my emotions to blue ink and a string of syllables. The alphabet drifts in a monotone clutter. It keeps the clock ticking. As I drink less, smoking becomes a complicated case of escapism.

As kangaroo paws blossom in marvellous ruby velvet displays, Charlie studies art at TAFE. We often hang out in her messy bedroom listening to The Doors, The Beatles, and The Stones. I curl up on her bed and write poetry. She dips paintbrushes in jars and swirls water into colourful tornados before enlivening blank canvases with intricate strokes. In the eye of the storm, we find solace through creativity. It is a way of channelling our unprocessed emotions as smoke meanders to the ceiling and bong water bubbles. So much between us is unspoken, yet so deeply felt. We are on a seesaw of struggle. As one spirals, the other supports.

Sometimes, Charlie's innate kindness is detriment. If giving from an empty vessel, she disregards her own needs, which depletes her self-worth to tiny splinters. Like me, Charlie is a victim of unconsented sex. Like me, the ashy aftermath entices her to lather herself with gasoline before striking a deadly match. Neither of us can fathom how to get to the roots of our darkness. With bleeding fingers, we dig.

When Charlie's dad marries her first love's mother, her life becomes a soap opera with cutting twists. There is so much she suppresses, so much she wishes to scream, but she chokes on the words behind her lips as all that is unsaid permeates the inky shadows. Sometimes she runs out of consonants and vowels to express the turmoil crashing within. Hours become seconds. Seconds become hours. Desperate to make things last, she stretches moments into infinity through her art.

Late one night I am driving us home from a party when she says, "I need some time to find myself, be myself. But I can't allow myself to be by myself."

Self-hatred twists and knots her insides, bound by an enormous amount of emotional energy. She often drinks and smokes to excess.

I nod at her paradoxical confession.

Then her eyes roll to the back of her head, and she slurs, "Jess, I'm dying."

I slam on the brakes as she retches. Hands to mouth, she tries to contain the anguish and grief lurching from her core. The vile smell of vomit cascades through my car as her heavy eyes violently shut. I hand her my water. Then I glimpse thick pink scars on her wrists, roadmaps charting the bloody war waging within her soft skin. The cuts emphasize the urgency in her words and encapsulate the emptiness that consumes her. I don't know what to do.

Charlie forgets the remark by morning. With vacant eyes, she shades a portrait with hefty strokes. Head spins mix with heart sinks. Her warmth is replaced by frost. Uncertainty finds its switch and dampens her radiance with overwhelming exhaustion. Years later, Charlie is diagnosed with borderline personality disorder. Eventually she moves through it and grows stronger, but in the interim, giving up and giving in seem more attractive.

The beer garden is lively, warmed by a Sunday afternoon sun. I scan the crowd for familiar faces, catching the gaze of a slender brunette. Sunshine drips off the top bun pulling her hair from her tanned face. I can't tell if it's a half-assed mess or elegant display.

She flashes a teethy smile and approaches.

"Is your name Jess?"

"Yes..." I eye her with caution. *What do you want from me?*

"Hi! I'm Ruby."

Her friendly tone tells me she wants to be my friend.

I glimpse *X.IV.XCI* on her wrist. "I like your tatt."

A flashback of my festival friend's warning to be wary of Ruby entertains me, but I continue graceful small talk. Ruby's outspoken humour makes me giggle. I can't help but like the blue-eyed beauty showing me her *"determination"* biceps tattoo before lowering her jeans to reveal a dove on her right hip.

We exchange numbers, and she comes over the following week. It's strange to us both that two strangers pre-drinking before a fun night isn't awkward. It evolves to us partying regularly and embarking on hilarious adventures. Despite what I've heard, I like her. She's the girl who pierced both nipples and clit with just a wild laugh. We instantly click.

Sunshine oozes with the warm nectar of Vitamin D as I laze on Jonny's springy lawn. Beside me are a dozen of his closest friends. It is January 2011. As they bellow happy birthday, my phone rings like an exasperated alarm. I excuse myself to a shady corner and answer to a sedated Charlie. My heart twists as she whispers that she's in hospital with a drip in her arm. She has overdosed on antidepressants.

I ask if I can see her while the guys devour cake. She lies that she is okay after a gastric suction and tetanus shot upon doctors noticing her self-harm lacerations from metallic blades. Even on her deathbed, she won't let me be present to support her. Even on her deathbed, the nurses dismiss her internal agony with stinky attitudes that questions why Charlie is taking up one of their beds. This is before mental health imbues social conversations. Instead of compassion and safety she is subjected to judgement and disdain.

Fear shackles me as I drive the guys to a club on the other side of the city. I am on autopilot as my mind seeks answers. *Why is this happening? How can I help?* Later it emerges that her rapist came to her workplace, triggering all her suppressed sorrow to rise. After weeks of striking it out, shoving it down, and slamming it away, she is caged by a thorny tangle of raw emotions beckoning her to be liberated from them by first allowing herself to feel them.

At the club, the bouncer examines Jonny's glazed eyes and giddy smile, shakes his head, and sends us on our way. My stomach warps into matted tissue as I drive the boys to the beach. They are rowdy and blithe, oblivious to my internal crumpling. On the warm sand, I bum a cigarette and inhale the trashy fumes. I don't usually smoke. The taste revolts me. But the toxic chemicals numb me from the reality of my closest friend willingly summoning death. Waves stir the shore with transient pulses. I am back at square one, pondering the stillness of the void that seeps between each briny reach-release cycle. There's something there. Something being whispered in the ocean's salty breath. Something waiting for me to hear it.

Eventually I strip to my underwear and swim beyond the break. In the water, I surrender my emotions to the silky rhythm. It cools and calms and drenches me in equanimity. Amid the perpetual percussion of each rise and fall, I see that Charlie's revelation of her worth is her greatest tool to seize the better that she deserves. In the overpronounced arches of cresting breakers, I see the detriment of the hard-skinned Aussie "she'll be right, gotta keep going" frame of mind that prohibits Charlie from processing the trauma at the core of her dense decay.

With retrospect, I recognise my realisations about Charlie deflect the fact that I too use coping mechanisms to avoid uncomfortable emotions. In doing so, I give power to my shadow—the unconscious parts of myself that I repress and reject because I deem them unacceptable. Ignoring and undermining our emotions doesn't make them go away. They continue trickling into our lives in intense waves that crash and churn and slash and burn until we find the fortitude to befriend our minds and welcome the myriad of emotions that make us human.

Charlie and I are united in our warped way of seeing our worth in men's desire that disconnects sex from emotion. We don't see it as this. Not for a very long time. Instead, we believe we are "using men for their bodies" because it twists society's narrative of women being unable to remove emotion from sex with the impossibly contradictory norm of commodifying women's sexuality by the way we are portrayed in media, discourse, and advertising. By viewing it this way, Charlie and I perceive that we hold the power when men lust after us.

Many years later, Charlie identifies that, "They didn't objectify me. I did it to myself." I agree and disagree. It holds truth. But that does not mean that responsibility to change it falls solely on women. For the deeper roots stem from a patriarchal worldview that taught us to objectify ourselves by deeming women as objects of men's gratification with secondary sexual needs. Yeah, we bought into it. But we don't know what we don't know. Until we do. Then we break free.

There are some things we are meant to know.
Others are revealed in time.

The mouldy pub reeks of spilt beer. Crusty men yell at greyhounds racing on the television. They roar in my periphery as I think about Charlie. Following her discharge, she resumes life like nothing happened. Still smoking. Still drinking. Still fucking the pain away. Through her actions, I grasp the disservice we've done ourselves by shunning, numbing, and running from our pain. Ever so slowly I am opening my eyes and learning to breathe amid the emotional undertow that once drowned me. It is the inception of me discovering an alternative path. One grounded in emotional intelligence and positivity. The first steps are visible to my weary eyes, but I can't yet fathom how to disjoin myself from the shrivelled trench that has been my life to spring into a new reality.

The clink of coins in my tip jar pulls me out of my thoughts and back into the bar. I turn and wave to Old Frank, the crabby barfly who I've slowly charmed into being my friend. He used to bark his order with a frustration burrowed in his bones. Now his saggy pink eyes ignite with dormant flames.

Later in the evening, a middle-aged man sparks up conversation from where he always perches in a dark corner.

"Can you read people well?"

I pour a pint as I lie, "Not yet."

I pride myself on observing microexpressions and nonverbal cues after years of poring over books and YouTube videos. It's easy to discern what people are thinking and feeling, but without understanding someone's personal context you cannot distinguish why said thoughts and feelings emerge. I don't want him to know this, though. I've hidden my intelligence behind a ditzy mask since the day I was assaulted. The less clued in people think I am, the more they'll unknowingly reveal. Therefore, I feel safer in perceiving their unspoken intentions.

"Three people in this bar have a gambling problem," the man remarks.

I nod.

"Three or four have an alcohol addiction. There were two rock spiders, one's gone now. One seeks a fight, and there are a lot of naïve minds."

"A *rock spider?*"

"A paedophile," he clarifies.

I stop wiping the scratchy metal bench and catch his silver eyes.

"See, when you read people, every so often you come across someone you don't understand. And it frustrates you, because they remind you of yourself. Either something bad happened to them when they were younger, or they've been through similar experiences as you. They've learned to hide themselves and mask their story."

I refrain from swallowing a sudden surplus of saliva that would reveal my unease.

He holds eye contact and clarifies, "I see this in you."

I open my mouth to argue, to protect the parts of me hidden behind my façade, but he continues, "The other barmaid has a big secret that she hasn't dealt with..."

Yeah, she's cheating on her boyfriend.

"...and I'm not talking about the affair. Everyone's telling her she's dealt with it, but she hasn't. It seeps through in all her interactions."

My mind ticks in double-time. I want to press for more details, but an almost empty beer steals me away.

Mid pour, the lights go out.

It's a neighbourhood blackout. The bar closes early.

At home, I chuck denim shorts and pastel dresses into a large pink suitcase bound for Thailand the next day. As colours scrunch in vivid disarray, I see my different personas knot and tangle. Something inside me shifts. For the first time on any account, I am compelled by the notion of letting the world see me without any masks.

Wrapped within rags might be gold.
- Thai proverb

Between two carriages on a speeding train, I grasp my hair behind my neck and vomit into the Thai countryside. A night of heavy drinking in Bangkok establishes the fortnight's theme as we venture south to Koh Samui. An old co-worker and our friends doze inside the sticky, rattling cart. I swear I'll never drink again, but the next night we're challenging each other to guzzle beyond intoxication. Amidst bustling markets and congested roads, I see a culture embodied in respect and self-control. Genuine Thai smiles humble me and trigger a shame that I'm not engaging as a traveller. I'm being a tourist. Retching most nights. Waking with vomit reeking from the hotel bathroom.

In the final days of our indulgent holiday, I spin around in front of the mirror and scrutinize my tanned, bloated reflection. I look alright in a bikini. This is what most skimpies wear. Could I handle that kind of work?

The inception of autumn roasts like a decadent Christmas dinner. I stick my head in the beer fridge to cool myself as sweat rivulets onto a bottle of lemonade. I exhale with quiet relief. Then the distinctive two-note glissando of a man wolf-whistling shrills. I pivot my head to a smiley blonde trotting around the pool table towards the bar. It is 4:45 p.m. on a Wednesday. She doesn't start until 5:00 p.m.

The girl introduces herself as Bec and chats with the locals before stripping down to a metallic turquoise bikini studded with golden rhinestones. My intrigue grows as she pours perfect beers with friendly service opposed to being provocative and hustling tips.

"What's it like being a skimpy?" I ask, without my usual sass.

"I like it." She smiles. "I'm with this new freelance network. We're cutting out agencies taking a bunch of money by acting as the middleman."

"Oh...What's that like?"

"It's great! We communicate directly with pubs so it's, like, more professional. Best of all, I choose where I work, when I work, how often I work, *and* if I don't like certain pubs, I don't have to return."

"That's interesting. Kind of empowering, I guess." I glance at the golden chains falling from the soft, stretchy fabric of her bikini. "Isn't it weird to be seen in your underwear slash bathers in a bar?"

"You get used to it. If anything, you get really comfortable in your own skin," she chirps. "Anyway, you see more skin at a beach."

"That's true..."

In her bright brown eyes I see a genuine, down-to-earth woman. An empty glass plonks on the bar. She skips off to fill it before I even notice. *If skimpy bartending can be women taking charge and working in a playful yet professional way, maybe I can do it.*

I voice this to Bec. She encourages me to call Nat, the savvy woman responsible for the industry's transformation to a freelance network. At the end of her three-hour shift, Bec hands me a tax invoice, and I change her tips to large notes that equal nearly half my weekly pay. Later, I retreat to the large, rusty storeroom and tap out a text:

Hi Nat, my name is Jess. I work at the Beach Tavern. We just had our first freelance skimpy. WOW, I loved her bubbly attitude and hard work! Do you have any openings for work?

Nat calls me at work the next day. I retreat to the same grubby storeroom to answer my phone. My eyes adjust to the pitch-black darkness as a crisp voice articulates she needs an emergency cover for a pub four hours' drive southeast. It is an introduction to Nat's efficient approach of getting shit done through a no-fluff filter. I apologize that my current shift at the tavern won't allow me to make it to the skimpy shift on time. Fifteen minutes later, Nat calls again, informing me there is a city shift available the following week. I agree to take it.

Our two weekend skimpies come from an agency. Friday's girl has a bird's nest in her hair. Every half hour she excuses herself to the bathroom to "touch up her makeup" and returns with pupils more dilated. Saturday's girl sports a leather bikini and elegant gold jewellery that adorn her body curving like an hourglass filling with sensual sand. She informs me she's also joined the freelance network of twenty-five girls who are quickly expanding their contracts with Western Australian pubs. When her three hours are up, she drapes a Gucci bag over her toned shoulders glowing like golden hour in the Louvre. Then she wishes me well for my first shift. Watching her hips sway as she saunters out the door in springy strides, I wonder what the hell I've gotten myself into.

Ruby and I get smashed at night, then I blunder a double shift. In my final hour, Ruby calls and begs me to come dancing at a nearby bar. I yawn into the phone and tell her I'll think about it. Usually, I'd veg after a day working without a break, but a sudden impulse to freshen up and slink into my favourite black dress surges through my veins.

At the bar, Ruby winks at men then guzzles the drinks they buy. Through a sober lens, I observe the bouncing dance floor with a closed-mouth yawn then decide on some fresh air. It's the same old scene. Liquid confidence fuels transient connections. I crave something new. As I wind through the giddy labyrinth of bopping people, a tall man with curly blond hair electrifies me with aquamarine eyes. I ponder saying hello but decide against it. A man that good-looking probably has a girlfriend, and I've moved beyond the incessant need to see my worth in the desire of men.

Outside, the chemical-laden air tastes stale. There's nothing fresh about city nightlife. As I ponder what I'm going to wear at my first skimpy shift in four days, a pink push-up bra flashes to mind. Then the ocean-eyed man sits beside me. I am struck by a bolt of lightning.

"Hello," he coos.

"Hi," I breathe.

His lips pucker slightly. "Do you smoke?"

"No, I just came out here for some fresh air."

His crow's-feet crinkle as he beams. "Oh...me too."

Suddenly, my tanned legs feel silky against my white dress shirt. His presence tranquilizes the incessant background murmur as he introduces himself as Jacob. He is visiting from Queensland to film a kitesurfing movie. I consider getting his number, but he's flying home in a few days and my week is filling fast.

Back on the sweaty, shoulder-knocking dance floor I explain to Ruby where I've been as guys watch us dance. If they aren't ogling, their feet point towards us indicating the direction they wish to walk, and a silent laugh reverberates inside me because I no longer care. I'm no longer chained to the value others perceive in me. I'm learning my own worth.

At 10:00 p.m. the music stops, and I skip towards the door.

"Jess, wait up," Ruby calls, running towards me in a tight dress that enhances her sculpted-from-ivory legs. "I just told that guy to get your number."

"What guy?"

"Oh, *come on*, Jess. You know who I mean."

With a coy smile I glance behind my shoulder. There he is. Jacob.

I tap my number into his phone, then feel his eyes follow me as I float down the stairs to the carpark.

Two days later, I meet him in a rented apartment near my work. His film mates snore as ocean tides crash into our whispers from the couch where we share our first kiss. He admits that though he'd only drank a few beers at the bar, he couldn't remember what I looked like. Apparently, he saw me as an illuminating ball of energy that magnetised him in.

After an hour of chatting, Jacob suggests we watch a movie. Maybe he doesn't have a hidden agenda, but my internal dictionary translates the suggestion to "let's have sex", so I politely decline and kiss him good night.

The next day, he visits me at the tavern before boarding a flight back home. I relish the elated beam that escapes him. It warms the dark room as I prance over and sneak a small kiss.

In the weeks that follow, he texts and calls most nights. There's an easy congruence between us with comfortable communication, similar humour, and curious zest for life. Despite living on the opposite side of the country, he lights up the mundanity of the daily grind. Something about him excites me.

To be fated means we are meant to meet.

To be destined means our meeting morphs into more.

Hours tick into minutes as I cake my face with makeup, clip hair extensions into my soft blonde waves, and inspect my nude reflection. Spray tan gives me a bronzed glow. I feel meaty inside my dainty limbs. By the time I feel moderately okay to prance around in my underwear, peak hour traffic stifles the city to a sluggish pace of fuming congestion. I attempt, and fail, to speed through stop-start lanes.

Ten minutes after my shift starts, I bounce towards a double, glass-panelled wooden door beside a fragmented beer sign. A crinkly man in a fluorescent-orange work shirt stubs out his cigarette then flounces into the pub to announce my arrival.

"SKIMPY'S HERE!"

All eyes are on me as I conceal my anxiety with a smile. A few locals sporting ripped flannelette shirts give toothless smiles. The girl behind the bar directs me to a tiny bathroom to undress. I emerge, strutting in a sheer-black lace babydoll. As eyes crawl over every inch of my bare skin, I feel constricted beneath the act of holding it all together.

The regular barmaid's kindness gives me the safety necessary to be vivacious and self-expressed, but every glance at the clock seems to slow time. A fat man in the corner chides that my outfit isn't revealing enough to be a skimpy. After brushing off the first few comments, I fume, "It's my first shift, give me a break!"

A bunch of Irish celebrating Saint Patrick's Day overhear my remark as they romp in. They are lively yet mellow and keep me busy with never-ending pints. Later in the game, I realise that appearance is secondary to social skills and an aptitude for business. When I become comfortable in my skin and figure out which pubs resonate with the friendly and hardworking skimpy that I want to be, my focus switches to witty banter and invigorating conversation. From that first shift—with the warm Irishmen tipping me with every drink—I begin financially backing myself in preparation to leave Perth in search of new adventures.

My skimpy work remains a secret I conceal with lipstick and lies. Eventually my confidence and charm grow as I carry a few funny stories up my sleeve and realise that everyone's favourite word is "you"— "You look well! How are you? What do you do for fun? Would you rather fight one horse-sized duck or one hundred duck-sized horses?" An outgoing personality, eye-catching costumes, and a fit body is essential, but so is growing a thick skin, reading peoples' energy, and proving oneself reliable.

There's an art to being simultaneously entertaining and empowered in the adult industry. You're walking a tightrope. Alcohol feeds ego. Sometimes men get out of line. Very quickly, I learn to hold strong boundaries and maintain high standards. It becomes easy to brush off brutish remarks, say no to stupid requests, and grasp that the pubs—and law—back me 100 percent. If respect falters, Nat cancels the contract.

Ruby hides her disapproval of the work behind inquisitive eyes. She even convinces me to let her drive to my second shift, three hours southeast from Perth. En route to the small forest town, she admits she's still high from a bender. Crystal meth is something some friends dabble in while I avoid. With goose bumps dotting my bare skin, I struggle to entertain rugged patrons with Ruby slouching in the corner as she withers into her comedown.

As we drive home, a thick fog looms between towering trees. The mist envelops us. It suffocates Ruby's playful nature. The three-hour drive extends into four as we inch forward in prickly silence. You could cut the space between us with a knife. She refuses to let me drive despite her exhaustion, snapping something about insurance. I am confused and concerned by her mental state, but I don't know how to navigate a conversation with savage dogs guarding her barbed walls.

When we finally emerge from the damp veil and city lights irradiate the horizon, I do not see their glistening light. The fog percolates inside me with murky disarray.

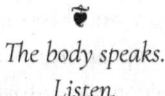

The body speaks.
Listen.

Vehicles crawl past Mama's shiny blue Monaro as she grips the steering wheel and speeds me to the emergency department. I wail in agony. My lower abdominal twists and stabs as my vagina bleeds gory cascades. The maxi pad I applied an hour ago already overflows in a relentless gush of vital life force escaping me. I observe the road like it is the Battle of Hastings.

At the hospital, doctors scurry in concern, unable to find a diagnosis. Every hour my pad is changed, until I'm given an adult nappy to contain the crimson surge. It is three days before my twentieth birthday. I wonder if I'll make it there before bleeding to death.

"Could you be pregnant?" the doctor asks.

Mama scrutinises me with judgemental eyes.

I groan with an anguish that is too painful for quivers. "No."

"Could you be having a miscarriage?"

"No."

The doctor looks at his clipboard. "Could it be appendicitis?"

"She doesn't have an appendix," Mama snaps.

The man scratches his head.

A morphine injection leaves a deep-blue bruise on my thigh but dissociates me from the pain with a euphoric rush whisking me into a fluffy bed of clouds. Despite the adult nappy, vaginal bleeding stains my white bedsheets in furious red splotches as CT scans, X-rays, and ultrasounds come back inconclusive to the pain that defeats me.

The day before my birthday I am transferred to another hospital in hopes they have an answer. En route, the young—and ridiculously good-looking—paramedic chats and performs routine checks. My pulse gallops in his presence. I fail to breathe into a slower pace.

He looks up from the monitor and gives a gentle smile.

"Your heart is beating really fast, but everything else appears to be okay."

I nod.

Fuck. He knows.

The moment shines fleeting rays into a distressing week. It is my sixth hospitalization in five years. The second to fall on my birthday. Once again, my suppressed emotional pain forces me to face it by defeating me with physical ailments I cannot ignore.

After a week of boiling bubbles bursting in my loins, I get an answer: a ruptured ovarian cyst. With retrospect, it's no coincidence that my sexual organs explode with anguished shrieks the same month I start skimpy bartending. The work can be empowering to boundary-speaking while shining light in dark places, but I don't know this yet. I'm playing with sexual energy from a disempowered space. But I don't want to look deeper and take responsibility for my actions. I do what most humans do—I project my shit outwards and blame something external for my pain.

On day six of beeping monitors and incessant needle pricks, I awake drowsy from a nap. A colourful bouquet blooms across the room. After contemplating it a while, I hobble over and pick up the small letter attached. *Love, Byron Bay.* I smile. Jacob isn't from Byron Bay. He lives three hours north in the Sunshine Coast, but often raves about the bustling bohemian town, convinced I'll love it and that I must go.

Until then, my affections for him are half-assed. I've chatted and flirted but don't expect anything more. After all, we live on opposite ends of Australia—4,400 kilometres away. The sweet floral fragrance changes this for me. It actualizes the notion of us reconnecting, and upon discharge, I book flights to see him the following month.

One small problem lingers: one of my managers from the tavern. A casual hook-up when I'm blackout drunk tangles me in his arms with the previous night's liquor lingering on my breath. It attaches me to his unspoken expectation that we've become exclusive overnight. His puppy-dog affection is generous and caring, but his possessiveness grows into a claustrophobic hold. I later discover I was given the job based on his attraction to my Facebook profile. It appalls me. When he visits me in hospital, he gifts an expensive gold bracelet that even he notes is a little excessive. I never wear it. When a gift is given with condition, it doesn't feel right to receive.

I'm caught between a rock and a hard place. He'd ensured my position at the tavern. Power differentials mean he could end it too. I don't know how to speak the truth, even if it hurts him. Even if it sets him free. And so, he continues bombarding me with messages when I fly across the country to be with another man.

Autumn rain patters across the windshield as Jacob drives us south to Byron Bay. It is thrilling and surreal to commit a week to a man I barely know, but I justify my decision with the money I've saved bartending and my safety net of nearby Contiki friends if shit goes sour. I glance at his joy crinkles as music swims through the speakers and merges with the rain.

"I like this song," we voice in unison.

Jacob gives a provocative sidelong glance. A tranquil silence follows.

Then I note the windscreen wipers moving in unison with the beat.

"That's a good omen," he states.

Jacob's sunny demeanour and down-to-earth vibe render an effortless connection. His adventurous spirit matches my innate impulse to meander off the beaten track and do secret things on secret beaches with no one around for miles. We hike rocky headlands, frolic in subtropical rainforests, and camp in the wilderness beneath the Milky Way. In the shadow of the moon's smile, we sing songs around crackling fires, and I befriend his ex-girlfriend, who is now dating one of Jacob's friends.

I know Jacob is older than I first presumed, but I don't want to directly ask his age. Towards the end of our week together, I slur the question to his ex. A chirpy crowd buzzes around us at the brewery.

"Are you sure you want to know?" the short brunette queries.
I feel Jacob's eyes on me as he sips a rum and dry.
"Yes."
She purses her lips. "He's thirty-six."
Oof! Sixteen years older than me...a decade older than I assumed.

Searching for emotions in my features, she remarks, "I hope this doesn't change things for you. You're good for him. I like you two together."

I smile at my beautiful new friend shining light on the truth that dawned my oblivion. Can a number change the way it feels to fall asleep with our limbs intertwined? Will it impair the gentle strums of his guitar as he serenades me beneath the moonlight?

"Age is just a number," I clarify.
I won't let it blemish our blossoming connection.

Know when to hold it, when to fold it, and when to mould it.

When I arrive in Perth, my "relationship" with my manager abruptly ends. To me, there is nothing to close because nothing mutually, officially, or exclusively started. He sees things differently though, and his relentless attachment shatters his heart into thousands of piercing pieces. For weeks he hurls the shards my way before I leave the tavern and become a full-time skimpy. That same month, Mama moves to Melbourne to pursue a yearlong air traffic controller course. This results in Papa spending his month off in Melbourne, and I sign a contract to rent their big blue house, complete with a $2000 bond.

With the house to myself, Ruby and I hang out most days. I smoke weed. She smokes crack. Inside us both, darkness grows as each murky inhale rips out tomorrow's page. At the start of winter, a week in Bali forces us both to be without our smoky poisons. Bored of cheap liquor, we order magic mushroom shakes from a local lady behind a blue picket gate. As the fungi kicks in, a bizarre telepathy connects us. In a night club adorned with crushed velvet walls, I purposely distance myself from a lone male dancer. His sexual energy is leaky. It repels Ruby too. Back in our hotel, waterfalls cascade from the walls, and we question whether situations gravitate towards us based on our vibe. Then she asks the question that breaks my brain: are we in the world or is the world within us?

The psilocybin tapers with daybreak. In our overtired, sticky state we fight over something finicky. We throw words with a fierce burn, and Ruby leaves Indonesia early, but not before placing a sorry letter by my bag.

Back in Australia, we hug and make up, but the undertones change. Neither of us are in a healthy state. Meth entices her into an inky pit that warps her intrinsic sunshine. Fun and games funnel into addiction and lies. Winter darkens. Tension grows. I delve deeper into skimpy work, burying the truth under a stinky pile of bullshit. The more I entomb it, the thicker it solidifies into a viscous tangle.

In my back, Ruby throws knives where she once placed feathers. She coaxes another friend to message Mama an exaggerated story that I'm a stripper and lying to Jacob about my age. Jacob knows how young I am. My friends' disapproval that he makes me happy and I finally trust someone enough to call him boyfriend is painful.

When my world pulverizes, he calms me with wise words: "You gain and lose friends through life. Sometimes there's too much water under the bridge to keep going back and forth. Time and space are good for turbulent relationships. Sometimes they heal. Sometimes they don't."

Mama doesn't confront me, but I'm two steps ahead of Ruby's game. When she stomps me out, I know she isn't going silently. Karma plays its part in what happens to us, but it's our reaction that kindles a new destiny. While she scatters rumours about me with pervasive venom, I hold on to her secrets with the confidentiality with which they were told. To my grave I will carry her closeted skeletons.

Midwinter, I book flights to visit Mama in Melbourne and mend the collateral damage. A hoarse cough hacks and wheezes in my throat. Storm clouds thunder. I tell Mama there is untrue gossip about me being spread. She admits a catfish profile messaged her saying nasty things, but she doesn't believe what is being said.

I return to Perth fostering a bizarre blend of invincibility and invisibility. I've preserved my reputation, but I feel sticky and icky from purposely withholding information from people I love. I don't know how to be truthful about work that is stigmatised rather than seen from a 360-degree view. My fear of disapproval and not being accepted for me burrows me behind masks and masquerades, but it's different from before. I've tasted the notion of letting my façade fall. I'm aware that there is another path.

Does the sun sink into the sea or levitate into a new morning?
In love, should we fall or grow?
Is the world falling apart or coming together?
The perspective we make impacts the direction we take.
What do you foresee?

Around this time, Laula returns to Perth after a wild backpacking-around-Australia adventure. She's chopped off her bleached-blonde hair and talks about "breaking up" with Landmark Forum—one of the world's largest personal development organisations—convinced that it's a cult. As we hang more, I notice something different about her. Something I can't quite articulate at the time. With retrospect, I recognise it's energetic. She's comfortable in her skin and growing an interest in holistic modalities, artistic pursuits, and spirituality. When one door closes, another always opens. It's our choice to yearn wistfully for the familiarity of what's been, or courageously leap into the next phase of evolution.

I continue working in "haunted" rural pubs with creaky floorboards and buckets catching leaks from sagging ceilings. It's like going back in time. I relish the taste of fresh country air amid dense jarrah forests. It dissolves the ache of my friends betraying me. Country patrons are kinder, funnier, and more down-to-earth than city folk. Sometimes it takes a little effort and time to open them, but once you do you've got friends for life. It's cathartic to leave the bustle each week and discover my resilience, calm, and capacity to connect with myriad humans in small outback towns. Over time, the job brings me multilayered healing.

Jacob and I take turns travelling across the country to see each other in ten-day stints. The same month we decide our relationship is exclusive, I am offered a job at a Canadian ski lodge with twenty-four hours to give my answer. Peak hour traffic keeps me on my toes as I phone Jacob to break the news. He listens with quiet resolve. After a reflective pause, he admits, "If I had things all my way, I'd have you over here with me." Suddenly the possibility of leaving Perth seduces me with a fresh slate.

A few weekends later, I am waitressing at a rustic wooden tavern in the hills of Perth. Early in my shift, a motorcyclist gang saunter in sporting jackets with their club patches. The feisty lady who owns the pub instructs they remove them as directed by law. Tension boils when they refuse, but no one does anything about it.

The blokes just want a cheeky beer. They are respectful, with the exception of a young new member who threatens to rape me in the carpark after my shift. Instinctively I know he's all talk. He's trying to impress the tough guys. But he's doing it all wrong. The stereotype of bikies being burly, tattooed assholes is too generic. People are more complex.

Moments later, an older member with kind eyes approaches me.

"Don't listen to that idiot." He points over his shoulder and rolls his eyes. "He's just trying to prove himself."

"Oh," I mouth. "Is that so?"

"Yeah...I'm second in charge around here. Miss, so long as I'm around, I guarantee you're safe."

I thank the man then continue waitressing tables with a composure I've learned to wear well. What surprises me isn't my lack of fear or the older man's goodwill. It's the flickering thought that I catch when the young dude first spits his words. I think I deserve to be raped because it's happened before. I've *internalised* something that should never be a genuine belief. That's when I realise the fallacy. I don't deserve it. No one does. It sparks a fiery conviction for anyone thinking otherwise. An unrelenting fire ignites.

The encounter is the final straw that prompts me to accept Jacob's invitation of leaving it all behind for tropical Queensland. In my final month in Perth, Laula ventures to a rural bar shift with me out of curiosity to the work. We bop along to '70s rock as trucks zoom towards the setting sun. An hour into our drive, she exclaims, "I love you unconditionally, Jess. No matter the decisions you make or the path you take, I love you."

The sincerity of her words strike me, especially in juxtaposition of Ruby's actions. For years to come, Laula's words echo in my heart and build momentum. She has always been a true friend.

Readying myself for Queensland, I commemorate my fresh start by dying my hair back to its natural brunette tinge. It's a step towards me embodying the real me. It's challenging to go, with Charlie still navigating her intense, internal ocean. Sometimes she sinks. Sometimes she swims. Slowly she grows stronger. Days trickle into hours as I wheel two chunky suitcases into the departure terminal on a warm January afternoon. With the reins of destiny in my hands, I wonder what I'll write on the next blank pages.

Chapter IV
EXPANSION

We write our lives with ink.

There is no eraser.

But we always have a choice
of where we tread
and how the pages thread together.

January 2012

Dawn trickles upon Brisbane's golden cityscape as the aeroplane's quiet hum propels me forward. Shivers ripple up my spine then drip down my back like liquid lightning. As peak hour traffic pulsates in a rhythmic panorama, clouds suspend me in a flocculent pastel world. I am in no-man's-land. Airborne between where I've been and where I am going.

Outside the terminal, I tap my feet and watch shadows shrink with the rising sun. When Jacob arrives an hour later, I embrace him and run my fingers through his thick curls.

Passing exotic pine plantations and silhouetted summits, we meander north to the Sunshine Coast. Jacob points out a fire lookout tower perched above the rainforest canopy and brags he had sex there. His words coil in my stomach. The smell of eucalyptus intensifies. As we pull into the two-storey beachside home he shares with a pharmacist and an engineer, I ponder if moving across the country is the right decision.

Rather than talk to Jacob about how I feel, I internalise my emotions. As he finalises graphic edits for a kitesurfing magazine, I stroll along the beach with our housemate's bounding Labrador and inhale the salty Pacific breeze. Seaweed drifts in the sparkling surf, not yet latching on to solid ground, yet too close to shore to be tugged back into its oceanic past.

A week later, Jacob and I drive back to Brisbane to fly to the Philippines. Two friends are marrying on picturesque Boracay island. The celebration stretches into a two-week adventure. Warm turquoise seas swish between outrigger sailboats, coconuts plonk from palm trees, and fire twirlers illuminate idyllic shores with choreographed shows. As honeymooners stroll along the beach beneath kaleidoscopic fireworks, I let my worries dissipate into Jacob's strong arms.

On the day of the wedding, rain strums upon our bamboo balcony with a purifying charm. Creating a stunning mosaic of ripples in the water, the precipitation percussion continues in a private cove.

When the bride and groom vow their love, rain clouds surrender to golden rays like a movie scene. As locals drum funky beats, a stunning brunette bridesmaid introduces herself as Blair. As small talk prevails, she asks my age. I glance at the massive sandcastle attesting the newlyweds love.

"I'm twenty," I murmur as water creeps towards the intricate structure.

"Oh. You're very mature for your age," she attests. "How old is Jacob?"

I swallow. "Thirty-six."

As the words escape me, a wave splashes the castle and swallows a turret of sand. I hold my breath for the bizarre look I've learned to shake off when people discover our large gap in age.

Blair peers at me with green eyes alight with a subtle flame of kindness. She doesn't even raise an eyebrow. Instead, she notes it must be difficult to move across the country and merge with your lover's world.

"I guess so..." I muse as another sand tower succumbs to the sea. "I guess I needed the change."

After a little more chitchat she suggests we hang out in Australia. I agree. Suddenly, it doesn't seem so bad that every grain of sand surrenders from the castle to mysterious currents that find a new home.

*Home is an internal space,
not an external place.*

"Jess! Jess, where are you?"

Jacob's voice floats into the large, walk-in closet from downstairs. I nuzzle my tear-stained cheeks into my arms and stifle a quiet sob.

"Jessica..." he sings again. I love when he calls me Jessica.

I gaze at my clothes squished on rails opposite his. Footsteps ascend the stairs. The bedroom door creaks.

"Jess?"

"I'm here," I croak.

The closet's sliding door rattles.

"*Thereeee* you are," he coos, giggling at where I've chosen to crumble.

I burrow my face deeper into my arms.

"Hey...what's wrong?" He drops to his knees and places a reassuring hand on my back.

Imploding on myself, I blubber for him to go away.

He attests he's not going to leave me in a bawling pile.

"We've got to talk about things," he appeals.

I peep up at him. *The last man I let into my heart ripped it to tiny pieces. Can I trust you?*

"Jess..." Jacob exhales and lets out a faint smile. "I can't help you if I don't know what's going on..."

This is true. "I...I miss my friends. I feel stuck here. I *hate* my job."

Wrapping me in his arms, he asks, "What's so bad about your job?"

"Every day people pass me with arms burdened by bags. I'm surrounded by people, but...I've never felt so...*alone.*"

Cheesy music, screaming children, and fried food wafting through impatient queues—there is nothing to like about shopping centres. Turns out the sales role I took for a holiday club is actually convincing strangers they've won a prize to coax them to attend a time-share presentation.

Jacob gives me a loving squeeze and suggests I find another job.

"In the meantime, why don't we go for a walk on the beach?"

I peer into his unblinking, guileless eyes.

"It'll make you feel better," he persuades.

"Okay..."

Across the road, we chase each other through the sand. Jacob gives me a cheeky look. Then he tears off his clothes and dives beneath the waves. I twinkle a smile, slide my dress over my shoulders, and splash in after him. The water is warm and silky on my skin. It's replenishing as I find his face amongst the waves and kiss him with tender passion.

🍂

Bathing in dim yellow light, I swim in sound. Jacob clutches his guitar like it's the Holy Grail and strums a funky melody. It bounces off music posters clinging to the walls as Blair seduces the dance floor with sultry sways. A fumbling dancer sprays me with beer. Jacob winks at me and beams. As the dreadlocked front man announces their last song, I slide Blair and a tipsy blonde two of my old work bras. Lacy black lingerie rains upon the seven-member band. They parade it like rock 'n' roll legends at Woodstock in 1969.

Later, Jacob motions for me to join him behind the DJ decks. I shake my head, shy to the attention. Whispering that a nearby cougar eyes him like Christmas pudding, he pulls me close and places headphones on my ears. I cherish that he makes me feel like a queen in his arms. His music touches me in ways human hands never could.

Sometimes he slinks into our bedroom when I'm writing poetry and plays his guitar. These are my favourite moments, us exploring creativity side by side. His instrumental cascades somehow awaken my dormant emotions in a soothing hypnosis that threads feelings into words. It is the release I need. Seducing my mind and entrancing my body, his songs loop into my heart with enchanting strums, slaps, and slides.

♥

> Love isn't waking up to a pot of gold beneath the rainbow,
> it's making your way there through the storm.

As the aeroplane zooms across Australia, the musty-smelling Italian man with no regard for long-haul flight etiquette stares at my screen.

"Excuse me," he interrupts. "I can't help but be curious to what you're writing with such sharp focus."

"It's a poem about love," I respond, piercing his saggy brown eyes with an unrelenting state.

"About love...hmm, what is love?" he muses.

"That's the question I'm dissecting."

He cocks his head to one side. "I'd love to read it once you're done."

"Sure...I'll email it to you when we land."

I continue writing, present to his lingering gaze. When the pilot announces our sunny descent, the man asks what awaits me in Perth. I explain I'm celebrating my twenty-first birthday with twenty-one close friends. Small talk delves into the soul's journey. Suddenly I see depth beneath his hungry eyes.

As we cruise along the smooth tarmac, he concludes, "You're an old soul. You're not like most twenty-year-olds."

♥

The small Maltese terrier prances around me on her hind paws. She resembles Jacob with shaggy light curls, relentless vitality, and a happy-go-lucky nature.

"Happy," I sing. "This way!"

She follows me to the laundry, still performing 360-degree spins.

"Sit," I direct.

Her tongue dangles from her jaw. *Pant. Pant. Pant.*

"Sit," I repeat in a firmer tone.

She does one more spin then obeys.

"Good girl," I praise, and place her dinner before her.

We adopt the hyperactive bundle of fur while Jacob's parents relocate back to New Zealand. She becomes my closest friend. Every morning, we have a ritual. She runs along the beach with me in joyful bounds. I gaze at the Pacific horizon and wonder what life is like in distant lands.

※

I scan the large amber bottle of whiskey while glancing at the time.

"That's $12.57."

The man raises an eyebrow.

"Oh, sorry." I chuckle. "That's the time. The whiskey is $79.95."

I place the bottle in a brown paper bag and tap his card. Then I continue daydreaming about stunning South American cities that fill the travel brochures I flick through on my breaks.

That night, I chat to Jacob about the possibility of travelling together. He smiles and nods. Eventually, he sighs.

"I'd love to travel with you, babe. I really would...but I can't. I'm in too much debt."

I digest his words. He's right. I waited six months for him to pay me back for his flight to the Philippines, but I can't keep postponing my calling to travel. It's getting stronger each day.

※

Healing is a soft process.

"Jess, wake up! There's baby turtles hatching and running for the ocean."

Afternoon sun drizzles from the window to Jacob's DJ decks scattered on a desk. I press my face into the pillow and stay in the stillness of my snuggly sanctuary.

Jacob returns five minutes later. "C'mon, Jess, you don't want to miss this! A fox dug up their nest last night...they've *got* to do this journey today."

"Okaaaayyy... I'm coming."

I leap out of bed and join our local community gathered around dozens of tiny loggerhead turtles. The wrinkled creatures peck at tennis-ball-sized eggs, then drag themselves to the surface of the sand and flounder towards the ocean. Kids build sand walls for the turtles' runway and urge the creatures on. I yearn to help the squirming hatchlings, but the struggle brings resilience. It strengthens their flippers which increases their chance of surviving the vast, open ocean where they will swim in a frenzy for days.

My insatiable curiosity for the Pacific horizon has evolved to me booking four back-to-back tours through South America and Antarctica commencing in a few weeks. Like a baby turtle, I'm cracking out of my shell so the wings of destiny can take me in her arms.

⁂

Jacob tugs my small blue suitcase into the airport, lips set in a grim line. It's the same bag I flung clothes in a few weeks ago when he returned from lunch with an old flame's lipstick on his collar. I questioned if he really sleeps on his friend's couch after his weekly DJ gig at a Brisbane strip club. I tell him I want to break up. His chest collapses in on itself. I've posed this three times in two months. On the surface, he soothes my insecurities as I find solace back in his arms. In the undercurrents, a niggly feeling lingers.

En route to the airport we chat about the boundaries and expectations of the open relationship I propose we enter. So long as we stay in honest communication, we are free to do as we wish for the six months I'm away.

Wondering where life will take us, I scan the departure screen as Jacob wraps his arms around me and kisses my forehead. A passer-by does a double take, scrutinizing Jacob's crinkled crow's-feet and my youthful complexion. I narrow my eyes on the man then give Jacob a slow, sultry smile.

Our final days brim with affection and appreciation, taunting me with the possibility that our connection will withstand the vast Pacific.

"I love you lots," he whispers. The words linger in my hair.

"I love you too," I reassure.

Final boarding for QF652 to Sydney.

His ocean eyes are bloodshot from surfing, or staying up late working on his business, or maybe it's that I'm leaving. Drifting down the airbridge, I glance over my shoulder and blow kisses until he's out of sight. His smile loiters in my daydreams as planes take off and touch down in Sydney, Auckland, Santiago, Guayaquil, and Quito. Farther I fly, as a strange sensation glides through me. My invisible wings extend. I am ready to reach new heights.

With sleepy eyes I blink in the sun. Two Australian accents float through my open window from the courtyard below. A guy and girl acquaint as they talk of the six-week Intrepid Travel tour trailing through Ecuador, Peru, and Bolivia. In the hotel's cosy common room, I meet fourteen other travellers—two young couples, two old couples, five solo ladies, an Aussie dude—and our bright-eyed Ecuadorian guide who leads us through the world's highest capital backdropped by Andean peaks.

With shaking legs, I feel invincible as we pant up steep cobbled streets and marvel at charming colonial plazas speckled with pigeon poop and pop-up juice stands. Jet lag spellbinds me in a disoriented blur. Adventure pulsates through my veins.

At night, we devour rice and beans at a no-frills eatery brimming with locals. Food is always better where a city's residents convene. Foreign sounds, smells, textures, and tastes stimulate my senses as exotic dialects mystify the oxygen-scarce air. Somehow it connects who I am to who I was and who I will become.

Life is an adventure we take.
Fear is an inhibitor we break.
Doubt is an illusion we shake.
Love is a habit we make.

Cool air blasts through the minivan as we meander through vegetated highlands overlooked by snowy mountains. An animated Kiwi chick, Miranda, has the van chuckling at her wild tales of peeing in thorny Serengeti bushes and being squirted by elephants in India. She later informs us that the yellow equator line we walked over is painted in the wrong location. It's a sham.

In the quaint city of Otavalo, a massive market stretching back to pre-Incan times buzzes with stalls vending alpaca scarfs, colourful textiles, and exquisite wood carvings. Andean folk musicians serenade bustling crowds with wooden flutes and panpipes made from aquatic reeds. I connect with locals dressed in long wool skirts, embroidered white blouses, felt hats, and blue ponchos. There is something wise and kind in their rich brown eyes.

I muse on Ecuadorian culture as we venture back to Quito. It is a unique intertwining of indigenous practises with colonial ways. I like it. An hour into our two-hour drive, we pull over to photograph snow-capped mountains peaking into fluffy clouds. As we absorb the scenery through digital screens, a hunched old lady crawls into my peripheral on her hands and knees. Cameras continue clicking. A crisp alpine breeze ruffles my hair. I glance at the group, oblivious to the woman inching towards us one hundred, ninety-nine, ninety-eight metres away. As they pile back into the van, I freeze and catch eyes with Lucas, the lone Aussie male. He mirrors my gobsmacked expression.

We look at the van, then back at the lady. A cascade of emotions crash. I feel sad. Then guilty. Then disheartened. I yearn to help her, but I don't know what to do. How can I reverse the ongoing consequences of colonisation? Giving her my lunch won't save global poverty or bring medical help to the oppressed. My spare coins won't change intergenerational trauma. As the driver calls out for us to keep moving, Lucas and I share a dismayed glance. We plod into the van with downcast eyes. While the others awe at highland scenes whooshing past the windows, I ruminate my actions, or lack thereof. She was helpless, but not hopeless. It shatters me that I did nothing. I'm finally being a traveller rather than a tourist, and with that shift comes the uncensored lens of culture shock that is difficult to absorb without ignorantly closing my eyes. In that moment I realise I can't yearn for global change if I'm not first proactive with *my* actions.

The insight of my own privilege is inevitable in that moment. Like fresh mountainous winds tangling in my hair, I've known that power imbalances exist, but the complexity and impact has been invisible. My mind flashes to friends back home, consuming and hoarding then complaining that they're broke. I grimace. But I don't know if it's their attempts to fill a bottomless void with materialism or my inaction to help the lady suffering from kyphosis that causes my disgust.

I'm still mulling it over when Miranda exclaims, "Look, to the right! There's a horizontal rainbow!"

Hovering above a snow-capped stratovolcano, a beautiful rainbow stretches horizontally between two clouds. Someone explains it's an optical illusion formed from light passing through wispy, high-altitude clouds. I gaze at the majestic phenomenon. My shoulders sink. It's not fair that I am bestowed this rare sight after what I've done.

Counting the rainbow's colours, I think of its symbolic promise, and a rich yearning to make an impact is born. From there on, I carry spare food and give it to those in need. I strive to listen not hear, see instead of look, and integrate rather than just skim the surface.

From Quito we take three hot, cramped buses that coil into the Amazon jungle. We practise our Spanish while playing UNO. At each stop, local vendors squish through the crowd with cobbed corn, chocolate, and fruit. On our final bus, I am sticky with sweat. A local lady clutches a flailing chicken, and an influx of passengers pushes us onto each other's laps. Kayla, a tanned Aussie, stands in the centre aisle breathing into her stomach beneath closed eyes. Locals stare at her. I do too. For a solid twenty minutes she continues her standing meditation until we arrive at our ecolodge overlooking the Rio Napo tributary.

There, we share a wooden bungalow. By candlelight, she discloses her recent divorce from a man hiding a nasty amphetamine addiction. It propels her towards spirituality. She radiates an infectious positivity that challenges me to see the blessings and lessons in every downfall. There is no artificial lighting or WiFi in the dense tropical rainforest. It is refreshing. Every morning, I awake to Kayla meditating in bed. Outside, I watch the river trickle past our balcony as the jungle stirs with the rising sun. There is something compelling about Kayla's daily practise. It inspires me to cultivate my own.

Out in the Amazon, nature in bloom
I think of you, in sun and moon
River flowing, metres from me
Birds chirping in virescent trees
I sit in this bungalow, peaceful and silent
And wonder how the world became violent
Is it because we are selfish with greed?
Or do we look, but choose not to see?

- 10 September 2012

On our last day in the Amazon, a local man leads us on a jungle hike. Monkeys howl. I am elated when a tiny frog jumps onto my open palm. As we squelch along muddy trails that drench our gumboots if we misstep, I fondle foliage and absorb our guide's words. He points out trees with cancer-curing properties and talks of the rich knowledge that medicinal shaman have of natural remedies. The word shaman sends shivers up my spine. It's like a long-forgotten truth is awakening. Then, with downcast eyes, the man sighs. He says that these holistic antidotes are being lost and forgotten as younger generations lose interest in favour of western ways.

Suddenly I am empathetic to Earth's leafy lungs and the disservice we are doing by attacking them like malignant tumours. I don't understand why we aren't doing more to protect the Amazon if there are trees with properties to cure cancer. I voice this to the man.

"That," he concludes, with dewy eyes, "is a very good question."

Kayla talks of the stillness meditation brings as we relax in a steaming thermal bath in Baños. "It's mind over matter," she says, as locals swim laps in the bubbling, mineral-rich water.

An array of adrenaline-fuelled activities tantalizes my taste buds before I decide on abseiling down waterfalls. It is rip-roaring to climb and slide down gushing cascades. Then I am balancing on the wet ledge of a clifftop at the plunging mouth of a fifty-metre waterfall. Lego-sized guides await beside rocky outcrops below. I feel constricted in my full-body wetsuit, wondering how I will descend the rapid torrents. Then the guide informs us. We will jump. Apprehension washes over the group, so I volunteer to go first. Kayla's words echo from the water's roar. *Mind over matter. Mind over matter. Mind over matter.* I plant my feet on the edge of the slick ledge with the precipitous drop behind me. I've mistrusted the world long enough. It's time to lean in. Over the abyss with bone-numbing water pounding upon me, I surrender into trust and jump with a high-pitched squeal.

Sometimes Jacob drifts to mind. We occasionally Skype when I have access to internet cafes, but our connection tapers with patchy WiFi. When asked where I am by our friend's ten-year-old, Jacob says I've run off and joined the circus. In travelling without a laptop or phone, I revere the world offline. Disconnecting from the *world wide web* enables me to connect with the whole wide world where rogue dogs patrol the streets and locals beam with sunshine smiles.

Our guide finishes her spiel on the Spanish Conquest as we dodge kids playing soccer on the steps fronting Cuenca's oldest cathedral. Inside the sky-blue domed structure, candles flicker against antique stained-glass windows imported from France. Hymns bounce off rose-coloured, Italian stone. But it is our guide's words that ring inside my head.

Hearing her talk of Spanish structures sitting on Incan ruins stirs a sadness in my veins. How can something built on bones be deemed a place of worship? How can man justify demeaning fellow humans to slaves, or corpses? It provokes a fire inside me because I connect the story with the English invading Australia. My heart shatters that the rich culture of Indigenous Australians trickles down the drain in mainstream education. I don't understand why more effort is not made to integrate the ancient wisdom of our ancestors.

Outside the cathedral, a wrinkled woman sits with open palms. I kneel and hand her my packed lunch. Her eyes smile. They warm my heart as I hike El Cajas National Park that afternoon. Dotted with hundreds of glittering lakes, the rocky terrain twists through paper tree forests and golden grasslands. As the fresh air purifies my heart, I see that temples are not made from wood and stone. Temples are made from the human heart.

❦

There is a question I pondered on long walks along the Queensland coastline: Is there something awaiting me beyond the Pacific horizon?

My answer arrives in laid-back Máncora, a small town in the north of Peru. It is sun-drenched and quiet. I appreciate the calm. Swaying in a knitted hammock, I undulate between holding on to Jacob and letting him go. I feel close to him here. Turquoise tides whisper a tale of a young girl and her lover frolicking naked in midnight waves. It feels strangely familiar, but like the salty breeze lingering on my tongue, it is invisible. I see it no more.

In Huanchaco, a slow-paced fishing village that is our next port of call, I stand on a long wooden pier as rolling waves drift into Jacob's horizon. It's been a few days since we last talked. I am resistant to chat. Did he really sleep on his friend's couch after those late nights working at the Brisbane strip club? Who is that young blonde he called for lengthy chats?

The next morning, Kayla and I stroll wide avenues of the colonial town. Amidst colourful porches opening behind iron rails, a monkey tied to a leash has us blink and giggle. The tiny creature swings from a balcony, half nibbling a lucuma, half dropping the creamy fruit all over the pavement in deep yellow splatters. It peers down at us. Then it reaches towards my open hand. Connected by paw and palm, we gaze into each other's eyes. I wonder what life is like, forever bound by a string. Then I exhale in relief. I know that constraint all too well. Only now have I cut my own figurative cord.

Midafternoon, we hike to a Catholic church overlooking the bay. The sun elongates our shadows as I express my appreciation for the golden chunks of Kayla's wisdom.

With gleaming topaz eyes, she responds, "If you spot it, you got it."

"Huh?"

"What we see in others is a mirror of ourselves."

I scratch my scalp. "What do you mean?"

"Sometimes it's easy to see the beauty in others and overlook our own value."

"Oh..."

Kayla smiles. "It works the other way too. Sometimes we project our weaknesses onto others because it's hard to see them in ourselves."

The bizarre new perspective has me present to an internal change. Two weeks ago, I didn't consider the noose of a consumer-driven world. Now, I see "developed" countries as hungry ghosts imprisoned by their perpetual thirst for more. We have everything we *want*. But a capitalist world gives us nothing we *need*: connection, meaning, creativity. Reed boats look miniature from the wall where we perch. They become intricate tapestries as I realise the cultural richness of letting nothing own you.

Gold, when beaten, shines.
- **Peruvian proverb**

Peru's dry capital perches on sharp cliffs crumbling into the Pacific Ocean. Clouds loom on the horizon, cats nap in immaculate gardens, and the last supper is depicted with a guinea pig lying paws up on a table in a Catholic cathedral. Lima is arid vibrancy bound by silver fog.

Beneath a seventh century monastery, human bones fill brick-and-mortar catacombs. The skeletal remains of 25,000 bodies are organised by bone type and displayed in decorative circular patterns. Ceiling grates allow glimpses of death from the cathedral above. A ten-metre, bone-filled well triggers tingling goose bumps as I walk subterranean passageways in the massive cemetery labyrinth. The bony blueprints show me our humanness. Beneath race, religion, gender, and class, we are made of the same elemental matter that composed in the heart of shooting stars.

After a short stay in Pisco, we traverse Peru's sizzling desert to Huacachina, a therapeutic oasis shaded by palm trees. Lazing by the pool while the others sandboard, I notice a pale Kayla doubled over in pain as she lumbers to the toilet. I ask if she is okay. She brushes it off while heating like the dunes encircling us. Our new Peruvian guide watches her with eagle eyes as we depart. As she continues withering into convulsive sweats, we veer off course to the emergency department in Ica.

As Kayla is rehydrated and medicated for gastroenteritis, the rest of us sweat outside the hospital in the switched-off minibus. Her blood pressure is critical after bad reactions to the first batch of antibiotics. Two hours pass. Crossed arms become clenched fists and heavy breathing. One guy paces the aisle. The group cohesion crumbles with each finger tap. I don't like it. Using the best remedy I know—laughter—I pull out a dozen woollen finger puppets that I've collected from city markets. Homer Simpson joins Pink Panther and a circus of monkeys in an animated show that has my friends in stitches and soothes the heat. Eventually Kayla is discharged, and we push forward to Nazca.

On a routine toilet break at a sewage-reeking service station, I notice another Intrepid tour travelling alongside us in a white van. As we prepare to depart, I peer out the window and lock eyes with an attractive stranger walking to the other vehicle.

His dark face beams as he asks in an indistinguishable accent, "How's it going?"

I don't know what to say. So, I lift my favourite finger puppet—Larry the lama—and reply in a high-pitched squeal, "It's going good, thanks!"

The man bursts out laughing as I make the puppet dance. Then our van meanders on in a theatrical exit that has us both wondering what the heck just unfolded.

High on a desert plateau, the Nazca Lines compel me. In a six-seater plane shaking with gusty winds, I awe at vast lines crisscrossing with geometric shapes like a giant has scratched the red pebbly dust to uncover light sand. Hundreds of giant geoglyphs elicit questions of how and why animals the size of the Empire State Building are etched into the thirsty earth. It attunes me to the mysteries in history and inspires me to scrape below the surface to see what I will find.

Just as the Nazca Lines intercept in beautifully rendered ways, we keep crossing paths with the other Intrepid tour. A one-night stay in Arequipa feels like we've teleported to an elegant European city bordered by three volcanos. Its white sillar stone buildings are our gateway to the world's second deepest canyon via potholed roads that bump us up high mountain passes into Chivay. From our modest hotel—where I befriend the chefs with Spanish as rusty as the dim, chilly kitchen—a muddy alley leads to the town square where street dogs lap at tiered fountains. The unkempt realness liberates me.

At the crack of dawn we sip on steaming coca leaf tea to ease the altitude and our trembles, then venture downstream to the Colca Canyon. Out the window, fluffy clouds shadow century-old terraces. I think of the cumulus castles suspending me above Brisbane nine months ago. My past feels so distant. No longer do I float between two worlds. I've entered a new realm entirely.

Condors soar on updrafts as we trek atop the canyon's steep walls. The dark, handsome stranger chats with Miranda and Kalya. I ponder speeding my pace to catch them, but I'm in a reflective mood. Brisk winds dishevel my hair, and the world's largest flying birds glide. The solitude is purifying.

❦

> *The tree of silence hands the fruit of tranquillity.*
> **- Peruvian proverb**

My love for Peru expands with every twist around winding asphalt roads. I relish its lush geographical diversity and genuine locals who integrate ancient ways into daily life. My appreciation deepens as we pull into Cuzco. The well-preserved colonial city nestles at the bottom of striking verdant mountains, enchanting me with locals bottle-feeding lamas, street vendors whipping up mouth-watering cuisines, and stray dogs patrolling the steep streets in packs.

From Cuzco, chiselled peaks and a labyrinth of cobbled streets pave our way into Ollantaytambo, a scenic old-world village home to unspoilt Incan ruins. Outside the stone city, an hourlong traffic jam crams us between grumbling trucks and honking buses, with no alternative route from Cuzco to the jungle. Exhilaration trickles through our white minivan as we crawl through the congestion. Beyond the mountain scape is the famous hike leading to the continent's biggest draw, Machu Picchu.

By booking late I fail to secure a spot on the Classic Inca Trail with a daily starting cap. Lucas is in the same predicament. The mishap turns out to be in our favour. As the others prepare for their four-day hike, we fill our backpacks with snacks for the less-travelled Quarry Trail reaching higher elevations with better nature scapes.

We begin at 4:00 a.m. by strapping our bags to mules. With us is our guide, three porters, an Indian couple, and Adam—an English guy from the other Intrepid group. Our guide has us in stitches as he informs us the correct pronunciation of Machu Picchu is Mah-choo *peek*-choo. This translates to Old Mountain. Mah-choo pee-choo, as most tourists say, translates to ancient penis.

Following a railway that trails along a refined valley floor, I notice Adam's British accent is laced with an Australian twang. He clarifies he is a Perth boy heading home after seven years in London. We stop chatting at our first ascent. The sun is sharp. The air is thin. I ponder turning back. Then we see two children strolling up the abrupt incline on their daily one-hour hike home from school. Their tenacity inspires me to move past my huffing and puffing.

Backdropped by snowy peaks falling into virescent valleys, I swoon at Adam's handsome Italian features as small talk deepens with each pant. It is unfamiliar territory to like someone when I technically still have a boyfriend. I ruminate on Jacob's and my agreement later while watching the sunset from my tent. Frigid air bites my cheeks and creeps through my gloves. My fingers crisp to icicles. Turning my focus to the stunning snow-capped vistas, I am inundated with gratitude as my spirit expands. Upwards, outwards, into the peaking white mountains' glow.

Breath is a conscious way of energizing my body as we scale a 4550-metre mountain pass the next day. Our Miranda-inspired high-intensity interval training pre-hike boosts my stamina, but nothing can prepare me for the altitude. Oxygen whisks the surface of my cells rather than flooding them with life. Chewing coco leaves numbs my tongue and relieves my heaves up the 700-metre incline. Then I find the secret formula: for every one hundred steps, I pause and take ten slow belly breaths. The searing feeling of suffocation gives way to stillness as my high-altitude corset unties and oxygen intake deepens. Each breath is a blessing. It connects me to my ancestors, nature, and future generations. Most importantly, it connects me to my centre.

At the end of the first pass is a remote Quechan village, where children peer from behind a stone wall with playful eyes. We give them cookies and fruit. They give us the warmth of connection. They are the only people we pass in three days. The lack of other travellers renders an authentic flavour as we zigzag over mountains brimming with mystery.

As we share citrus segments in the sunshine atop a grass summit, our guide teaches us that everything is shared in Peruvian culture. This "what's mine is yours" mentality stems from ancient times. One of the porters gushes, "Me encanta la vida! Todo lo que necesito esta aqui."

I love life. Everything I need is right here.

That evening, Lucas and I watch the sun melt into snow-capped mountains above a canopy of clouds. Comfortable silence enriches the view of a silhouetted Incan Sun Gate perched atop the sheer valley filtering fleeting rays through its tall rectangular opening. Eventually we are pulled out of our reverie by salty stir-fry and mulled wine from camp set up beside large granite boulders.

I later wonder if we're safe from falling rocks as I rub my hands together for warmth in my sleeping bag. I crave the body heat from a man. But it is not Jacob I yearn for. It is Adam.

After winding back down to Ollantaytambo—sweaty, smelly, and sleepy—a train packed with middle-aged tourists pulls us into Aguas Calientes. In the tourist town where souvenirs are triple the normal price, we shower and settle into bed. The river meanders around cliff faces lined with lush cloud forests. Hearing only the crashing rapids and sound of my heartbeat, I close my eyes.

Birds *cheep* and *tweet* with the promise of a new day as we board a bus to Machu Picchu. The lost city of the Incas sprawls across the green saddle of two mountains. It is the most beautiful man-made wonder I've ever seen. Hundreds of layered grass terraces slope to a misty valley where the Urubamba River snakes. We are at the juncture of the Andes' eastern slopes and the Amazon's tropical rainforest.

Early in the day, something compels me to slip off my shoes and explore the mesmerising masonry masterpiece barefoot. Some tourists raise their eyebrows at me. Others nod and grin. Dodging poo from fluffy sun-bathing lamas, I run my fingers over polished dry-stone. The walls are cool. They fit together with advanced precision.

Engineered to avoid landslides, erosion, and flooding with absorbing topsoil and an advanced irrigation system, Machu Picchu is filled with massive rocks enabling astronomical observations and wise agricultural decisions. I ponder the shock of the explorers who discovered the crumbling city wrapped in centuries of vegetation before the world declared it one of the new Seven Wonders. Wonderment silences me.

※

Back in Cuzco, reintegration comes with honking streets and a plan to meet the other group for celebratory drinks. Miranda informs me the mysterious spectator of my finger puppet show is Jabari, an Egyptian living in Canada. They walked the Classic Inca Trail together. He intrigues her, as Adam does me.

Sleepiness trounces me as we wait for them at a booming nightclub. None of us have phones with WiFi to make contact. I stifle a few yawns then stroll back to our hotel to sleep. In the morning, Miranda informs me they arrived just minutes after I left. A strange relief floods my body. Though Jacob and I agree our relationship is open, it's difficult to do when we still have ties connecting us.

An overnight bus brings us to Puno, a rugged town on the shores of Lake Titicaca. As we drift across the world's highest navigable lake, thoughts somersault through my mind. I know I have to talk with Jacob. It's time to rip off the label keeping me shackled. But I don't know how to say it. Alone on the ferry roof, I plug into my iPod and let my feelings drip to the lake floor. I'm in the womb of South America, being held as we sail. On the deck below, a Canadian man chatters with his wife. He says the lake's water residence time is 1343 years. That means the water molecules cleansing the Incans are still present today. I wonder what dilemmas they released into the serene liquefied opal that stretches through the Andes.

Like the twenty-seven rivers flowing into Lake Titicaca, a continuous stream of new information enters my awareness, with only one small river draining water out. I funnel my experiences onto journal pages and flow with ancient currents to a small island where we stay with local Quechan families and help with daily farm duties. Amantani Island has no machinery. All agriculture is done by hand. Grinding quinoa with a ten-kilo rock beneath the biting afternoon sun has me present to the privilege of having convenience and choice of food. Later, we peel the skin off beans. The crust clogs in my nail beds and bleeds for days. I've never deeply pondered how supermarket food reaches its packaged form. I've never had to.

Our local host is an angular man in his forties. He has two children and sad eyes. I try but fail at making him smile as we lead cattle through small fields separated not with fences but by tiny stones. At a community volleyball game that evening he twinkles his first beam. Another family tells me his wife recently died from an illness that was late to receive medical attention. I suddenly understand his despair. As daylight dwindles, we layer up to combat the freezing night. Lightning strikes the sky as we walk to the candlelit hall for dinner.

Pitter-patter. Splish-splash.

Crack. Clash. Boom.

I awake to a donkey braying outside our window. After thanking our family for their hospitality, we board a boat back to Puno. Something weighs on my heart for the entire ride. I still feel the sorrow in his deep-brown eyes.

Back in the hilly port city, we commemorate our final night in Peru with the other tour. At a local club I get red wine tipsy and embrace my inner goof by dancing like Mr Bean and placing my puppets on Adam's fingers to perform a play.

Later, Jabari walks Miranda and me to our hotel on an abandoned cobbled road. He quizzes my agreement with Jacob and asks why he isn't with me.

"Do you love him?"

His mixed accent verbalises what I've been asking myself for weeks.

I pause. "Yes, I do. But I'm not in love with him."

Alcohol is an elixir for truth, tugging words from my mouth before I realise it's me who said them.

"Is he good to you?"

I ruminate for a moment. "Yes."

Jabari eyes me like a detective examining a crime scene.

Outside our hotel I slur, "Why didn't Adam come?"

Jabari flashes a compassionate smile. "Oh, Jess...come here. Give me a hug."

May the sun set on where my love dwells.
- **Bolivian proverb**

Sailing into Bolivian waters, I muse on Jabari's questions. Why isn't Jacob with me? He's good to me, but is he good *for* me? On the quaint southern shores of Lake Titicaca, water birds welcome us to the dusty colonial town of Copacabana. I sunbake on the hotel roof then excuse myself to bed with an upset stomach, trying to digest the situation.

The next day, I stop eating meat. This is prompted by a stray dog chewing raw sausages in a neglected milk crate at the markets. It later becomes a decision based on human welfare and environmental ethics. Coming from warm and welcoming Peru, I'm initially jarred by Bolivia. It's hard to swallow with poverty intensified and different cultural norms. I try catching locals' eyes and sparking smiles, but they toil away and keep to themselves.

Surrounded by snowy altiplano peaks, make-do buildings cling to steep slopes overlooking affluent apartments in La Paz, Bolivia's gritty de facto capital. I am bewitched by The Witches' Market, where dried lama foetuses, aphrodisiac formulas, alpaca blankets, and potions ensuring love fill tiny stalls that trickle onto precipitous cobbled streets. It is here a bittersweet turn in the winding road has half the group disembark, while the rest of us continue south. I share a room with Wren, a gorgeous Brit of Indian descent. Something coy in her bulging brown eyes compels me to dig beneath simple chitchat. With glee, she confides that she and Lucas shared their first kiss while rooming together at our island homestay.

"What?" I shriek. "That's great!"

"Shhhhh." Her British accent soothes as she presses a finger to her lips.

I link my pinkie finger to hers, joking that I want to be the flower girl when they marry. They do, five years later. It is a traditional Indian wedding in Goa, where we all reunite. The intensity of their budding travel romance shows in their final days together. Their love is palpable, even in the early days of not knowing how they'll make it work living half a world away.

On our third day in La Paz, Adam and Jabari swing by our hotel. Their tour has ended, but they're continuing solo travel. Lounging on a double bed, sipping on wine at midnight, Jabari convinces Miranda that he doesn't know what the haka is.

Miranda's jaw drops. "No way! Haven't you seen the All Blacks play?"

Jabari shakes his head then winks at Adam and me.

He knows what it is. He just wants her to perform it.

With a little persuasion, Miranda gives a very animated version of the traditional Maori war cry dance. As our neighbours bang on the wall and yell in frustration, the rest of us shake with laughter.

It's not my intention to kiss Adam. I let it go. I'm happy just chilling. But as the night draws on, we kiss in a shaky elevator then trot off to sleep. My communication with Jacob is instantaneous. He admits he's "reconnected with someone from the past," but we still don't end things. Perhaps a string of hope keeps us tied together. Our connection is fated, but our love isn't destined long term. If we truly, deeply loved each other, would we have agreed to be with other people? Or is that what true love entails—allowing the other to be free?

I now see true love as two birds in a cage with the door wide open. Free to leave yet choosing to stay. There for love, not obligation.

Amid passionate soccer fans on our final day in La Paz, we bicker whether to cheer for Bolivia or Peru. The crowds roar with a fiery spirit as both teams score a goal. I miss both. I am entertained by the antics of the Bolivian coach who resembles an angry Mr Bean. Strolling back to our hotel, I notice there are no glowing gold McDonald's arches. The country closed all restaurants and recently announced the expelling of Coca-Cola to celebrate the "end of capitalism" with the close of the Mayan calendar. I respect those decisions.

Sunrise bursts hope into the tail end of a twelve-hour bus ride into Sucre, the refined valley city that is Bolivia's actual capital. Elegant streets with whitewashed buildings soothe the chaotic pulse of La Paz to a serene rhythm. The switch happens in a mere blink of an eye in terms of deep time. In grand cosmic cycles, it is only yesterday that dinosaurs stomped and plodded. Just outside the mountain-surrounded city, is the world's largest concentration of dinosaur footprints on a 1.2-kilometre-long cliff. Gazing at the world-record-setting 347-metre trail from a baby Tyrannosaurus Rex, I wonder if creatures will one day ponder our footprints—questioning what we run from, quizzing what we run for.

I'm still running from life in some regard. Yet I'm running towards things that make me feel alive. The delicate balance of creation and destruction becomes real as we pull into Potosí, where extreme poverty doubles the national average in what was once the America's wealthiest and largest city.

A poignant documentary forewarns us of the tiny, dust-congested tunnels oozing with toxic substances inside the Cerro Rico mine. Dubbed "Devil's

Mountain", it looms over the rickety city that slouches on a desolate plateau. Legend says a bridge could be built from Cerro Rico to Spain with the extracted silver that fuelled Spain's wealth for 300 years. The same legend says another bridge could be built with the bones of eight million indigenous people killed inside "the mountain that eats people". Pressing bandannas to our mouths, Miranda, Wren, and I inch and sweat through cramped tunnels. We are here by choice. It devastates me that children are forced into labour without protective gear.

Outside the mountain, most workers are Catholic. Inside, they worship El Tio, a part-devil, part-goat deity who is "Lord of the Underworld". A miner tells us the name is twisted from "Dios"—the Spanish word for God. For centuries, this warped depiction cajoled exhausted workers to slave harder, threatened that Tio would take their lives otherwise. That the Spaniards corrupted spirituality into a terror-based reality boils my bones. God is love. Not fear. Conditions in the 500-year-old mine are horrendous still with miners often coughing blood to death at age forty. It breaks my heart to pieces as fine as dust particles that stagnate inside the tiny tunnels we crawl through.

Sitting in pitch-black darkness with one of the guides, I breathe into my abdomen as he asks what Australia is like.

"Different. Very different," I say, suddenly feeling guilty to live in such paradise while the entire mountain threatens to collapse in on itself from centuries of plundering a death trap of tunnels.

"We have everything we want, but nothing we need. People have no idea what the world is really like..."

Maybe I don't either. It's eerie that the same country millions run for is the place I run from. Like the poorest of poor living on Bolivia's richest mountain, it's a contradiction.

I emerge into the high Andean sunshine a changed woman. My sweat dries, my breath deepens, and empathy expands my heart—whole, but broken.

The journey is changing me. And the journey is constantly changing.

᳀

People brush past my aisle seat on a local bus bound for Uyuni, a freezing town beside the world's largest salt flat. Leaving malnourished, begging children and severely polluted rivers in Bolivia's harshest region, I watch the world whizz by. The tides of transformation tug at my skin. They reveal a deeper layer of me as I surrender to the steady stream. Daydreams sway between Queensland with Jacob and Perth with Adam as we disembark in the desolate desert. It feels like the end of the world.

Beyond crowded markets inspiring creative photography ideas with buckets full of trinkets, a white wonderland of salt stretches into the horizon. Buckled into four-by-fours, we speed across the blinding desert to a rocky outcrop of land brimming with gigantic cacti. It was once an island in a prehistoric lake. From the island's peak, the crusty salt flat glistens in all directions. We snap perspective photos with beer bottles and toy dinosaurs then layer up in a hotel built entirely from salt.

Breakfast is stale white bread and strawberry jam at sunrise. Then our captivation of the high desert plateau continues with vivid mineral lakes lapping at lofty Andean mountains. The terrain is cinematic. In the morning, Wren sketches flamingos flocking in a bright-blue lagoon. In the afternoon, I gaze at rock stacks perched beside a shallow red lagoon and discern that Bolivia is a country of stark contrast. The harder my heart shatters, the deeper it opens.

Lost amongst mountains, my thoughts drift back to you
Peaceful pink flamingos, gentle shades of blue
The tranquil essence of nature calms my restless heart
Your presence stays with me, all these miles apart

- 20 October 2012

On our final day in Bolivia, I face the bitter morning with five layers and wait for dawn to crack the day open. A bumpy road leads us through the twilight to a remote geothermal pocket where hot steam spouts into frigid air. We are free to roam the geyser basin, dodging boiling mud baths as we hold our noses at the pungent sulphur smell. Then the sun's first rays cascade over the horizon, illuminating billowing fumaroles and silhouetting people in mystical steam. It's so potent and raw, yet so otherworldly. I have to pinch myself to make sure I'm not dreaming.

Rustic mountains climb towards the sky as we cross the border into Chile for just one night. In the lively town of San Pedro set high on an arid plateau, dusty streets are festive with a local football game airing on TV. Just 30 kilometres from Bolivia, the juxtaposition is palpable. The air isn't cut with tension. Locals don't hide their intrigue. I feel a confidence and buoyancy that is irresistible to embody.

The liberated cadence becomes me as we drive to Argentina. Our fourteen-hour bus ride extends to twenty with a late departure and broken fan belt midway. Cruising south past a mosaic of mountains and cacti, I feel the tantalising draw of a current pulling me somewhere new. New desires. New destinations. A new destiny is emerging.

The need for deep sleep oozes in my eyes as we pull into Salta. Outside our hotel, purple jacaranda trees bloom with a woody, herbaceous smell. Dropped flowers create an indigo trail that we follow to a cobblestoned square with shimmering colonial architecture held by wooden eaves. It is definitely the most European city we've been to, yet the charm of the nation's blended heritage is distinct from the West. We embrace it with lips painted red, sipping Yerba mate as a bandoneon gives sound to the tango with sensual sentimentality. Traditionally dressed dancers invite us to sidestep and swirl as we click our fingers in time to the beat. I find a cathartic release in slow and sultry steps as my cheeks dilate with happiness, and I think of all the wonderful humans whose journeys intertwine with my own. Old souls. Young hearts. Kindred spirits. Fated friends. All with something to teach. All with something to learn.

Wind whisks through Caramello's cinnamon mane. She flicks it and neighs, then trots in front of the other horses patiently waiting for the obstruction on the forested mountain trail to clear. I stroke her strong neck and giggle at our similarities. I don't like stagnation or being told what to do either.

Enchanted by leafy vistas, I ruminate on Miranda's suggestion to write a "plus, minus, and interesting" list of staying with Jacob. I love his playful sense of adventure. I relish the new perspectives he empowers me to see. I am eternally grateful for his wholehearted inclusion of me in Queensland life for it pulled me away from drab and drug-fuelled Perth circles. But I want to travel, and he cannot fulfill that destiny with me. Caramello swishes her tail as she walks forward. The answer is deep within the earth she sets her hooves on. I'm not ready to swallow it.

Nonetheless, it weighs heavy on my mind as nineteen hours of tarmac twists into Mendoza. As we cycle between sunny vineyards renowned for delectable Malbec wine, I am alone with my thoughts. Warm zephyrs breeze along leafy roads. They exhilarate me as I feel complex layers of reality shift and shake.

The next day, a small shaggy dog follows Miranda, Wren, and me around the city's central plaza as we revere in nostalgia.

"I've never had someone *really* close to me pass away," I remark.

As I say it, I touch the wooden trunk of a nearby tree.

"Touch wood..."

Next week is the three-year anniversary of my suicide attempt. The rawness of waking sunburned on the sand with a second chance influences me more than I know. It compels me to embrace life and not let it slip away. Time is transient and our bodies are temporal. If it were otherwise, would existence have the same potency?

This is what I ask as I attach myself to a tandem paragliding harness, jump off a cliff, and do somersaults through the sky. Gliding over luscious mountain foothills and high viridescent plains, I observe the world with a bird's-eye view as adrenaline revives me with life.

While the others fly, I perch on a sunny rock and watch the flamboyant mannerisms of Argentinean men. They embrace each other with brotherly love that conveys their appreciation with uninhibited warmth. I like it. It feels like home. I understand why it's said that Argentineans are Spanish-speaking Italians who think they're in Paris. If you feel something, express it from the broth of your bones burning with untamed liberation.

As we bump back down the mountain, one of the hunky paragliding instructors joins me in the dusty Ute tray.

"I like your smile," he chatters. "You're always smiling at everything."

Bearing witness to others' perceptions of who we are is interesting. The "what" is obvious, but the "why" is hidden, often from ourselves too. His observation broadens my beam, but I do not explain that a close encounter with death influences my cheerful demeanour. I'm still figuring it out myself.

The unexpected is what changes our lives. Let it.

The mighty Andes separate Chile and Argentina with soaring white peaks. In the coming weeks, I crisscross the mountains on a new tour heading south to Patagonia. Pulling into Santiago, Chile's charismatic capital, I look at my friends with dewy eyes. The strangers I met in that cosy Quito hostel have become dear friends. Now we venture different ways.

As they prepare for Buenos Aires, I speedwalk across the cosmopolitan city to meet my new group. In an elegant hotel lobby, an eighty-seven-year-old Dane and a middle-aged Indian introduce themselves as two fellow travellers on my new tour. Beneath my cheery exterior, I'm jarred. I know that tours need four travellers to embark. The thought of being stuck with two old men for three weeks jolts me out of my comfort zone of travelling with similar-aged travellers from Commonwealth countries.

As soon as I let my judgements go, the couches fill with a dozen others from Germany, Thailand, Canada, England, and Finland. Most are in their thirties, forties, and fifties. Ironically, it is the two men I first meet that I grow to love the most. A thirty-something-year-old Englishman with a wide smile and shaggy hair introduces himself as Olly. He will be leading us off the beaten track to Ushuaia, on the southern tip of South America. In a bright-orange Mercedes-Benz overland truck self-sufficient with camping gear and a fold-out kitchen, I soon learn that the journey is the destination.

We acquaint in a grey meeting room upstairs. I smile with my eyes as each person states their name, country, and occupation. It's a common way to introduce yourself on the road. I wish we'd do it by: *What lights you up? Why are you travelling? What is your most treasured memory? What is your most terrible?*

Amidst two middle-aged couples, two young women, and a few lone men is a handsome European man.

"I am Kai, from Finland. I don't work now. I'm retired."

My torso warms. His confidence is alluring. The table chuckles with surprise. How can a thirty-year-old man be retired? I later discover the ex-professional motocross rider lives off his winnings as he travels the world.

I feel free as I skip across town to the vibrant eco-hostel where my old group stays. It's the first time I've been alone in months. I realise how much I miss my solitude. At the hostel, I hold hands with Miranda and Wren as we share precious last words. Then I check my emails on the shared computer to discover that Old Frank, my favourite barfly, has died. Around the time I "touched wood" in Mendoza, declaring I'd never had someone dear to me pass, Frank took his last breaths. He wasn't found for three days. The news hits me like the tree I touched falls upon me. Slowly, then all at once.

Just after midnight, I taxi back to the elegant downtown hotel and tiptoe into the pitch-black room I share with the two solo women. Trying not to make a sound, I lie on my creaky single bed. Their agitation strikes me with each subtle turn.

We wake at 4:00 a.m. to beat the city traffic. I am mourning with morning's soft, honeyed rays. The feeling of forward motion is invigorating and insightful, but suddenly it feels like life moves too fast and if I don't hold on, I'll get left behind. Slowly the sun rises, and I grow accustomed to the truck's sputter and squeal. Physically, I'm on a long, bumpy ride into the untamed wilderness of Patagonia— Chile and Argentina's sparsely populated, majestic bottom-half. Emotionally, I'm in a discombobulated shamble.

❦

If countries are people, Chile is a supermodel. The long, thin nation extends from an arid northern desert to a maze of glaciers, fjords, and islands. After chugging past some of the Andes highest peaks, we detour off the highway to a waterfall descending in shimmering white cataracts. Bianca, a German lady who still appears disgruntled at my late-night arrival, cackles at Kai's jokes. I feel their eyes on me as I slide under the wooden rails. His, warm with intrigue. Hers, cold as ice.

Perched on the cliff edge, I wipe mist from my face and watch water tumble into rocky outcrops below. Destined somewhere new, just like Frank, the water flows in nonchalant surrender. A nearby flower compels me to pluck its yellow petals. I momentarily hold them between my fingers before the wind carries them into the cascade. I think of the twinkle in Frank's glazed brown eyes as the river perpetually glides in reflective strips. Then we move onward to Pucón, the adventure sport capital of Chile perched beside an azure lake.

The picturesque town is shadowed by a fire-belching volcano. Tourists buzz on hiking to the crater, glimpsing hot bubbling lava, then ice sledding down. As boots, helmets, gas masks, and ice axes are dispersed to do this, I realise I'm not excited by the experience. Not one little bit. My need for solitude outweighs my need for thrill, so I catch a ride back to town and stroll to the lake instead.

Lazing on gravelly black sand, I watch birds fly into the horizon as Frank drifts onward in their flapping wings. Somewhere beautiful. Somewhere unknown.

Sunshine replenishes my tired body, and I acknowledge November for the introspective season it is for it reminds me of my dance with death. Diving into deep, fixed waters of the underworld shakes up what I must realise to release. This beckons me to grow.

❦

Disintegrating into nothing leads to integrating everything;
becoming one with the stillness beyond the veil.

Transformation isn't easy. Anyone who says that shedding a skin is painless is still wearing it. As emotional tsunamis crash within, I realise that I am breathing underwater rather than drowning in my depths. Waves of sadness mix with intense realizations that ooze through ink in journal pages. Paper is my only keeper.

The next day, I log into my socials on the hostel computer to a frustrated message from Jacob. He is concerned by the space growing between us and my "disappearance into the void you so often run to". He says I should talk to him instead, not understanding that the void is my safe space—to be with myself, by myself, free from others' emotions and expectations that absorb into my bloodstream with effortless precision. It is my space, my temple, my home. For me and me alone.

I don't have it in me to reply straight away. Some people process their internal state through external dialogue, careless of messy articulation for they find clarity through listeners' ears. That's not my style. I need stillness and space to be present with what arises. Only when connected to my deeper essence, the part that brims with gentle wisdom, am I ready to share what I've found.

As I prepare a group breakfast, boiling water simmers with the freedom I feel being half a world away. For so long I blamed Jacob for the choking feeling of constriction, but he was a steppingstone from dreary Perth to where I am now. He facilitated my expansion.

The truck grumbles as we leave Pucón. It reflects my inner terrain. I miss the depth of my old group who would hold me in my realisations. Suddenly, my heart skips a beat. Down the road is my old group, strolling with backpacks bulging as they blink in the leafy canopy.

I bounce to the window and haul it open. A refreshing burst of air enlivens my lungs as I open the portal to my past and scream.

"MIRANDA! WREN!"

I am acutely aware of the new group's shock that the quiet girl I've shown them has a voice charged with impassioned zeal. I don't care. The only thing that matters is my friends' loving eyes as Olly slows the truck to a quiet rumble. There's no time for words. Everything I wish to say—*I love you, I miss you, I need you*—seeps through my dewy eyes as Olly gradually accelerates and my friends shrink into the path that they chose but I did not. The moment lingers in my mind for years.

As rain pitter-patters through gaps in the windows en route south to Puerto Montt, the gateway to Patagonia drenches me with a scene from memory lane. I am driving home from a gig before leaving Queensland when Jacob moans that his ex-girlfriend, who I met in Byron Bay and remain close with, is angry at him. I ask why. Jacob discloses she questioned if he cheated. His confession that he did infuriates me—not because it happened, but his lack of remorse and stubbornness to apologise that jeopardizes their friendship. The windscreen wipers swipe into a rainy black abyss, out of time with the music that was once in perfect unison. It is in that moment I realise our relationship is dying for my trust in him swiftly dwindles.

Showers hammer upon me as we assemble tents in the pitch-black, soggy campsite. Hammering pegs past the top squishy layer, I exert my anger into each heavy clank.

Fuck his hedonistic ways.

Clank.

Fuck his over-the-top, pushy, pornographic behaviour.

Knock.

Fuck his sexual exploits.

Ding.

Fuck him for working at a strip club.

Clang.

Fuck him!

Bang.

And fuck...me.

Fuck me for me for putting up with that bullshit.

In our early-morning pack down, I am unable to remove one silver peg. Olly tries dislodging it. Then Kai attempts. It's futile. I've wedged it too deep, too hard. Eventually we must leave it in the ground and continue our journey. Over time, I realise the anger stems from my boundaries being crossed by Colton assaulting me and that trickled into my relationship with Jacob because I hadn't yet healed that pain. Like the stubborn tent peg, there is simultaneous potential for my rage to splinter and rust inside me or be purified through healing tears and rain.

Aboard a ferry across the Reloncaví Sound, a crisp Pacific breeze whisks across the deck. I awe at clouds drifting across glaciated summits and shake my head at my naivety of strolling along the beach, questioning what was on the other side. Past me feels so foreign. So far away.

I gaze at the boat's white, foamy trail and wonder how long the Pacific Ocean unified minuscule water molecules into something larger than mere atoms. What wisdom does it carry? Inundated by mystery, my fire subsides into the cerulean currents. Finally. Ripple by ripple, wave by wave, I surrender into my softness. I surrender into the answers.

⚭

Soy sauce wafts from fold-out camping tables as the food team chop carrots. Revering that I have no idea where we are, I wander into the wilderness, enlivened by dewy grass kisses on my bare feet. In unspoiled solitude, I follow the frigid shores of a glacial river to a fallen trunk overlooking forested mountains. The blur of iconic peaks, jagged coastlines, and quaint towns where we stock up on food solace my nebulous mind.

Our days start before sunrise and end around moonlit campfires. Toasty flames dry hand-washed clothes with smoky aromas as music coils into the icy air. A German photographer—who sticks out his tongue each time he snaps a photo—is convinced that "Cabernet" means "better", so we sip full-bodied Cabernet Sauvignon. The "better" Sauvignon melts language barriers into the mesmerising gleam of fire and deepens our sleep on rocky ground. Bianca and the other female traveller share a tent. I cherish the introspection that isolation enables.

Chilean Patagonia is wetter than windswept Argentina, with jagged peaks protecting the latter from Pacific rains. On an overgrown mountain trail, we cast the first footprints of the season in crunchy snow as raindrops bead leaves. Crystal flakes pirouette through the forest canopy, catching on my eyelashes and melting into my shoes. I'm in an ivory wonderland, tiptoeing across the crispy sheet in enchanted bliss when I fall through. Bianca laughs. Kai extends his gloved hand. My frozen fingers electrify as he pulls me up into his arms. This makes the corners of Bianca's lips curl.

Kai teaches me Finnish as majestic, glacial scenes fly past the truck window. When he invites me to Finland for the summer, a Plan C weaves into my Queensland versus Perth daydreams. With music silencing my internal chatter, I flow with feelings in a dreamy curiosity of what I will write in my journal's blank pages.

Sometimes we open the sunroof at the back of the truck and strap into roof seats where we admire the 360-degree view. These are my favourite moments, sitting with Kai in stillness as crisp winds invigorate us with confident lashes. Turquoise lakes and unclimbed alps connect towns in our flexible itinerary, but to me, the dots connect when looking back.

My soul is a river.
You became the sea.

On a rocky lakeside beach near our campsite in Puerto Rio Tranquilo, rain trickles in iridescent showers. Torrential overnight downpour bogged the truck, so we trudge back and forth to the craggy shore collecting large stones to create an escape path beneath the tyres. A lanky English traveller who talks incessantly about himself frustrates me as he watches the rest of us sweat and pant. Meanwhile, he lazes on a wooden bench sipping tea. Two hours after we manoeuvre the truck off the soggy soil, I sit alone on the gusty beach, sublimating my agitation through breath.

As waves serenade in swishing plops, I question how I can be angry in a place so peaceful. At the time I don't realise I'm invalidating my emotions and thus making it harder for the discontent to leave. With retrospect, I understand that naming our feeling lessens the charge, for it creates emotional distance through the activation of different brain regions.

As the clouds clear to a revitalising sunshine, Kai joins me by the water. His unguarded eyes sparkle with unknown constellations as he tells me his story. Married for eight years, then diagnosed with cancer, he rethought his entire life and divorced on good terms. Years of hardcore motocross riding have damaged his internal organs, and he regularly pisses blood. Apparently, he only has a few years left to live.

That night, we sleep in a dusty graveyard by the Argentinean border. Sipping red wine, we watch the hypnotising dance of tangerine flames telling tales of what's to come. Beneath a billion twinkling stars, our legs touch, and in the moon's reflective shine our bodies complete what daydreams began.

What is simple by the moonlit campfire is complicated with morning's embers. It is my day to cook for the group, so I emerge from the tent early. It is a gusty morning. Dirt blows into our food as I balance pots on fold-out tables. It is messy and squally and slightly comical. Then Bianca sees Kai surface from my tent, and her eyes catapult fire into the dusty disarray.

Clouds veil snowy summits on a lonely highway that brings us to El Chaltén. Exhausted from the midnight escapades, I snuggle into my top bunk in a female-only wooden chalet. The soft yarn blanket is warm and toasty upon me. As my eyes start drooping, Kai slips in and kisses my forehead with tender chivalry. He suggests we say we are a couple and share a room at our next destination. I toss in my sleep. His blue eyes blur with Jacob's like a cerulean whirlpool drawing me in and pulling me under.

In the morning, I stroll to a café and decode a Sudoku puzzle, hoping it will solve my real-life dilemma. I drum my fingers on the table and flick away crumbs as numbers mesh and matte into formulas with hidden answers. I respond to Jacob's message with veracity and grace, but we still haven't broken up. As I meander through a world-class hiking trail beside the vibrant alpine village, blossoming yellow flowers remind me of Frank. Off the trail is a shady hollow where a shallow river cascades past a complex labyrinth of roots. Suddenly the transience of it all becomes transparent. The entangled maze is temporary in the river's endless flow.

Back in the frontier town, I dye my hair a darker brown. Olly later chuckles that he saw me waltz into the bathroom wearing a rain poncho.

"I was wondering why you were having a shower in your raincoat."

*

> *Clear eyes and starry skies,*
> *Swallowed by your hollow lies*
> *Words rise like smoke and drip like ink*
> *They stick to me and make me think*
> *Beneath these waves that hold me under,*
> *The truth lies close; silent in slumber*
> *I may fall and I may fumble*
> *But truth prevails while darkness crumbles*
> *Far below my comfort zone*
> *Take my hand, bring me home.*

- 12 November 2012

"You're a hippie. You need a flower," Kai proclaims as he tucks a tiny blossom behind my ear with a loose brunette strand.

Inhaling its sweet deliciousness, I unknowingly stain my nose yellow as ice-dominated landscapes enchant us into El Calafate. The picturesque town is named after a delectable berry that, if eaten, promise one's return to Patagonia.

Atop a sunny park hill, I laze alone and watch toddlers in the playground below. They flounder and fall, but they get back up each time. In their novice perseverance, innocent and brave, I see that the joy of losing ourselves is finding ourself down unsuspecting paths. The grace of falling is learning to fly. With a relieving exhale, I decide to stop swimming against the currents in a struggle for familiar shores. By surrendering to the fact that everything in my life is unknown, I release the desire to control. This allows life to authentically unfold.

The next day, we chug past stunning subpolar forests to Perito Moreno, a gigantic blue glacier advancing from distant granite mountains. "The White Giant" appears as a glistening ice castle crested with jagged sapphires. Unlike most glaciers, the world's third largest ice cap grows rather than retreats. From steel-grated balconies opposite the mammoth phenomenon, we awe as building-sized chunks of ice creak and groan before calving into pristine waters with thunderous crashes.

Our miniscule existence in a gigantic world is palpable in the magnitude of chunks swiftly detaching from the icy façade that was home for millennia. As ice ruptures and melts, its watery form remains. Everything around me shifts, but through the transformation my internal essence stays—mind sharp, emotions soft, spirit strong.

On the deck of a tourist boat, I shiver as we sail past towering glacier walls and hold my breath as deep rumbles pre-empt thunderous splashes. Kai cups my icy hands in his. I melt into his warm embrace as he proclaims that tonight he will take me on a real date.

Back in town, stray dogs lead us past boutique chocolate shops to a colourful café, where I savour Calafate berries rolled in creamy vanilla ice cream. We talk about family and religion and philosophical views. I am fluttery yet calm, grateful to connect away from watchful eyes.

Patagonia is the perfect place for introspection with glimmering lakes studding the vast steppe with wild silence and barren beauty. Before our final crossover back into Chile, I discover my water-saturated passport in the safe. Bianca's hate shudders down my spine. I pierce her with you're-an-immature-bitch eyes. She smirks, then scowls as I move to the front of the truck and cosy into Kai while Olly sings along to The Kooks. Somehow, I get across the border with the splotched photo.

Topaz lakes and rugged grey mountains welcome us to Torres del Paine National Park where Kai and I sip red wine atop a hill with howling winds. Between kisses, we gaze at the iconic granite spires that he will hike in the following days. I don't have appropriate equipment, so I walk him to the ferry where his adventure begins in the morning. As we snuggle up on a wooden bench, a lone white horse gallops along rocky shores bejewelled with radiant blue icebergs. The shapes are obscure, like cryptic letters from a long-lost language.

With Kai absent, I can no longer distract from my finger-biting reality. Miscommunication led him to ejaculate inside me during a steamy shower escapade. We didn't use a condom, and I no longer subject my body to the health risks of birth control pills. The anxiety is dizzy and pounding. I find solace in a forest ravaged by a recent fire where the complexity of surviving trees enthrals me. The roots protrude above the soil, forming intricate patterns and wooden lattices. Every leaf, twig, flower, and branch mesh together with answers to my unasked questions.

At night, I watch the sun melt behind imposing granite towers and envision

Kai charging through the three-day hike. Olly and I bond around campfires and absorb inspiring travel tales of the eighty-seven-year-old Dane. Somehow, the fact that I might be pregnant to a travel flame in a foreign land amidst breaking up with my long-distance boyfriend doesn't feel so heavy.

Two days after Kai departed, we return from an afternoon hike to him lazing in the sun at camp. My inkling was right. He raced through the hike to buy an extra night together before the truck's inevitable screech into our final destination, Ushuaia, the world's southernmost city.

Antarctic icebreakers dock in the harbour where the Andes meet an archipelago strait. Sipping red wine, Kai and I wonder which ship will take me to the icy continent. I ponder verbalising my concerns, but I don't want to cause unnecessary worry. It's a conversation I'll have only if needed.

Travel romances are bittersweet because we're pushing time zones and comfort zones. We savour each moment with vivid tenacity, but we don't know if—or when—we'll ever see each other again. I am the Pacific, wild and untamed. He is the dense, salty Atlantic embracing me in an unrestrained collision of rough currents and roaring gales. Meeting but not merging, it is time to go our separate ways.

Chapter V
FLOW

South America and Antarctica reach for each other like star-crossed lovers, separated by the furious waves and howling winds of three oceans converging. In the world's largest and roughest current, 1000 kilometres of wild undercurrents crash in a clockwise motion.

Three hundred million years ago, when Antarctica was warmer than California and covered in lush evergreen forests, the world existed as one massive supercontinent, Pangaea. In this Permian period of unity, South America and Antarctica fell in love. It was an impassioned affair. An era of eros. A soft and slow journey, enriched with the sweet nectar of tender devotion. The Ice Queen adored the quiet warmth of South America's ardent touch. Her Latino Lover cherished the unwavering safety in her cool façade.

As earthquakes, volcanic eruptions and subterranean movements caused the supercontinent to stretch, thin and fragment, the lovers were pulled apart. Their separation was painful. Physically, they could not touch. Emotionally, their bond remains in oceanic tides that keep them connected.

Today, South America and Antarctica extend themselves into the wild waters that simultaneously separate and connect. From beaches they reach, but they can never quite meet. Pondering the could haves, would haves, should haves—is it better to taste true love and lose it, or never touch it at all?

Wednesday 21st November 2012

Wild seas crash against the rugged headland of South America's southernmost tip as the ice-strengthened expedition ship rocks with fierce waves. I watch Cape Horn's striking black cliffs shrink to nothingness from the frigid deck while biting winds freeze my nose to a dripping ice cube. From my vantage point, I see where the Latino Lover long ago barricaded his heart with rocky ramparts in cynical hope it would prohibit him from future pain. He soon learned, as I am now, that being guarded and suspicious doesn't stop us from hurting. It stops us from loving. And that hurts more.

Our journey across the Drake Passage takes three days. Amid the fluid intensity of the Pacific, Atlantic, and Southern Oceans converging, a strange calm consumes me. In my single cabin, I unpack my entire backpack and lie down. Water churns against my round cabin window like a washing machine with hurricane force. The perpetual sway soothes heartache's jagged edges and smooths my pain with tender memories of treasured days.

When dinner is announced on the intercom, I wobble down passageways peppered with barf bags to the dining hall, where white slip-proof cloths drape over bolted-down tables. I scout for the two travellers from Perth I coincidentally sat behind on a bus to the port that morning. Amidst the monotone buzz of Mandarin Chinese wafting into boisterous American accents and aromas of freshly baked bread, they wave me down and introduce me to Tane, a Kiwi living in Brisbane. I giggle as redheaded Earle photographs every dish of our four-course meal, and wonder if freckled Deseree is anorexic as she pushes vegetables around her plate.

Waves pummel over the bow as we steer down the latitudes. Up and down. Side to side. The ocean's extremity cleanses me with each rise and fall. It's like being in the womb, completely immersed by water before being birthed into a curious new world. The in-betweenness is strange. The planet's southern frontier distances me from the mess I created. Under the covers, I am scared and alone. I regret not sharing my hopes and fears with Kai. I wonder if my words move and breathe inside him, as his touch does in me. Soon, half the boat doses up on seasick tablets and excuse themselves from meals. Relaxing into the undulating sway, I explore the ship's layers. A library on level five absorbs me, and I watch daily presentations in a large lecture theatre with cinema-style seats. With each quiver of the ocean's emotion, my understanding of Antarctica's unique geology, biology, history, and politics expands.

Slowly, we arrive in crisper waters, and my world stops shaking. The sky coils with streaks of molten lava before the sun dips behind majestic white slabs of snow. Being this far south in summer means sunset is a two-hour prelude for sunrise. I chuckle when an American lady asks if it's light all year round, moments after another passenger questions if we'll see polar bears.

Before we step foot on the glowing white ice sheet, our landing is approved by the Antarctic Treaty. In a presentation titled *Who owns Antarctica?* I learn no one does. Despite several countries claiming sovereignty over overlapping slices of land, a 1959 treaty declares peaceful scientific investigation.

Exhilaration ripples through the boat as we step through disinfectant trays in sturdy, knee-high boots for our first landing. As we zoom around turreted blue icebergs on zodiacs—ten-seater, rigid, inflatable boats—I unglove my hands and trail them through bone-numbing waters. Seals sunbake on ice floes, stretching blubbery flippers towards dramatic white cliffs glittering like precious stones. As icy splashes dot my signature yellow expedition parka, the troubles furrowed in my brow melt into the larger, unknown mass looming underwater. There is nothing I can do but wait for the sun to liquefy my internal iceberg so I can immerse in its reflective pool.

Crunching onto the kingdom of ice and snow, I giggle at the hilarious courtship displays of chinstrap penguins. As they collect rocks to build nests for the season, a lone male suddenly stretches his head towards the sky and beats his chest with small, stiff flippers. This compels the other penguins to echo the braying squawk, creating a symphony of screeching trumpets that drifts through frosty winds. Rocky nests are smudged with trails of brown faeces, and the odd prankster steals rocks from other penguins. Earle and I giggle that we are a colony of yellow penguins, sporting our weatherproof parkas as we climb scintillating mounds.

Back on the ship, an Englishman living and working in Antarctica for thirty-six years sits next to me at dinner. I ask him to share a story from the old days as a bowl of freshly baked bread entices us with doughy aromas. The warm, grainy roll is crunchy and irresistible with butter melting like velvet salt. The man's eyes light up as he talks of huskies sledding over parts of Antarctica that no longer exist.

"No way!?"

"Yes. Actually, Antarctica was once much bigger," he notes with a lowered head.

"Really?"

He nods.

I look at my golden-brown crust, suddenly not hungry.

"Global warming is *very* real."

As a waiter asks what soup we'd like, excited chatter bounces around the dining hall. I wonder if my children's children will have the opportunity to explore the magnificent white ice shelf before it completely melts.

He must sense my sadness because he gives an empathetic smile then addresses the table. "You guys are lucky. In all my years working here, I've never experienced such perfect weather."

Chili and tomato waft from a nearby table.

"You mean it's not always still and serene like this?" I ask.

He chuckles. "No. Oh, no, no, noooo. Antarctic weather is *notoriously* unpredictable."

He explains the changes from treacherously turbulent, to grey and gusty, to pristine and peaceful in mere minutes, then notes, "Let's hope it stays this way for the next few days!"

Be here, now.

Hot water drips down my back as I rub my bloated belly. It is our final day harboured beside titanic-sized glaciers. I wake feeling as numb as the continent's subzero interior. My period still hasn't come. I don't know if my stomach is full from indulgent buffets or if there's a tiny human growing inside me. Rationally, I know the early signs of pregnancy wouldn't cause a bump this big. But the swelling amplifies my fears of what I will do if I really am pregnant to a man who lives half a world away.

Through the intercom, the captain invites us to wear bathers under our thermals if we wish to polar plunge. I stay immersed in the shower's healing drops, letting my fear drip down the drain. Steam fogs the bathroom as I blink back warm tears. I should do the icy jump. It'll make me feel alive.

As our zodiac lands on shore, I convince Tane to jog up a frozen hill to warm our shivering bodies. Panting at the peak, we gaze upon glassy grey waters reflecting metallic mountains. The ocean is an iridescent mirror dotted with ice.

"Are you going to plunge today?" I ask, wiping sweat from my brow.

"Maybe..." he ponders. "This might be my only chance."

I jog on the spot to maintain the heat. "What if we plunge now? While we're warm and it's easy to strip down?"

He chuckles.

"Yay?" I grin.

"Maybe..."

"C'mon, Tane. It's now or never! Let's run down and see if they'll let us go."

He shakes his head in disbelief, then finally nods. "Okay, Jess. Let's do it."

Zipping down the icy mound, we pass Deseree and Earle.

"Where...where are you guys go-going?" Deseree's teeth chatter.

"Polar plunge," I call out, jogging away slowly.

Her eyes widen as she tugs her thermals over her hands.

"You comin'?" I swivel around and jump up and down.

Earle examines the icy water.

Deseree shakes her head.

"Sprint up that slope," I suggest over my shoulder. "It'll warm you!"

At shore, the expedition leader agrees to let us plunge. While he arranges a lifeguard and towels, Deseree and Earle trot towards us.

"We're doing it with you," Earle explains with a beam.

Soon the four of us stand on flattened rubber boots, shivering in our bathers.

"Alright, who's first?" the expedition leader asks.

Four sets of eyes land on me. In my fluorescent-yellow bikini, I step forward. Three zodiacs linger nearby with dozens of cameras ready. I wish they'd grant me privacy to plunge without digital eyes.

Gazing into the glacial water, I convince myself I'm jumping into a thermal pool. My toes cower. I take a deep inhale. If I am pregnant, this could be the end of my freedom to live life solely for me.

3, 2, 1...

Splash.

All senses invigorate as I dive. It's cold. So cold, it burns. Underwater, my problems dissolve. Four strong breaststrokes. One long exhale.

Onlookers applaud as I emerge for air.

"It's not that cold!" I exclaim.

"It's not *that* cold?" a voice quizzes.

"It's warm!" someone jokes.

Back on shore, I wrap myself in a towel. Deseree swears as she prepares to plunge. Sixty-eight others jump that day, the most from any expedition.

That night, we convene in a giant lounge as the captain—on his final voyage—gives a toast.

"To Antarctica and her beauty. To the friends and family who could not join us on this journey. And to the friendships formed on our beloved Ocean Diamond."

"Cheers," we echo with camaraderie and excitement, lifting champagne glasses as we prepare for another shaky ride.

⚓

The Drake Passage bestows a calmer journey back to Ushuaia. I attend more presentations, learning about climate change, biological prospecting, research, tourism, and mining.

Supposedly the world's third largest oil reserve lies untouched beneath Antarctica's thick ice sheet. Suddenly, I understand why so many nations fight for land claims. In 1998, a fifty-year mining ban was signed. As we cruise north, I pray humanity will never drill through kilometres of chunky ice to then transport oil across the dangerous Drake.

Antarctica's riches are not in her reserves. She is the treasure.

> *We have everything we want, but nothing we need*
> *Our vision is jaded by consumption and greed*
> *Pay cheques increase, stomachs expand*
> *The less that we give, the more we demand*
> *As our toxins form smog in the skies*
> *Temperatures increase, and sea levels rise*
> *Our mother, she cries alone in neglect*
> *But still, we do not see the effect*
> *The planet is warming, water's harder to find*
> *Are we that ignorant, or just merely blind?*
> *The trees we cut that help us to breathe*
> *Are replaced by pollution that we leave*
> *While economy is priority and nations "prevail"*
> *Our planet, our mother becomes very frail*
> *The white and blue continent, contains so much mystery*
> *Give it a century, will this be history?*
> *Entertainment over the environment is what we choose*
> *And thus it is precious life that we lose*

Salaries increase to some who call this fiction
By corporations themselves; what a contradiction
How much longer can we pretend?
Will our ignorance be mankind's end?
When the last tree falls, it won't be so funny
When we are hungry and cannot cook money
I wonder, will you hear my rhyme?
Or will the clock tick out of time?
We live in a nation that needs information
to make a transformation, and save our population

- **29 November 2012**

Amid the ship's therapeutic sway, I find stillness in my blanket cocoon. My period still hasn't come, but I relinquish the fear holding me captive by breathing into my womb with a loving presence. This creates safety in my body. People trot past my locked door, chatting excitedly about breakfast. I'm about to join them when a ship-wide announcement floods the intercom.

"Ladies and gentleman, we have a rare sighting of a humpback whale breaching on the ship's starboard side."

I leap out of bed and peel back the curtains. Right outside my window, the giant creature spouts water through its blowhole. I smile and awe. Then it dips back into the ocean and sings a long, loud lullaby in pulsing grunts and rhythmic groans. Its song moves inside me long after it disappears. It serenades me with the notion that everything will be alright. I've simply got to surrender.

At breakfast, Deseree pockets fruit and cereal, preparing for her journey home. I follow suit, making the most of the all-inclusive dream as I fill my backpack with napkin-wrapped food from the buffet.

With snug-fitting clothes, we hug the crew goodbye at the harbour. Then Tane walks me to a pharmacy to get a pregnancy test. In a dim outdoor toilet, I piss on a plastic stick and hold my breath for the results. Outside, in cloud-filtered sunshine, I sigh in relief.

No embarazada.

Not pregnant.

With a day to waste before my flight to Buenos Aires, I upload photos and check my emails at an internet café. A lengthy write from Jacob reflects on our beautiful journey together but acknowledges what we've danced around for months: it's time to call it quits.

With no ties binding me to either man, I study my itinerary for another bright-orange overland truck awaiting me in Argentina. A smile illuminates my tired heart. I am reborn. Finally.

☙

Bound for the city that doesn't sleep or tire, I feel my convolutions disperse into the stratosphere. Buenos Aires welcomes me with tango parlours perched on cobblestone sidewalks where locals kiss cheeks and lick dulce de leche. Juicy steaks sizzle from parrillas on street corners, and buildings boast a European flair. I enjoy it. I relish the passionate celebration of life bursting with delight. It reflects and reinforces how I feel inside.

Night is always young in the "Paris of South America". In a restaurant that opens at 9:00 p.m., I meet my new group and our English guide, Bran, who devises an itinerary to Brazil. The new group is friendly, but this will be my last organised tour. I yearn for exploration without the constraints of time. With the truck's incessant chug away from the waking city, I befriend first-time traveller Rebecca from Adelaide. Remote villages and open plains breeze the day away until we park beside the Uruguay River at dusk.

After bathing in murky grey waters, we cook dinner beneath twinkling constellations and set up tents beside the silty stream. Halfway through the night, rain pitter-patters. It soon intensifies to heavy plonks. Then lightning rips open the sky and thunder rumbles in untamed reverberations cracking into my dreams.

We wake to the river lapping beside our tents. Rains still strum. After a quick pack up on squelchy shores, Bran starts the truck. Tires upheave slushy puddles. The engine moans. The truck is stubborn, static in the mud. We unload our bags to lessen the load and try again. Showers drum. The river continues rising. Again, nothing. We place stones under the tires and try pushing. Still, nothing.

In a dryish bush, Rebecca clasps her head in her hands. I prance over and ask if she is okay. She grumbles about the unwarranted delay, then confides her recent bipolar diagnosis. She is challenged by sensory overload. I empathise that uncertainty causes us to catastrophise novel situations because we have no prior context to inform future decisions. It is dense and discombobulating. But it is in these spaces we grow.

Some of the group hike into a nearby town while the rest of us scavenge more rocks. Eventually we give up and scrutinise the river's ominous rising. What will happen if our beloved truck is pulled into its persistent flow?

My daydream is interrupted by our companions' return with a tow truck. Turns out, they met the town mayor who fed them tea and biscuits, then sourced a truck to rescue us from our muddy bedlam.

Our journey resumes with sticky heat and soggy cloths. The seats are prickly. Mud smears every crevice. But I feel closer to the group because we've overcome a blood-pumping obstacle. When we reach our hostel near Iguazu Falls at midnight, I am placed in a dorm with Rebecca.

I knock softly on the door.

An Israeli girl in a tight-fitting dress flings the door open. She snarls like a leopard.

"Hi, sorry to arrive so late. We had…truck trouble."

I step towards her, glimpsing another girl wiping lipstick from her mouth and two topless guys crouched behind a bunk.

She blocks my entry to rest and rejuvenation. "It is too late for newbies to enter!" she yells.

The other girl nods with a smirk. A faint chuckle escapes one of the dudes. I can't be bothered fighting that they've snuck two guys into bunks that would be ours.

Back at reception I get a key to another dorm. It is away from the other buildings, down an unlit slope. In our new room, a man paces in the dark. As soon as we enter, he leaps onto a bunk above a passed-out girl. I flick on the lights, but the bulbs are detached. One is warm on my bed. The man lies still and silent, but wide awake. His head storms with static. The lightning strikes my bones as I slide my valuables under my pillow and feign sleep. In the morning, the room is empty. With a drifting focus, we venture to the roaring cascades of Iguazu Falls.

Straddling the Argentinian and Brazilian border, the watery spectacle is girdled by a lush rainforest delta. An ancient legend speaks of a god lusting after a beautiful Aboriginal woman. Alas, it was unrequited. She loved a mortal man. As the beloveds escaped in a canoe along the Iguazu River, the enraged god severed the stream and condemned them to an eternal fall.

Gazing at the 275 two-step waterfalls cascading in misty white streams, I can't help but think that the lovers won. Fall they do, forever plunging deeper in love. The everlasting love of their evanescent lives thunders with silky tears that spray my sunburned skin. It beckons a trust in the mighty flow.

There's a reason for every season.
When life ebbs, go with the flow.

"When people travel for extended periods of time, there's always a reason. Why are you here?"

I peer at the bubbly British chick and shrug with intended nonchalance. Why does it matter? I don't owe the world an explanation.

I try to ignore the question, but it reverberates between the deafening percussion of plummeting water on Iguazu's Brazilian side. Portuguese dances like a ballerina seducing her Romeo on metallic catwalks that overlook hundreds of watery curtains. Twinkling as they tumble, the falls don't answer to anyone or anything. They move without apology. For a while I push a middle-aged, Australian man around on his wheelchair. We have fun dodging lizards and opossums until I venture into the subtropical rainforest alone.

Following my feet, I find myself in a bird park. Inside massive enclosures with flamingos frolicking beside shiny mirrors, I cannot avoid the question. Why am I here? Am I running? Meandering past palm trees and ferns with no fence separating me from exotic birds of vivid colour, I'm lost in thought. So much so, I'm certain the toucan beside me is a simulated sculpture with a blow-up beak. I look around, expecting a cheeky-grinned local to emerge holding a remote control. Instead, the bird looks at me, croaks, and flies away. Later, a purple-crested jay examines me with all-knowing, yellow eyes. Just as I think it might speak to me like the taunting macaws, it leaps towards a butterfly and devours the winged insect with one massive gulp. As it digests the omen of transformation, I ruminate on how the trip has changed me.

In 100 percent humidity, we continue north to Bonito. Amid green fields rimmed by terracotta-toned earth, herds of cows block the road as whip-cracking cowboys wink through the window. The hostel pool takes the edge off 45°C heat, where I release my emotions into the liquid body.

Wisdom seeps into every fibre of my flesh while I float. Suspended by water with the world on mute, I stay there for a long time. Sometimes I sink to the bottom of the pool and hover as long as my breath allows. It's quiet there. It's soothing. As the world moves and morphs inside me, I see that being stretched is how we expand.

From the adjacent bathroom, a man sings "Three Little Birds". His voice is deep and lyrical. It swims through the ceiling cracks and dances in the steam eddying from both our showers. I bask in Bob Marley's lyrics for a moment then find the courage to sing along. For a moment, he falters, then his voice harmonises with mine. We are two strangers, naked in adjoining showers. Unable to see each other yet connected through song.

The music echoes in my bones as I swing in a hammock and mosquitos feast on my skin. Back and forth, I question where to settle in 2013. All my belongings are in Queensland, but without Jacob, do I want to stay there? Left to right. East to west. The answers undulate in the hammock's sway.

❦

The next morning, I sit at a bench, half journalling, half gazing at Portuguese-dubbed Simpsons on TV. Homer's stupid antics disappear from focus when Rebecca's tiny hands embrace me from behind. I feel her heaviness before I hear her sad sniffle. Lack of sleep, sticky humidity, and constant delays compound her in a thick tangle. I hold her as she sobs, then attend to her despairing word jumble. Much of the group judge her jagged moods. She can be prickly, but I empathise with the distress of her need for stability being unmet.

I listen as she explains the different stages of her illness, without invalidating her emotions. I try to make her laugh then reassure it will roll over like a wave. An hour later, she still sweats with quivering sobs. I'm lost for moves. It's getting more intense. Then I spot Bran and pull him over. He directs me to grab a frozen bottle from the kitchen and places it behind Rebecca's neck.

"Icy water on the base of the neck lowers blood pressure and gives a shock value," he reasons.

Rebecca takes a gasping inhale.

"This will stop you hyperventilating and calm you."

As he talks her down from her heightened state, her breath deepens and slows. Eventually, colour returns to her face and her eyes flicker with light.

That night, we find a traditional rodeo afterparty in a rusty barn. Live music blasts as cowboys square-dance and bootylicious locals twerk on all fours. In a tipsy blur, the others leave. Rebecca and I balance a stumbling Bran between us as we walk home. Locals survey us, two petite foreigners carrying a short, intoxicated man. I scan the streets with eyes paralysing potential threats to rubble. In his intoxication, Bran admits a former two-year heroin addiction that prompted him to leave the UK.

Midway through our walk home, a car approaches and slows. Bran uncoils himself from our arms and bolts down a side street, yelling that "they're after me". Rebecca and I search for him to no avail. Eventually, we find him cowering behind a bench and balance him between us again. A few steps farther, he stops in his tracks and gives me a sobering look.

"Jess, you are wise beyond your years, because you are strong beyond your years."

His articulation is crystal clear. Then he continues mumbling about British drugs. Maybe I am. Maybe I had no other choice but to make portals from potholes. What's the point in staying stagnant when we're given opportunities to flow?

We expand by being stretched.
We stretch by departing our comfort zone.
We vacate our comfort zone by farewelling what we know.

Smack back in the heart of continental South America, Brazil's Pantanal springs to life from a landlocked river delta. The world's largest interior wetland is an ecological paradise homing thousands of species in open marshes that annually flood with torrential rains. As we zoom along desolate dirt tracks in a four-wheel drive, I spot a bird perched on a capybara—the world's largest rodent—as it maunders across murky waters. The two unlikely pals reveal that nature functions best uninterrupted with humans simply observing its natural flow.

Nature has always been my greatest teacher. Everything has a season. Everything has a reason. The beauty in simplicity is profound. Just when we think we've found solid ground, the earth shifts and shakes, revealing deeper layers. Beneath earthquakes and landslides, massive tectonic plates reveal what's stronger and more substantial. We're reminded of the many situations we cannot control yet encouraged to keep on growing.

The next day, we canoe across waterlily-brimming streams. As my awareness undulates with the timeless mirror, I sense there's more beneath the surface. The beady eyes and broad snouts of caiman alligators camouflage in ripples that wrinkle the reflection of trees. Later, on a floating raft, the others lure them out with bait and fish for piranhas while Rebecca sits with me and chatters.

"Do you believe in soul mates?" she asks.

Gazing into the water, I nod. A comfortable silence ensues.

Then she whispers, "I think we have many."

The notion has me blink and tilt my head. "I've not thought about it like that before. Makes sense, though."

Some connections are fleeting. Others are retreating or repeating. It's the ones that stay we should treasure as sacred.

A three-day, two-night voyage steers us away from the Americas' highest concentration of wildlife to the ocean. Forward movement comes with card games, upbeat playlists, and boundless introspection. Away for 100 days, I reflect on the belongings I packed into the tiny blue suitcase that I left with. Over time, the contents changed. So did the bag. My attitudes and opinions have evolved. Some remain as glaring as my favourite red tights, but most are worn, torn, thrown, or disowned.

In the silent space of my heart, I find home. It is on this three-day journey I decide to move back to Perth. No longer do I feel homesick for places I've never been. I long for the land I ran from.

Peace washes upon my heart as we pull into the halcyon bay of Paraty, cradled by lofty, jungled mountains. Monkeys scream from distant canopy. Men strut in hot pants. Women parade in G-strings like catwalk models. As the sun melts behind pop-up beach bars overlooking tropical islands, live music merges with the warm evening breeze.

Cruising through the island-studded horizon the next day, I absorb the sun's toasty kisses and shove seaweed down my bikini bottoms to crack up my friends. Rain sprinkles in patchy increments as we swim in private coves. Then we cruise back to the hip harbour. A pungent fishy aroma wafts through uneven cobblestone streets connecting picturesque colonial homes. I notice the sidewalks elevated a foot above the streets. Supposedly the below-sea-level town is cleaned every full moon with high-tide floods that leave watermarks of the ocean's perpetual motion.

Following a tiny hand-drawn map given to us by a local, we bump along a narrow rainforest trail to—well, we don't really know. Based on his wide eyes and grand hand gestures, we're in for a treat.

Emerging from palm trees, a wobbly suspension bridge leads to a massive rock trickling with water. Locals hike to the top, then slide down the smooth, algae-covered boulder. We follow suit. Climbing up, then sliding down, the cool pools offer a refreshing thrill.

As the shadows of trees grow, I follow a stream trickling away from the torrents of people playing. Around a bend, I sit on a mossy rock and watch the rivulet glide towards me, grateful for the journey leading me here. Then I face the other way, watching the water flow onward. It is unwavering and unafraid. Jacob once said that prayer is like meditation. Both render a sense of peace and connect us to a higher power. Where the former entails us reaching out, the latter requires us opening to be reached. I never really understood what he meant, but I get it now. As I tap into the divine, I let the divine tap into me. Asking for my life to be

forever guided,
Help me help the world, I pray.

☙

After piling into the truck one last time, we watch narrow streets with salty zephyrs congest into polluted city highways. Churches perch on distant hills. Brazilian men beam from droning trucks. We stop-start through peak hour into Rio de Janeiro. Forward movement comes with acceleration, then brake, just like life. Amid six lanes of traffic, Bran wipes sweat from his brow. Locals seem unphased by the sluggish flow. In fact, they embrace it.

There's a question I sometimes ask: if you could live in the mountains, forest, city, or sea, which would you choose, and why? Often, people combine two options. Sometimes three. With Rio, you've got it all. Perhaps that's why the cinematic city is the most visited in the southern hemisphere. Forested mountains roll into the city then protrude from the sea like fertile breasts and pregnant bellies. Golden beaches kiss shimmering seas dotted with sunbakers, and African-influenced samba infuses passion into compact streets.

As my days in South America trickle into hours, the mental grime of returning home strains me with the unknown. I shake it off on a dance floor until the time comes for me to hail a taxi and go.

A short flight brings me to Sao Paulo, followed by a long flight to Johannesburg. Feigning sleep on my fourteen-hour layover, I nap on a different chair every hour, often passing a huge billboard with an African proverb: *If you want to go fast, go alone. If you want to go far, go together.*

I integrate the words on my flight to Perth. I embarked solo, but I've never truly been alone. We always meet people along the way. Amid the endless stream of faces, eventually I looked within and met myself. I know now that changing locations won't erase my problems. I now grasp that I've been running for so long, I forgot what I was running from. It is in this moment I feel a switch. I'm no longer travelling to find myself. I'm travelling to create myself.

Descending into Perth, I gaze at vast coastal suburbia. The questions I left with are answered, but in those answers, new questions open. They roll into the city on salty zephyrs from the sparkling sea.

What comes next? What am I creating?

☙

If you think there's more, there's more.

Two days later, my excitement dwindles as I stroll past coastal mansions. The once-familiar city feels foreign. I don't understand the mammoth houses or why society is absorbed by consumer-driven greed. There's so much space. I don't understand the fear of impoverished people from war-laden countries finding asylum on our rich shores. I feel distant from social norms. I even feel shame in calling myself Australian. I can't help but wonder if ignorance and arrogance have always been the standard, and I'm noticing now because I've changed.

Plodding loudly to keep snakes at bay, I take an overgrown shortcut through the bush. I don't stop walking until I reach the rocky groyne. The sun sets in a peach pastel dream. Wistfully, I yearn for the horizon, where daylight stirs hope into a stranger's morning.

Christmas jingles in at my grandparents' two-storey home with explosive Christmas crackers and strategic water fights. Dogs bark. Young cousins squeal. Barbequed vegetables sizzle. Solar lights illuminate a tall pine in the front yard, and we canoe across the river in graceful slithers. Amid games of UNO backdropped by the cricket playing on TV, a friend texts and asks what I got for Christmas. *The presence of family*, I reply.

Most of all, I enjoy hanging out with my sister, Emily, who is pregnant with her second child. We watch her oldest daughter peering at the world with untainted blue eyes. Not yet corrupted by consumerism, she shares her smile with all. I learn much from the way she interacts with the world. Pushing the bottle away when she's had enough, she isn't afraid to show her emotions. Every moment is new and exciting. Basking in her imagination, she lives with her heart open and is unafraid of change.

Several times a year, the Moore River's water level reaches a height to break the sandbar and discharge into the ocean. On Christmas night, the warm blue river creeps towards the cool turquoise sea. Papa and I are curious to break the thin sandbar, so we embark on a midnight walk to the brackish estuary and dig a shallow path. An innocent rivulet runs towards the ocean. Then it becomes a churning channel ripping sand from banks. By morning, the bar widens to a gaping twenty-metre chasm.

When Grandad discovers that we disrupted the river's natural cycle, his gentle brown eyes storm. He fumes that if the sandbar is broken in the wrong place, thousands of litres of surging water can permanently sweep the beach away. We apologize with downcast eyes. Though the beach is okay, I realise we can't force a process before it's ripe and ready. We must be attuned to life's currents and willing to flow.

Integrating into western society is challenging after such a soul-stirring journey. In the last days of 2012, Charlie insists on a night-time beach adventure. This helps consolidate my transformation. Sprawled on soft, sandy shores, we watch waves oscillate from the horizon. Birds fly in motion to my gliding thoughts as the moon hums a gentle tune. Through it I drift, floating in an eternal daydream.

Between adoring glances at Charlie's dark curls and perfect button nose, I realise that life isn't about finding the right pieces. Nor is it about crushing and contorting chunks into unattainable expectation to fit certain moulds. Life is about staying open and trusting that the pieces will appear when and where they're meant to. It's a receptivity rather than a pursuit.

True flow is understanding that the world is in constant motion. What's right for us in one moment may switch in the next. In letting go of old pieces that have taught their lesson, sung their song, I create space for the new. Life is changing. The pieces are rearranging. I am exchanging outdated beliefs for new dreams.

As midnight approaches, we swim topless in the moonlight. Moon dust trickles through Charlie's veins, shimmering with a tenacity I always knew was in her. Finally, she sees it too. It's the first time I return feeling that everything and everyone has changed. It is refreshing and delightful.

As we walk home across the carpark, we pass a father and son from Syria. They both wear green T-shirts. Trauma brims in the tragic ocean of their wide-eyed alertness. My heart jerks with empathy when they say they arrived in Australia today. Just the two of them. I don't dare ask if they left family behind. After friendly small talk, we leave them staring sightlessly into the inky ocean. Charlie and I are walking away from our dark pasts, but for them, the horizon is sinister and foreboding.

Just before New Year's Eve, I reunite with Laula. We last saw each other at my twenty-first birthday. She embodies her usual earthy elegance, but there is something different about her essence. She seems lighter, somehow. Laula chatters about some recent plant medicine ceremonies with San Pedro and ayahuasca. I'm curious, as is she, about my time in South America. We stay up late fusing our creative juices into collaborative poetry and dancing to the Red Hot Chili Peppers' funky beats. We are both seeing the band in different cities in the coming weeks.

Laula suggests we wrap poetry around tennis balls and throw them onstage.

NYE rolls in at a Carnival-themed house party. Amid the merry stream, an old friend pulls me aside and exclaims, "You're so vibrant, Jess. Like you've found yourself at your core. You're actually glowing!"

"Oh, thank you, darling. That must be because I'm around you!"

Though her words are genuine, the attention is overwhelming. I hope she'll change the subject, but instead she continues.

"I'm inspired to travel after seeing the change in you."

At the afterparty, I watch the first rays of 2013 rise from a massive trampoline. Ready to face the year with passion in my heart, power over my mind and a cleansed soul, I later realise the potency of that intention.

In a retro nightclub, my girlfriend wraps rhythm around her body in a sensual sway. I've always adored her infectious moves. Ruby-red heels enhance her toned legs that write poetry on the dance floor as she flings her brunette mane. I'm lost in the music, absorbed in the moment, captured by her body speaking in artful arcs. Then the two Syrians sweep to mind. Suddenly I feel sticky and heavy. I can't shake the pained look in their eyes.

En route home, I chitter-chatter with our Lebanese taxi driver. I ask his opinion on what's happening in the Middle East.

"You want to know *my* opinion?"

"Yes, please. If you are open to sharing."

The man smiles like a distant relative gives an unexpected gift. He replies, "We all have the same God. Enough is enough. Muslim, Jewish, Christian: One God. Up there. We don't need anyone trying to rule the world down here. It's not about justice or welfare. It's about the oil!"

I'm one shot and three rums in, but his response sobers me.

On my street, I thank him for driving us home.

He smiles then gives another chunk of truth. "The world was made without borders. It is greed that's made it this way."

The soul hums in quiet hues. Listen.

With half my life in Queensland, the time comes to collect it in mid-January. Before leaving, I apply for a job with Australia's largest travel retailer. I'm certain I'll be successful. I'm wrong. My travel escapades don't matter. They're more concerned about my sales experience, or lack thereof. The rejection turns out to be a disguised blessing, an ironic one at that. Instead, I get a job fundraising for different charities. Meanwhile, two friends working for Flight Centre regularly seek advice based on my on-ground expertise.

Hours after the job rejection, I Skype Jacob. He is DJing on a cruise ship while I'm in town. This smooths my transition, until he suggests I move back to Queensland. When Blair seconds the notion, I find myself back on the pendulum of belonging to more than one place.

In my old beachside home, Happy greets me with loud pants and a wagging tail. It looks like Jacob hasn't bathed her in months, so I scrub her trembling body with soapy water, feeling my mental grime clear as my fingers run through her matted fur. Before my mind can sway, I pack. Jacob has half-boxed some of my things, and it hits me that while I left to wander, he was left to wonder, with all our memories lingering.

With seven small boxes bound for Perth, I drive south in Jacob's Subaru to meet Blair and her ADHD-energetic friend, Jack, in the Gold Coast. We have tickets to Big Day Out, headlined by the Red Hot Chili Peppers. En route, I drive through Brisbane, where Jacob's ship docks for the afternoon. Traffic chugs and moans around me as I crawl through putrid exhaust fumes, looking for a *Port Side Wharf* sign.

When signs for the Gold Coast appear amongst massive billboards, I realise I've driven too far. Without GPS navigation on my phone, I call Jacob and declare it's too chaotic to meet. He asks where I am. I don't know. The engine whines with salty corrosion. Sirens wail in my periphery. Jacob takes a deep breath, then directs me to him using his own phone as navigation.

By the time I arrive, we have just ten minutes together. His teary eyes and tight hug tell me he still cares for me. In my heart, I know it's over. And yet, my chest expands with the tender nectar of romance gone, before crystalizing with a cool stoicism. While Jacob sails into the cerulean horizon, I drive to Surfers Paradise where Blair and Jack await.

In a high-rise hotel room, I wrap handwritten poetry around six tennis balls and share my plan. Blair shrugs it off. Jack listens with jaw ajar. Then he chimes in with another idea. We are going to sneak backstage. His enthusiasm ignites my own as we waltz into the festival with optimism and daring. Midafternoon, Jack leads me to a small stage backing onto a two-metre fence. Beneath it is a gap we can slide under. It will be dark and empty here during the Chili Pepper's encores. This is our entry backstage.

The day blurs with pumping bass and dreamy dance mixed with scantily clad girls and shirtless muscleheads fuelled with testosterone. When Chad, Flea, Anthony, and Josh take the stage, a fire sparks in my veins. As they crank up the crowd with funky melodies, Jack piggybacks me on his shoulders, and I throw five tennis balls towards the stage. As each one dissolves into the sea of bopping people, I see the foolishness in my plan. When the encores come, I motion to Jack. This is our cue to go.

He steps towards me. Then he falters.

"Let's just see what the next song will be," he drawls.

The crowd sways like a unified ocean. I want to be part of it. So badly, I want to be a molecule in this enlivened sea. But I can't sink in. I cannot surrender. I am inundated by a calling to go as "I Could Have Lied" rolls through the speakers. I kiss Blair's cheek. She doesn't want to come. Then I grab Jack's hand and lead him to the back of the crowd where people taper. Invisible zephyrs guide me to the dark, empty stage. At the fence, Jack and I stand in silence. We share a knowing look then roll under.

On the other side, we pause to gather our bearings. I expect to be caught and escorted out, but there is no one around to notice. Forty metres away, a dozen demountable buildings perch beside the bridge off stage. We're about to dash towards them when four finishing-their-shift crew emerge and linger by the structures.

Jack pierces me with striking blue eyes and whispers, "Kiss me."

Behind his head, the workers sing their goodbyes and disperse.

"No, we can't miss this. We've got to go."

I grab his hand and run to a dark space between two buildings. There, I reach into my bag for the last tennis ball, wrapped with lacy yellow lingerie. The music stops. Flea hollers gratitude to the crowd. Without knowing why, I tear off the panties and write my name on the ball.

"Walk like you're meant to be here...no one will question otherwise," Jack instructs.

This time, he leads. I follow him straight into the floodlights where heat plummets like a midsummer sun. A few metres away, a tall figure strides towards a white van. He is escorted by a security guard.

"There's Chad," Jack whispers. Then he shifts focus to a short, purple-haired man. "Oh my God... It's *Flea!*"

I freeze. Suddenly the absurdity of our actions become clear.

"Give me the ball."

It takes me a moment to process what Jack says. I'm comprehending Chad leaving and Flea sliding into another white van where something delays his departure. Through squinted eyes, I see him unclip a microphone from his shirt.

"What? It won't—" *work*...

I don't finish. Jack snatches the ball and throws it inside the van with a bold whizz. A microsecond later, the door slams and the van drives away. Jack and I look at each other, gaping. Mission successful—I guess? We melt into a heartfelt hug, then slide under the fence to the diffusing crowd where Blair awaits.

In the days that follow, we float through the Sunshine Coast's canals on a blow-up boat. Jack raves about his perfect aim to anyone who will listen. I do too. The miniscule chance of the ball sliding inside the van as the door shuts seem inconceivable. Yet it happened. I daydream of meeting Flea and apologizing for what he likely perceived as a small grenade. In retrospect, I see a boundary was crossed and hope no one was hurt by the balls.

༈

Back in Perth, I start my fundraising job at the airport. It's challenging to shift between midnight-ending and four-a.m.-starting shifts while staying upbeat and respectful of jetlag-induced moods, but I love it. Inspiring people into monthly charity donations makes me feel that I'm doing something good for the world. Finally.

As the band continues their Australian tour, I buy a ticket to Perth's Big Day Out to see them again. Meanwhile, I hop on Twitter and tweet Flea, explaining why the tennis ball mysteriously appeared beside him. I don't think he will actually read it, let alone reply. But he does. His "thank you" sits in my inbox for weeks before I discover it. When I do, he's un-followed me, and I am unable to respond.

At Perth's Big Day Out, I stand on a brick ledge at the back of the crowd with a girlfriend when the band takes the stage. She was enthused about the mission when sunshine dripped down her crown like liquid gold, but her passion fades as the encores sound. I stride to the high chain-link fence alone.

My jaw drops as I search for a way through. The positioning of one fence ending slightly in front of the other creates a tiny-person-sized gap. It is invisible. Unless you seek it.

Squeezing through, I take a deep inhale. A passer-by spots me and calls for his friends to follow.

"Hey! Jack, Lach...that chick just snuck backstage!"

His friends' single-minded focus on something renders me invisible.

"What, cunt? *Where?*"

"Right *there!*"

I adjust my posture to a confident stance and begin my navigation of the demountable building maze without looking back.

"Oi, fellas, let's sneak in too!"

I've approached the third demountable when the dude lets it go and continues walking with his mates.

From the stage, applause erupts as the Chili Peppers play their final song. I've timed it wrong. I'm early. They still have to finish up and give their thanks. Dazzled that I've once again walked through undetected, I perch beneath a tree and call Jack.

After explaining the situation, I ask, "What do I do?"

His spirited chatter calms. In a low tone, he directs, "Stay there. Keep on doing what you're doing. Call me after!"

After we hang up, I text a guy I'm dating the same question. As the band finishes playing, I glide up an asphalt path the four white vans will take to depart the festival. Two security guards watch me from a ledge above. I fake a phone call asking when a "friend's shift ends" and "give them my location". As I finish, a text dings: *Have sex with Anthony Kiedis.*

A few seconds later, two eyes rest upon me. Through the open window of a crawling white van, a dark-haired man with a thick moustache examines me. Only, he doesn't look at me. He looks in me. I meet his gaze with equal intensity and fall into his strength, vulnerability, determination, and pain. In his steady eyes is a moment of unguarded human connection. It is timeless and tranquil, yet it penetrates me with a magnetic blaze.

Then a thought bubbles: *That's Anthony Kiedis!*

In an instant, the sincerity of the moment bursts for I'm no longer seeing him through an untainted lens. I'm seeing his famed projection. Anthony must feel the shift from innocence to hunger because he motions for his driver to move on, leaving unspoken words to linger like winter mist.

Thirty seconds later, a short man with purple hair approaches me with a security guard. My heart lunges from my chest. It's Flea.

His electric-blue eyes emit a quiet confidence like lightning in a summer sky. His infectious gap-toothed smile dissipates my unease. Opportunity opens yet another window for me to applaud his compelling musicianship or at least give a high-five. But I am shy and star-struck and divert eye contact to an inanimate object behind his head. He walks on by.

Eventually I plod back into the festival and realise that opportunities don't seize themselves. It's up to us to claim them. When we're in flow with the universe, it pulls us where we need to be, but we must never discard our oars.

Life's perpetual unravelling is what makes it so damn beautiful. For once a moment has passed, it will never be again.

*You're not shedding a skin,
it's the illusion being stripped.*

February is a blur of unpacking boxes and acing my new job. Sipping coffee as vivid hues enlighten the hilly horizon, I chat with strangers leaving home, returning home, finding home. I am moved by people's philanthropy as the art of conversation generates thousands of dollars to charity.

Friends keep noting that my year away altered me. I haven't changed, not in essence. I've simply shed the faux facades. My sensitivity and bravery are innate, I just didn't want to show them. Approaching the moonlit Zig Zag to dig up my nearly three-year-old time capsule, I realise authenticity is refreshing.

Shovel in hand, I pass two photographers capturing the moonlit cityscape.

Thud. Scrape. Clang.

I dig for an hour. Beneath sturdy garden gloves, my hands blister.

Clank. Thump. Thwack.

There is no sign of the cylindrical tin. With a heavy sigh, I exhale the idea of digging up my past. Maybe it's meant to remain entombed.

As I leave, I explain myself to the photographers.

They chuckle. "We thought you might be digging up a dead body."

A text from Charlie entices me to a 1920s-themed party where we stay up all night. As dawn dissolves the darkness, I find myself back at the red quarry with three mates. Dressed in Gatsby-era suits, the boys scale a boulder that shadows my small hole. Persuading me to join, they watch the city wake. I love adventures, especially ones involving climbing, but I can't see a safe way back down, so I decline and continue digging. Eventually the boys descend the rock. At least, they try. With no ledges to steady their feet, jumping is the only option.

Two boys rustle down and land with a pitter-patter.

Then *a swish, thud,* "OWWWWWWWW" cuts through the air.

I turn to my mate blinking tears in an agonized heap. We later discover that he's broken two bones in his ankle. I fling the shovel aside and start carrying him to my car. One of the guys runs to help me. The other continues digging. A few strides in, a yell has me pause and swivel.

"Jesssssssss"

"Yeah?"

"I found it!"

He hands me the rusted coffee tin at my car. Later, I read the ink-blotted letters. It's disconcerting to peer into my past and observe the stormy undercurrents that once ruled me. My scribbled words encompass me with mute resonance, but something is missing. A deeper part of me is still embedded by the rich red earth, waiting to be discovered.

―

At the beginning of March, my boss notices me pouring my heart into every interaction and invites me on a five-week fundraising road trip through remote mining towns in the Pilbara.

Before packing my life back into a backpack, I meet Deseree at a holistic bookstore café. Since Antarctica, I've been sharing snippets of my writing online. She resonates with my words. One of Deseree's friends, Alyssa, organises monthly networking events to motivate Perth women. Each event hosts three speakers—for mind, body, and soul. Deseree invites me to be the soul speaker at the next event, occurring three days after my return.

Before my "Fuck yes!" bubbles, a whirlwind of fear clouds me with doubt. Uplifting others with words that infuse spirituality with passion is a path I want to take. The opportunity awaits me on a silver platter, but something holds me back. I soon discern that it's my own limiting beliefs. Deseree believes in me. Alyssa believes in me. And so, I silence the niggly voices in my psyche and give my word to be there.

Two days before my departure, my sister births her second daughter. My newborn niece's innocent coos melt my heart as I spread my wings and leave Perth in a campervan with two other girls. Scottish Paighton naps in the back while English Karen and I navigate an isolated highway into the dry red earth of the resource-rich Pilbara. On Karen's stints, I gulp water and brainstorm my "soul" talk. After two days, we pull into Newman, a small town beside the world's largest iron-ore mine. I have a rough draft ready.

With a night to rest before our first thirteen-hour day, we meet our other teammate, Mags—a bubbly Kiwi with shimmering blue eyes—at a caravan park. We fundraise as a pair in the following weeks, alternating between airports and local shopping centres. I relish her worldly insights and peaceful heart. It is a blessing amidst a high-energy month. While Karen and Paighton drink at the pub after work, Mags and I chat under the stars in fold-out camping chairs. I later realise she plants keys to awareness and self-development in my fertile mind. They shimmer gold but remain underground, waiting for me to unearth the right doors.

"Excuse me," I call out to the worker lumbering past in a hi-vis yellow shirt.

The man spins around, wiping sweat from his brow. Different charities frequent the shopping centre each week. I understand that he, like many others, just wants to purchase groceries after a strenuous day. But I also believe in what I'm doing.

I hold out a small teddy bear wearing a yellow charity shirt and feign a confused expression. "You dropped this."

The man looks from me to the teddy then back again. He's unable to restrain the corners of his mouth upturning.

"Ya got me." He chuckles with a subtle wink, then eyes the banner behind my head.

"I donate to these guys already, good on'ya, love. Thanks for makin' mi smile."

I nod and grin, as another worker edges into my peripheral. He approaches on Mags's side. He is hers to pitch to.

Soon a sunburned man plods towards me.

I hold the teddy out again, and joke, "Look, it's your mini me! You're cuter though..."

The man ignores me and continues walking. Then, registering what I've said, he turns around and guffaws with twinkling eyes. Cocking his head to the side, he reads the charity banner.

"I'm here to inspire you into your philanthropic nature via small, monthly charity donations," I explain.

After signing him up, he leaves the table with a skip in his step. This is what I find most rewarding—seeing people's demeanour shift by transforming privilege into benevolence.

Two minutes later, another man cruises towards me. I hold out the teddy, then throw it to him. As he receives it, I sing, "Now that the catch is over, let me tell you why I'm here..."

The man chuckles and tosses the teddy back. Then he motions to the grocery store and rubs his belly.

"Just here for some tucker."

I smile and let him be, concealing a small yawn. Maintaining vigour is tiring, but I am energized by infusing joy into people's day.

On our last day in Newman, Mags inspires a charismatic Indigenous man to donate, after a compelling conversation about the potency of Western Australia's land. I am curious to the noninvasive way Mags engages with people and the language she uses. After the encounter, she uses the term "original people" lightly in conversation. I ask her what she means.

"Well," she begins. "What does *abnormal* mean?"

"Not normal?"

"Exactly. So, if abnormal means not normal. And Aboriginal Australians are the oldest continuing culture in our world today—the original people of this land—why did the English coin the term Aboriginal?"

She pauses for a moment to let the statement simmer.

"It's a subtle language twist to distort the true meaning."

I ponder her words as we drive to Karijini National Park for our one day off before another seventy-hour workweek. Although "Aboriginal" stems from the Latin word "ab" which means "beginning" or "origin", I follow her logic and feel an amalgamation of anger, compassion, and despair at the ongoing oppression of Aboriginal and Torres Strait Islanders.

Driving along the Warlu Way Trail, Mags speaks of an Aboriginal Dreamtime legend in which a sea serpent emerged from the Ningaloo Reef. As it slithered inland, the serpent carved crevices, creeks, and waterholes. From the flat, dusty plains our lonely highway meanders, a mountainous horizon soars. Excitement energizes us all as we park up beside iconic red chasms and go walkabout through some of Earth's oldest geological formations.

Clambering over natural terraced staircases leading to cool freshwater pools, I awe at the network of ancient rocks towering over sheer ravines in chunky stacks. After lying on a warm, weathered rock decorated with intricate swirls, I dangle my feet in an emerald pool and imagine First Nations tribes mapping the land with dance, song, and Dreamtime stories of creation. Everything and everyone has something to teach. Wisdom is at the heart of all things, for wisdom is in the heart of all things. I wish my schooling promoted more cultural inclusion. I wish our government wasn't the only Commonwealth nation to never sign a treaty with its First Nations people. I wish that Australia, like Germany, faced up to the attempted genocide of the 1905 Act so that institutional racism and the ongoing oppression from colonisation can be healed at its roots. I don't believe we can create a strong national identity and move towards a reconciled future if we haven't yet faced up to our past.

Mags and I chat about it as we drive to Karratha. Off a coast that was illegally possessed under the lie of "terra nullius", cashed-up bogans play on expensive boats and jet skis. Over the week, I bump into a few old friends. Mags notes the synchronicities unravelling around me.

"When we bump into people," she says, "often it's 'cause we're embodying a similar energy. Sometimes they have a message for us. Other times, we have one for them. Either way, it's a sign you're on the right path."

En route to collect the girls that evening, we watch the sun set behind a three-kilometre train that hauls hundreds of carriages brimming with iron ore. Thousands of tonnes of precious Australian earth chugs past, bound for a boat to China. It saddens me that neither country truly understands the potency of the land. Economically, maybe. Spiritually, no.

At the shopping centre, Karen and Paighton meet us with excited eyes. They've befriended some locals who've invited us to spend the week on their handmade houseboat in Dampier, a pretty port town nearby. Each night after our shared dinner, I work on my speech on the upstairs deck as twilight blushes like a soulful hearth. Then the ocean rocks us to sleep in our wooden bunks. The salty sway is rejuvenating between dynamic days.

On our next day off, we drive to tranquil Point Samson. Our long shifts plus the hours I put into my presentation reduce me to red eyes and tightened nerves, so I join Karen and Paighton at the pub. My tension uncoils as I sip on alcoholic elixirs and watch Karen zip around pool tables making friends. When the pub closes, we wind up at an afterparty on a fishing boat reeking of seaweed. The night is blurry. It gives me the release I need.

In the morning, cool saltwater rejuvenates us all. The others continue drinking. I refrain. I also neglect drinking sufficient water, so when we arrive at my friend's house in South Hedland that evening, my head throbs and I'm drenched in sweat. The others work. I stay in bed for two days. My body has reached its threshold, forcing me to slow down, rest, and be.

When I return to work, I am three kilos lighter but ready to kick ass. Jazzy and juiced, it is my most focused fundraising fortnight yet. Mags often speaks of the potency of attention when grounded with intention. I'm curious about the notion and try it on our final day. As the music store pumps Red Hot Chili Peppers, I set an intention to inspire ten individuals to donate enough money to cover monthly transportation for remote cancer patients to receive treatment. To my amazement, it works, to the dollar, and we finish the month with spirits high.

Before we doll up to celebrate, I read my speech to the girls. They are dewy-eyed and silent. My veins buzz to speak so authentically. And be heard. I still feel invigorated as we meander along the shimmering cerulean coast to the glassy waters of Turquoise Bay. That night we camp on blow-up mattresses beneath a labyrinth of stars that appear as tiny twinkling pinpricks on an inky canvas. The ocean swooshes in salty serenades, and I thank each shooting star for the wishes they bestow.

Move with life's currents, don't fight the flow.

Rain drizzles from stormy skies as I sprint down a slippery Perth footpath. Mama navigated peak hour's stop-start rhythm for twenty minutes before I jumped out of her car. As I bounce into the venue, Alyssa introduces herself and hands me a glass of champagne. Attached to the stem is an elegant tag that reads *Invigorate*. Women chitchat while I eye the chairs facing a microphone and projector screen. On the surface I am calm. Beneath my skin, my cells whir with electricity.

I ground myself by making small talk with a nearby lady.

She talks of the other two speakers, then says, "I haven't met the soul speaker, yet..."

"Oh, that's me," I chime, relishing the air of mystery.

In the front row, I sit between Mama and Mags, chewing my lip as the speaker to "inspire our minds" delivers her message that ends with an elaborate sales pitch.

In a brief intermission, I duck to the bathroom. In an ornate full-length mirror, I scan my peach beach dress and flip-flops, feeling underdressed. Brushing back my long brunette mane, I peer into my hazel eyes, giving myself strength to leave the dimly lit bathroom.

You've got this, Jess.

Back in the venue, a confident Columbian lady begins the journey of "energizing our bodies" by positioning us in a power pose. As the minutes tick, I feel the urge to pee again and expect another short break as Alyssa takes the mic.

"We're running a bit overtime, so I invite our next speaker, Jessica Sierra, to come up and invigorate our souls."

My heart gallops.

Mags smiles and reassures, "Just be you."

Tucking my hair behind my ear, I take the stage and instinctively slip off my flip-flops. I'm about to shed my soul. There's no other way to do it than barefoot and soaked in rain. My larynx contracts with emotion. Using palm-sized cue cards, I begin.

"Depression is a disease of loneliness affecting more than 300 million people worldwide. Once upon a time, I was one of those people..."

Five minutes in, tears started falling. Not mine. A lady in the front row. Steadying my breath, I slow my pace and talk of my attempted suicide. My body caved from the downfall of my mind. But my soul held on.

"Rain is all the pain we cannot let go of, all the tears our souls cry, falling upon us to remind us we're alive. And doesn't it feel invigorating to be drenched by rain!" I laugh, running my fingers through my damp hair.

"The soul gives life to our body and inspiration to our minds. When we separate body from spirit, we end up a corpse. Even if still breathing. Creativity is our soul's expression. Intuition is the language. Our eyes are the window. So, smile often. Smile at strangers. Smile with your eyes. Let your expression linger in a stranger's soul, if not for a nanosecond, for a lifetime."

Suddenly my tone, pacing, and sharing my presence equally with the dewy-eyed crowd dissolves into the focal point of the moment where I stand before the projector screen—raw, real, me. Time and space melt into a radiant tapestry that wraps me in a technicoloured spell as I conclude.

"The light isn't at the end of the tunnel. It is within."

The room applauds as I slide into my shoes and sit down next to Mags. At the end of the night, I am approached by several women. Some thank me for my brave sharing. One seeks advice for her daughter who is suffering with mental health. Then a radiant brunette requests to meet for coffee and discuss where I want to go with my words.

That weekend, I celebrate my twenty-second birthday. The next day, Mags and I leave Perth to fundraise in Kalgoorlie for a week. Once a notorious hotspot for brothels and skimpies, the Wild West town perches beside the world's largest open-cut gold mine.

On our first day, a kind Maori bloke offers us his place while he spends the week in Perth. At night, we feed his dog and two cats. By day, Mags's cheeky laugh is music to my ears as we inspire strangers into their charitable benevolence.

Back in Perth, the brunette lady from my soul speech invites me to public speaking events around the city. "You could go far with this, Jess. I can see you doing a TED talk."

At our next meetup, Louise connects me to a public speaking coach. They are the first two people I tell of my plans to write this book. The coach proclaims I can finish it in three months if I wish. I laugh. Even before I know that the real story is yet to come, I know it deserves more than a lets-smash-this-out-fast approach. I'm in it for the long haul.

As autumn leaves crunch up the footpaths, I fly to Queensland to surprise

Blair for her thirtieth birthday. Straight off my red-eye flight, Jacob meets me for breakfast on Mooloolaba's lively Esplanade. I push avocado around my plate as he asks if our sexual dynamic was destructive or awakening. The ocean rolls in a glassy swell of cerulean. I don't answer. I'm yet to peer into the past's reflective pools. From above, it seems like waves continuously crash forward, but undercurrents simultaneously draw the water back into itself, allowing it to become one again.

Jacob drops me at Jack's place, where I hide in a big cardboard box and jump out at Blair with a "Surprise!" It is a beautiful week reuniting with old friends and connecting back to the Pacific Ocean. Salty zephyrs kiss my cheeks. The moon sheds a silver trail back to South America.

Beneath a billion glittering stars—on the same beach I once wandered, wondering what was on the other side—I float in the cool, winter waves as the world mutes to a monotone buzz. With just the sound of my heart pumping, my thoughts dissolve into the very water keeping me suspended. All this time I've been seeking home outside of myself. All this time, it's been within me in my own beating chest.

As the ocean washes away my footprints in a choreographed flow in tune with my emotions, I see that the answers are in my willingness to surrender, immerse, and feel. In a language that transcends words, I finally understand what the ocean always knew: we must live into the answers.

PART II

AFTER

Chapter VI
REBIRTH

Lately you've been
living in your dreams
and dreaming wide awake.
Dissolving deep into dreamland:
the land of lucidity greets you with
infinite possibility of what the
computer in your cranium
can consciously create.
The abstract astral awakens
on the other side of your conscious mind.
As your ego slips into slumber
subconscious reflections
reveal the remedy.
You remember
who you are
where you came from
and what you came to do.
"I believe that we can do this.
I believe we can do this, so we will."
We all have this power;
awake and asleep.
It's all a dream.

You're just awake in this one.

Friday 19th July 2013 - Lesley Myburgh's magical garden, Peru

The harmonic jingle of metal chimes beckons me to open my eyes. Ripping the blanket cocoon off my face, I blink in the light and examine the garden. It contains eight empty mattresses and a lone man meditating besides a cluster of San Pedro cacti. Serenity ripples through my cells in oozy waves.

The golden nectar of sunshine bestows me with warmth. Dazzled by the bold glow, I feel myself behind my eyes, observing my own awareness. Just as I ponder getting up to explore, a hummingbird shoots across the garden. In its beak it carries the corner of a blank page. I don't see this. I feel it. It is all-encompassing as it places me on an empty stage with the innate knowing that my fate is mine to create from hereon.

I stare at my dainty piano fingers as though recognising them for the first time. Gratitude undulates through me with buoyant elation. I want to find Laula and thank her for instigating such a soulful journey. Wrapping the blanket around my back, I straighten my crumpled wings and transform from caterpillar into butterfly. My spirit expands beyond the stratosphere.

In the archway between the two gardens, Laula appears beaming, as though magnetised to my heart's call.

"Jessica, you're up!"

The golden flakes in her protruding chartreuse eyes shimmer like nebulae exploding with starry wisdom. She looks into me like she's already witnessed the moment unravel in totality yet allows it to organically unfold. She sees me. She sees all of me, peeling back the layers until only my true essence remains. The epiphany that she always has, and always will, bursts my heart open with resplendent rays.

Free from mental chatter, I discover infinity in her irises. Her presence grounds me deeper into the moment as silence eddies into a reciprocal transference of emotion. I breathe in the fresh alpine air. The inhalation fills my chest but doesn't reach my belly. Instead, the instinctual part of me that wants to maintain control by understanding all the variables pipes in.

"What time is it, Laula?"

As the words tumble from my mouth, each syllable shatters our tranquillity like clock hands clacking into the stillness of not knowing.

Laula's hesitant shrug signals for me to let it go. But I'm curious to how long we've been journeying and continue peering at her doe-eyed, like she has all the answers.

She looks at the clear blue sky and focuses on the sun.

"Two o'clock?" she guesses, with an upward inflection.

"It's been three hours?"

"Yeah, babe. The journey's still going...we're still in it."

She delivers the message in a graceful tone that rekindles a timeless space. Then she excuses herself into the garden fronting Lesley's home with an enigmatic smile.

I look down and become enchanted by a shallow pond filled with convoluted seashells. Her words echo into oscillating ripples from insects dancing on the glassy surface. The journey is still going. There's more to learn and discern.

My tranced exploration of the garden halts on a lone yellow flower. Lesley mentioned it's common to purge and welcomed us to vomit in the flowerbeds. It all gets recycled back into the Earth, she said. I heard people retching while in my cocoon. Suddenly, my stomach feels like a cement mixer groaning from stirring the same old shit. The nausea is heavy, but I cannot vomit on cue. Lesley also noted it is sometimes difficult to purge. My default pattern of repressing emotions stagnates energy-in-motion within me. This prohibits release. Lesley and Gui have a tea to settle the stomach. Therein, a new dilemma arises: speaking my needs.

Plants brush my arms as I meander along the winding path to the other garden. Lesley stated we get more from the medicine if we don't converse because silence allows a deeper plunge into our internal terrain. My muscles relax with this knowing, but I also feel raw with my masks, layers, and stories crumbling. For so long, they've been my armour. Only now do I see that a warrior's strength is in vulnerability, for we are free from protective layers defending the ego's delicate skin.

From a shaded porch fronting Lesley's home, I hear laughter and spot Laula, Lesley, Gui, and the Canadians lounging around a wooden coffee table. The hostel's receptionist sits on a couch beaming. She slices gooey columns of cacti into small chunks. I join the circle with a quiet "Hey" as conversation bounces around me. Music carries a downtempo beat. I zone out on a melodic cascade as one of Lesley's huskies rests her head on my knee. Sweeping my fingers through her fur, I am soothed by the silky tactility of my hand's repetitive motion. I tune back into the conversation as Lesley describes the day the dogs accidentally drank San Pedro. Now they regularly lap it up. I wonder if this is why their lucid eyes are so deep.

A sweet, intoxicating aroma interrupts my thoughts as Gui emerges with a platter of fruit. I didn't even register that he left. Riley straightens from the couch and licks his lips. I plonk a grape in my mouth, savouring the syrupy juices as it melts into a zesty fusion. My stomach momentarily settles with each crisp bite until only the oozing green flesh of kiwi remains. Riley eyes my leftovers, so I scoop them into his bowl. He thanks me with a smile that births butterflies and stirs up my nausea. I open my mouth to verbalize my need to purge, then promptly shut it when no words come.

Feeling like a fish out of water in my inability to ask for what I want without feeling like a burden, I glance at Lesley. She is resplendent, even in the shade. I wish she'd read my mind and spontaneously offer tea. Suddenly I notice a lump in my throat. It grows with my awareness. I try to dislodge it by swallowing it down, but my fruity saliva thickens the phlegmy build-up.

With a quiet *"Ahem,"* I attempt to nudge it down my oesophagus, but it solidifies in position, stubborn to move. My insides flip, endeavouring to turn a page and write a new way of being, but unable to digest new words until I purge my musty tales.

Just ask for the tea, Jess. Then you can go and be with yourself again.

I open my mouth, this time determined. "Hey, Lesley, do you have any of that tea?"

My torso softens as she extends her hand to two teapots on the table. "Of course. Do you want berry or green?"

"Which is the one that helps you throw up?"

"Oh. I'll get Gui to make you some now."

Her empathetic smile unveils a belief I created long ago that I'm the only one I can count on and asking for help makes me weak. Gui leaves and returns with a ceramic cup filled with steaming liquid. I blow into the potion and drink. Each sip dissipates the sticky build-up in my gut. For a moment my insides are still. Then my stomach lurches, and I excuse myself with a faint, "Thank you."

Down the stone path I walk, quickening my pace once out of sight. By the entrance to the property is a small house with a bathroom. My butt cheeks have barely touched the toilet when a stream of diarrhoea surges. Relief at last.

As I wash my hands and look in the mirror, my stomach continues to gurgle. My skin appears pale but twitchy, like dozens of microcosmic worms squirm beneath my pores, motioning for me to peer beneath the surface. My scrutiny ceases in my hazel irises as my reflection becomes a window into the past and a gateway to the future. I see the tormented teen I once was. I see the wise woman I am becoming. Beneath long lashes, my almond-shaped eyes swirl with warm honey, rimmed with a blue circle that contains the story of my life and all that is yet to come. The dazzle of welling tears illuminates my fearlessness and fragility as my soul pierces through illusions like a diamond blade.

    With the door closed, I crumble. Yet, in that moment, I realise it is no weakness to let myself fall. Sinking into my sensitivity and letting it encompass me is what makes me strong. I blink back the struggle of keeping it together. I allow the first tear to drip. Released from the cage of holding it all in, I see the pain of an innocent girl being caught up in the affections of the wrong man. The tiny drop becomes a warm, salty stream. My stomach knots with memory lane playing out like a strange array of Polaroid pictures showing me snapshots of my past. Each photo portrays me from the age of sixteen, saying yes to sex when my soul screamed no. Beliefs that I long ago buried are being uprooted and challenged for their validity. Am I worthless, or is it just a repeated thought that's festered into a toxic belief I've kept hidden from the entire world, including myself, until this moment of discovery?

    I feel the density of sadness and shame I've unknowingly carried with me for years, and for the first time, I see my trauma for what it is: not mine to hold on to. The truth paralyses me. My tears become a rejuvenating waterfall in tropical heat. For my sexual healing to begin, I must transcend the idea that I'm worthless and learn to love myself again. I lean into the bathroom sink as my insides come up in vile chunks of acidic residue. For a moment it is still. Then comes another surge, and the stench of stomach acid pervades.

    Clusters of unhealthy thoughts unravel and upheave, no longer poisoning my perception by cementing my psyche with lies. A foul taste evades my mouth. Yet, I feel clear. The importance of inner journeying flashes like lightning zigzagging through an inky night. In one month, I will step onto my seventh continent, but this experience, where I am right now, is pivotal to the evolution of my soul.

To evolve we first dissolve.
Disappearing into the darkness,
we discover the doorway to a new world;
an inevitable evolution into the light.

Across from Lesley's home, a big grassy hill covers two ancient caves that contain the Incan Temple of the Moon. Clouds roll in fluffy wisps as Gui leads us there through the valley. I walk close as he divulges his former life as a gaunt zombie addicted to heroin. His triceps bulge, but not in a king-of-the-jungle, gym-meathead way. It's a healthy expression of wellness and vitality. He's so gracious, so deeply embodied in peace, it's hard to imagine his before. Huachuma showed him the root cause of his addiction. This empowered him to change.

His authenticity warms me as I unclasp my hands inside my alpaca-wool sweater. A crisp mountain breeze sweeps through golden wheat fields. With it are melodic zephyrs of ancestral songs that breathe the world into creation. I become mesmerised by the grandiose grey mountains rising on the horizon, witnessing me amid eons of evolution before my birth. With each step, my legs connect with the earth like moving trees.

Standing on a bulging rock leading into the caves, I am the entire universe experiencing itself. Timeless, in my tiny human form. Bound by no mental chatter containing egotistical inflammation or limiting beliefs, I am fully present with the multifaceted macrocosm playing out around me. Each inhalation contains vital life force that circulates within my cells. Each exhale releases what I do not need. Through rhythmic breathing, I generate profound internal vitality. Appreciation ripples as millions of seeds scatter into my being that connect me with every heart of every human, every cell in every organism, and every particle in every star. Every atom in my anatomy vibrates with unconditional love and enthusiasm for life that somewhere along the way I've lost or forgotten.

Inside the cave, I wrap my striped blanket around me. My eyes adjust to a darkness that dissolves my shadow and enhances sunlight trickling through contrived cracks in the ceiling. A dozen figures stand silhouetted. I scan the cave for Laula's slender physique. With a flashlight, Gui forges a luminous pathway from finely carved altars in the walls to a rock-carved archaic throne. Beside it a set of stairs leads deeper into the cave. In his French-American accent, Gui explains the Spanish never found the temple. This is why the incredible stone masonry remains intact.

In single file, we amble down the steps to a small hole at the subsequent cave's entrance. One by one, the others press their ears to the hollow and awe before stepping through. I wonder what Earth whispers. When my turn comes, a mellifluous whistle coils into my ear from a vertical flute stemming in her core.

The second cave is smaller, with sunrays striking a flat rock where the Canadian guys sit silhouetted. Their seat is an ancient altar where mummies once lay. On certain nights, moonlight pours onto the altar, giving the temple its name. Free from hordes of rushed tourists and temporal entrance fees, the sanctity remains. The others must feel it too, because a reverent silence eddies between us.

A mix of emotions brews as I close my eyes and brush my fingers over the cool, concave walls. The sensation renders a vision behind my eyes of Spaniards galloping horses through mountain valleys—looking for gold, looking for glory. I feel the devastation from the Spanish invasion compress inside the hollow. Its poignancy swirls, softening me with compassion until I feel the urge to leave.

After emerging from the temple, I sit with myself atop the grassy mound. Arid summits backdrop the panoramic valley with amplified hues of terracotta, olive, and saffron. I see the mountains as sentient beings, whistling from jagged slopes and murmuring in subtle undercurrents of the breeze. It is Earth's unyielding peace, patience, and perseverance that shaped the striking sierra. I am humbled and honoured to be a tiny speck of consciousness in the grander scheme.

As warming rays subside, I drift back to Lesley's home. Cauliflower clouds drift overhead. At the bottom of the hill, a guy hugs a tall tree. Dark cornrows cover his hazelnut cheeks, but through a gap I see his eyes closed in meditation. His admiration for nature makes me smile as I wander back to the teepee where this all began.

In the circular structure, I reflect on my tendency to repress my emotions because the potency scares me. Instead of being radiantly expressed, I've suppressed who I am at my deepest level. This causes me to contract into my fears instead of expanding into love—into my full potential. I wonder if the others are experiencing similar epiphanies. I get an inkling they understand concepts I'm yet to embody. Riley, in particular, is a mystery. There's an enigmatic intensity to him that's sparked my curiosity. I'm musing on the knowing look that he and Laula shared en route here when something rustles by the door. It's him.

Scanning the room, he asks, "Do you mind if I join you?"

"Not at all." I grin and pass him a cushion.

I contemplate conversation but have no idea what to say.

Perhaps Riley's psychic antennas hear my inner dialogue, because he reassures, "It's nice when you can sit with someone in comfortable silence."

My breath slows as I turn my attention to the chimes. Sporadic winds rustle a soothing melodic symphony. Then it echoes into a stillness that feels like home. It is here I realise that the space between the chimes is the stillness between our thoughts. It's always there. We can return to it at any time.

Tuning in to a part of myself that is deeper than the mind's constant chatter, I become aware of my own awareness. I have thoughts about my thoughts, feelings about my feelings, and beliefs about my beliefs. With this realisation, I become the architect of my life. Until this point, subconscious beliefs ruled the content and foundation of my mind. With my new awareness, I can reroute the path I'm walking by rewiring neural pathways firing in my brain. Creating new thoughts will break my I'm-a-victim-of-this-depressive-spell-with-no-control-to-change-it cycle. In the space between the chimes, I decide I no longer want to wallow in self-pity and rely on antidepressants. I want to fuel happiness from within.

I excuse myself from the teepee and run up the stairs of Lesley's mountain retreat to scribble the insight on paper. Four empty beds occupy the room. I switch on a gas heater to warm my shivering body then rummage in my bag for a pen. That's when Trey appears by the door.

"Oh, hey," he drawls in a dreamy tone, meandering towards me.

I wish he had the same courtesy as Riley to ask if I want company before entering. I'm in an introverted space and want to collect my thoughts before they drift away. Inwardly, I groan. But I sense the innocence in his ignorance as his eyes grow at the heater's fiery orange rectangles. Ceasing my search, I make room for him to hunker beside me. We soon get talking about the boys' journey through the Amazon, where they are going next, and the different places that I've called home. My world map tights are an effective visual prompt to trace our movements around the globe.

"So, after Peru, you guys are going back to Canada?" I ask.

The heater hums while it toasts our hands. I feel cradled by the world while acutely grounded in my body.

"Yeah, we're back to Calgs next week..."

"*Calgs?*"

"Calgary." Trey motions to a city between the west coast and central Canada.

"Oh, cool."

"Yeah, it'll be summer, nice and warm. Then we head to Shambhala!"

I cock my head to the side. "Where?"

Trey's face lights up as he talks of the transformational music festival nestled in the forested mountains of British Columbia. Pressing his fingers into my knee, he maps the location and rants about a funky spaceship stage set in an old-growth forest. He suggests I come. I'm tempted. The Canadians are cool guys, but it's the same weekend as a San Francisco festival headlined by the Red Hot Chili Peppers. I'm not missing it.

"Maybe next year," I proclaim light-heartedly.

"After Shambhala, we're going to Kelowna for a week," Trey describes, sliding his finger north-west. "There's a massive lake. It's super chill."

I raise an eyebrow. "*Car-loan-ah?*"

"*Kel-own-a!*"

His accent makes me giggle. "Cool, maybe I'll come visit..."

In retrospect, my intention of figuring out where I'm meant to be is salient in the conversation.

I leave Trey contemplating by the heater, hoping he'll have the sense to turn it off when he leaves. Outside, I cushion myself into a chair swing idling beside the teepee. Riley also spots the vacant seat and is en route towards it before I sit down.

We swing in silence. I like the ease between us. I wish we could bask in it longer, but the others mosey into the garden and gather around us to watch daylight fade into the sun-streaked sky. As the almost-full moon rises, Lesley appears. She invites me into the teepee alone.

The medicine is waning, but I feel buoyant and present to her love. She asks about my journey, nodding slowly as I share my mental breakthroughs. When I'm finished, she reaches into her shrine for a heart-shaped crystal.

Cradling my hands in her soft palms, she says, "Green represents the heart. Yours is healing." Then she slides the jade between my fingers.

The crystal is cool and smooth. I keep it close for years to come.

"Have you heard of Dr Emoto and his experiments with water crystals?" Lesley queries.

"No…"

"Dr Emoto is a Japanese researcher who has done *incredible* studies on the effect different words and prayers have on the molecular structure of water."

A light breeze rustles through the teepee.

She continues, "Examining different compositions and shapes under microscopic photography, the results speak for themselves."

I lean forward.

"Water stamped with 'I love you' or 'Thank you' produces *beautiful*, symmetrical crystals. Negative phrases like 'You make me sick, I will kill you' quite literally distorts the crystals."

She pauses.

I intuit the importance of her next words.

"We are sixty percent water. The words we speak are so important. Our self-talk creates beliefs about ourselves and can change the structure of water molecules inside of us. If there's *one thing* I want you to take away from this conversation, it's this…"

She waits until I meet her eyes.

"Every day, you must look at yourself in the mirror and tell yourself you are beautiful, strong, and full of light."

I nod and exhale, realising that I've been holding my breath.

"How are you feeling about your antidepressants?"

"I don't know if I need them anymore. Life is…beautiful."

The words are as bracing as my Antarctic dip.

"You are cured of depression." She smiles. "Your heart is open now."

I sense a "but" coming.

"But…"

There it is.

"...if you stop taking them, you must do so slowly and with medical supervision. Your body has grown accustomed to them after seven years."

My stomach recoils as my lanky GP flashes to mind. I've never felt safe or seen by him. He's methodical and stony. There's no way in hell I'm letting him in on my plan.

"Take your antidepressant as usual tomorrow, then see how you go. If you still feel you want to go off them in a couple of months, taper your dosage gradually. With support from family and friends."

"Okay." I smile. "Thank you."

Lesley examines me with iridescent sapphire eyes. "The bad days will still come... Let them. Sit with the feelings. Acknowledge them. Allow yourself to feel."

I absorb her words as she clarifies, "It's a three-step process: acknowledge, feel, release. Let it come, so you can let it go."

"Okay."

"Sometimes it might take a whole day before you feel ready to release the feelings. But the power is within you to do so. It always has been."

Love has no limits.
Boundless.
Timeless.
Infinite.
Free.

As stars stream the sky, Gui calls taxis for everyone but Laula and me with prior arrangements to stay the night. Trey and Riley ruminate with Ben and Conner about also sleeping in the mountain retreat, but only two beds are spare. They linger until finally deciding to leave together. Drifting into a restful sleep, I feel their intrigue in gentle waves of deep contemplation.   Over breakfast, I gulp my antidepressant with steaming black coffee and share my plan to taper off the pills. Laula notes it'll be a big change after seven years. I nod. But I am absolute in my decision.

Eyes sensitive with fresh insight, I adjust to the brightness of day as we navigate dusty streets to the hostel. A thought bubbles to complain that I've forgotten my sunglasses, but I recognise it as a negative notion I wish to break free from. With heightened awareness, I find gratitude instead. I'm alive and free, walking through Cuzco's hills with my dear friend after a life-changing journey. This conscious switch calms me, even when we take a wrong turn that extends our walk by an hour.

Back at the hostel, my newfound positivity lulls to discover the four Canadians moved to a different hostel. Just fifteen minutes ago. Had we caught a taxi, left earlier, walked faster, or not gotten lost we wouldn't have missed them by mere minutes. While Laula naps with the afternoon sun, I journal on the second-storey balcony outside our new room and ponder if we'll ever see them again. I glance over the stone wall below with every passer-by, hoping it's the guys returning. I felt such a cordial connection with them. Surely our story has more pages to fill! My torso momentarily heats with an anger disguising the sadness that it's out of my control if we ever see them again. Then, a deeper awareness beckons me to detach from my desires and surrender to the unravelling.

As soon as I let it go, a knock comes from the wooden gate. I peer over the balcony and glimpse four heads. It's them.

"Hola," I sing, amazed at the timing.

"Yo!" Conner calls in a low tone.

I bounce down the stairs and open the gate, beaming. Apparently, Trey left a single shoe, so all four returned and sought our whereabouts from reception. I wonder if his forgetfulness is purposeful. When I ask many years later, he says, "No, I genuinely forgot it...but we were always going to meet again."

That night, the six of us laze in the annex's moonlit courtyard. While travelling Peru, Laula and I cowrite poetry then record the "raps". Amid chitchat, I spontaneously share one that we uploaded to YouTube. I'm passionate and zany. Laula's a gnarly gangster. It's hilarious and raw, and I'm pleased that the guys find us insightful and funny. From there on, I'm unafraid to express my quirk, wit, and sensitivity. This creates a sturdy foundation for connection to effortlessly deepen.

Nearing midnight, Trey suggests we get coca leaf brownies from a local store. Three heads slowly pivot, followed by a dramatic pause.

Ten seconds later, Conner concurs in an unhurried tone, "Yeah, bro, that sounds like the go."

Three more head turns.

Another reflective pause.

Twenty minutes later, after more head pivots and gazes into the horizon, we move. Later, Laula and I write a poem about it.

With moist chocolate decadence salivating our mouths, we make a plan to meet in the morning and venture to Pachamama, a music festival in the Sacred Valley. Then we hug good night.

The galaxies in your eyes tell a story that never ends.

I awake refreshed from a dream where Riley kisses me. I share the vision with Laula as we stroll to Cuzco's main plaza to meet the boys. Traffic fumes blend with Spanish lingo, and Peruvian flags dangle in creases of red and white. Luxuriating beside a bed of yellow flowers, we record a rap while we wait. Half an hour after we planned to meet, the four Canadians dawdle over, and we taxi to the bus station. Three silver soles buy a fifty-minute bus ride to Pisac. I slide into a window seat, joined by Riley, who first asks permission to sit beside me. I love that he does that.

On a bumpy bitumen-sealed road, I curl my hair around my finger and proclaim, "I have a confession."

A humble yet confident smile curves. "I think I already know."

I look at him deadpan. *Did Huachuma give you the power to read minds?*

Riley straightens a crease on his pants. "At least, I think I do..."

"Oh."

"What's your confession?"

"I had a dream about you last night," I coo.

He cocks his head to the side. "Oh. I didn't know *that...*"

I examine the stubble on his well-defined jaw. *What do you know then?*

He catches my eye. "What was your dream about?"

"It's a secret," I breathe.

His face warms as we veer conversation elsewhere. When we pull into sunny Pisac, I pause by the open bus door. Looking directly into his green eyes, I purr, "I had a dream you kissed me."

I glimpse him smile as I leap out the door. We exchange knowing looks between bustling market stalls selling ceramics and alpaca-wool clothing, then venture into the untamed wilderness surrounding the charming colonial village. Following the winding path of the Urubamba River in the direction a festivalgoer gives in town, we maunder along dirt trails dominated by mountains. With ears alert for cut-up melodies layered over complex timbral sounds, the first hour is silent. I link arms with Laula, noticing the boys' slow amble. The pace frustrates me. Occasionally we stop, allowing them to inch closer as summits shadow us with late-afternoon sun.

We feel the electronic *wub-wub* coursing through the valley before spotting people hula-hooping and dancing under psychedelic shade cloths. Beneath a tree decorated with funky ornaments, we watch as an African drum circle morphs into tribal beats and bohemian-dressed women start belly dancing. I watch in fascination of their confident self-expression. Being in environments where it is customary to move free from judgement becomes a catalyst for me to shake away my rigid conditioning and let my true essence shine. It is a slow and steady journey, but it is evolution nonetheless.

Eventually we roam the other stages in twilight, leaving the rapid gallops of psytrance in favour of melodies interwoven with slower riffs. The four boys awe at the full moon radiating into the valley. Laula prances between festivalgoers, making friends. Later in the night, she approaches me in hysterics and informs, "Some guy just offered me cocaine or LCD."

I burst into laughter. "LCD! Did you ask if he has 110-inch?"

"No." She chuckles. "I should have."

As Laula plays with poi balls, a ticking clock in the back of my mind inches towards an alarm signifying the last bus home. When the six of us finally gather and navigate the pitch-black countryside, I already know we've missed it. Nonetheless, we pierce into the darkness, guided by a vague recollection of the way we strolled in. Laula notes a eucalyptus smell rippling from a dense patch of trees. Twelve feet crunch over a loose gravel track. Then a dozen vicious barks snap into the abyss.

Packs of wild dogs are common in South America, but my previous encounters have always been within the bounds of city streets. I face the others with one eyebrow raised. The barks echo into our thoughts. Retreating isn't an option. We must push forward. Without words, I pull my shoulders back and focus on the love inside my heart as I march forward. In my peripheral, a dozen stray dogs linger beside a ramshackle stone building. The potential of ripped flesh being infected with rabies becomes palpable as we edge closer and they hungrily stare us down.

"Don't let them smell your fear," I instruct. "They're going to let us through."

Carrying the feeling that we'll cruise past unscathed, I stride on. A few metres ahead stands a low stone wall. One by one, we step over. Relief floods us on the other side.

Soon the streetlights of Pisac shine upon us, and we face our next hurdle: we've missed the last bus back to Cuzco. My instincts were right. The guys throw around ideas. Taxi? Too expensive. Hitching a ride? Too dark. And there are six of us. Retreat to the festival? Not with those dogs. We're out of options when a white van slows beside us. Behind the wheel, a local man enquires, "Cuzco?"

"South American time" is a term reflecting the rarely punctual culture that happily moves at a slower pace. When you've got somewhere to be, it's annoying. In that moment, the lateness is a godsend.

Back in Cuzco, we huff up steep cobblestone stairs to the boy's hostel. While the others lounge in a cushioned booth, I cartwheel across dewy grass and count the seconds of my handstands. Riley lingers nearby, intense green eyes upon me.

Eventually I walk over and meet his gaze. Without warning, he steps forward and kisses me. A moment later, Ben approaches. Riley and I jump apart. A nervous giggle escapes me as he passes. Then the others appear, with an exhausted Laula beckoning me to Casa de la Gringa, across town.

Two days later, Trey and Riley book a room beside ours while Ben and Conner trek to Machu Picchu. Though the attraction with Riley is palpable, nothing else happens, but I do commit to meeting them in Kelowna after Shambhala next month. San Pedro helped me realise that my warped beliefs have collapsed intimacy into a mere physical act. In my mirrored reflection, on our last night with the guys, I promise myself I will break the cycle.

The four of us are smoking weed through an apple bong when Laula clips an infrared qi-light in her nose to ease altitude sickness and congestion. The device turns her into Rudolph with a bright-red light that has us all in stitches. We talk metaphysics and philosophy and eat good food.

When bedtime comes, I ponder asking Laula to bunk in a room with Trey so I can hang with Riley, but I refrain. Deep down I know I must sleep alone to unlock the handcuffs binding me to the same traumatic sexual scenarios. It will be a long time before I'm intimate with another. I feel it when I sing good night to the guys and snuggle into the warmth of my own body on that cold Cuzco night.

Before the guys leave Cuzco, they continue a poem Laula and I began. For years after, Riley's green scribble echoes in my mind. *You are beautiful and perfect and in control.* Amongst the seeding, feeding, and weeding of my inner garden, his words fertilise empowering beliefs.

᎒

A week later, Laula buses back to Lima with me where we whisper tender goodbyes. On a rainy street corner, I peer into the profundity of her cosmic green eyes and discover hidden worlds. I relish that she catalysed such deep transformation. Without her, the journey might've never unravelled.

In the airport-bound taxi, I catch my reflection in the window. There is something in my gaze that could cut glass. It is soulful yet sharp. It tells me that this is just the beginning.

Chapter VII
THE SEVENTH CONTINENT

Australia revealed that the world was made without borders.

In Africa I realised interdependence is better than independence.

Antarctica taught me that Earth is our collective common ground;

it's all of our responsibility to help heal our planet.

Asia illustrated that the power is in the people.

South America showed me how to live;

how to give; how to forgive.

North America taught me how to love and how to let go.

Europe revealed that history always repeats,

unless we change that cycle.

If we can consciously co-create a human narrative

that unifies, empowers and loves...

we can rewrite our ending.

We can change the world.

Are you crazy enough to know that we can?

Wednesday 31st July 2013

North America is the last continent I meet with a soft yet purposeful stride. Merging into different cultures with wide-eyed perception is my norm. Feeling foreign is familiar. The unknown is what I know, and it enlivens every cell. For it is in this space that anything is possible. In a city where no one knows your name, you can be anyone.

As the captain announces our descent into sunny Los Angeles, I gaze upon congested freeways connecting crammed gridiron neighbourhoods on a hilly coastal plain. A murky smog taints the city with gritty filth. I taste it as I trek past honking and humming traffic leaving LAX. It permeates my cascading sweat.

Outside the terminal, a bus screeches to a stop. I hold out a fresh twenty to the stout driver. Her nostrils flare. I glance from my money to her knitted-together brows.

She snaps, "It's *one* dollar. We *don't* give change. The next bus comes in twenty minutes."

My stomach contracts as I blink at her scowling from me to the door. Perhaps it's a line she repeats frequently at this stop. I understand her frustration. But the first local interaction imprints assumptions of a nation's people. I wonder if everyone's attitude stinks like a blocked sewer in 100 percent humidity.

A lady from Panama overhears the commotion and covers my ticket as we cram inside. I feel like a waste of space with my bulging backpack as I squeeze myself into awkward compressions every time the door jolts open and a concoction of hot rubber, spilt motor oil, and crisped fries waft in.

An hour passes. The bus slowly empties. I scan the inner-city streets for signs of Santa Monica. Time ticks on. Eventually the drivers change, and I realise I've missed my stop. The new driver directs me to other buses bound for the coast, and a Lebanese shop owner converts my twenty-dollar bill to smaller notes. One taxi, two flights, and three buses later, I check into a multistorey hostel in the heart of Santa Monica.

Late-afternoon sun streams through the window as I plonk my bag into a steel locker between two wooden bunk beds. After bouncing down the stairs, I breeze out the building and take a burning inhale. I observe the aesthetic of the palm-lined streets. Then I do a 180 and saunter towards the ocean, where I sink my feet into soft sandy shores. A warm breeze ruffles blonde strands free as the world's largest ocean breathes blessings unto the land. I gaze into the horizon and think of my loved ones back home. In an instant, my nervous system calms. Sometimes I wonder if they can feel me loving them from afar; if the wind is nuanced with all the words unsaid.

Facing the iconic Californian palms swaying in golden hour's rays, I whisper to myself, in slight disbelief, "You did it, Jess. You're here. You've made it to the seventh continent."

*

Santa Monica is perfect to ease into the fusion of diversity that is L.A. The charismatic city is expensive and expansive. Contoured from desert, mountains, and valleys, it brims with an optimism so rich it becomes lonely. From its coastal edge, I can breathe.

Winding along a sandy footpath on a hired bike, I feel invincible with winds eliciting possibility. I soak in the monumental pier from afar, relishing the tourist-bustling scene without somatic overload. Ahead, tanned beach volleyballers spike and dive. Behind, a shrill metal scrape comes from a carpark with hefty fees. To my right, the vegetated mountains of Malibu roll towards the ocean. With legs on automatic, I turn this way and cycle.

My mind is free to daydream as tyres meet the path and carry me forward. To my dismay, the beachside bike trail ends at a quiet waterfront before the wealthy city. It is a psycho-geographical barrier imposing exclusivity from that point forth. Sitting cross-legged atop a circular picnic table, I smear avocado onto rice crackers then sprinkle salt from a sachet I pocketed on the plane. Earlier in the day, a friend emailed to say that she feels me in the glitter of the sea. Gazing into the vivid hues of the ocean's rolling shimmer, I assimilate that I'm never really alone.

After lunch, I glide under the pier's silhouetted wooden beams to Venice Beach. The paved boardwalk is buzzing with freak shows and free spirits moving to an amalgamation of music merging with the salty breeze. It is an interactive circus liberated with eclectic expression. It enthrals me. A grey-haired pianist flits his fingers along a grand piano set up in the middle of the street. Then I'm bopping my head to rock-and-roll riffs from an electric guitar. A few pedals later, a T-shirt shop pumping funky reggae competes with the acoustic serenades of bright-eyed buskers. Skaters leave whiffs of marijuana in their trail. Artists unveil their imagination in acrylic shapes. This raw and all-encompassing stream of creativity activates the streets, and unlike Malibu, I'm *included* in the hustle. If Venice is the birthplace of art—the passionate heartbeat of individuality—Malibu is where you go when you've "made it". Somewhere along the way, charm and soul get stripped away. Cardiac pulsations stale to mundanity.

My glamourous expectation of Hollywood detonates as I lug my backpack and a paper bag filled with food down the boulevard. Once again, I miss my bus stop. Once again, it's an American immigrant who helps me. He spots me wiping sweat from my brow and offers a ride to my hostel. Usually, I'd decline. He's a stranger. I enjoy getting my bearings while walking. But it's sticky hot and I'm weighed down by my I-was-too-hungry-to-sensibly-shop-for-just-two-days groceries.

I'm jaded by the faded streets desperate to stay relevant with adverts rotating on giant screens and neon lights flashing at every corner. Every gutter and alley reeks of a commodified thirst to suck money from polluted air. It's like God plonked a paintbrush inside a hexed tin of consumerism, then ditched the brush and kicked the can to saturate the greedy varnish all over town.

I know it's dangerous to get into the car. I've seen *Taken*. But I bank on my ability to grab someone's attention on the pedestrian-swarming streets should I need. The man retains a straight-to-the-point Russian-style communication, and I'm grateful for my fake wedding ring. Convincing him my beloved awaits me doesn't stop him from insisting we meet later. When he asks for my number, I lie that I've forgotten it. In truth, I'm travelling without a phone. But he doesn't need to know that. Since San Pedro, I'm learning to trust the world, but my safety nets remain securely tied.

Like a vexed adolescent etching curses into wet cement, my time in Hollywood chisels the challenges of travelling alone as a woman. Later that evening, I zip to a nearby convenience store to buy wine. Skipping back to the hostel that boasts free live views of movie premieres at the Kodak Theatre across the road, I scan the names inside five-pointed, coral-pink terrazzo stars embedded in the sidewalk. I'm finally sinking into Hollywood's vibe, when a man behind me bellows, "Your ass is out of this world!"

His verbal explosion has me shrivel inside my baggy grey T-shirt and world-map tights. For him there are no consequences. He walks on. I'm tight-lipped as I focus on the brass-blocked letters inside the stars again. Four "immortalised" names later, another voice barks, "I've been there, and there, and there...but I haven't been *there* yet."

At the red light of a pedestrian crossing, four lanes of traffic roar. My heart pounds like a war drum. My back and shoulders tense as he continues hollering sleazy remarks. It boils my blood to molten lava. I ponder gracefully letting it go as the traffic lights tick, but the inferno inside me sizzles with a blue flame. Slowly and purposely, I turn and look straight into the scrawny guy smirking behind me.

It's been forty years since women's rights movements sought equal opportunities and greater personal freedom. Four long decades, and we still have a way to go. I, like many women, am no stranger to the nauseating shivers induced from uninvited leers, ogles, and utterances from men. Unwanted sexual attention is sickening. It pains me that some men are so oblivious to the effects.

Without words, I project poison into his eyes. His jaw drops. He even steps back. Then the little man in the box flashes green. I stride on, knowing he doesn't dare follow. I am free from his lewd presence hovering like a horsefly persistent to pierce my skin.

Back at the hostel, I swish the encounter away with a swig of wine. It seems to work. But not really. Deep down, it fuses with every other sexual harassment and embeds the notions that I am not safe, this patriarchal world is untrustworthy, and men value my physique but not my psyche.

Talk to fill your spirit, not the silence.

I meet my roommates after smudging the dorm with palo santo. The sweet-pine-and-mint-liquorice odour diffuses from the windowsill. On my thin, bottom-bunk mattress, I hunch over my laptop and copy diary entries into Word documents so I can post journals home and lighten the load I carry. It is cathartic on an emotional level too. Humming air conditioners and wailing sirens become background noise to my tapping fingers. Laptop keys unlock something within. It is the inception of writing this book by gathering raw material from blog posts, iPhone Notes, and sentiments scribbled on paper pages. It is the first of many days I sacrifice my adventurous spirit for the discipline needed to pour my heart into these words. I'm here for hours. My neck is strained and shoulders tense, when the door squeals open and a beautiful Brazilian lady says hello.

We bond over her enjoyment of the uplifting fragrance stemming from the continent where she was born. Not long after, an attractive Austrian chick breezes in and joins our conversation. My search for authenticity is quenched in the profundity of our conversation. I'm sick of being asked the same five questions by every new person I meet: *Where are you from? Where have you been? Where are you going? How long are you travelling for? What do you do back home?* When I began travelling, sharing the where and why was invigorating. As the journey continued, the novelty waned. I desire depths not everyone is comfortable to dive, let alone on first meetings. Post Peru, an enigmatic exploration of spiritual ideals and expanded awareness becomes my comfort zone. It is refreshing to skip small talk and satiate my need for connection and meaning.

Tipsy from wine, we skip and slide along Hollywood's smooth terrazzo pavement. The surge of sightseers dwindles with the night. This increases visibility of the street's stars. Inside a classy bar, I chat with a man from San Francisco, picking his mind to what I'll find in the golden city. I get the inkling Northern California has a different vibe. When I enquire to the differences, my new friend simply smiles and asserts, "You'll see."

The first thing I notice is the weather. Outside the Hilton Hotel, a crisp midnight draft seeps under my layers as I stride through the empty Financial District. It's eerie. Alert for sudden movements, I zoom in on my Google Maps photograph and scan street signs. Beneath the moon's tiny slither, I monitor my shadow. Two blocks from the contained safety awaiting me at my hostel, a man with tattered clothes slumps over a trolley laden with his processions. A vacant look occupies his eyes. Though he doesn't penetrate my sphere with an uninvited gaze or pestering words, I am confronted. Not by his presence. It's the situation.

In Australia, homelessness is less seen and less known. If you're sick, you get free medical care. If you can't work, you get unemployment benefits. Countries poorer than the USA uphold a similar social security. It's not about affluence. It's about ideals. To witness this firsthand, alone, on a squalid midnight street, is goddamn confronting.

In my final year of high school, my quirky media teacher showed us an image illustrating the wealth gap. The rich feasted in skyscrapers while the majority are malnourished on the street. Behind me are towering corporate skyscrapers. Before me is the gritty ghetto of San Francisco's most notorious neighbourhood, the Tenderloin, dubbed its name a century earlier due to officers' "hazard pay" that got them a good cut of meat. As I buzz myself into the hostel, the image disintegrates in my mind's eye. I no longer need it to visualise inequality. I'm standing inside it. I'm breathing it in.

My inspiration to venture to the USA is a three-day music festival, Outside Lands, headlined by Paul McCartney and the Red Hot Chili Peppers. When I book accommodation for just one night, I don't consider that non-local festivalgoers will flood the city. This mishap means I bounce between three hostels and one couch-surf in my nine days in San Francisco. All four temporary homes dot the crazy cesspool corners of the Tenderloin district that compounds the density of destitute into just a few blocks. Wealthy neighbourhoods border the soft underbelly of vice where vagrants huddle beside ramshackle buildings, setting up their little corner of pavement on trash-cluttered streets. "Massage parlours" and liquor stores droop beside cheap hotels, Asian restaurants, and ethnic grocery stores. Yet every morning, the famous San Francisco fog creeps in. It purifies the anguish with a clean canvas for the day ahead.

On my first relocation, I map an extended route to avoid the open-air drug-bin bundled in the centre of the district. A few strides in, a man walks into my peripheral. His voice babbles between acoustic melodies gliding through my headphones. I turn the music down but keep the headphones in as I pace towards the Tenderloin's outer rim. The man follows. I don't sense a violent air, nor does he appear altered by substance. But he's there. He's not going anywhere with me ignoring him, so I unplug and spark a smile to dissipate potential conflict. To different degrees, humans are sensitive to the sentiments of others. Either we take on the atmosphere around us or imprint our own emotion.

Beneath raised eyebrows, the man's eyes and mouth gape. Then his expression softens into a genuine beam. This broadens my own smile. Now I don't know who is mirroring who.

After a brief introduction and comment about the weather, he insists on walking me to my hostel. I agree. The part of me that's tentative to the possibility of abduction is overridden by curiosity to where he came from and what he is doing.

After a bit of small talk, I query, "What are you grateful for?"

I ask partly out of interest to his response, partly to make conversation, and mostly to attune us both to the goodness of life. I've recently started a morning gratitude practise after reading about the multilayered benefits. It's a dull day. I woke with a mood matching the weather. I don't want to stagnate in this sticky space. Gratitude can shift this.

The smell of fermenting urine and garbage has me hold my breath for his answer.
"I'm grateful I'm free."

His answer renders a digestive silence. Freedom has so many interpretations. He's free from the constraints of capitalism, yet his homelessness maintains the system's power through fear. I'm free to gallivant the globe yet still a prisoner of the system. We're both free to choose who we want to be. In his response, I see that freedom is more than an emancipation ideal or a way of being. It entails an awareness to not oppress others.

"What are you grateful for, miss?"

His husky voice brings me back to the moment.

"I'm also grateful I'm free. I'm grateful I have freedom to see the world through whatever lens I choose. I'm grateful I have legs to take me where I wanna go. I'm grateful for friends around the globe."

I sense my response lands with the sincerity intended because he ruminates on my words. A few strides farther, he nods at four women huddling by an empty shopfront. They smile. One waves. He nods in acknowledgement. I can't maintain eye contact. Their massive, glazed pupils make my stomach contract, yet simultaneously, compassion oozes warm nectar in my chest.

"You don't want what they're on," he whispers after we pass.

I glance at his drooped body, empathetic to his bottom lip's slight jut.

It feels right to revert conversation back, so I ask, "Do you think we're free in society if shackled by its norms?"

He pauses for a moment then responds in an uncertain tone, "I guess it depends on your perspective..."

At the intersection of Ellis and Jones, he motions south with his head. In a firm tone he instructs, "Miss, don't go down that way."

I glimpse a man spitting on a passer-by and divert my gaze forward.

"Okay..."

Across the road is a dingy dead-end alley shadowed by apartment blocks and hotels oozing an old-world charm. As we approach, sunrays start drizzling through the clouds. Suddenly the day doesn't seem so gloomy. I stop in the last centimetre of sunny pavement and thank the man for walking with me.

"This is you? Down *here?*"

Steel air-conditioner tubes trail down medium high-rise hotels to wrought-iron bars guarding the street-level windows and doors.

"Yeah," I confirm. "My hostel is at the end."

"Are you—are you sure?" He surveys an abandoned mattress flopped beside a bunch of bins reeking of cheap liquor.

"Yeah, see that small white sign above the doorway at the end?"

"Oh. Will you be okay?"

"Yes." I smile. "Will you?"

"I'm always okay," he chirps.

I face the man and spread my arms with an invitation to hug. He freezes and stares at me with wide eyes. Then he exhales and embraces me. Gently. Slowly. With tender respect.

In the alley, I spin around and sing, "Enjoy the rest of your day."

You too, miss," he replies, still looking bedazzled. "Keep on smiling..."

Beyond fear, liberation awaits.

The day before the festival, I hire a bike from a charismatic Irishman in the one-block grassy plaza of Union Square. Surfing hills, I pant upwards then hurtle down. Colours and shapes flash by. Obliged to no set route, I am free to swerve in different directions depending on the feel of each street. I soon notice an atmosphere changes every few blocks. It's relieving to witness vibrant murals, pagoda-topped buildings, craft cocktail lounges, old-school taquerias, upscale boutiques, pungent fish markets, decadent gelato shops, and Victorian homes luxuriating around the gritty apex of dirt and crime. It is also unnerving.

Cycling to the waterfront, I am enticed by worldwide cuisines steaming from every corner. Cable cars rattle. Buses moan. Foreign chatter minces sonic undercurrents as I whir around the edge of the bay. Revitalised by the afternoon sun, I catch whiffs of marijuana from young dreamers and old hippies. Eventually I stop my thigh-burning extravaganza for lunch in a springy grass park that overlooks the iconic red suspension bridge spanning the Golden Gate strait.

I remember reading that the Golden Gate Bridge is one of the most popular suicide sites in the world. Sinking into nature's lush carpet, I gaze at it and trail down memory lane. My eyes are dry. But I can taste salty tears trickling down my cheeks as I reminisce on the inky night beckoning me to gulp down pharmaceuticals. Families picnic in the sunshine. Kites dance in the sky. The pages of my past feel like someone else's story. Life plummeted into a dreary darkness. But I came back.

There's a reason you're reading these words. Become present to your next breath. It's reminding you you're alive. Your mission is not over yet. There's still a purpose you must fulfil. Your calling is so strong I felt compelled to add this paragraph in, despite the disruption of flow. These words aren't mine. They don't belong to me. I am merely the messenger who beckons you to come home to your heart and feel its pumping beat. You have purpose. Your life matters. You are loved.

How do I know?

You're still alive.

You're still breathing.

You're still here.

⚭

"Excuse me, could you tell me where the Rose Garden is?"

The young man's fruity voice glides into my daydreams as I lounge on a sunny patch of grass in Golden Gate Park.

"Nah, sorry...I'm not from here."

I examine his untamed blond hair forming ringlets beneath a backward black cap. He slings a guitar over his shoulder while balancing a skateboard on the ground. Dimples dot his freckled face as he explains he just moved here from Colorado. He approaches just as I'm smearing avocado onto rice crackers with a pocketknife. I've been riding all afternoon. I'm hungry. Yet despite my grumbling stomach and minimal rations on hand, it feels absolutely necessary to invite him into my picnic.

His name is Stephen, and he oozes an infectious awe for life. He lives in a small apartment on the outer edge of the Tenderloin and also has a ticket to Outside Lands, but no one to go with. I pinch the skin on my forearm when he says it. How serendipitous to meet in the very park the festival is held the day before it begins. It seems fated that we go together.

The next day, we meet amid the smell of burnt coffee at a Tenderloin café then stroll through the hippy heartland of Haight-Ashbury into the city's lungs. There, the festival's expansive layout with multiple stages and 65,000 people render three days of choose-your-own-adventure. On the first evening, I lose my toenail in a mosh pit, so I leave Stephen for a calmer vibe. Soaking up every guitar change of Paul McCartney's set, I stand behind a young couple cradling a toddler, thinking my foot is safe. Then the dad accidentally stamps on my toe. I barely comprehend his apology between blood erupting like a volcano. For two songs all I can fathom is pain. When I focus on the music, the agony subsides. This inspires a hack I start attuning to: focus on the music rather than the misery. Of course, there are times we must acknowledge and allow pain. But when we're accustomed to ignoring life's magic, something must change.

I take the festival shuttle back to the city that night, crashing on a futon beside an Indian man I'm couch-surfing with. Having never couch-surfed before, I message him after skimming through one-hundred-plus positive reviews. When I arrive at his small open-plan apartment nestled in the Civic Center, I'm baffled that we'll be sharing the futon and wish he'd communicated that clearly. The alarm bells dwindle when I remember the reviews and recognise different cultural norms.

His sexual energy isn't leaky, and I trust his invitation for consented cuddles is just that. I am starting to process and thus heal my sexual trauma as revealed by San Pedro. It's a hard no. But I do appreciate sleeping with our toes touching.

My love for Stephen grows deeper each day. He is a freedom-loving daredevil and a gracious dreamer with sudden urges to stop and revere trees. On the festival's final day, we are ten people from the front of the crowd when the Red Hot Chili Peppers take the stage. Squished in a sea of people swaying in high-energy waves, I suppress my urge to pee and lose the spot we claimed hours earlier in the previous act. Feet trample all over my bloody toe, but my burning passion to be in the presence of my favourite band conquers. The sky darkens. The band plays songs from six of their ten studio albums. A fellow fan motions for me to climb onto his shoulders. I do. Warm sweat trickles down my legs as I lock eyes with Anthony Kiedis. His gaze lingers on my blue-and-green Red Hot Chili Peppers T-shirt I purchased earlier that day. I wonder if he remembers me until a voice of rationality kicks in.

When the encores come, I am content to stay and listen. To be stroked and soothed by the sweet caress of funky melodies dripping down my spine and absorbing me in a lyrical spell. Then "I Could Have Lied" begins. The emotions inside the music carry me back to their Gold Coast show. Impulse kicks in.

I squeeze myself to the front of the crowd, then leap over the metal rail separating the swaying swarm from the stage. Pain shoots into my knee as I fall on the concrete. My tights rip—my favourite world map tights. Blood oozes through Kazakhstan to the Caspian Sea. A security guard spots me and escorts me down a railed path, away from the stage. This is my plan. From the front to back in thirty seconds. Now I'm free to run towards a path backstage where clocked-off crew members walk my way. As I near the security-guarded partition, I push my shoulders back, lift my head high, and direct my gaze forward.

The burly security guard is distracted by a man chatting to him on a bike. I waltz on by. My advantage is that the festival ends in five minutes. It's cake. Music pours from giant speakers like stardust trickling onto galactic skies. I follow the sound to a bustling road where workers communicate on walkie-talkies and trucks beep. Amid the commotion, the realisation dawns that a higher force didn't pull me there. Not this time. It was ego. I did it because I knew I could.

My desire to stand in the band's path as they stride off their public platform and step into their private world crumbles. I suddenly see it for what it is, intrusive. As I take a road with exiting cars, the crowd applauds, and I pause beneath a blinding lamp. Flea and Anthony's uplifting verbal ejaculation of gratitude becomes background hype as I befriend a worker who helps me get back into the festival.

At our meeting point beneath a giant windmill, Stephen and I begin a playful walk home. An abandoned office chair becomes a venturesome ride that rattles up and swishes down the steep hills of San Francisco. My abs contract with deep belly laughter. This is where I want to be, having fun with my friend.

When the time comes to say goodbye on a dim Tenderloin street, my cheeks mould into happy curves as we devise a plan to drive into the heart of California when I return to the city in a rental car. Gazing into Stephen's starry blue eyes, I'm moved by the way he lets me strip back the layers and see him, without touch and without words. It's bizarre to think that life existed without him just three days ago. If the attractive Irish guy in Union Square hadn't rented me a heavily discounted bike, would I have zoomed through the city on wire wheels? If Stephen asked someone else for directions, would our paths still cross on a different day in a different way? If we were closed off to the magic of life, would our auspicious meeting still occur?

I don't know if there's a plan B. I don't know if there's a hidden order threading our hearts to those we're destined to meet. What I do know is that every moment is a portal, and we never know what'll unravel next.

Life becomes fuller, richer, and deeper as trust perpetually blooms.

"Excuse me," a voice behind me murmurs. "I don't mean to bother you, but you wouldn't happen to have any spare change?"

I turn around. The speaker is a scrawny young woman slumped beneath a baggy shirt. Morning rays revive Vancouver with ambition for a new day, but the streets are yet to fill. I blink my dry eyes and digest the question. With me is just a small carry-on bag. Amid flight delays leaving San Francisco, my backpack is MIA. Everything I own and packed for the next few years is lost in the conveyor belt vortex linking cheery air hostess welcomes, restless wandering, and snailing cues. All I have is my passport and the clothes on my back.

My stomach sinks as I count the goose bumps dotting her arms and lament, "I'm sorry...I don't."

She manages a small smile. "Thanks anyway. Have a nice day."

The interaction lingers as I navigate the historical Beaux-Arts-style building that is Vancouver's Pacific Central Station. Even destitute, she is well-mannered. It is an introduction to the courteous culture that brings me into a more gracious way of being.

An obnoxiously icy air-conditioned coach carries me to Kelowna, where the four Canadians vacation after Shambhala. My bloodshot eyes fixate on the window's evolving panorama with pristine lakes caressing evergreen forests that climb snow-capped mountains towards dreamy skies. The colours of spirit are shown in nature's cool, calming hues. It floods my veins with awe. As the bus purrs across a pontoon bridge, my chest twitches like my heartstrings strum for the glistening lake bestrewn with sailboats and kayaks. We're here. Canada's sunniest city, Kelowna, springs to life from the sensation of Trey pressing his finger into my knee during the ceremony.

My hostel perches behind a white picket fence and tall, multidirectional signpost with vibrant city signs. Weary from my sleep-deprived journey, I find sanctuary in a hammock hanging over a shaded wooden deck and reminisce on my novel adventures of late. Memories before July feel like misty pools from someone else's life. As stillness becomes me, tiny twigs and fallen leaves poke patterns into my back. With nothing but the sound of my heart beating, abstract thoughts entertain my sleepy mind. Am I in the world? Or is the world in me?

When the muted hum of a vehicle stopping is followed by the predictable pause of the four guys taking their sweet-ass time to get out of the car, I poke my head out of my cocoon and jolt into an energised state. We reunite with excited hugs then venture to a lakeside park. As we catch up on the past months' escapades, a gentle breeze rustles branches above our heads. I assume our time together will be tranquil. I'm wrong. As darkness swallows the sky, we drive to Morgan's house—Ben's part-time lover, full-time friend. Liquid gold trickles down her luscious blonde crown. She oozes warmth like solstice sunshine. My presumption swiftly pulverises into powdered MDMA we scoop into tiny squares of toilet paper, fold into "parachutes", and swallow.

Initially, I'm present to restless visceral tension. I've not tried MDMA. I'm still haunted by the experience of losing Courtney to addiction. Ecstasy with Jarred once, methamphetamine with Courtney once, pills with friends twice, LSD alone, mushrooms with Ruby—my dabbling has been out of curiosity not escapism. I enjoy dissecting the physiological and psychological effects of altered states, and if there's anyone who'll enthuse that, it's the Canadians. This is why I partake. As my head soars into the clouds, I keep one foot on the ground. My promise to Konrad five years ago still lingers.

Morgan's pristine sapphire eyes remind me of an alpine lake. In them I feel safe and seen. To my relief, the airline delivers my missing backpack. I move it to a dusty corner in Morgan's lounge room in the two-story townhouse that she insists we all stay in for the week. While she's waitressing, the word "chilled" takes on a frustrating new meaning. The guys are languid after Shambhala. I want adventure buddies to explore. A short walk into town becomes a whole-day mission that requires several prompts from my part. It's like trying to persuade a bed of sloths to leave a decadent, all-you-can-eat feast to run a marathon without water. I am grateful for Morgan's fiery spark and forthright nature. It keeps things fresh as she saunters in after work, proclaiming, "I'm coming in hot!"

The others ride the euphoric waves of MDMA most nights. I do not. I take a transitory ride while the others keep commuting. Conversation between the six of us is abstract. We talk of quantum physics and the notion of every human, plant, and animal being specks of consciousness stemming from the same central source. My itch to understand the deeper meaning of life is satiated, but sometimes it is challenged. When they present the idea that we create our own reality, I get lost in the stories my mind generates. Rather than focused presence or mindful intention-setting, I remain fear-shackled to express my heart's desires. This becomes apparent late one night as I curl myself into a tiny ball on Morgan's couch, trying to look cute as I furl both hands towards my face like a sleeping kitten.

As Trey, Ben, and Riley laze upstairs, discussing who will sleep in the loft, Conner kneels beside me and enquires, "Where do you want to sleep tonight, Jess? You can sleep beside Trey, Ben, myself, or Riley? It's *your* choice, just let us know..."

I peer into his deep-set hazel eyes, noticing a striking green swirl within the brown. He's not asking to force me into bed with anyone. The question is practical in nature. Beds and couches at Megan's are limited, and we all want a good sleep.

Conner and I bond that we both fly in our lucid dreams. He's always the easiest to inspire action, and I feel a safe brotherly presence in him. It's my own aversion to ask for what I want that shackles me.

I clear my throat to say "Riley". I often daydream of his lips breathing me in again. Now and then, his green eyes lock on mine, releasing every bit of breath from my lungs as time collapses in on itself and distant galaxies eddy into the smoke-filled room. Earlier that evening, Riley ran around piggybacking me in the alley outside Morgan's home. I couldn't hide the joy from my smile, even when we tumbled onto the cracked road shimmering with broken glass. The crumbly asphalt grazed my open palms, but our fall wasn't catastrophic enough to draw blood. Vital life force surfaced but remained contained. That's how I feel in my inability to say his name.

Maintaining eye contact with Conner, I swallow and respond in a dumb tone, "Ummm...I don't know..."

The crinkles around Conner's eyes soften. His eyebrows lift as he maintains a warm gaze that invites me out of my shell. I feel him feeling the undercurrents brewing in our conversation—the subtext, the unsaid, what I feel so intensely I'm certain it pours from me like blood-red passion. I smile sweetly, grateful for his kindness. Then I sleepily close my eyes. I'm tired of the lump in my throat blocking me from expressing my true desires. It rips and constricts like hardened gum under a school desk. Conner places an assuring hand on my shoulder, then jogs upstairs where conversation muffles. Meanwhile I dawdle into the empty downstairs bedroom and get cosy under the covers of the un-sheeted bed.

When I wake in the morning, Riley is passed out on his stomach beside me. Morning rays drip through the curtains. I rub my eyes and notice a fluctuating hunger. Within my grasp, I no longer crave him. When the distance between us grows, I'm drawn in. Perhaps in some distant recess of my mind, it's safer to only want him when I cannot have him because then I cannot be hurt by love.

Nonetheless, the energy between us is heady with possibility. That afternoon, I brew a big pot of cacao on Morgan's grimy stove. Riley dances into the kitchen dressed in baggy harem pants as electronic music booms with bass that has us all bouncing. His face lights up as he proclaims, "These pants make me look like a genie!"

I twist around to face him and gush, "If I rub you, will my dreams come true?"

His eyes glimmer as he traces my contours from my feet to my collarbone and replies, "Maybe. It depends what they are..."

My torso ripples with an exhilarating warmth.

Then his eyes meet mine as he concludes, "Mine would."

*To get what we want, we must know what we want
and have the courage to name it.*

That weekend, the guys drive back to Calgary to wash their post-festival clothes and return—minus Ben—with what they need to pick grapes at a nearby vineyard. As soon as they leave, I scrub and sweep every surface in Morgan's home to thank her for hosting us so pleasantly. The task takes all day. Rubbish in one pile. Empty bottles in another. I'm sprawled on the couch when she returns with her friend Aimee, bright-eyed and bouncing, ready to party. After a brief freak-out moment that I pocketed her remaining MDMA, Morgan finds her hidden stash and the fun begins. I've refrained from partying since that first night but decide to join the girls. After weeks of hanging with dudes, I want to immerse in feminine energy.

Aimee is a short, half-Filipino beauty. She's sophisticated and elegant, yet her smile holds unexplainable tension. In my inebriated state, her huge grin and wide eyes resemble the Cat Bus from my favourite childhood movie, Totoro. I blurt this out in a gas station carpark on our walk into town. With lowered inhibitions from the MDMA, I don't realise what I've said until the words have tumbled from my mouth.

"What's the Cat Bus?"

Morgan doubles over in hysterics with air wheezing from her lungs.

Aimee's ear-to-ear smile vanishes. "What the fuck?"

I open my mouth to put her at ease. When consciously choosing, I speak with profundity and eloquence. This is my default on first meeting. As time goes on, my filter drops in congruence with my level of comfort. In this moment, my ability to weave articulate words escapes me. I feel Aimee self-consciously drowning in my lack of filter, and suddenly I feel constricted inside my skin as traffic whooshes past on the highway. I convince her it's not a bad thing—the Cat Bus has a contagious smile—but a visceral strain lingers.

The friction eases as we get higher. MDMA dots sweat on our skin and electrifies every cell. The flash of a selfie has us all smiling together, then swaying together, soaring closer to an artificial bliss with each swing of our hips. Flashing lights break dancing's uninhibited flow down to robotic movements that freeze moments in time. Then it is 7:00 a.m. Pastel-pink clouds imbue the sky with opportunity as I walk back to Morgan's while the girls continue partying.

Morning crisp upon me, I cross my arms over my torso to stop shivers vibrating through my being. With each tremble, memories from the night flash like the strobe's intermittent images that cut up time. Nostril burns. Black hole pupils. That toe-curling taste of bitter drips. A ramshackle house with piles of dirty dishes. Each shudder dissolves my steady footsteps into the sensation of levitating over the footpath. It's time to stop. I'm not grounded. Continuing will be a violation of my promise to Konrad. I need solitude and sobriety for my mental and physical wellbeing to prevail.

After passing out in the silent house, I pack my bags and check into the hostel to give myself some space. Then I explore the predictable grid-pattern of streets where children sell homemade lemonade and busking musicians serenade my stroll. Since Peru, coming home to myself is a dynamic and cathartic journey. I'm nervous yet courageous to explore the parts of me unknown. This puts emphasis on quality "Jess time" to immerse in nature, track my breath, tune into my emotions, and process uncomfortable feelings. These times I cherish as sacred.

I find this refuge in the lake. Submerging into balmy waters, I let stillness settle around my broken being. The lake provides a sanctuary for me to soften and slow, but it's on me to turn inward and be patient with what I find. Allowing notions to come and go, I float. I can't hear the world above the water. I can only hear my own thoughts. Reflecting on the love that San Pedro awoke in my heart, I imagine a life of creativity, vitality, and connection. My vision is clear as I emerge from the lake with skin shrivelled like an old prune. Placing my feet back on solid ground, I am grounded once more, rejuvenated and ready to face the world again.

The fire dances tangerine in the cool, summer air. I sit on Riley's lap, hypnotised by the primal crackling of stored sunlight releasing in soft hisses and whistling pops. It is my last night in Kelowna. A local friend insists on commemorating this with a lakeside bonfire. As wisps of smoke curl and unexpected twists give the fiery strokes a life of their own, I wonder where the journey will take me next. Figuratively, I mean. Literally, the coming weeks will bring me from Calgary to Vancouver to California to Turkey to then settle in the UK with Blair.

It's a strange feeling to not know when I'll see my friends again. What starts as a flash of orange inevitably cools to golden embers twinkling amongst the blackened coals of what was. The moment is so vivid. The fragrance of burning wood. Flickering flames reflected in my friends' eyes. The toasty warmth as I hold my hands up to the golden glow. I press myself into Riley's thighs, wishing he'd wrap his arms around me. I don't know why I feel I must keep my feelings for him secret. Maybe imagination is always better than reality because we don't daydream about the icky or mundane. We romanticise the fire—dancing in burnt apricot and honeyed gold—forgetting that when it dies in smoky tendrils, a new moment will spark.

Back at Morgan's, I cosy into her sister's empty double bed downstairs. While I showered, someone constructed a blanket wall separating the bed in halves. As Riley slides in beside me, I wonder if it was him or one of the other guys. The whole scenario confuses me. The boundary is clear, but whose is it, and why isn't it verbalised without the passive-aggression? I keep to my side as sweat dots my skin like delicate spring rain. Slowly it thickens to a tropical storm. Eventually I strip my damp clothes and fall into a dreamless slumber.

Early-morning rays trickle through the window as Conner's deep voice wakes Riley for their first day of work. Forgetting I'm naked, I sit up, quickly pulling the white sheet to my chest. Four eyes are on me. Conner gives Riley a knowing look that he returns with a blank stare. In the rush of the guys leaving, there isn't space for an explanation. Not that I know what to say. As Conner leaves the room, Riley turns to face me with a dumbstruck expression blending with wonder as the sheet falls and reveals my naked body. Beneath the skin baring my humanness whole, I am a nude landscape of beauty in my vulnerability to be seen. Truly seen.

Eyes soft on mine, Riley's handsome face warms when I wish him a happy first day. Then he leaves with, "I'll see you...after..."

*

At the hostel, I ask if there is a printer for my bus ticket. There isn't, but the athletic owner offers to drive me to a printing store instead. On the way, I acknowledge her for the homely and artistic aesthetic. It's by far my favourite hostel.

"Thank you," she chirps. "It's come a longggg way. When I bought it, it was a rundown crack house with dirty syringes covering the yard."

"Oh, wow. You wouldn't know..."

"Yah, right? We bought it with good intentions. For six months our mantra was 'Build it and they will come'. It took a while...but we got there."

I nod.

"Now it's travellers who make the place flourish. I just pop my head in every few days. When things are meant to be, they will be..."

Her closing sentence brings Riley to mind. I acknowledge the thought then blink it away. Now is not the time to daydream.

Later that afternoon, the guys collect me from the hostel and drive to a park near the bus station. Instead of his habitual aloofness, Riley faces me directly. Meanwhile, Trey and Conner sit back-to-back just beyond our bubble, allowing the space for connection, I guess. But what is there to say? I'm venturing east, west, south, and then north, followed by a great big unknown. As the clock hand strikes our inevitable goodbye, we amble to the station until it's time for me to walk my own way.

"Onward and upward," I burst, concealing my sorrow with a smile.

Trey and Conner grin and wave.

Riley lowers his head and furrows his brow. Then he stands tall and catches me in his steady gaze. His mysterious green eyes linger in my daydreams for months as bittersweet tinctures simmer.

Travelling begins and ends with goodbyes. We farewell our family when we leave. We adieu our amigos along the way. I'm accustomed to the nomadic lifestyle, but I've never gotten used to goodbyes. I know I'll see the guys again. There's no doubt in my mind. I just don't know when. In the oceanscape of my emotions, I break and grow, ache and flow. The goodbye sweeps through me like stormy tides.

🍎

Poignant feelings drip through shedding skin that births a brave new world.

As the bus trundles away from the city, I marvel at forested mountains and glistening lakes until darkness dissipates the light. Windows rattle with every rotation of the tyres fondling the road. A foul smell wafts from the toilet. Some people read. Others feign sleep. Most periodically check their phones as we commune across the no-man's-land of where we are and where we will be.

When we arrive in Calgary at 6:00 a.m., I hop on the C train and watch the stale, grey city wake. The manic-depressive weather is in a good mood, shining hope into the concrete jungle backdropped by snow-capped mountains. Across from me, a foreign traveller checks his phone. As the train catches speed, his suitcase rolls into an unsuspecting local girl walking down the aisle. She turns to him, or the suitcase—I can't be sure which—and apologises. I stifle a giggle. Canadian etiquette is growing on me fast.

With just three days left in Canada, my priority is basking in nature. After a day hanging in Calgary with Ben, we venture to postcard-perfect Banff. Ben is easy to get along with, embodying a cheekiness and charm that lightens any mood. His quick wit blends with an insightful depth, fusing high ideals with analytical thoughts that he delivers in a sincere and tactful way. He sees the forest and the trees. As do I, in deep appreciation for the dense coniferous forests and lofty alpine meadows surrounding the popular alpine town.

Away from the havoc of tourists clogging Banff Avenue, we chill by a slow-flowing stream. Ben says choosing love over fear is the most important decision we'll ever make, one that we can attune to at any moment. His words make me present to the crisp breeze and stillness of the mountains. Is it possible that fear has been my default, pulling me away from life? What will it take to burst my heart open and embrace life with unshackled joy?

The moon shines a silvery path upon the trickling stream, and from there on, I question whether my thoughts stem from fear or love. Every time a thought bubbles, I envelop it in a bigger bubble that questions if it's empowering, true, and kind. If not, I dissolve the smaller bubble into the bigger bubble's devotion to positivity, growth, and peace. By bringing awareness to my subconscious patterns, I rewire the foundations of my life.

The river surges over dramatic granite rocks in a satin wall of white. Thundering and churning, the glacier melt tumbles into a cool turquoise stream. There it collects itself. Then it keeps on moving. Is there a final destination, or is it one continuous flow? I ask myself this same question after we leave Bow Falls, and Ben drops me on the Trans-Canada Highway. He's staying in Banff with friends. I have three days of back-to-back transport taking me from Calgary to Vancouver to Sacramento. As his smiling reflection in the rearview mirror fades from sight, I sculpt my hand from an open-palmed wave to a single thumb saluting the sky.

The superhighway stretches into the horizon before me, seemingly parting the mountains for vehicles that waft smoky black fumes. The heat of the sun plummets down. My backpack weighs heavy on my shoulders. In between beats bouncing through my iPod, cars zoom towards me then glistening windshields shrink from sight. For a moment, fear kicks in. What if no one picks me up? Or what if it's a twisted soul and I'm never seen again? I observe my fear, then evaporate it into an empowered intention to make it to the bus station safely and on time.

As my thoughts transform, I giggle as "Life is a Highway" plays from shuffled songs. With a skip in my step, I enter a trance as I soak up the mountains. I don't like aimlessly waiting by the side of the road for a ride, so I walk forward with my thumb outstretched. A few songs later, a car pulls over and drops me near the next town. Usually, I text the number plate of the car I hitch to a friend. In a different context, electronic breadcrumbs have been handy in the past. Travelling without a phone—and the absence of this safety net—kindles a deeper trust in the journey. Often it is fellow travellers who help along the way. A Spanish-born Israeli man living in Calgary picks me up next and drops me at the Greyhound station, where I ready myself for another long, cramped, window-rattling night ride.

Delirious and drained, I arrive at a no-frills hostel near the bus station the next morning. I've never gotten the hang of sleeping with a vertical spine while moving forward at 100 kilometres an hour. A strange blend of Chinese food and urine wafts through the window as I catnap on my top bunk. When I awake, I explore Vancouver in my favourite manner: following my feet to see where I end up. Usually this leads to awe-inspiring adventures that connect me with foreign customs on exotic streets. For whatever reason, on this first visit to North America, I find myself in defeated and depleted neighbourhoods. To my detriment, my conceit that I'm a "true traveller" means I think I'm beyond the guidance, or warnings, of Google telling me which way to go.

In Chinatown's bustling vibrance, I understand how the smell of hot vegetable oil and spicy soy sauce wafted into the hostel. The place is buzzing with live seafood stalls and mural art encompassing the stories of early Chinese pioneers. I continue walking, noticing the odd building boarded up with thin plywood sheets. A few blocks farther, the zombie apocalypse is upon me. Litter-clotted gutters skirt sidewalks that home hundreds of dosed-up, strung-out, inebriated, narcotised vagrants. My awareness instantly sharpens, for I understand that perpetrators will rarely go after someone who has noticed them first.

In just two blocks, sprightly Chinatown dwindles to a drab district filled with junkies yelling. I am in a state of dis-ease. My first instinct is to get the hell out of there, but every way I turn the pungent smell of urine pierces my nasal cavity as I dodge cockroaches scavenging through the trash. No one says anything to me. No one looks me in the eye. One guy hobbles past in sporadic steps, talking to himself in gibberish. I keep my demeanour strong but composed, observing the hunched stance of passers-by protecting themselves from the dense energy encompassing the dirty streets. There's an imbalance. I feel it as a heaviness in my chest as my rib cage collapses in. Eventually, the clusters of slouching people are restored by pedestrians walking with erect spines. It's disturbing how swiftly the streets become business and residential hubs again, like the compacted human misery I just experienced doesn't even exist.

I stroll away from East Hastings then watch the silhouetted city darken to metallic reflections on a small inlet of water. On the shorelines of my consciousness, I sense myriad possibilities twinkling in the floating echoes of the water's timeless mirror. For the first time in a long time, I feel like I'm home. I know I'll be back. Sooner rather than later. I am encapsulated with the knowing that my time in Canada has just begun.

Vulnerability is the key to authenticity.
Authenticity unlocks the door to connection.
Connection unlatches our world to love.

On board a lavish high-speed train, 1970s rock 'n' roll is my soundtrack to the dazzling panorama whizzing past the window. For twenty-one hours, I relax into my spacious seat and extend my legs horizontal on the adjustable cushioned leg rest. Waterfalls trickle in aquamarine curtains in time with the rhythm and rhyme of lyrical lines that drip down my spine and make me shiver in my skin. Alpine lakes glitter with sapphire ripples. Zephyrs breeze through alpine meadows shadowed by crumpled peaks. Sometimes dense forests cut up the idyllic scenes as aesthetic chills from the music pulsate in pleasurable waves that enthral me in a dreamy spell.

It is on this ride I realise windows are my television, my gateway to the outside world. I relish this. In my periphery, people scroll in relentless fixation as dopamine-inducing buzzes and beeps rob them of the present moment. This digitized world exploits consumer behaviour through rectangular devices of artificial light. Amid a generation of Facebook addicts and Instagram influencers, I love travelling without a phone and experiencing life with all senses engaged. I'm free to follow scents down memory lane, immerse in lullabies of exotic sound, and surrender to tactile sensations that evoke the feeling of home.

It pains me that social media usage increases emotional loneliness as most kids prefer liquid crystal display to real-life adventures. The irony of my generation is the enhancement of technology made for us to communicate and connect, yet the breakdown of both through these very devices. True connection isn't dependent on WiFi detection or virtual likes. It's the realness and rawness of opening our hearts and letting ourselves be seen. When we press the off button and tune into the sounds of our beating heart, we reclaim our sovereignty over our mind.

For some reason, I picture Sacramento as a small beachside town. Sniffing for swaying palms or a revitalising salty balm, I follow a quaint road shaded by oak trees. This brings me to a four-storey Victorian mansion. Grand stone steps lead to a wraparound veranda supported by detailed olive-green columns. It's one lavish hostel. Inside, a chandelier dangles from vaulted ceilings with skylights that drizzle rainbow rays. Beneath a mahogany staircase is a polished wooden desk, where the receptionist explains it is an 1885 gold rush mansion. She also clarifies, after a confused pause, we are nowhere near the ocean.

Upstairs, I park my backpack on a wooden bunk between human-sized windows that cast midmorning light onto a boarded-up fireplace. I feel like I've stepped back in time, half expecting to walk into a decadent party with rich merchants eating damper and mutton.

After a quick whizz through the well-preserved Old Town, I find sanctuary by the turbid river. It is infamous for flooding the city with its swift, strong flow. As opaque waters drift by, I close my eyes and reflect on the tides leading me here. I'm in a restful state. Then an uneven scuffling accompanied by a pervasive sweat splinters my stillness. I open my eyes to a shaggy homeless man hobbling past the cement slab where I sit. He perches in the shade of a nearby tree, and like me, watches the murky brown water gush past.

For a moment it is silent. Then, without warning, he splashes in. Rapidly doggy-paddling to stay upstream, he swims to the middle of the river. I feel liberated watching him. My concern shifts to awe as the same currents tugging on the riverbanks eddy around him as though avidly welcoming him home. Then an epiphany cascades over me. I'm drenched in it, like I too have jumped in. He isn't homeless. He is home. There, in the water. On this planet we all call home. Who am I to judge him for not having a home? We all have home. We all are home. For we are all born unto this Earth. Colonisation is essentially cultural ego pointing at the common ground we share and claiming it as one's own. In riches or rags, our bodies decompose back to the earth from which we came.

Listening is how we learn.

In the refurnished communal kitchen, I slice juicy tomatoes on a marble bench and chat with Marco, an attractive Swiss backpacker, about the hostel's old-world charm. It's all small talk, until I mention the synchronicity of my North American leg. This widens his squinty eyes.

"Did you just say *synchronicity?*" he asks with an Italian accent.

"Yeah..." I stop chopping. "You're familiar with the word?"

"Yes! Have you read The Celestine Prophecy by James Redfield? It's fictional," he explains as his forehead puckers. "At least I *think* it is..."

"I've heard of it," I bubble. "My friend Laula raved about it. And these four Canadians I met in Peru..."

Marco tilts his head and verifies, *"Peru?"*

I nod.

"It's funny you say that." Marco smiles.

"Why?"

"Peru is where the book begins."

I lean forward. "What's it about?"

"An ancient manuscript found in Peru has nine...what's the word they use... *insights* predicting the evolution of mankind."

"Interesting," I muse. "Tell me more?"

Marco's eyes crinkle. "I want to get my water from my room. Shall we meet outside once you've eaten?"

"Okay, see ya soon." I grin.

Feeling satiated, I find Marco in a patio lit by elegant lampposts and a disseminating moon. As I settle into a metal chair, he begins.

"The first insight talks about a large number of humans encountering a spiritual awakening. Mysterious and meaningful coincidences—*synchronicities,* as you said earlier—guide us forward."

"Hmmm...I see why the book being fiction confuses you. It does seem quite real," I agree, thinking of the strange coincidences guiding me since I left Australia—my dreams preceding Peru, Lesley's resonance with depression, and meeting Stephen in Golden Gate Park. Even now, being in Sacramento and meeting Marco, might not have happened if I'd known it wasn't a beachside town. These events can't be tossed aside as mere coincidences when they connect the dots like twinkling stars forming constellations in the night sky.

"The second insight looks into human history over the past...what's the English word for one thousand years?"

"Millennium."

"*Mill-en-um?*"

"*ee-um.* Mill-*en-ee-umm.*"

"*Mill-en-ee-um.*" He chuckles. "So, anyway, in the first 500 years, in the Middle Ages, only representatives of the church interpreted our spiritual reality."

"Oh, yep."

"But unfortunately, priests and royalty abused their power and violated their own oaths to God. This caused common people to—*ah,* what's that word?"

Marco looks at me blankly.

"Get angry?" I offer.

"Yes, it's something like that but there is another word..."

"Do something about it?"

"Yes, actually."

I giggle at his use of the word "actually". Throughout my travels, I've noticed Europeans frequently use the word.

"Do you mean *rebel,* Marco?"

"Yes! It was the start of the European Renaissance..."

I nod, catching sight of a trickling stone fountain. Marco's eloquence and detail captivates me as he describes mankind sending explorers into the world in the second half of the millennium.

"We discovered the world isn't flat, nor the centre of the universe. No longer suppressed by medieval times, science rapidly developed, and soon the Industrial Revolution progressed. Somewhere along the way, though, we *forgot* our mission to seek the answers and got *distracted* with obtaining a more comfortable and convenient life."

I chuckle wistfully, thinking of our collective fixation with screens.

Marco continues, "While exploration and experimentation have been essential to our evolution, it has created a void in our human experience."

"Yah! Consumerism is at an all-time high."

"Exactly. After 500 years, we are *remembering* our age-old quest to discover the spiritual meaning of life and our purpose on this planet."

Gentle winds rustle through garden beds skirting the red-bricked patio as Marco continues with the third insight, "Where attention goes, energy flows."

I nod. The Canadians once described the universe as a dynamic field of energy. With focus and intention, we can project our energy in our desired direction. Each day my sensitivity to people, situations, and dynamics increases. I've always felt something beyond my five senses. I can't touch, taste, see, smell, or hear it. I feel it. All around me. Since leaving Peru, I've strived to emanate love and be a vibrant fountain of joy. Sometimes vitality surges through me. Other times, it is draining.

Cool zephyrs trickle over my skin as Marco talks of humans unconsciously stealing energy from others when they feel low and disconnected.

"By manipulating or forcing others to give us their attention, and therefore energy, we feel full. However, the feeling is temporary and damages both people," he clarifies. "The book calls it...*ahh, damnit* I've forgotten the English words again. It's this thing that underpins all human conflict."

"Ego?" I suggest.

"No, that's not it. Actually, it is two words but I can't remember what they are." Marco presses his lips together and momentarily palms his forehead as though trying to extract the words from his brain.

I later discover he is searching for "control drama".

"This is the part of the book that confuses me most. I see it everywhere, in others and myself. It feels so true!"

I absorb his words like an ancient oak soaking light from the sun. The metal chair presses patterns into my butt, but I dare not move in case my shuffling distracts me from the words he speaks next.

Marco explains there are four ways we steal energy, four "control dramas". The "intimidator" steals energy by direct threats that project fear. The "interrogator" steals energy by probing others with questions conveyed in a judgemental or critical way. The "poor me" constantly whines and plays victim, making others feel guilty. And the "aloof" steals energy by withdrawing and playing coy.

I roll my eyes to a large white umbrella in the right corner of the garden as my head cocks left. In my teens, my parents interrogated me by snooping through my chat logs and eavesdropping on my phone calls. Then they summoned me to family meetings, where I felt cornered and criticised. This made me detached and distant. I became aloof.

"But we don't need to steal energy from others," Marco continues. That's the fifth insight."

His voice swirls around my thoughts and brings me back into my body.

"There is an abundance of energy available to us that increases by remaining in a loving state. When we are full and in flow, we feel light and buoyant. This increases the occurrence of synchronicities."

I nod slowly. "My Canadian friends often talked of eating well, unplugging, meditating, and exercising to 'raise our vibration'. I think this means... fundamentally...to heighten our mental and emotional state, so we can flyyyy through the sky!"

I add this last part in as a way of testing Marco's comfortability with our conversation's depth. It is something I often do—say something light-hearted amid deep and meaningful discussions—to allow people to choose which way they want the conversation to go. Sometimes they take the playful route out. Other times, they delve deeper.

Marco smiles and chooses the latter, explaining that it's easy to transcend our control dramas once we realise they stem from childhood.

I inch closer as he clarifies, "Someone with aloof parents who didn't have time to be fully present could easily become an interrogator, because continuously asking questions as a child was their way of gaining energy. This goes both ways. Someone with interrogating parents could easily become aloof."

"I was *just* thinking this!" I exclaim, then stroke my chin and note, "I see the connection between the intimidator and the poor me too. You can't have a victim without a bully..."

"Yes," Marco notes with a perplexed knot twisting his forehead. "I think there's an art in mastering the ability to *not* play into them."

My eyes dry for I fear missing something important if I blink. "I see. If someone is intimidating, how do you not submit to becoming a poor me, yet not fire up their ego by mirroring their agro behaviour?"

"Agro?"

"Oh, sorry, it's Aussie slang. It means aggressive."

Marco chuckles, then exclaims, "Actually, when we learn to stop playing into our own individual dramas, we clear the past and discover how to stay connected to this subtle energy infusing all things. The seventh insight is knowing our personal mission and being clear with our energy. Every experience is an opportunity to raise our vibration and engage with the synchronistic flow of life. Mystics from all traditions describe this connection to the divine—*whatever name* you wish to give it...."

"God, Allah, Brahma, Jehovah, the Universe, Source—a rose by any other name would still smell as sweet."

Marco nods.

"I've always felt that different religions have more in common than we think. I think it's the same divine spirit being encountered by *different* cultures at *different* periods of time, thus being interpreted in slightly different ways. I think these differences are exacerbated because it's human nature to fear what is different and unknown. But at the core, there is love."Marco continues listing intently to my words.

"Love is the source of this omnipotent, omniscient, omnipresent force that connects all things..."

We both gaze upwards as my words trail into space. The tiny constellations that witnessed the start of our conversation are no longer in sight. A different sea of stars watches us.

"I feel lighter, since we've been chatting," Marco divulges. "It's funny, the book talks of people along our journey delivering synchronistic messages. By uplifting those around us and seeing the beauty in every face, we boost others into their wisest self."

"Yeow! Thanks for appearing when you did."

A wide smile crinkles the crow's-feet around his eyes. "You too, Jessica. It seems strange that we may never see each other again. Yet, it makes sense...for it is exactly what the book speaks of."

I nod.

He pauses for a moment, then asks, "Where are you from?"

"Everywhere." I grin, stoked that it's midnight and only now does that damned question arise.

Somewhere far away, a swirling gas storm twice the size of Earth rages on Jupiter's skin. Maybe the answers to all life's mysteries are within the Great Red Spot. Appearing to us as a tiny twinkling speck in the midnight sky, maybe it illuminates the truth in languages we can't yet fathom. Conversation veers a different direction, and we don't delve into the eighth and ninth insights.

They come later in the journey, when the time is right, and I'm ready to receive them.

Two days later, my local friend picks me up from my hostel in Santa Monica. We met nine months ago on the boat to Antarctica. Now he's taken two days off his firefighting job in Tustin so we can journey to another great wonder: the Grand Canyon. Congested city traffic became a desert horizon on Interstate 40 as my friend nods to distant peaks, noting that Southern California is one of the few places you can ski and surf in the same day.

We arrive at Grand Canyon National Park in perfect time to set up camp and watch the sun set. Stunned into silence at the depth, distance, and dimensions the canyon spans, I wait for the perfect words to capture the canyon's beauty. Nothing comes.

Three years later, I sit outside my wooden A-frame home that was once Robert Juniper's art studio in the hills of Perth. It is a crisp winter day. I am writing this book's second draft. An unrequited love weighs heavy on my chest. Basking in a brief moment of sunshine and an unquenched yearning for romance, this story unravels.

Once upon a time, about five or six million years ago, the world's greatest love story began. Before the magnitude and magnificence of the Grand Canyon became visible to human eyes, the Colorado River fell in love with the rich, red rock. Long before we began to awe at sunsets melting into striking strata—as vistas stretch beyond our line of vision—the river had a vision of what was to come. Meandering along the canyon floor, cutting and carving channels through chromatic crust, she never lost focus of her dream.

Carefully caressing the land she loved, she stretched her entire body across him. The earth was firm and fixed in his ways, stubborn to her loving touch. She did not falter. She knew the beauty that lay beneath his skin, long before we could see. As she persisted with her gentle, undulating flow, the earth softened. He allowed her to undress him. Soil and sediment safe in her embrace, she carried him across the continent. Giving her solid ground beneath the myriad of tributaries she extended over his limbs, he held her, and constellations formed explanations for the exploration that their bodies embarked.

Two elements, meeting and merging, passionately intertwining. Sensually and slowly, just as she had known all along, the earth opened, revealing his warm inside and exquisite layers of vividly coloured rock. Layer upon layer of ancient history held within his body, he was venerable with his vulnerability to expose his insides for all the world to see. Each stratum is a different colour, representing a different era of time—reds, ochres, yellows, buffs—intricate lines seemingly painted onto the walls he let crumble. For her, and her love. Her soft, soothing strokes continue to deepen and widen the canyon today, as the grandeur of their love is put into perspective. For all the world to see.

Driving into Orange County on Labour Day feels like a dream. Palm trees lining bustling roads soon replace tiny rain pellets sliding onto my friend's van from leaves. I appreciate the peaceful silence as he takes me to a viewpoint on a secluded hill. It is a place of emotional security to think and feel and be, away from people. Like my Kalamunda Zig Zag, city lights stretch into a 360-degree panorama below rupturing fireworks and humming planes.

I journey across it the next morning, after we part ways at the train station. He has fires to fight. I have the passionate burn of fresh adventures to tend. Sitting amongst commuters glued to their phones, I gaze out the graffitied window. Backdropped by a baby-blue sky, thick black plumes billow from factory chimneys in a toxic stream. Despite the glassed partition, I hold my breath.

Part of me wishes I had a device to distract me from the pollution poisoning our planet. I feel so helpless, like I'm the only one watching the world slowly suffocate, unsure how to save future generations from the destruction of mankind. I later realise that small changes by many hands are the way to progress. In the moment, all I can fathom is getting away from it. Far, far away. And so, I do, in the small Kia Rio hire car that becomes my home for the next week. Adjusting my bearings to right-side driving amid seven surging lanes, I grip the steering wheel with knuckles white. I drive all day. I drive all night. Stopping only for bitter, vanilla-flavoured service station coffee and short periodic naps squished in the backseat, I drive up the 101 until I reach the north-western corner of California.

The day is a paradox. In the morning, I pass towering skyscrapers arranged in linear blocks, burdened by the chemical soup of the city's own filth. The megalopolis is a liver unable to detoxify and excrete chemicals from its own system with ease as everyone tries to get ahead in a fast-paced rat race with frenzied deadlines and static buzz. It's tense as fuck. Twelve hours later, I inhale oxygen-rich air, surrounded by the tallest trees in the world at Redwood National Park. If highways are blood vessels, my car is a red blood cell that becomes oxygenated in the forest—the fully functioning lungs that rid the system of carbon dioxide. City chaos becomes a regenerating stillness. My body softens as I melt into the timeless space.

The botanical giants stretch into canopy clouds as I walk along a moist forest path, where a cleansing breeze rustles into a choir of chirping birds. Sunshine illuminates moss between thick sequoia and redwood trunks, and ferns drape over the forest floor. Shivers slide down my spine. They rouse a supernatural feeling that has me present to Earth's largest and longest living beings whispering in the winds above my head.

Many years later, my then-boyfriend and I climb the lateral branches of a giant oak tree. We talk of mankind's belief that we're the most advanced species on Earth. The notion he presents: we're not. Trees are. A universe of their own, trees support their own existence. And ours. Their decaying leaves give them nutrients to thrive. They store sunlight for millions of years that humans are now burning as oil and coal fuelling the growth of our civilisation. They generously inhale carbon dioxide and provide us with oxygen using only the light from the sun. He ponders if the destruction of old-growth forests will be the beginning of the end for us humans. Then he speaks of Jesus and Buddha—both admired for their spiritual connection and inner stillness—and concludes that all trees are naturally in this state.

With lives spanning for hundreds, sometimes thousands, of years, my presence is inconsequential to the forest's grand existence. Yet, each step feels so vital. So meaningful. Not just to me, but for all humanity. Every crack of tiny twigs with the earth's dewy embrace is a sacrament to the trees and their importance for future generations. We can survive for days without food, water, and sleep. Some people survive years with a lack of love. Without oxygen? Life ceases to exist in a matter of minutes.

One day, our ancestors will walk on our ruins, as we do our predecessors. What will they say? Are we the generations to create life or take it away? We can detach and distract, glue our eyes to our devices. Or we can walk in reverence and reset the path we have paved. Unplug. Take a walk in the forest. We can stand tall and proud for what we believe in. Let our roots grow deep and intermingle. We can stretch out our arms and choose love, like our planet's virescent lungs.

No matter our actions, or lack thereof, the truth remains: we need nature. Nature doesn't need us. Nature will rebirth and regenerate, eventually. For it is in sync with the cycles—autumn's fall, winter's introspection, spring's promise, and summer's kiss.

The world needs you.
The world needs your love.

Twenty minutes into my drive south to San Francisco, I pull over for a hitchhiker. He is smiling and dancing. I think it's a great way to attract a ride. At the billboards lining the highway exits to Santa Rosa, I realise we've been chatting the entire drive.

At one point, I go into a service station to pay for petrol then move the car to a nearby car bay so other drivers can refuel. He emerges from the toilet looking flabbergasted until he spots me waving in the car. I know that I'm trustworthy and considerate of others' possessions. From his perspective, everything he owns is in the boot of my car that was momentarily MIA. Hitchhiking renders a deeper trust in the journey.

It is almost midnight when we park up beside half a dozen cars in Golden Gate Park. Just as we've reclined our seats and dozed into our first breath of slumber, a loud knock jolts us awake. I rip down the travel towel I placed over the windscreen to block out the streetlight. A security guard blinds us with her torch and, after an amused smile that suggests the towel was erected for other reasons, commands us to move on. With a weary wave, I manoeuvre our chariot a few streets away and reverse park on a steep hill. It's the best sleep I have in that car. Tilting the seat back creates a wide V that holds me like a quirky crib.

In morning's light, we hug goodbye, then I reunite with Stephen at our usual café. In wide beams, we skip across the road to a seven-storey apartment block where white fire escapes zigzag to a black wrought-iron gate. Sculpted into the concrete header is an ornate beige owl, protecting everyone who enters the brown-bricked building. Stephen shares a tiny one-room apartment with three other men. Two bunks, a small fridge, sink, and wardrobe are stacked like Tetris inside. The communal shower is one big room with a three-minute timer that starts ticking as soon as I enter. When time is up, the lights go out, and I fumble for my clothes in darkness. I am humbled by the simplicity with which Stephen lives as we leave the city and venture east.

At the first sight of iconic granite bedrock soaring over pine forests, I exclaim, "Welcome to Yosemite!"

Stephen bursts into uncontrollable laughter.

"What's so funny?" I giggle, amused by his amusement.

Between fits of laugher, he explains, "It's pronounced Yo-sem-*it-ee*. Not YO-SEE-MIGHTY."

"Oh," I remark, but continue enunciating it as I had. It's a mighty national park. It deserves that in its name.

Hanging with Stephen is a combustion of curiosity, spontaneity, and enthusiasm softened with whiffs of creative waves. On the fringe of the national park, we stop beside a slow-flowing stream and watch glacial meltwater glide over fallen rocks. Perpetual flow rounds the debris over time, making the healing quality of surrender potent. Stephen's first instinct is to honour the trees by playing them a song on his guitar. Strums from fingers and thumb create soothing melodies that move over meadows, mountains, and moraines. They melt my thoughts and still my mind.

As dusk greys the park's lush mosaic, we roam the forest and find sanctuary on the bank of a shallow rivulet. Silhouetted by silky peach skies, the Sierra Nevada Mountains rises before us while birds sing the day's final symphony. On flattened peaks, trees appear as stick figures on a pilgrimage into the setting sun. They remind me of my internal voyage, slowly but steadily moving across bumpy terrain towards a radiance that inspires me to thrive. I am content and inspired. Then a nearby branch cracks and I spin around to a doe and her fawn eyeing us as they prance through the trees. A brown squirrel with white specks burrows into the ground nearby. I chuckle and tell Stephen that squirrels are my spirit animal. Inquisitive and resourceful, they have an abundance of energy, always have a stash of food, and know how to balance work, rest, and play.

We sleep in five-billion-star accommodation that night—in a parking lot beside a five-star lodging. In the morning, our escapade continues with artful surrender. Other sightseers watch us duck under safety rails to sit on the edge of glacially fashioned granite cliffs. Giant sequoia trees sprawl before us, backdropped by bold bedrock striking the sky with an awe-inspiring certainty. Brimming with adventure, a tune grows in our heart, inspired by an old-school Red Hot Chili Peppers song, "Flea Fly". One particular lyric in which the young musicians bellow "Bee-stay!" has us in hysterics as we mimic it on our walk. Eventually it inspires us to write a song. Melodies find a musician in Stephen. Lyrics find articulation through me.

Destination unknown
Going somewhere we don't know
Sitting on a rock, we have seeds to sow
Out in nature's where we grow

Oh, not the bee-stay
Now we're home
Oh, no, no not the bee-stay
My soul grows

Pick me up and let me be
Free like the chirping birds in the trees
Whispering wisdom through the leaves
Falling down on you and me

Catching wisdom with our hands
Turning it into this jam
Flowing with the currents, everything goes
Growing and glowing and going and going

Home is here, home is now
Everywhere, home is dear
Do not fear, for love is here
Follow the music until it's clear

Music moves through us. It moves us into a higher state of being. Lured off the beaten track swarming with tourists panting uphill towards the distant thunder of Yosemite Falls, we prance over partially submerged rocks to a series of hidden rock pools. Water cascades through our peaceful nook, half illuminated by midday sun and half shaded by forest canopy. We swim in cool currents, lounge on warm rocks, and sing our song as foliage falls upon our secluded paradise. Somewhere throughout the day, Stephen misplaces his guitar pick, and I lose my pen.

Eventually we stop rummaging through watery chasms, and Stephen proclaims, "I have this theory that when we lose something, it's because the universe has gifted us something else."

"Yeah?"

"Yeah, this is proof. Today we were gifted the inspiration to write a song, then we both lost something. My guitar pick symbolises the music. The lyrics, your pen."

His theory makes sense. Nothing is ever lost. It simply changes form.

En route back to the carpark we explore a lush forest trail boasting remarkable views of towering granite domes. As evening creeps in, the path becomes a two-lane bridge bordered by a low stone boundary. Two women and a man slump on the other side. As we ramble closer, a tense air is palpable with the man's loud complaints of the park. Arm in arm with Stephen, I feel a tornado brewing in my butt. At the exact moment we pass, I let it out—a long, loud fart ripping in a trumpet of methane.

This'll give the grumpy old fart something legitimate to complain about!

The bombardment of grumbles ceases. Stephen erupts in a fit of silent laughter, yet we don't miss a beat. We continue striding like nothing happened.

As soon as we're far enough away for our laughter to not be audible, I chuckle. "I'm so sorry, Stephen, they probably thought that was you."

With twinkling eyes, he guffaws, "Jess, I can't believe you did that. That was one of the funniest things I've ever seen. You know you ever so slightly turned your bum towards him as you farted?"

Oops.

That night, I'm woken by another loud knock on the car window. It isn't the man from the bridge seeking revenge. It's a park ranger. She warns us that bears may rip the doors off if they smell food inside. So it is, we embark on a drowsy midnight drive to a visitor's centre on the fringe of civilisation, nap, then quest west to Santa Cruz.

Seeking a college party has us happen upon a quaint cul-de-sac where a cluster of vibrant caravans nestle in a grove of redwoods. The quirky, bohemian community is part of the student accommodation at the University of California, Santa Cruz. It feels like a portal to Wonderland. Prayer flags dangle over wooden decks adorned with pot plants, small sculptures, and inviting outdoor furnishings. A group of students playing music on a picnic table chatter that university doesn't start for another week, so our mission to party fizzles in favour of an enticing forest trail.

Amid a small clearing with crunchy leaves slumps an abandoned queen-sized mattress. Stephen suggests we sleep on it tonight. It's a great idea—being cramped up in the car renders restless nights with tense muscles yearning for release through back-cracking spinal twists. On the surface it is pristine and clean. But something about it makes me uncomfortable. Maybe there's bed bugs lurking inside. The more I look at it, wondering how long it's been there and why someone dragged it so far into the forest, the eerier it becomes. Though I have no tangible proof, I can't shake the feeling of it being a place of rape. I voice this to Stephen. After a moment of silence, he too acknowledges the sinister vibe.

We shake off the chills with some standing yoga and the singing of our song. As I focus on opening up space in my spine, the unease settles. For me, at least. For Stephen, the presence looms, growing in power as fear widens his eyes. Daylight drains to a dark-grey hue. My heart thuds. I am sensitive to others' emotions. Without self-attunement, it is sometimes difficult to distinguish where I end and others begin. Three belly breaths centre me in clarity that the energy will amplify depending on my next thoughts. I choose them wisely.

Peace. Power. Protection.

Taking Stephen's hands, I lock him into my empowered gaze.

"Just breathe…"

His chest rises then falls in one shallow cycle. The surrounding air stagnates. Even the trees seem to stiffen in anticipation, as the sky compresses upon us. This is it. This is the moment to flick the switch from fear to love. Connecting to my heart, I call for protection from a higher force.

"Deep inhales. Deep exhales. Breathe into your stomach, and out through your heart," I affirm.

Breath fills Stephen's stomach, but his eyes dart to the canopy.

With softness and certainty carrying my words, I pray, "In the name of Jesus, go away."

I haven't been to church in years, but the words my dorm leader, Amber, shared long ago stuck. I pray this when my surroundings feel edgy or eerie. Though I don't believe in the way fundamentalists use religion as a motive for death or war, I've never stopped believing in the peaceful love at religion's core. When the layers of control are stripped back, when we look beyond elitists' misuse of power, I find solace in my connection to something more powerful than any pain experienced on this earthly plane. Something that listens and responds when we pray. In that moment, a gentle rustle moves through the leaves. It revives serenity from the tense stance of the forest opening.

Back in the car, Stephen and I plunge into a sea of secrets. The grime of our dark pasts find understanding in each other's eyes. Stephen doesn't judge me for my trauma-ridden promiscuity, my dark pits of depression, or my job as a lingerie barmaid. I don't judge him for his addiction to heroin and cocaine that led him to be incarcerated, until a few weeks before we met. I don't fear being alone with a convicted criminal. I am moved by his authenticity. I am proud of his tenacity to rise from the darkness. I am inspired by his will to grow. As he shares his journey into meditation and mindfulness behind locked prison doors with the help from another inmate, I blink back tears. A single drop spills from my eyes. It is followed by a racing cascade. Briny and inundating, the tears bring new insight.

From our confessions, a new song is born. It reaches a cadence as we pull into Monterey Bay the next day. Perched on a rocky groyne, we serenade the glassy blue sea as gulls glide on waves of wind, rising and falling with the crescendos and diminuendos of our song.

Roaming the globe;
A quest I ponder
the question of home
Is over yonder
where I should wander?

And this I wonder...

Porque no
Go with the flow
Release your peace
Piece by piece

Like music, life's raw emotion is expressed in crescendos and diminuendos. When Stephen and I say goodbye at Fremont Train Station, life decreases in volume and becomes still. Four eyes well with emotion.

"I love you," he marvels, in a low, sincere tone.

"I love you too," I whisper.

He locks his arms around me. Melting into the protective hold of his freckled biceps, I snuggle into his chest and rest my head on his beating heart. The perpetual thump softens the goodbye. Then the first twinkling tear falls, followed by a warm stream that rolls down my cheeks as I turn on my night vision and drive south to Los Angeles. Between sniffles and sobs, music undulates through me as I sing our songs until eventually the time comes to find solace in my dreams.

With one day until I must return the car, I venture to San Diego. At least, I try. Cruising through congested city traffic, I get as far as Orange County when a wave of exhaustion prompts me to pull over and take a nap. In a shaded corner of a quiet beachside carpark, a blissful breeze carries the conversations of attractive surfers through the window. My body's need to rest subdues my will to continue surging forward. Sometimes I move so fast even I can't keep up. In a diminished but caffeinated state I ache for sleep with eyes alert for the parking inspector sure to fine me for not paying the hefty fee. After an hour of restless tossing, I drive north to the Hollywood Hills for sunset.

Seeking a quiet space to park overlooking the illuminated city skyline is impossible in the labyrinth of security-surveyed streets. Narrow winding roads have me driving in circles for an hour. I want to spend a night in the Hollywood Hills. It's a Californian experience I want to seize. But in the car, with the psychogeographical barriers, it is impossible. With one last glance at the stunning stretch of city lights, I swallow my ambition and descend the hill. Beneath a leafy suburban street, I block out the windows with clothes and curl into the foetal position on the backseat. The next day, I return the rental car then bus to the Santa Monica hostel, grateful to finally sleep with a straight spine.

I awake with excited tingles to hop on a plane to Turkey. Tucked under the covers, I flip open my laptop to confirm what time I must leave for the airport. My heart shoots to my stomach. I had to be at LAX...yesterday.

By memorizing my arrival date in Turkey, I overlooked the two days lost in transit and assumed I left America a day later than I was meant to. A strange blend of aggravation and acceptance washes over me. A new flight costs $1000. There is nothing I can do but pay it. I apologize to Blair, who awaits me in Istanbul. I'm still coming. But I will be three days late.

Swallowing my dismay, I walk to the ocean and sink my feet into the sand. The power of the Pacific absorbs me. As I watch light particles dance on sea's shimmering surface, the realisation dawns that it's time to taper off my antidepressants completely. Since Peru, I've halved my dose. It's time to lower it again. If the sun can keep half the world warm when it's hidden from view, I can find solace in the darkness. I can befriend my mind. But first, I must let it unfurl...

Chapter VIII

THE UNFURLING

Music is medicine.

Songs soothe. Mixes move.

Audio alchemy redefines art.

My mind melts into melodies as

sonic tonics drip down my spine,

caressing me with instrumental poetry.

Time travel becomes tangible

gliding through the galaxy

on waves of sound.

Bursts of bass

pulsate with my heart

intertwining into a universal

language that we all understand.

Rolling with rhythm, I flow with tunes

tuning me in and out of reality.

Melodies in motion are

my chosen potion,

the elixir of life;

the soother

of strife.

Friday 13th September 2013

I used to wonder why intermissions break up great musical performances. I always thought it was for the performers. It's not. It's for the spectators. Mozart once said, "The music is not in the notes, but in the silence between." Suspended in disbelief, it is in this space our hearts and minds move in a synchronised beat. Dramatic pauses are essential to mould meaning—in music and in life. Just as audiences need an interval to integrate sound, we need an interlude to process the past and plan our path ahead.

My intermission comes in a twelve-hour plane ride traversing the Atlantic Ocean. In between continents, I process the teachings and transformation of the past two months. Soulful melodies swim through my ears as I contemplate amongst calligraphy clouds. I wonder what life will be like, free from the "need" to ingest a prescription drug each day. Can I train resilience and optimism into the same brain that caged me in fear?

When dinner arrives, I snap my orange antidepressant into three chalky chunks and swallow just one. Music delivers high-frequency healing vibrations that allow me to create new neural pathways as I surf sonic waves. My belief that antidepressants are the remedy because they've artificially regulated my brain chemistry for seven long years crumbles.

With the plane's descent, I come back to earth with a fresh perspective: I am determined to do more than survive. My commitment to thrive is unshakable.

Outside Istanbul International Airport, a local bus fills with people. Some glance back at me. Others look at their phones. Most gaze out the window into the dark night. I close my jet-lagged eyes and make a silent intention to bring more music into my life. Stephen awoke my dormant love for playing with rhythm, timbre, and sound. I want to create more. I want to immerse in foreign tones. When I open my eyes, the man beside me on the backseat smiles and holds out a headphone. Something in his burnt umber eyes beckons to be seen beyond surface shallows, so I nod and place the earpiece beside my left eardrum.

Surging through the wires connecting us, an angelic voice, mellifluous flute, and guitar carry us across the suburbs. With music, language is no longer a barrier. Though I cannot understand the words being sung, I feel a richness in the message being conveyed. It bridges the gap between us. I can't help but imagine myself as Lieutenant William Bradley dancing hand in hand with Aboriginal Australians in Sydney Cove in 1788 before centuries of interracial misunderstandings begun. Like my interaction with the mysterious Turkish man beside me, the encounter was friendly. Song and dance have always been a connector for different cultures through time. I love that.

As invisible sound waves vibrate liquid in my ear, thousands of tiny cells move to commute a memo to my brain. There is love etched into the melodies. It drips from the computer in my cranium to the ever-expanding centre of my heart.

I later discover the musician is the man beside me. He scribbles his name onto a blank page in my journal, and we communicate through broken English. When the bus reaches its final stop in a large, cobbled courtyard, he insists on walking me to my hostel. People fill the midnight streets. Homemade simit and car exhaust hang heavy in the air. At the edge of a bustling square, I stop and gesture that I am okay to walk alone. I don't want him to get the wrong idea by ending up at my hostel.

In retrospect, I realise he doesn't have an ulterior motive with me. His energy is clear. He signals with his hands that he is protecting me. But I am a fiery, intuitive, well-travelled woman. I don't need a guard.

My journey is one of exploring the world but also learning I can trust the people in it. As I lean forward to hug my new friend goodbye, he blocks me with an outstretched hand and steps back. With flushed cheeks, it hits me: I'm not in a western culture anymore. The cultural norms are different. I scold myself for not familiarizing myself with Turkish etiquette and farewell him with a nod instead. Change is the only constant, and on the road our ability to adapt must be swift and strong.

Change is inevitable
for the evolution
of our souls.
Shedding skins,
transforming into
something more whole.

At the hostel, Blair greets me with an excited squeal. Her chestnut bob has grown from when I surprised her for her thirtieth birthday in Queensland four months ago. We chat until the early hours of the morning then succumb to a short sleep in our sticky bunks. My eyes reluctantly open with morning's rays. Even the strong Turkish coffee simmering with an enticing, spicy aroma can't feign my body to stay awake. I feel bad for missing my flight and making Blair wait three days, so I force myself to explore the polychromatic city through a muted lens.

Charismatic carpet sellers and spicy bazaars trickle into my sphere like a movie playing in half time. I need rest. I need the nurturing cocoon of clean sheets to regenerate. In hindsight, I should have communicated this to Blair. I'm trying to be the nice girl, but I'm bypassing my own needs. Instead of sleep, I get streets. Bustling, cobblestone streets. Local dress shops become a repeated scene of Blair trying on outfits and whining about the fit. A palm to my forehead soon replaces complimentary words. Constantly offering reassurance is exhausting when someone always seeks external validation. I feel I'm being whisked into her decisions, rather than creating a shared adventure.

On our second day in the modernised old-world city, Blair yells at me to wake up. She's adamant to explore a cluster of picturesque islands known for their romantic horse-drawn carriages. I blink and mumble that I need sleep. I'm jet-lagged. Without a solid recharge I have nothing in my tank to give. She growls that I'm wasting time in bed. I lift the sheet over my head and roll over, leaving her to storm off alone. When Blair returns, the hostility melts. I've slept. She's explored. We apologise for expecting each other to compromise our individual needs. Sometimes it's healing to do your own thing.

I finally get a feel for Istanbul on our final day as I sip coffee on the sunny hostel roof. Minarets and domes bejewel a charismatic cluster of orange roofs that stretch towards the glistening blue strait connecting Asia and Europe. On the other side—a different continent, but the same city—mosques and churches adorn the photogenic skyline. It is a cultural and political frontier where Christians and Muslims have intermingled for centuries. As a loud, melodic call to prayer erupts from large speakers at a nearby mosque, a wave of serenity washes through the streets. It muffles the hum of air conditioners balanced beside satellite dishes atop most buildings. My nervous system regulates.

I think of acquaintances back home who may never witness Turkish culture because they fear different norms. Musing on the biases and assumptions that either enable or obstruct genuine connection, I stare at a red and white flag flapping softly in the wind. For the first time since landing, a sense of ease trickles through my veins. I've been swimming against the currents instead of surrendering to the flow.

Just as I'm sinking into the city with a slow exhale, an apprehensive chill rolls through my body. I instinctively scan nearby windows before knowing why. Then I see him. The man across the road stands naked by his window in full-frontal view. Dick in hand, he devours me in his hungry gaze. My muscles tense as molten lava spews through my upper body. I leap out of sight and extend my middle finger above the parapet. Then I crawl towards the stairs and retreat to my dorm as horror simmers to disgust.

Under the covers, I unfurl. Memory lane takes me back to Perth, four years ago, when a young dude followed my car along a highway in broad daylight, jerking as he drove. Simmering with fury, I scream into my pillow and kick my legs. I let the fire soar through me. I let it encompass me completely. Then I deepen my shallow breaths. Pulling the sheet over my head, I become present to the discomfort of my internal state. It is the compounding effect of these experiences that intensifies my pain. Rolling out my tangled emotional knots is liberating, but it also unveils all the shit I've swept into those stagnated bundles.

I understand it is up to me to heal my sexual trauma. I know it is up to me to create healthy boundaries so I can express them in an empowered way. But in the profundity of my inner terrain, I see this goes beyond just me. There needs to be a shift in society and accountability from men that this behaviour is not okay. It is time to create a new paradigm where women worldwide are treated with the equality and respect that we deserve. It's time for the patriarchy to crumble.

I crave wide-open spaces with room to breathe. At the end of an overnight bus to Göreme in Cappadocia, my wish is granted. On the high plateau punctured with volcanoes is a troglodyte village hollowed from caves and tall, thin rock spires called "fairy chimneys". Lack of sleep enhances the otherworldly feeling. I am stepping into a vivid fairy tale.

At the time, the Australian government advises reconsidering the need to travel in Turkey, especially the east near the Syrian border. Last month the Assad regime unleashed rockets filled with nerve agent on their own people in Damascus. The news stings my chest as I remember the Syrian father and son on the beach nine months ago. Their tortured eyes torment me as I toss in bed at our picturesque hostel that backs into beige caves. My head throbs with static buzz. My eye muscles spasm. Sharp zaps electrify my brain like lightning storming in frenzied blasts. I later understand these are my first withdrawals from tapering off antidepressants.

Despite government warnings, Cappadocia fast becomes one of my favourite travel destinations. By day we explore moonscape valleys, vacant caverns, and subterranean tunnels etched within the soft fawn stone. Locals offer us rides through the whimsical landscapes. They don't ogle or hassle. Their respect renders a safety that allows me to drop into a dreamy space. It is from this serenity that this story unravels.

Once upon a time, only about one or two million years ago, dragons nestled in the picturesque troglodyte village we now know as Göreme. It was a time after the noble dragons left, departing this world for another. The hearth in their hearts was no longer fuelled with excitement or rich creative spark. It was rage. It was greed.

The colossal creatures were restless. They were reckless. Their wisdom was deep, but their gluttony was toxic. Despite their capacity to zoom in on prey far away, they could not foresee their own wrath. Hungering for the jewels nestled within Earth's skin, they clawed into her crust with their sharp, razorblade talons. An innate and all-encompassing peace emanated from Earth's core, enriching her with patience, empathy, and understanding. In a low tone with slow articulation, she warned the dragons to stop.

"You must look within yourselves to find gold. Not pillage the planet."

The dragons knew better. They chose not to change. Quenching a thirst that they could not satisfy, they always wanted more. They continued thrusting their tails into Earth's crust, selfishness hardening their once-soft skin. As they cracked Earth open, a deep, stabbing pain oscillated into her core. Through steaming chambers, her mantle and crust connected in volcanos mounding from the lacerations. Her skin was broken like a sundered shield, revealing her sheltered heart to the vulnerability of her rupture that was her rapture. For being broken is how we open. We must destroy the old before we create something new.

Shooting hot magma from three volcanoes formed from the dragons' claws, she watched it stream into the dragons' nest. The gases she excreted were poisonous to the beasts, for her love-filled breath was a medicine the dragons did not know how to swallow. Slowly but surely, the dragons withered and waned, destroyed by their own vile greed. The dragons couldn't change their ways fast enough to save themselves. But maybe we humans can.

When the ash settled and their era evanesced, Earth was fragile. The entire Cappadocian plateau was strewn with destruction. Volcanic ash consolidated, creating light porous rock, and from the rubble, the rebuilding began. The Earth continues to change face, transforming through time. She promised she would never crack open her heart in that part again. In reverence for the mighty beasts, though they lost their way, she plateaued part of herself where the dragons' lair once lay.

In the years that followed, she allowed herself to cry. To heal by letting herself feel. To find peace through release. Sometimes her tears cascaded from the sky in torrential rainstorms that drowned out her rational mind and eroded soft layers of lava and ash into spindly stems of surreal enchantment. Other times, she iced over, becoming cynical to love *and life in despair of the destruction. Eventually she found hope. She always found hope. Her demeanour warmed with the golden nectar of dripping sunshine that melted away her melancholy as she embraced the future's mystery with optimism and pride. It was her swift climatic changes—her courage to embrace all facets of her emotions—that transformed the ruin into the riveting rocks we see today.*

It was the captivating caverns carved from wind and water washing away the warfare that compelled the fairies to come. When they arrived thousands of years ago, they built chimneys from their underground homes in tall, thin rock spires protruding out from the arid Anatolian Earth. They fluttered with joy and flattered Earth for her beauty. Her inherent power. Her unwavering poise. Her inspiring perseverance.

Filling the sky with song, the vivacious creatures sent healing vibrations deep into Earth's core. The Earth resonates with the pure of heart and sprouted wildflowers for the fairies to tie around their naked bodies. Delighting in the floral fragrances, they played chasey in the sky. "Tag, you're 'it'!" they cheered, coating Earth's contours with honeycomb and cream fairy dust. Different eras of Earth's emotion streaked the strata. Yellow tips show the fairies' joy. Layers of pink and red—the bleeding of her heart—stratified over the white and grey wisdom and purity she gained from her pain.

Eventually, as with all inhabitants of Earth, the time came for the fairies to go. Transcending the lunarscape they loved so dearly, the fairies relocated to the moon. From there, they admire Earth with tender love. Sometimes you can glimpse them fluttering across the night sky in a glistening stream of light. Their airborne magic often appears as shooting stars glistening in streams of light. Look a little closer. Listen a little deeper.

Can you hear the fairies singing for us to treat our Earth with the reverence she deserves?

After a sunrise hot air balloon ride with clouds maturing from fuzzy mauve to milky white, we venture to Alanya. To my dismay, it is a resort town filled with scantily clad Europeans. I miss the intricately eroded, stratified layers of the Cappadocian plateau that bestowed my eyes with stunning panoramas of rippling crevices and branded ravines. In Alanya, flabby red butts wobble to the ocean as topless sunbakers dots sandy Mediterranean shores. I dislike resort towns because the construction of luxury buildings inevitably pollutes the authenticity that was once the draw.

In our hotel lobby, white tiles reflect the tenth-storey balcony. The receptionist smiles as the man before us takes his key. As we step forward and Blair hands over her passport, a sudden zap strikes my skull like lightning striking a rocket moving a lightspeed. I am shocked by the source of the sensation. It is not external. It comes from within.

"Whoa." My voice sounds foreign, like someone else is talking. Holding my spinning head, I look at my feet planted firmly on the floor.

Blair whirls around, examining me with caring eyes. "Are you okay?"

"Yes," I soothe, not wanting to cause concern.

Then my ears start ringing like Sunday morning church bells. I lunge towards a grand piano and collapse on its spongy stool. My hands and feet tingle. I can't shake this heavy, depersonalized feeling lugging me down like a weighted vest.

I feel like a walking dollar sign as Turkish men eye us like candy. Yells from hassling shopkeepers are clappers inside my skull that intensifies to a gigantic bell. I'm dizzy then drowsy. My head throbs then fogs. But I keep on smiling. Partly because I don't want to ruin Blair's holiday and partly because triggering facial muscles with a smile—even if fake—releases dopamine and serotonin which trick the brain into happiness. It's alchemy, so long as I don't permanently bypass dark emotions and the lessons they hold.

I am happy to leave Alanya for Antalya, another Mediterranean city that stretches towards turquoise shores. We sleep in a finely restored Ottoman house in the old city where vines climb medieval walls. Cobbled streets wind in an endearing labyrinth that connects bars, bazaars, and boutique stores. My external reality mirrors the grey matter meshing in my mind. Blair and I take familiar roads that trail past the 13th century six-domed mosque and late-night dondurma vendors daily. Inside my brain are imprinted patterns of thought and behaviour. Externally, we can take a different path. Internally, I can reroute neural pathways by choosing better thoughts.

On a day trip to Düden Waterfalls, I contemplate medicine transcending something we package and mass-produce. Sunshine on my skin triggers the uplifting release of serotonin in my brain. I feel clearer on days I skip the sugary spreads, processed meats, and glutenous baked goods at breakfast in favour of fresh cucumber, vitamin-rich tomato, tasty olives, and eggs. I see the correlation between basking in nature and a balanced mood. As white reflective strips spray me with tranquillity, I ponder the link between high-speed internet and mankind's waning connection. I can't help but think that our mental health epidemic is a consequence of the technological evolution.

Blair is content to sit with me and gaze into the lush green hinterland containing the small cascades. Slippery spiral stairs lead to a cave behind the waterfall where a Facebook post Riley recently scribed echoes in my mind: *The pilgrimage of the headspace to the heart place. It's not a race, we get there at our own pace.* Maybe the maze I'm trying to master begins with undoing the knots of my mind. Maybe then I can sink into the stillness of my heart.

The idea warms me, like mineral-rich waters trickling down glistening white terraces that resemble giant steps in Pamukkale, the inland village we venture to next. Hiking shoeless up the thermal travertine pools, we periodically dip our bodies in warm aquamarine waters. Above the remarkable geological phenomena are first-century ruins. In the colonnaded streets connecting ancient temples, bathhouses, cemeteries, a well-preserved theatre, and a necropolis with sarcophagi, eastern Europeans pose provocatively in G-string bikinis to get Insta-perfect pics. It's bizarre to witness the sacred city that was once the holy end of a long pilgrimage dotted with bare flesh. First, confusion clouds me. Then, a fire erupts.

The busloads of day-trippers dissipate as evening kicks in. I walk slowly down the mountain, charmed by the feeling of water gushing past my feet as it cools with the setting sun. It's like walking on dried-up cotton candy, where giant dollops of the sugary dessert have been scooped out to create the pool steps. At the bottom of the terraces is a shimmering turquoise lake. Thinking of Riley's words, I envision mineral-rich waters trickling from the ruins of my mind—the remains of the ancient city—into the peaceful reservoir of my heart.

Thorns and roses grow on the same tree.
- **Turkish proverb**

Short stays in Izmir and Çeşme bring us to Chios, a unique Greek island with fortress-like architecture blending into citrus orchards and glossy seas. The sun-soaked serenity puts us in good spirits. We hire a car, laughing as we pull in the side-view mirrors to squeeze through narrow cobbled lanes in medieval mastic villages decorated with black-and-white motifs. At night, my withdrawals continue with night sweats drowning me in abnormal dreams, but finally there is a positive: the return of my lucid dreams.

From Chios we're at a crossroads of where to travel next. Blair dreams of Santorini. I want to explore somewhere new. Eventually I yield, and we set sail to the world's most beautiful volcanic creation. Our journey composes of two long ferry rides, in which the first departs late. As we disembark in Athens, seagulls screech and heavy metallic creaks crash into salty gales. The commotion mutes when we realise our next ferry is anchored two kilometres away. It leaves in five minutes. We both have fifteen-kilogram backpacks containing everything we'll need for two years. There's no way we can sprint there in time.

Nearby, a worker loads baggage onto a truck.

"Geia sas, sir!" I call. "Do you know anyone who can give us a ride to gate nine?"

He looks up and spots two sexy locals motorcycling towards us with takeaway coffees in hand. He yells in Greek. They holler back. He says something else. Their eyes bulge from their heads, then they screech to a stop and gesture for Blair and me to board their bikes. It's impossible to balance us, our bags, and their fresh coffees, so they fling them aside and speed us across Europe's largest port. We arrive in cinematic timing. Ten seconds after we step onto the ferry, the loading ramp inclines. Heart pounding, I meet Blair's bewildered green eyes and burst out laughing.

"I guess...we *are* meant to go to Santorini..."

Long ago, before we created navigational compasses enabling us to chart our location in the open ocean and thus map the world, an innate wisdom was known and revered by our ancestral tribes.

It was that of the elements—Earth, Fire, Water, Air—the four fundamental forces that create our fabric of life. In a time when our family tree was much smaller, our ancient forefathers gathered every dusk and dawn. Sunny, snowy, stormy, or still, they sang into the tangerine twilight:

"Earth my body
    Water my blood
    Air my breath and
    Fire my spirit."

Each element is composed of deep-rooted shadows and gifts. Strong and stable, Earth takes steady strides to build substance over long periods of time. She teaches the others patience, allowing them to ground into her solid being and giving nourishment to grow. By nature, she can root so firmly into dried-up beliefs, she crusts into a deep trench that is unyielding to change.

With a dash of daring, Fire inspires her to open with his illuminating spark. His warmth is invigorating because he stirs high ideals with an infectious zest for life. Fire is bold and bewitching. The speed with which he ignites with tremendous passion is thrilling, unless his fuel is rage.

Water's calming currents cool Fire's heat when needed. Fluid and flowing, completely drenched in feeling, her psychic depths are a blessing and a curse. Her acute sensitivity enables compassion and care that cleanses away impurity, allowing an osmosis of intuition and imagination to flow. Sometimes, though, she swims too deep, drowning in a desire to escape it all.

That's when Air breezes in, with a curiosity and charm lightening the load. He transcends the murky world of feelings to the clear mental stratosphere, where fresh ideas and information glide into his invisible skin. Omnipresent and oxygenating, Air is empowered by Earth's ability to bridge his ideas into reality.

Every month, the elements convene to commemorate life. Beneath the inky black sky of each dark moon, they meet on a beautiful island in the Aegean Sea. Earth gifts Fire broken branches to fuel his golden glow. Unto the flames, Air exhales the mysterious mist gathered in his lofty trail. Water warms her salty seas, giving rejuvenation and replenishment for her elemental kin.

One cloudy evening, a sudden vision ignites in Fire's flames. In a ravenous frenzy, orange flickers twist and curl into obscure shapes, hypnotising the elements like a plasma TV. Burning branches become images of human hands relentlessly slicing old-growth forests with no reverence for the wisdom in each splinter of every tree. As man strings massive wooden trunks together to construct ships and conquer the world, images of death and destruction entail. They massacre indigenous tribes. Poisonous gases gush into the air. The oceans fill with toxic pollutants. All in the name of evolution.

The vision extinguishes, leaving golden embers in its wake as a wave of unease crashes the party.

Air gasps for breath, gagging for a long, deep inhale, as though the irritated tingle of carbon monoxide already seeps into his skin.

Earth ruptures into a fit of thick, phlegmy coughs, as though trying to rid the infections that land degradation will bring.

A single, silent tear falls from Water's eye in a salty trickle. It ripples into her entire being.

Fire flares into a wild inferno, outraged by the vision that flashed to life in his flames.

With a scorching heat, he roars, "We must burn them! We must destroy all humans, before they destroy us."

Air breezes backwards, detaching from the emotional charge with an aloof air that refuses to fan Fire's flames. The conversation makes him anxious, as information speeds through his nervous system like a falcon diving towards prey.

Water remains silent. On the surface, she is calm. Beneath her composed exterior, she plunges to benthic depths. Fire's words echo into her psychic realms as she searches for deeper meaning.

It is Earth who breaks the silence, concluding in a firm, dry tone, "No. I gave an oath to provide for all beings who call me home."

Fire sizzles, "You saw the vision in the flames. These monsters don't deserve you. It will be the beginning of the end!"

Earth ponders Fire's raging plan with an admirable practicality, stoic in her emotions. Enduring a stubborn self-control that is sometimes necessary, Earth breathes into her core and responds, "No. My word is my word."

Before Fire can fume back in a vindictive spark, Air gusts in, "I understand your anger, Fire. But destroying humans will go against our elemental vows. Let's send a message instead. A warning of the devastation that will come if they lose their humanity to greed. I can stretch my body thin. I will send messages in the whispers of the wind, as I scatter pollen and seeds...."

A ruminating silence follows.

Finally, Water gushes in. "Yes, it's the only way. The vision is real. It's inevitable for humans to sail across my seas. It's inevitable for the world be to be connected. Yes, there will be death and destruction. But there is more. When humanity remembers how it feels to love each other, there will be unity on Earth."

The primal impulse of Fire does not rule Water. She is guided by her intuition, flowing into every crack and crevice, then becoming one with her container. When Water speaks, Fire listens. For the ancient elemental codes enable her to cool his heat and extinguish him, if necessary.

"A message with magnitude is vital," Air breathes. "It will require a sacrifice from us all. For the world to hear us, we must each give a part of ourselves to birth something better..."

The elements solidify their plan until twilight. Together they fuse Air's ideas, Fire's passion, Earth's ambition, and Water's depth of understanding. Then the sounds of singing fill the morning air, and they embrace in a bittersweet goodbye.

In the time that follows, Fire and Earth join forces to create magma—hot molten rock—that Water deliberately embraces. Magma's heat turns Water to steam, creating a volatile pressure with transferring thermal energy. As steam expands explosively, Magma tears apart in a monumental volcanic eruption.

Rip. Rumble. Roar.

The eruption is equivalent to the detonation of forty atomic bombs.

Thick rivers of lava became blood baths for the island's original inhabitants. Water crashes in massive tsunamis. Every half hour, titanic waves strike the shores of Crete, crashing ships into the mountains.

Air bears the burden of ash and dust, along with the roaring acoustics that are heard in modern-day Delhi. After two days, magma chambers completely empty. This causes the volcano to implode, and thus creates the glimmering caldera of water connecting what we now call Santorini. Grey pumice coats the ocean. Volcanic ash pierces the stratosphere, starving Earth of sunlight and clean air. It is a cataclysm bringing a global winter for two years. Temperatures drop. The sun sets in strange colours. Famine breaks out in modern-day China. Then there is silence.

Eventually, white Cycladic houses sprinkle over the crescent-shaped island, and the world comes to see. Every year, two million tourists awe at tangerine sunsets melting into sapphire seas while snapping postcard-perfect selfies.

Santorini is more than just a stunning metaphor of the beauty created from utter destruction. It's more than just a tourist hotspot enchanting us with iconic images of whitewashed villages clinging to photogenic cliffs. Direct from elements that knit the tapestry of our lives, it is a message. A reminder to open our hearts and feel the world's collective beat. To love our Earth and live with reverence for the mother who homes us.

En route to our hostel from the port, we meet a tall Californian blonde. She is fluent in German and speaks basic Russian and Greek. One night she immerses us in a theatrical opera show in the hostel courtyard. It's hilarious because there isn't much warning. Amid deep but pleasant conversation about world politics and our different spiritual or atheist beliefs, it arises that she's learning the art. Thirty seconds later, after a little persuading from myself and another traveller, she shows us how the human voice is an instrument that tells a story. Two new arrivals scurry past like they're walking over a freshly mopped floor. Then some other travellers join and watch the performance with dropped jaws. Just as she's hitting a high hammer vibrato, a nearby window slams open and a man who retired early yells to keep the volume down.

One evening, after an exhilarating day zooming around the island on hired quad bikes, we stroll to a nearby bakery. While I lick my lips at the mouth-watering display of cheesy pastries, custard tarts, and chocolate chip cookies, the man behind the counter shoots a fiery, "Where are you from?"

My stomach cringes, but I bubble, "Everywhere."

His upper lip curls. As he snaps the question again, I notice his hands clenched into fists. Our personal identity doesn't matter to him. He's looking for a fight.

"I've been living in Germany for the past five years and I'm about to relocate to Athens—" my Californian friend begins.

"But where are you from? What does your passport say?"

"The United States."

Her answer is fuel for his short fuse.

"I don't like *Americans*. They killed my best friend."

The man fumes that his best friend was in NATO and America forced him to go to Somalia, where he died. The freshly baked aroma of cookies and cakes becomes sickly as he spits each word.

I don't understand what he's raging about. She does. In a restrained tone she apologizes for his loss. She's sincere, and it's noble considering the way he's snarling at her with misplaced spite. Then she explains NATO is a conglomeration of multiple countries, thus the responsibility would be on all nations involved, not just the USA. Somalia had a terrible drought that year, causing widespread famine that prompted people to flee to neighbouring countries. This led to vigilante groups taking over and aid workers being unable to deliver supplies to starving people, which is why soldiers entered. She clarifies that to blame the individual people of a country for military choices is unfair. She had as much control over what happened as he did.

Her rationality shifts the situation from unpleasant to awkward. The man is silent as we pay for our pastries. I'm grateful we have exact change.

Outside the bakery, I console, "I'm so sorry that just happened."

She sighs.

There is a long silence before she gulps. "It's okay. I'm used to it... People *love* judging Americans..."

How you make your bed is how you are going to sleep.
- Greek proverb

Santorini is a sun-kissed crossroads of where to go next. Months ago, Blair and I agreed to move to the UK after travelling. She has a visa and job transfer. I have a British passport. As her starting date approaches, I'm uninspired to start anew in London's gloomy weather. I'm not ready to settle. It takes a local bar offering me work on the island to realise this. When I voice it, Blair erupts like old Santorini. I feel guilty for bailing on our plan, and I understand her fear in making the move alone. But I cannot ignore the whispers of my heart telling me there's something else in store.

Eventually she comes around. With wet cheeks and compassionate smiles, we hug and make peace with the decision to venture different ways. It's new for me to assert my wants and needs, rather than diminishing my desires by people-pleasing. With seasoned wisdom, I see the links with my sexual healing and cultivating confidence to say no when sparked by visceral body sensations.

As the sun melts into the sea, we revel in tomorrow's promise with our collective holding of breath. The horizon twists into a golden reverie. I get clear on my direction. It entails a ferry and three back-to-back buses into Bulgaria.

❦

An exhilarating spark to explore somewhere new accompanies the usual fatigue of overnight travel. I arrive in Sofia midmorning and stroll uneven cobblestone roads to my hostel. It's the first time I've ventured beyond Western Europe. I'm instantly enthralled by the broken realness as I dodge potholes in cracked sidewalks that connect an eclectic blend of architecture conveying the city's complex history. The putrid smell from garbage piles is not so attractive.

Coincidently, my Bulgarian friend from high school is in Sofia on an annual family visit. They are on a mission to issue her a Bulgarian passport. I tag along, climbing dim stairwells encrusted with graffiti to lawyers' offices and government buildings. Her dad—a warm, bright-eyed man who I've always admired—greets me with his customary excited "Jessi!" and chats about the Bulgarian government's corruption while we pursue a wild-goose chase of under-the-cover deals. He says that seceding Soviet control, there practically isn't a government anymore. The people were left in ruins. Bribery is the only way to get things done.

Locals are regularly protesting in the streets, tired of political elite's lack of transparency and the inequality between wealthy and poor. Two attractive guys sleeping in my cosy attic dorm—Australian Max and American Mike—attend the protests and note the intensity thick in the city's air. I bump into them shortly after farewelling my old friend, and we stroll the chilly streets together. Beside a lavish church laden with turquoise and gold domes, we scout flea markets filled with communist antiques, fake Roman coins, war medals, and rare 1936 Olympic medallions that inconspicuously stud every second stall. They bicker like a married couple as we meander through the strange jumble of grey Soviet-era apartments, excavated Roman ruins, Ottoman mosques, and Eastern Orthodox cathedrals. Mike calms Max by feeding him the odd Prozac. But he doesn't give it up easy.

That night we embark on a pub crawl. I'm committed to sobriety while tapering off my medication, so I sip water while the guys gulp beer. By not indulging in escapism, I empower my mind with clarity amid moods that secretly swing from optimistic and determined to suicidal thoughts that tantalise me with the allure of ending it all. The boys induce my wit with their down-to-earth cheekiness that sometimes edges on cocky. It's a trait in young Western men I have not missed. Yet as I share my awakenings in Peru, I sense intrigue, depth, and maybe even resonance in Max's striking steel-blue eyes. Outside a lonesome bar at the end of the night, he sets his gaze on me and quips, "So, what's the go? Are you just a tease, or...?"

Half joking, half arrogance, the question is sobering because it stirs my new ideals into old ways of being. I am enticed by confident approaches. But something in me has shifted. I'm learning to love myself, to stand for what I want and don't want, and to be in this power without apology.

I look him dead in the eye and respond, "I'm not going to sleep with you, but I'll be your friend."

We collapse into our separate beds that night, set up in two straight lines beneath an A-frame roof suspended by thick wooden pillars. I snuggle into myself, beaming wide. It's the first time I've confidently said no and directly expressed my boundaries when provoked for sex. It feels fantastic.

The next morning, we eat breakfast at a local cafeteria sizzling with minced meat. The guys invite me to travel south with them to a famous Eastern Orthodox monastery. I'm tempted, but I stick to my northern plan. Back at the hostel, I ready my bag then spot Max nursing his hangover in his bed across the room. Sunlight streams through the windows. He motions for me to join. There's an innocence to the gesture, and my celibate stance is clear, so I lie beside him and curl into a ball as he wraps his arms around me and holds me tight. It's been months since I've felt the warmth and tenderness of a long embrace. As I soften into the affection, I am imprinted with a new notion of intimacy being more than just sex. I also come to realise that at our core, we usually seek the same thing: human connection.

Draw water from the new well, but do not spit in the old one.
- Bulgarian proverb

It is dark when I arrive in Belogradchik, a sleepy village in the north-western corner of Bulgaria. I trot past closing shops on empty streets to my cosy yellow guesthouse. No one is home when I arrive. I am unsettled to pierce the thick darkness in search of a more substantial dinner, so I microwave some oats in the communal kitchen. My audacity is coupled with intuition. I often stroll alone, it's part of travelling, but tonight, a niggly feeling tells me to stay put.

Shortly after I've eaten, Mariyana—the slender guesthouse owner—breezes in. Her flabbergasted expression morphs into a warm smile as she takes me in. Apparently, she was waiting for me at the bus station to chauffeur me here free of charge. I'm not used to the kindliness. She's not used to the independence. We laugh it off and wish each other a pleasant night. In my private room, I cosy into bed while absorbing an article on the transformative power of affirmation. I appreciate that science backs the concept of programming our subconscious mind with positivity to access new belief systems. With space to sink deeper into my thoughts than a shared dorm would allow, I'm reminded of my conversation with Lesley post-ceremony.

I've been resistant to the mirror work that she directed I do. Maybe it's time to begin. I push my laptop away to take the first brave step of facing my reflection, but instead of jumping out of bed, I sit there, body frozen. My eyes dart around the room. I seek distraction. On the wall, a circular light cover depicts a jigsaw puzzle with a missing piece. It is abstract and unique and captivates me with its symbology. I can't tell if it means I'll find the missing piece by looking towards the light, or if there will always be more pieces to discover.

At any moment, I can switch off the importance of Lesley's homework. But the more I look at it, the clearer it becomes: dimming the light keeps me in stalemate, in limbo between wanting to love myself but lacking empowered action. It's a poignant realisation. Enough to have me rip the blanket off and march towards the mirror. In my hazel gaze, I see a determined young woman, faced with the decision to be her own best friend or most feared enemy.

"You're beautiful," I mutter.

My reflection blinks and ever-so-slightly grimaces.

Lifting my chin, I clarify, "You're beautiful."

It takes every ounce of will inside me to resist the urge to laugh or run. I breathe through the stiffness compounding in my muscles. Then I meet myself with a fixed gaze.

"*You*, are fucking *beautiful*."

It's raw and vulnerable and very uncomfortable. But I push through. If I can't see the beauty that is inherent in every human, no others' words will ever sink in. Finally, my eyes crinkle. I release a grin.

In the morning, I wake late and slam myself for sleeping in. I'm making progress integrating healthy habits, but it takes patience and practise to assimilate a new norm. Dull grey clouds loom over the Balkan Mountains in the horizon outside. *Don't make yourself wrong, Jess. Tomorrow is a new day. Today, you needed the sleep.*

From the crisp foothills where I stand, I embrace a winding trail. It leads to gigantic grey boulders striking the sky like a mammoth rock castle. Nudging closer, I notice the fortified walls of an ancient fortress strategically built around the rocks. Stone steps and metal ladders lead me to a smooth rock pile at the top. There, I perch. An eerie fog slithers close. Then it creeps around me. I stand there for a long time, gazing into the dreary haze that camouflages the lofty drop below.

What happens if I jump? Will the veil lift?

Be humble for you are made of earth. Be noble for you are made of stars.
- Serbian proverb

Travelling alone, far from family and friends, is testing at the best of times. When your brain is rapidly adjusting to neurological changes that disrupt your body's normal function, it's agonising. The decision to continue travelling while tapering off antidepressants is mine. I therefore take accountability for the anguish merging with travelling's enchanted waves. At any moment I can fly home or continue taking my "medication". Deep within myself, I know that this is the path I'm meant to take.

The part of me that is tenacious beyond reason becomes salient at this time. No matter the external circumstance, I am bound by resilience and resolve. It's how I survived at fifteen/sixteen. It's how I survive now.

During this time, seemingly meaningless actions have lasting effect. The kindness of strangers, particularly Mariyana, is light in the abyss. She insists on driving me to the bus stop the morning I leave Belogradchik and arranges to collect me after breakfast. I agree, despite it only being a ten-minute walk. Mariyana is a warm ray. I am about to again embark into the murky unknown.

As I sip coffee in the ornamental courtyard, my eyes dart from a grinning terracotta gnome to my small digital travel clock. The minutes tick to my bus's departure. I ponder walking into town, but Mariyana was adamant to take me, and I don't want to offend. Maybe the bus is running late and she knows this because word travels fast in tiny towns.

Fifteen minutes later, Mariyana rushes into the garden. The usual silky cascade of her mousy-blonde locks is a dishevelled mess. Her chest collapses in when she sees me.

"Jessica, I'm so sorry," she blurts. "I slept in."

A strange peace trickles over me. "That's okay," I reassure. "Obviously I wasn't meant to be on that bus."

Mariyana makes me coffee in her home around the corner, then asks her husband to drive me to the Serbian border. I try to oppose it. It's an hour away!

Before leaving, I snap a photo of Google Maps to gauge where I'm going. Twelve kilometres from the border is a small Serbian city with a bus to the bigger city of Niš. In the car, I make small talk with Mariyana's husband in broken English as we cruise past lush verdant meadows. Fresh air breezes through the window. It tastes delicious.

At the border, he declines the money I offer for driving me so far. With a tired wave, I stride towards a lonesome building that is the border crossing station. Truckers nap on the side of the road before another long drive. A sleepy-eyed man stamps my filled-to-the-brim passport. Then he scratches his scalp and watches me with bulging eyes as I walk across the invisible line into Serbia.

Crunching over fallen leaves, I take a single carriageway that snakes through green fields dotted with the occasional stone house. Irregular drizzles fall from overcast skies. Sometimes I catch the drops on my tongue. Sometimes I plonk my backpack beside the damp road and sit on it to rest while pinching the skin on my forearm. This is so absurd. No one knows where I am or what I'm doing. Anything can happen. Yet the rural stillness puts me at ease.

A few hours into the enchanted walk, my shoulders collapse beneath my backpack. With the hum of the next approaching car, I swing out my thumb and catch eyes with a local couple. The woman shakes her head apologetically, nodding at stacked firewood cramming the backseats. I return the smile and continue walking. Shortly after, a loud truck squeals to a stop ahead. I recognise it from a parking bay at the border and decide to suss the vibe before committing to the ride.

Climbing the passenger-side ladder, I set my gaze on a wide-smiled, crinkle-eyed man.

"Where you going?" he sings, with an open palm.

He's clearly quite amused, and I'm unable to contain my smile because the situation's humour suddenly becomes apparent through his entertained eyes.

"I...I don't know," I bubble. "Where are *you* going?"

"*Belgrade!*" he exclaims, pronouncing the Serbian capital *bell-graad-aye*. "You come?"

I ponder the offer as combustion fumes from the diesel engine waft behind me. A photo of a young girl on his sun shield catches my eye. It's either his daughter or a purposely positioned image to make me think this way. In a split-second decision stemming from my gut, I settle on trusting him.

Shrugging my tired shoulders, I chirp, "Okay."

For the next five hours, we communicate in short sentences and exaggerated facial expressions. The man is transporting timber from Bulgaria to Germany. He teaches me that a head nod means no in Bulgaria, while a head shake means yes. As the truck groans forward, trees drip in scarlet cascades and rich orange veils. I awe at their ability to shed their skin with the seasons but dare not scramble through my bag to capture the choreography of colour on camera. I don't want to miss a moment of the vivid montage.

Two hundred fifty kilometres later, we pull into a petrol station on the fringe of Belgrade, and the man points to a bus stop that will take me into the city. I gift him a small bottle of rose oil for his six-year-old daughter. Then we wave goodbye.

Dusk deepens Belgrade to a noble solemnity as I disembark the bus an hour later. Seeking a hostel amongst haggard socialist blocks, I am charmed by massive murals that embellish cold concrete walls. Zebra crossings become literal with African equines painted over the road's black-and-white stripes. After a few laps around a gritty, old-world neighbourhood, I set my eyes on a man with a furrowed brow trudging towards me.

"Excuse me, do you speak English?" I ask.

"Hm, ah, yes," he replies in a thick Serbian accent.

He smells like an ashtray.

"Do you know if there is a hostel nearby?"

His stony expression morphs into a wide grin that surprises me as he directs me up the road. The encounter introduces me to the helpful, blunt, and passionate nature of Balkan locals. At first glance I take them as stiff and rude, but these traits aren't baked into their DNA. It's more like a resting bitch face combined with tough cynicism from the decade-long misery of ethnic conflict that shook the region.

From that first interaction, I decide to stay in Belgrade a while. There's something fresh and alive in the audacity of an unpolished city wearing the scars of its past without explanation or apology. History is written in stone, between pine-lined avenues bridging the remnants of Ottoman relics, art nouveau architecture, bombed buildings with candy-coloured facades, and small shops selling babushka dolls amid other Russian memorabilia. Golden leaves pirouette in the wind. Wrinkled men play chess beside elaborate Orthodox churches. I understand why Belgrade translates to the "White City" for white is made by mixing all colours of the rainbow.

Merging with the perpetual rhythm keeping spirits high, I fall in love with the art coating valiant concrete streets. It's an open-air art gallery where freedom flourishes in the full expression of generation Y coming to age while witnessing the blood of civil war. It compels me. The graffiti isn't your typical vandalism at the hands of teenage rebels. It's creativity in its purest form, sparking new ideas and elaborate visions through intricate brushstrokes and layers of sprayed paint.

Looking back, it's strange to reflect on the way the photographers, dance-crew members, raki drinkers, explorers, and friends I meet in Belgrade perceive me. Just like Belgrade—enduring 115 wars where it was burnt down forty-four times—I am rising from the ashes and remembering the strength of my own flames. My softness and sensitivity aren't traits I reveal to strangers. To them, I'm a vivacious wild child, who hitched a ride there and is down for a fun time. I've been diving deep into my inner terrain. It's refreshing to come up for air amid the diversity of new friends who lounge with me on ancient stone walls while the sun sets over the confluence of two mighty rivers.

*

> *The eyes of all cheats are full of tears.*
> **– Bosnian proverb**

On a small white shuttle bound for Sarajevo, a local lady insists that I'll love the Bosnian and Herzegovinian capital. A French man also living in the city agrees. I ask what prompted his move, but an American traveller interrupts us to announce that Franz Ferdinand's assassination on a Sarajevo bridge instigated World War I. The French guy rolls his eyes. The American repeats his interjection like he deserves a big gold star for today's fun fact. He seems oblivious to the tension he's sparked, thick in the burnt-clutch-smelling silence as the driver navigates steep cobblestoned roads. After a little rambling about Serbia holding Sarajevo under siege for four years, the guy turns to me and inquires, "Where's the favourite place you've travelled?"

"South America." I yawn, repelled by his invasive energy. There's a difference between talking *with* and talking *at*. I wish more people understood this.

He leans in and gloats. "Oh yah, I've been there."

"Where's your favourite in South America?" he demands in a tone implying countries are something to collect.

"Peru." I cringe and stare out the window at nothing in particular. His incessant need to be validated is giving me a headache. It reminds me of the interrogator control drama detailed by Marco in Sacramento.

An awkward silence entails so I add a polite, "You?"

"Antarctica."

Oh, this isn't a conversation to listen or learn. It's to place-name drop. I get it, dude, personal growth for some, bragging rights for others, but...

"Antarctica isn't in South America. It's a different continent."

The guy slumps back on his seat, lips pressed in a thin line. I'm not giving him the bright-eyed, secretly begrudging response he wants. Nor am I admitting that I've been there because I'm avoiding ammunition for his close-ended questions.

It's a time before social media amplifies ostentatious selfies, backdropped by iconic vistas. At least, I don't notice it because I don't own a phone. When

I eventually get one, it seems everyone has a reality channel that filters out the gritty rawness of travel. I want insight, authentic encounters, and stories of transformation. I travel to drink it in and connect with others, not trump them by one-upping their experiences. I can't be fucked combing his delicate ego. I'm stripping back my own.

Tapping on my dorm door, I'm wary of my late-night arrival. Two voices beckon me to enter. Other than names, I'm too tired to further acquaint myself with the tall Chinese man blinking behind black glasses, and the tiny gap-toothed Canadian adorned with a silver cheek piercing. Kasey and Ge. They seem nice, I think, as my eyes close.

In the morning, I learn Kasey is a professional accordion player, embracing some downtime after an international tour. A local fling has kept her in Sarajevo for a month. Ge is on holiday from his home in Germany, where he works as a computer scientist. They are chalk and cheese. I'm chili chocolate. Sweet. With a fiery kick. Strangely, the three of us thoroughly enjoy each other's company, and we form a curious camaraderie.

By day, Kasey leads us to the local hotspots where we sip coffee from copper pots and indulge in baklava. It is difficult to maintain a gluten-free, vegetarian diet in the Balkans, with limited options and the crispy phyllo pastry of scrumptious burek pies encasing spinach and feta cheese. Outside a bakery enticing me with sweet fried deserts, Kasey smokes a cigarette, despite the rest of the Balkans not giving a fuck about smoking indoors. On the pavement, a few metres from where we stand, a large splotch of red catches my eye. I spot Kasey stepping away, so she doesn't ash on it. I squint at it curiously. It looks like blood.

Kasey sees me gawking. She centres herself with a long exhale, then notes, "It's one of the Sarajevo Roses."

I cock my head to the side.

"*Oh*," she exclaims as tears well. "You don't know..."

Toying with a lock of her bleached-blonde fringe, she explains, "The Sarajevo Roses are small concrete craters filled with red resin. They mark places where three or more people died from an explosion during the siege."

Mid chew, I freeze. Suddenly, I'm not hungry. It seems people walk at half-speed as my abdomen constricts. Kasey clarifies that the siege the American dude spoke of was the longest in modern warfare. She suggests Ge and I partake in a walking tour the next day.

Bundled up to embrace the crisp autumn morning, a passionate student with impeccable English leads us through the city. Flowing beneath the infamous Ottoman bridge whispering to me its memories of the First World War, translucent green water reflects grand symmetrical edifices decorated with geometric shapes and ornate balconies. A few blocks later, pockmarks dot minimalistic concrete buildings with the city's tortured past. It's confronting. My chest rips and writhes with every shelling crater and bullet hole that our charismatic guide points out. They are open scars. Yet, strolling vibrant streets that were once deadly sniper alleys, I get the impression that the city is emerging rather than frozen in despair. These visible wounds do not evoke sorrow. They convey a resolute strength.

Between handicraft shops and open-air cafes wafting espresso aromas into bustling pedestrian courtyards flocking with pigeons, the Sarajevo Roses splash war-torn memory in what is known as the "Jerusalem of Europe". An old Orthodox church perches behind a stone wall, just down the road from a Catholic Cathedral, in the same neighbourhood as a finely crafted mosque and Jewish synagogue. It makes sense. Geographically, Sarajevo's religious roots stem from the Ottoman, Roman, and Byzantine Empires.

The tour ends beside a sculpture of a naked man pulling the meridians of the Earth together above his head in a circular grid that encapsulates his entire body. *Multicultural man will build the world,* the words below him inscribe. I love it. I resonate with it deeply. I relish the tripartite government representing Bosnian Muslims, Orthodox Serbs, and Catholic Croats, and I hope that peace and tolerance remains. Diversity in fragmentation divides. But in understanding that new things are learned from others, diversity unites.

Walking back to our hostel, I notice thousands of skinny, white headstones stretching across the verdant hills towards mountains no longer rife with snipers. The resilience this conveys tears my heart to pieces yet simultaneously sparks hope for better days. If an entire city can rise from its horrific past with wise undertones and a tenacious spirit, then maybe, just maybe, I can too.

At night, Ge and Kasey venture out drinking. I stay home and research how to rewire the way neurons fire in my brain. I don't want to live a half-life anymore. I don't want to numb my emotional responses and overlook the triggers that cause my mood to dip. I want to feel what's been pushed beneath a pharmaceutical duvet so that my healing journey can continue with space for vibrance and vitality. In realising what must be released, I delete old programs from the software of my brain. In instigating behavioural change, I alter my brain's hardware through corrective neuroplasticity. On the road, there are variables I can't control. Instead of wallowing in sleep disturbance and disruption to diet I ask myself:

What am I putting into my body?
What am I doing with my body?
What am I saying to my body?

These three questions become the building blocks in which I reprogram maladaptive behaviour and build myself a new world.

In the early hours of most mornings, Ge stumbles in, slurring a mix of Chinese, German, and English. Kasey giggles. I place a glass of water by his bottom bunk. He wakes without a hangover, ready to embrace another day. It's invigorating and easy hanging with them both. Ge is an open-minded genius who evades all questions about Chinese politics. Kasey is an eccentric artist with growing suspicions about her lover's fidelity. And rightly so. Turns out he has a long-term girlfriend. After convincing her to leave Sarajevo with us, I up my funny as we board a slow-moving train.

We arrive in Mostar under starry skies and seek a place to stay. Tourist season is dwindling with autumn's falling leaves. Many hostels are already closed. Kasey—who toured here last month—recommends a hostel on the other side of an elegant arch bridge, so we lug her accordion over. It's a hilarious mission, even when we discover the hostel is closed. Back across the bridge we hobble, as a mouse squeaks and scrambles in a cobblestone corner, to the side dotted with medieval minarets and domes. Far below us, still waters reflect the midnight moon. In the distance, electronic music thunders. We follow it to the only open hostel and finally rest our weary eyes.

In the morning, Kasey leads us to a riverside café where we sip coffee and savour the view of the stunning, medieval bridge that we crossed last night. She explains it was once the jewel of the Ottoman Empire and took nine years to construct. For 427 years, the bridge was a phenomenal architectural work. Then the Yugoslav Wars broke out. After two years of fighting together against Serbia, their common enemy, Croatia turned on Bosnian Muslims. In 1993, two days of fierce Croatian barrage gave the iconic wonder its fatal blow.

People were incredulous, remembering the exact moment they heard the tragic news. Eventually the bridge was rebuilt using stones extracted from the same quarry, but it could not unify the broken city. Now, it divides Mostar with Croats and Bosnians living on different sides. To the west, a tall crucifix perches on a hill. To the east are damaged buildings.

In between, young men leap from the white parapet into the turquoise river twenty metres below. Their boldness is captivating. Watching from afar, we too courageously plunge into the crisp waters of new adventure. Ge is soon starting a new job with Microsoft. Kasey has finally liberated herself from the affair. I am fighting for freedom from antidepressants.

> *Without suffering, there is no learning.*
> **– Croatian proverb**

Kasey is an adorable pocket rocket with immense regional knowledge. I cherish her super-chill approach to life and the way she giggles at Ge's quirky mannerisms. En route to Dubrovnik, she explains that during the war the medieval old town—known as King's Landing from *Game of Thrones*—was filled with refugees and left unprotected under the impression it was safe as a UNESCO World Heritage Site. Alas, Yugoslav forces attacked with months of shelling that continued even as agreements to end the fighting were signed. I'm wide-eyed. It seems nowhere was out of bounds.

When we arrive in the picturesque port city, a swarm of yelling locals shove accommodation flyers in our face as exit the bus. My ears ring like a rebellious child swinging on the rope of a school bell like they're Tarzan. I step away from the commotion and inhale sunshine as Ge and Kasey pick a homestay near a crystalline harbour. Slowly I'm building new thought and behavioural patterns, but my brain is still neurologically adjusting to life without pharmaceutical regulation. Sometimes I seize the day. Other times, the days seize me. Lately it's been more of the latter.

When we venture into the medieval walled city, I fantasize of fire-breathing dragons cleansing me of these damned withdrawals. The reality is a pounding head and a majestic tourist mecca of expensive cafes linked by slippery marble streets in a labyrinth of narrow alleys. Turrets and towers perch beside orange roofs that are protected by high city walls and ringed by an azure horizon. I am Dubrovnik's old town in 1992. Beaten and bombed, while peace treaties are conjured.

As Ge's snores roar across the room and Kasey cosies into the double bed beside me, my withdrawals heave me to a deep cavity. Dark thoughts extend into me like the smoky tendril fingers of a cursed phantom. They coerce me to end it all. The breakdown always comes before a breakthrough. I think of life, then death, then imagine my nieces growing up with the explanation, *Aunty Jess Jess is no longer here because she let the darkness consume her.* My trembles intensify.

Kasey and Ge are warm and kind, but we're soon parting, and I'm not comfortable letting them in. I feel guilty for the ways my symptoms trickled into Blair and my adventures. I'm desperate to not repeat it. I consider calling friends and family for help. Then I anticipate them telling me I shouldn't be tapering off the medication, so I withdraw from connecting as my symptoms spread like venom. Night fevers mix with silent tears, drenching me in a hot ocean of dismal blues. It feels like my heart's been yanked from my chest. The pain is agonising as I fumble for meaning in a perplexing abyss.

One night, after Ge's flown home to Germany and Kasey breathes in deep slumber, I'm struck with a sharp abdominal pain. It feels like I'm being repeatedly stabbed by a psychopath with a trench knife. Drenched with sweat, I crawl to the bathroom. I barely make it before I collapse on the cool tiles and spew a vile stew. I'm there a while. Throat burning, mouth dripping with bile, I'm shrivelled and dishevelled with each wretched retch.

The next morning, I Skype Laula in Peru. I'm burning for compassion and understanding, but she seems upset by something, so I shut up and listen.

Brow creased over wide eyes, she discloses, "I'm going home early, babe. Something *fucked up* happened..."

"Oh, darling. What happened?"

"Well, I was walking around just out of Iquitos when I spotted what I thought was a little local stall. You know how it is in South America—small brick pop-ups in the middle of nowhere."

I nod.

"So, I made my way down, thinking I'd grab a snack, when this guy starts *yelling* at me in Spanish. I don't know what to do...his energy is really hostile, so I freeze. Next thing I know, he's pointing a gun right at my solar plexus!"

"Holy freaking shit, babe!"

"Right? I freak out and put my hands up, saying *'Lo siento. Lo siento. No entiendo.'* Thankfully, he registers I'm just a lost tourist and lets me go...but I'm so rattled, I've booked a flight home next week."

"Completely understandable," I soothe as I swallow my conundrum. "I'm so grateful you're okay, physically at least... That's terrifying."

For the rest of the chat I console her. Later, we discover that my abdominal pain peaked at the exact moment the gun aimed at her stomach. The timing feels too uncanny to not be connected.

After the encounter, I notice a gradual change in Laula. She shifts from being too unquestioning, to always seeing the best in peculiar characters, to being more discerning. Meanwhile, I am transforming from scepticism and suspicion to gaining confidence in mankind. As I trust more, she trusts less. We are meeting in the middle in a happy equilibrium.

After we hang up, I call Mama and ask if she'll meet me in Croatia. It's gruelling and confronting, but I need help. She's off work and in the ravines of my gut feeling, I know I'm not ready for Australia. It'd be too easy to slip into old habits with friends still drowning wellness with endless parties. I need to solidify the foundations of my new life. There's a freshness on the road that's helping this process. Mama agrees—but refuses to let me buy her ticket—and arranges flights to Zagreb in four days' time.

My head throbs as I kiss Kasey goodbye and board a bus for Split. A breathtaking panorama of lush green islands dotting glistening turquoise waters slide past the window as the road twists around mountainous terrain. It's calming.

I disembark at Diocletian's Palace and seek a hostel with golden hour upon me. The massive Roman fortress buzzes with cafes, bars, and apartments burrowed within cobblestone streets, but renovations clamour behind wooden beams blocking every hostel doorway. Everything is closed for the season.

The sun is caressing the sea as I dab sweat from my forehead and do another lap. In lustrous marble courtyards, I feel heavier with each step. This is futile. My body temperature is rising. I need a place to rest. With tears forbearing, I amble away from the ancient city walls and decide I will sleep in a nearby park.

Just as I'm about to toss my backpack on the springy grass, a handsome middle-aged man pushing a bicycle spots me.

"Hey!" he calls. "You need place to stay?"

I eye him through narrow eyes, make a snap judgement to trust him, and mumble, "Yes."

His face erupts in a broad beam that instantly puts me at ease. "Come." He motions across the park. "I take you to Mama's."

Charlie may have had three angels, but divine intervention brings me the man himself. Mama, his sister-in-law, rents me a small rooftop room where I sweat out my fever and awe at a nearby litter of cats. Before settling in, Charlie hands me a business card for a local restaurant, with his name written on the back.

"You get discount, only if you bring this card," he explains.

I never eat out, but I do that night, knowing Charlie will receive a small commission for referring me. The rich vegetable moussaka is the first meal I manage to keep down in days.

In the morning, Charlie insists on taking me adventuring around town as he chirps about his amazing Split. Maybe he sees the anguish in my eyes and senses I need a friend. Or maybe he's like this with everyone. Either way, his enthusiasm and kind-heartedness are a godsend.

Soaring beside an octagonal cathedral girdled by marble columns is a Romanesque bell tower. Charlie leads me up the winding tower, instructing where to duck as we pass tourists rubbing bruised scalps. Eventually the steep stone steps turn to flimsy metal stairs spiralling over the internal void. My body is weak from days of vomiting. I stop often to catch my breath and gaze into rugged Dalmatian mountains. At the top of the belltower, Charlie climbs through a large, arched window to a sunny ledge. There, we dangle our legs over the edge and awe at the

Adriatic Sea glimmering beside an ocean of orange roofs gaping with alfresco dining.

"Every Sunday I sit here in sunshine," Charlie proclaims, then switches to Croatian to shoo away a security guard eyeing us on our high perch. I love it. I love the novelty of sitting where I shouldn't be sitting because I'm with my local friend. The air tastes salty as Charlie gazes upon his city with pride and talks of pristine beaches, untouched islands, and limestone caves. After carrying my backpack to the bus station, Charlie assures, "You will come back to Split. I know it."

My sweats and nausea subside when I arrive in Zadar, so I take to the streets and follow my inner compass. With unkempt hair and makeup reserved to a single sweep of mascara, I enjoy passing through life unnoticed. It's refreshing to feel at ease in my own skin after years of hiding behind a cosmetic mask. My goal on the road is to blend in. Not stand out. I observe more when my attention isn't pulled into a cognitive frenzy of feeling others eyes, judgements, and expectations on me. This renders a more authentic experience because my focus is uninterrupted.

En route to the town centre, however, I spot a hair salon and decide to polish up my regrowth. Taking care of ourselves externally has a symbiotic effect with our inner world. And vice versa. Emerging with freshly dyed, blow-dried hair, I continue walking. A gentle ocean breeze caresses my blonde locks like I'm on a catwalk fitted with a studio fan. The emotion I spot in women passing by is not one I am familiar or comfortable with. Envy.

Self-worth and self-love stem from within, of this, I am sure. However, the intrigue cast my way is the boost I need to remember—people notice me. People will notice if I'm gone.

The city meets the sea on a wide, open promenade. Perched on an elegant white bench, I am a silent witness to the sun's luminous kiss that sprinkles glitter into the cellophane ocean. Gulls glide on a satin breeze that sweeps hope into the silver sky. Mama is meeting me in two days. She is flying across the world to be with me. Everything is going to be okay because I drew courage to be vulnerable and ask for help. This is just the beginning of my valour. In the planning of this book, it becomes salient that I must be candid with those I love most. I intend on telling Mama about my skimpy bartending past. She must hear it from me rather than read it in a book. The sheer thought of that conversation terrifies me.

Farther along the boardwalk, tourists gather on large marble steps that lead into the ocean. The sweeping synthesised reverberation of an organ fills the air, like Davy Jones plays a song on his mellifluous underwater organ. I look around for the musician. All I see is delighted people, some with ears pressed to the stairs. The music seems to flow with reaching and receding tides. Then I realise why. It's the ocean's melody.

Underneath the steps, polyethylene tubes of different lengths allow water to push air through architectural blowholes and create sound. I'm brought to a humbled space within as mankind's interaction with nature gives the symphonies of the sea an instrument for its voice. And a stage.

The ethereal melodies stay with me as I reach Zagreb, Croatia's inland capital. I'm committed to moving my body every day to empower my mental state, but it's challenging when the sky is stale and uninspiring. I awake drowsy, eavesdropping on bubbly chatter beyond my private room. Instead of leaping out of bed, I plonk the blanket over my head and groan into my cocoon. The day is fresh on my eyelids. It's up to me to embrace it. Nothing and no one barricade me in. The cage is constructed in my mind. Letting go of limiting beliefs will dissolve the illusionary bars around me. But knowing this and cultivating the will to take action seem worlds apart.

After a few hours of intense inner dialogue—*c'mon, Jess, you can do this, no I can't, yes you can, but I don't want to, yes you do, no I don't, why, why not, because it's good for you, no it isn't, yes it is, no, yes, now, do it*—I flop out of bed and drag one foot in front of the other. Forward movement isn't about how far we leap, but that we keep on moving. Rather than criticise myself for taking three hours to get out of bed, I celebrate the small win of simply starting. I don't deflect accountability by blaming my hormones, brain chemistry, or the weather. I take responsibility for the direction I want my life to veer. If I'm not changing it, I'm choosing it. And if I'm not choosing it, I'm changing it.

In a nearby park, I blink in muted daylight and watch the world go by. Crispy golden leaves return to the earth from which they came. They pirouette and glide, with no fear of falling. I am an autumn tree. Letting go of what no longer serves me, I make space for new growth.

The next day I meet Mama at the airport. Her bulging hazel eyes are bright despite being jet-lagged. Her long red hair drapes over me like silk as I rest my head on her shoulder. The part of me that needs to be quick-thinking and independent as a solo female traveller instantly softens. Since childhood my default mode is to withdraw when the world is overwhelming. The part of me with highly attuned psychic and emotional antennas eventually reaches a point where I must disconnect in order to renew. It stems from childhood. When upset or throwing a tantrum, Mama and Papa instructed us to cover our eyes with our hands and count down from three. At the end of the countdown, we'd open our hands and say, "I'm happy now." If the tone didn't match the words, we'd repeat the process.

There wasn't much awareness around the healthy expression of different emotions, but this was a 1990's societal snare rather than a family pitfall. The process taught me to turn inward during despair and be my own safe space, a habit perpetuated during the assault's aftermath when I had only myself to lean on. With an otherwise bubbly persona, my retreats are blatant. It is rare I trust others with what I call my "water moon moods". Mama is one of them. I relish that she doesn't need an explanation as to why I'm suddenly still and silent and serene. She understands it's not personal, leaving me to flow with my emotions like ocean currents: unrestricted, unrelenting, and unafraid.

Once Mama has rested, we explore Plitvice Lakes National Park. It's spectacular. I'm dazzled by nature's beauty amid a complex network of unrailed wooden boardwalks winding for kilometres around pristine, terraced lakes. Ducks glide across reflective emerald streams. Waterfalls trickle beneath an invigorating breeze. From cool caves, we awe at forested hills bursting to life like fireworks frozen in time. Explosions of rich russet, bronze, scarlet, and gold tint the forest floor in a mosaic of crunchy colour. This is what doctors should prescribe: nature therapy regulating nervous systems to a state of ease. My withdrawals continue with brain zaps, headaches, and insomnia. The latest addition is the odd, irregular beat inside my chest. It's daunting and disconcerting, but my heart is tenacious. It pulls me through.

A doorstep is the highest of all mountains.
– Slovenian proverb

Mama is chatty by nature, but abandoned houses rife with bullet holes put us in a digestive silence as we traverse into Slovenia, the forested-green heart of Europe where snow-capped Alps meet the balmy Mediterranean. As remnants of the war dwindle to vast forests backdropped by distant mountains, she perks up and we pull into the real-life fairy tale of Ljubljana.

Unlike its Balkan siblings, Slovenia untangled from Yugoslavia in a mere ten days. The contrast of avoiding years of bloody torment is palpable with small-town friendliness and undamaged buildings. Charismatic cafes flourish inside baroque facades. Bright-eyed musicians serenade an art nouveau bridge that is guarded by stone dragons. Every corner thrives with a unique creative flair. I love it. Slovenia fast becomes my favourite pocket of Europe.

In the heart of the city, a medieval fortress crowns a massive forested hill. The dreamy, pedestrianised streets of old town become orange roofs that shrink to Lego-sized homes as we ascend in a glass funicular carriage. From this angle I notice the absence of Ottoman-influenced architecture as Baroque buildings increase.

Ambling through the elegant castle, I discover an art exhibition titled *Reality*. A large painting of a man lying down with his shoes resting nearly beside him has me stop and ponder the meaning. From his face extends a long, dark funnel that glimmers with stars. I am captivated by him exhaling his vision, then breathing it back in, no longer a slave to the mundanity of his polished, black shoes that imprison him in capitalism.

Mama finds me there staring. She is silent—I don't think art touches her as deeply as it stirs me. But who am I to assume another's experience? After a moment of relishing the quiet tranquillity, I ask her what she sees.

"Someone breathing the darkness out."

What? How?

I look at her, then back at the art, and see that we're both right. Reality, like art, is shaped by our assorted interpretations. We see the same image, but our differing lenses account for diverse meanings.

Perhaps the single truth of life is that there are many.

Ljubljana is a base for us to explore three of Slovenia's exquisite caves in a hire car. Rolling down forested hillsides, I half expect a pack of unicorns to prance from the fluffy clouds. The novelty of exploring one of the world's largest underground canyons, an immense subterranean city that was a refuge for WWII soldiers, and a Renaissance castle perched halfway up a vertical cliff that backs into the gaping mouth of a cave feels relevant for I am pilgrimaging new territory in my inner terrain.

Navigating dimly lit, slippery trails is invigorating. As is crossing a 100-metre bridge over a vertigo-inducing drop, listening to bats communicate in ultrasonic clicks and watching water drip off stalactite chandeliers formed over millions of years from an open-carriage electric train. It reminds me to listen beyond my normal range of hearing, be patient with the slow process of internal reconfiguration, and most importantly, have fun along the way.

The fairy tale continues in the idyllic town of Bled. I am enthralled by the lake's glimmering alpine waters, ringed with lush forest and backdropped by snowy peaks. In the centre is a picturesque islet with a quaint church perched on top.

Ducks, dressed in iridescent emerald feathers, glide across the silky surface where motorized boats are banned. Beneath the surface, they paddle relentlessly. From above, they compose their demeanour as ripples oscillate the watery mirror.

Ambling through tourist shops with Mama, I find a tiny mug magnet that reads: *I'm in Slovenia*. In red letters, another message is revealed: *I'm in love*. I pack it into my backpack and ponder gifting it to Riley. We have tentative plans to move into a Canmore rental with Ben in the new year, and the unravelling possibilities excite me.

When nothing is certain, anything is possible.

Travelling with Mama is taxing at times. I'm in my comfort zone but she's out of hers, so I take responsibility for our logistics and accommodation. My cognitive function is low, with insomnia drying my eyes to sandpaper. Each night, artificial light streams through my closed eyelids while my ears hiss and buzz from no external source.

My own research later reveals that by snapping my antidepressants into smaller pieces, I am inadvertently breaking the extended-release mechanism built into the matrix of each tablet. Rather than my body slowly absorbing the medication in a sustained and balanced way, I'm unknowingly dose dumping. Getting one big hit every twenty-four hours explains why my emotional peaks and troughs are so intense. Doing this with an SNRI antidepressant formulated to make serotonin and norepinephrine available by blocking reabsorption means I'm fucking with the neurotransmitters linked to stable moods, brain function, concentration, sleep, appetite, digestion, and response to stress. Balanced proportions of serotonin and norepinephrine produce endurance. Ironically, I am enduring the hell of my neurotransmitters being severely out of balance as a calm ocean becomes a succession of crashing tsunamis.

My decision to taper off antidepressants without the help of medical professionals is not one I endorse. Though thousands testify the same hell when easing off the same medication, a stable environment and smaller dosed tablets may have reduced my symptoms. My mindset at the time is *I will be without the medication*, but also *fuck you western doctors for putting me on these pills and telling me I need them for life*. My resolute spirit allows me to thrive without medication in time, but my single-minded focus refuses to seek expert advice because my trust in pharma giants is dwindling. And rightly so. Around this time, the largest pharmaceutical company in the world settles a $67.5 million class action lawsuit directly linked to Pristiq, the antidepressant I'm tapering off. It shatters me to read that Pristiq is linked to liver problems, blurred vision, sleep trouble, abnormal bleeding, somnolence, and increased blood pressure. That health care officials are bribed, babies are born with birth defects, and suicidal thoughts increase when on the medication. Thus, even if I did seek psychiatric advice, I'm not convinced I would trust it. Like everything in life, this is a blessing and a curse, and again I reiterate that though this path worked out for me in time, I *do not* endorse that it is right for you. That's not for me to decide.

While I continue braving each day, Mama's love for music reignites my own as we explore Imperial Vienna. The city's history is drenched with soul-stirring melodies, and memory lane connects me to my high school music tour just months before my antidepressant prescription became a norm. It feels symbolic to retrace the steps my younger self. No longer consoling my distraught best friend at midnight, I'm becoming my own best friend and consoling myself. The impressive cityscape blends the innovation of contemporary times with lofty Gothic towers, elaborate Baroque palaces, and stark minimalistic buildings. Bicycles whizz around marble sculptures. Canal waters murmur. As we warm our freezing fingers on steaming mugs in traditional coffeehouses, I try to summon the courage to disclose my past to Mama.

Mama's ability to read something once then file it into the vast library in her mind amazes me. I'm an absorbent for emotions and intuition. She's a sponge for cognition. Her mind is sharp, analytical, and ceaseless, allowing her to give wise advice in a practical way. If the world can't stimulate her mentally, she turns to her iPad. This pains me. I want her presence—to me and our surroundings. I can't comprehend that it's her way of finding comfort and safety amid foreign environments in constant flux.

One evening, I ask her to stop scrolling while we eat. She flicks her hand and tells me to hush. Pushing sauteed vegetables around my plate, I roll my eyes. I have something to tell her. The unspoken truth suffocates me. By the time she puts her iPad down, I'm seething in quiet resentment at what I judge to be a relentless attachment to screens. I blurt out something light-hearted. Deep down, I retch on what I need to confess.

During a train change en route to Budapest, we gather our bearings on a bustling platform. Unfamiliar customs whizz past. This stresses Mama out. She starts swearing about the lack of English speakers and having to lug her suitcase through the jam-packed station. Asking locals for directions, I veer us where we need to be. My head pounds. I'm sick of being the voice of reason while she roars about matters that I deem ridiculous and entitled. I forget that this lifestyle is normal for me. Eventually, I snap that she's only burdened down by her own materialism. With compassionate hindsight, I realise Mama is inundated with culture shock while I drown in the tempestuous ocean of my now-unveiled emotions.

Bitter silence drenches the train ride until Mama makes a light comment about a solar farm out the window. I respond in a gentle tone. It's the ones we most love who get the brunt and burn of our bad behaviour, for with them we feel safe to be ourselves unrestrained. This is true for us both. Not everyone is cut for the backpacker life. Though we've progressed from private hostel rooms with paper-thin walls to cheap hotels, we're still on the go in unfamiliar domains. I commemorate Mama for buying the ticket and taking the ride. The trip is a catalyst for our relationship to evolve. By the end, we're no longer just mother and daughter. We're friends.

If you don't cherish the little, you don't deserve the more.
- Hungarian proverb

Budapest welcomes us with a smiling crescent moon illuminating a stone bridge with a subtle sway. The cycles of conquest and liberation through time curate a treasure trove of architecture beside the Danube that glides past flat urban sprawl. I savour the gothic arches, baroque extravagance, Renaissance geometry, Roman ruins, art nouveau from the golden ages, and gigantic Soviet statues displaying the Iron Curtain's gloom.

The city is sophisticated in an unpretentious way. It is evident in the shabby-chic ruin bars adding an eclectic edge to the city's unrivalled nightlife. American Mike from Bulgaria is in town, so I leave Mama to play solitaire on her iPad and embark on an adventure with him into the old Jewish Quarter. Inside an abandoned apartment block, cigarette smoke breezes through a sprawling labyrinth of rooms fitted with mismatched furniture and weird antiques. It feels like we're clubbing in a giant thrift store. I love the artful disorder of themed dance floors flaunting psychedelic light shows. There's even a room with furniture stuck to the ceiling.

When we leave, Mike invites me to a daytime pool party in the refreshing thermal waters of a Roman bath. I'm compelled by the location but repelled by the thought of being sober around heavy drinkers. I hang with Mama instead. Walking home from dinner on a dim one-way road, *The Celestine Prophecy* flashes to mind. I take note to seek the book in the UK, the next English-speaking country on our itinerary.

A few steps farther, a second-hand bookstore emerges behind a crimson façade.

Mama doesn't need much persuading to enter. She loves the doors that literature opens more than me. Inside, I ask the small man behind the counter if there's an English section. I expect a small corner. Instead, he directs me to the basement, where two dozen shelves entice us with the musky sweetness of preloved books.

As I scan each row, a forest-green cover catches my eye. There, to my open-mouthed delight, is *The Celestine Prophecy*, patiently awaiting me.

Better to eat bread in peace, than cake amid turmoil.
- Slovakian proverb

I flick open the first page on a train to Bratislava. Out the window, the Danube undulates through the countryside while simultaneously caressing ten other countries. Slovakia's small capital lacks truckloads of camera-clicking tourists. This creates novelty with an unpolished charm. Unexpected quirks keep me on my toes as my local friend, Petr, shows us around. We met in Belgrade a few weeks earlier and bonded over me travelling to Bratislava, a city that most travellers skip. Petr leads us around uneven sidewalks sprouting grass as he shares childhood memories of the bloodless, self-determined split of Czechoslovakia that infuses peace into quaint medieval streets.

Absorbed by his stories, I nearly trip over a human-sized bronze man leaning out of a sewer hole.

Petr chuckles and explains, "This is Cumil. He represents a lazy communist worker."

"He looks like he's trying to look up women's skirts," I joke.

"That's one theory. Another is that he grants you a wish if you rub his head. It will come true so long as you keep it a secret forever."

"Forever?"

"Forever."

I look from Mama, smiling with amusement because she knows what's coming, to Cumil, then back to Petr. "Have you ever made a wish?"

"I did when I was a child," he remarks with a wink.

I cock my head to the side and peer into Petr's eyes.

"Are you going to make a wish?" Mama asks. She knows I want to.

I look down at Cumil. "No, that's okay..."

I don't want to seem childish by believing in wishes, so I join Mama and Petr as they walk away.

A few strides in, I stop, run back, and brush my hand over Cumil's cool, polished head.

When I look up, Mama and Petr are chuckling.

"What did you wish for?" Mama asks.

"I can't *tell* you!" I exclaim with feigned shock. "Then it won't come true."

Every time you feel yourself being pulled into other people's nonsense, repeat these words:
"not my circus, not my monkeys."
- Polish proverb

Zigzagging north, we pass flourishing lowland forests and pull into a gloomy-grey Krakow. Piling on extra layers, I gear up for a tour through Auschwitz. Emotionally, nothing can prepare me for the world's largest death camp in what was German-occupied Poland.

Chills creep under my skin as I walk through a deceivingly beautiful courtyard that leads to an iron gate baring the false promise: *work sets you free*. Inside double-electrified, barbed wire fences are concise blocks of two-storey brown brick buildings. Tuning into my headset, I listen to the atrocities of the Holocaust, to the extremities of hatred that man succumbs when there is an "us versus them" mentality. Sometimes it is too much and I unplug. I am met with a ghastly silence drenched with solemn sniffles.

In places of considerable murder, colourful bouquets are arranged. It is a paradox that something so beautiful signifies utter devastation. The haunting floral aromas have me silently collapsing in on myself and blinking back tears. Inside an icy gas chamber, clicking cameras shatter the poignant silence. It is sobering. In mid-November, I shiver under four layers. I shudder that people were branded with numbers and trudged barefoot through the snow while loved ones passed as black smoke through chimneys.

It doesn't feel right to pull my camera from my pocket and diminish the torture of history's largest killing machine to pixelated images. Until I spot a group of Israelis parading their white-and-blue flag as they walk towards the crumbled remains of gas chambers and crematoriums from a railway junction with forty-four parallel tracks. It's the same route that one million Jews, Gypsies, Poles, and Soviet prisoners of war unknowingly took to their death. The strength and solidarity is a sight that I wish Hitler saw.

Back in Krakow, a full moon shines hope into the tragedy as we explore the Royal Castle. Mama chats about a legendary fire-breathing dragon living below in a karst cave. I'm half present as I seek the silver lining. We can't change history, but we can learn from it. Remembering our past inspires us to create a better today. An undeniable resilience lives in those afflicted by the hostility of forgotten humanity. Imagine if we vowed to leave people and places better than we found them. Imagine what we can create.

Every cloud has a silver lining.
- **English proverb**

The night before Papa arrives in London, Mama and I sprawl across a motel bed. The truth stings my tongue. I have to tell her. I can't let her discover it in a book. I think Papa already knows. After all, his background is in intelligence, and he once hung a pair of lacy suspenders over my bedroom door as though draping the truth for me to know he knows. Maybe they just fell out of the washing machine. But I'm more vigilant than that. Regardless of whether he's told Mama, I need to find the words myself.

I peer at Mama lounging beneath the covers, iPad in hand. Her face shines with artificial light. It illuminates her hazel eyes.

With all the bravery I can muster, I ask, "Mama, can you put the iPad down for a moment?"

As much as I get triggered by her preoccupation with screens, I appreciate her unwavering presence when asked.

Peering into her wide eyes, I swallow my fear. "I—I have something to tell you. It's difficult to say, but important I tell you..."

As I fumble for words, Mama rubs my back with a soft reassurance that inspires me out of my shell.

"Before I moved to Queensland, I worked as a skimpy barmaid..."

I pause, expecting her to fire up. She maintains a loving gaze.

"I never got into topless or nude work, but I regularly bartended in bikinis and lingerie. It was a big reason why I moved away."

Opening like petals to the sun, I feel lighter as I liberate myself from the weight of my secret.

Mama's welling eyes mirror my own. She waits to make sure I have nothing more to say then asks, "Is that it?"

I nod.

"Jess, we might not always agree with the decisions you make in life, but as parents, we love you unconditionally. You can always come to us if you need our love and support."

Suddenly it seems so silly that I let the worry stew. I snuggle up beside her as she strokes my arm then eventually turns back to her iPad while I drift into the most restful sleep I've had in weeks.

※

As Papa grounds into chilly London, I meet with Blair and introduce her to Adam and another friend I met in South America. Blair is settling into the city's rapid rhythm, Adam's been bouncing between Perth and London, and my other friend has just published her first book. December fast approaches. I'm dazzled by Christmas lights as I meander to an 18th century pub that miraculously escaped bombing in both world wars. The original brick and stone add a timelessness to our reunion. It reminds me how quickly life moves.

Tipsy from red wine that melts winter's frost, we hug goodbye beside the massive network of train lines that brought us all together. Nostalgia hits me as I watch the world go by from an almost empty carriage. Will the four of us ever be in the same place at the same time again? Life has a funny way of twisting in different directions to what the signposts read.

※

The old know and the young suspect.
- Welsh proverb

On the eastern fringe of England's oldest oak forest, Papa retraces memory lane all the way back to his childhood home in Cinderford. Mama sits in the hire car with an upset stomach as Papa and I skip down the road to the two-storey house. Just as I snap a photo of Papa grinning before the stone façade, the front door opens. The homeowners scrutinize us on the footpath with narrow eyes. Without context, our presence seems suspicious.

"Hello," I chirp in a tone intending to disarm them. "This is my father, I just wanted to get a photo of him here because he grew up in this house…"

After a few testing questions, they welcome us inside for a tour. Papa's eyes flash with sentimental memories. This continues as we cross into Wales and cheeky second and third cousins brighten the weather with their smiles. Rolling green hills open up to evocative Medieval ruins. Rainbows beam across the sky. Unbeknown to anyone, I make my first attempt at cutting myself off my antidepressants completely. It's not pleasant. As we venture north to Scotland, my withdrawals spiral like a wild storm.

Failing means you're playing.
- **Scottish proverb**

Papa's playfulness is a blessing amid grey skies and a regimented travel plan that sometimes feels stale. Mama is in bed sick the day we explore Edinburgh Castle, so Papa and I run amok as canyons become toys and we hide behind exhibits to scare each other inside the stunning stone walls. Our dynamic has always been bouncy and mischievous. He eggs on my spontaneity. I excite his inner child. Back at the motel, Mama brags that our family tree links back to Robert the Bruce who led the first Scottish War of Independence and whose statue guards the castle gates. If we look back far enough, we are all royal leaves on the tree of life.

Short stays with family in Nuneaton, York, and Herne Bay prompts me to maintain a small dose of antidepressants. I can't yet face the storm. Back in London, we return the rental car, and Mama and Papa fly home. Lounging on Blair's couch in Clapham Junction, I prepare for my move to Canada by peering into the past's iridescent pools. It's been five months since I met Laula in Peru. Somehow it feels like years.

As memory lane undulates into the very waters that hold me, I realise just how much I've grown. All because I chose to stretch myself beyond my comfort zone and shed my conditioned layers. In letting go of all that is not love inside of me, I discover the greatest voyage: the unfurling of my mind's knots into the peaceful expanse of my heart.

It is here I find fortitude, hope, and freedom. Finally, I find home.

Chapter IX

TRANSCENDENCE

I think of thoughts

as cords or codes

tuning us in

to our chosen channel.

Magic or tragic;

the webs we weave

are threaded from

the thoughts we believe.

Ask yourself:

What's worth seeding?

What's worth feeding?

What's worth weeding?

December 2013

Out the aeroplane window, I watch the Northern Lights dance across an inky-black sky. It's my first time seeing the auroras, and even more riveting to see them at eye level as I glide above Canada's snowy northeast. Wide-eyed, I want to shake the entire plane awake so others may witness this giant shimmering canvas of blue-and-green streaks swishing through the stratosphere in live time. Alas, I am surrounded by bobbleheads, snorers, and unoccupied-middle-seat dominators as people nuzzle into the tiny leather confines of economy seating. With my feet wedged in between the seats in front of me, I awe at the mesmerizing phenomenon, silent and alone.

Calgary welcomes me with a bone-rattling cold and a customs officer slamming me with routine questions—how long do I intend to stay; what is the purpose of my visit? I pretend to know the answers to his questions, then chirp, "I'm writing a book. Maybe you'll be in it."

On the cold, bumpy bus to Nelson, I befriend a deep-voiced local man. I am delirious yet unable to sleep. Chit-chat takes the edge off the cold, bumpy ride as I watch tall evergreens standing frozen in time. Draped by white blankets of snow, broken branches become writhing stick figures that have jumped from the trees. Naked and stripped bare, they are shackled from flying by white pharmaceutical coats lining their grave.

Someone once told me that the Ancient Greek's root words for pharmaceutical translate to sorcery and poison. I understand that doctors do not enter medicine with malicious intent to cause harm. Most are doing the best they know how for their patients. The same can be said for physicians in the early 1900s who locked up, lobotomised, stigmatized, and socially isolated the mentally ill, until we learned the value of talk therapy and community care. I don't pretend to know all the answers. I'm simply examining our approach to mental health with curiosity of how it will shift over time.

Maybe this means a transformation in our collective response by normalising mental health conversations and prioritising not just physical and mental wellbeing, but emotional and spiritual too. When I look out the window again, I see colonies of trees pulling through winter together by reaching for light from the sun. Standing up to bitter winds while snowy peaks overlook the stark, knotted forest, the forest is still. So still. Amidst a slippery subzero world, ancient wisdom solidifies in the trees' now-frozen limbs. Though denuded, the magic in each wand is limitless. It grows stronger each day.

My tentative plan to live in Nelson with Ben and Riley crumbles, so I stay two nights then venture onward to Kelowna. I've teed up a bed at Kelowna International Hostel. There I will work in exchange for my accommodation while I apply for a working holiday visa.

As we part ways, my friend from the bus warns, "Be careful."

I think it's ridiculous that people, mostly men, assume I need their unwarranted advice to venture off into the world, like I'm endangered and impressionable and haven't taken a grown man to court, entertained numerous country towns in lingerie alone, or backpacked seven continents while getting a sharp read on the world around me. I often play to it. By allowing others to underestimate me, it puts me two steps ahead for they unintentionally reveal more of themselves and are dumbfounded by my assertiveness if I ever need to call them out or uphold a strong boundary.

I cock my head to the side and feign naivety. "What do you mean?"

"Kelowna is a fast-paced town. Don't get sucked in."

"Okay." I smile, concealing that I already know. "I won't."

I guess it's sweet that he's watching out for me.

Pain shapes us,
Experiences bond us,
Awareness liberates us.

At the bus stop, I shiver under four layers and wonder if the water in my eyes will freeze as two local girls sporting miniskirts chat nonchalantly. Inside the hostel's vibrant walls, I remove my top layer, and a tall, redheaded Dutch girl shows me my room in the chilly basement dubbed "the dungeon". In the peak of summer, working travellers occupy the three other beds. With fewer guests in winter, it's just me.

The dungeon's only window is boarded up to retain heat. With the owner's encouragement, I paint windows on the walls with panoramic nature views. Along with three girls also exchanging work for accommodation, two Aussie men live at the hostel while working in town. I hear about Ronnie before I meet him. He is a notorious ten-minutes-after-the-pancake-mix-is-packed-away-bed-emerger who sooks when he can't get breaky.

At 10:10 a.m. a few days later, a bald guy with a full arm tattoo sleeve pouts in the empty kitchen. Without saying a word, I unlock the office and slide him some pancake mix plus extra for a hideaway stash with a *shhh* finger. It's the start of a deep and playful friendship. Ronnie's wacky sense of humour has me in fits of giggles as he helps paint moonlit mountains and balmy beaches on "the dungeon's" walls. During our artistic endeavours we discover that my first skimpy friend later became his girlfriend when she moved to Darwin. I love how certain people are magnetised towards each other.

The week I move to Kelowna, Morgan moves to Australia. I'm ready to ground. She's ready to fly. In our overlapping days, we hang with Aimee and reminisce on our growth since summer. Before she goes, Morgan gives me her phone. Then she extends her wings into perspective-widening experiences not found in one's comfort zone.

The following week, Trey invites me to a party in Calgary. The bus is sold out, so I rideshare with a Serbian girl. As we crawl across snowy roads, she asks me about my time in Serbia, having never met someone who has travelled there. After ten hours navigating glassy mountain passes and icy turns, she drops me at Trey's campus residence at the University of Calgary, and I reunite with the four guys.

It is a pleasant evening making new friends as soft white snowflakes dance outside. My favourite is a lively girl with emerald-green eyes. She feels strangely familiar though we've never met. I relish the soft wisdom that emanates from her as she talks of an upcoming ayahuasca ceremony that Trey invites me to join. My heart expands while my mind bleeps at the thought of drinking another plant medicine.

When the night ends, I curl up in Conner's boot as he drives a carload of people home. Water slides horizontally on the back windshield. It forms a glistening lattice with snowflakes liquifying in vertical drips. The melting gridlike dispersion stops as the car comes to a halt in Riley's driveway. He starts his goodbyes. I sit up and face him.

"Can I come?" I ask.

A penetrating silence follows. Every ear is burning.

"Uh," he falters. "I was just going to go inside by myself...and chill."

"Okay," I compose, and lie back down.

In retrospect I wish that I'd approached Riley in a quiet corner at the party and expressed my emotions. Rather than feeling knotted and tied by conflicting tides to both reveal and conceal.

In Ben's bathroom, I scrub my face and peer into my tired eyes. Residual mascara stains my eyelids with circles of black tar. I can't keep doing this. I can't keep shunning my emotions out of fear of vulnerability. Doing so imprisons me in barbed metal bars that spear and smoulder as I slouch in on myself. Ben wishes me sweet dreams as I ride waning waves of sentimentality on his couch and vow that I'll get better at courageously speaking my feelings, needs, and desires.

The next day, Ben and I watch *The NeverEnding Story*. With a cheeky smile he giggles that we don't need the "television" to "tell (us) a vision". We can create our own. Orange flames crackle in the hearth while snow pirouettes like angel feathers outside. From an ornate rug I watch the fire flicker. It whispers wisdom through the tempered glass, talking in tongues that the pain will pass. *Give time, time. Let go. Detach from expectation.* It expresses that I will feel a warmth inside me again. But we are speaking different dialects. All I can fathom is how broken my heart is.

I did it to myself, I was never unaware of that. Expectation and attachment are recipes from the ego that never result in true love, because love is unconditional and cannot be controlled.

Tearing my gaze from the flames to Ben, I declare, "I guess, as long as you believe in love, that's all that matters."

"And yourself, Jess." His chocolate-brown eyes deepen. "Believe in love and believe in yourself. The rest is an illusion we create out of fear."

His words hit me like the soft flakes outside bundle into an avalanche and crash upon me. With the potent blow, I understand that everything is already okay, and I smile for the first time all morning.

It's a redirection, not rejection. Sometimes the branch breaks to show us the strength of our wings.

The art of letting go allows better things to grow.

Back in Kelowna, my first white Christmas glistens with dangling frost-spikes and crystalline snowflakes transforming the city into an ivory moonscape. Ronnie and I run through the powdery streets, hurling snowballs at each other in a carnival of laughter. With a rejuvenating sweat, we retreat to the hostel's toasty common room and bask in the sweet cedar fragrance of the tinsel-adorned pine tree. My cheeks hurt from smiling. It's a good pain. It inspires me to completely cut my antidepressants in the coming days.

With fresh home-dyed brunette locks, I bring Ronnie to Aimee's house up the road to celebrate NYE with her friends the following week. It's a pleasant evening of mingling with new friends and building community around me. In the first hours of 2014, I support Ronnie's wobbly body on mine as I guide him back to the hostel and tuck him into bed with a glass of water. Then I skip back to the party, unaware that I'll soon call the house my home.

The next day, I ponder Trey's invitation to drink ayahuasca. Guided by moonlight, I meander the same footpath I strolled in summer, piercing memory lane with fresh insight. There's no point getting stuck on past pages when an entire book beckons to open. Water shimmers in silver trails as I perch on the frosty shore in front of a tall totem pole in someone's yard. My iPod beeps with low battery. Then it dies. This forces me to be alone with my thoughts. Observing the ebb and flow of mental chatter, I realise every word I tell myself is a spell. Can I learn to build myself up, rather than break myself down? Can ayahuasca empower me on this journey?

In my dungeon room, I stretch *into* my body. I'm new to a regular yoga practise and love that it makes me feel calm and grounded. With equal pressure of fingers and toes pushing into the carpet, I feel connected to the earth. Fresh energy revitalises my cells as I inhale into my belly. Long exhales release the chaos clouding my mind. Relief shoots into my calves, creating space in my hamstrings, and tension in my neck subsides. The world is lucid. I feel Earth holding me from deep within her core as a musky smell from the corner wafts with summer's memories. By tuning into breath, a soulful fire ignites. It is in this space that I decide to partake in ceremony.

In that first week of January, I connect with the essence of ayahuasca, asking her to be gentle with me. It is the day I officially stop taking antidepressants. Within me is a profound internal shift. My physiological withdrawals cease and my moods stabilize as I focus on daily yoga and meditation while cutting out processed sugar, gluten, meat, and dairy.

As I observe the thoughts occupying my mind, I question where, how, and why each belief formed. At what point did I plant each seed? Have they become weeds or are they creeds I should feed? By catching my default responses, I rewire cranial programs with empowered thoughts. Choosing to see life's lessons allows me to grow.

In mid-January, I board another cold, cramped overnight bus to Calgary. In the early hours of the morning, I venture across the frosted city to Trey's residence where he and Riley snore on the couch. They partook in an ayahuasca ceremony last night and are drinking again with Ben and me tomorrow. Beside a rubbish pile reeking from last month's party, I gaze out the kitchen window and get clear on my intentions.

Release the illusion I need antidepressants for life. Rid myself of negativity. Be filled with love and positive energy to share with the world. Transcend what I think I know, so I can transform into who I need to be.

Slowly, the sun rises and illuminates icy twigs on a nearby tree. When Riley and Trey wake, we chill on the couch and chat about their ceremony. It's the first time I've seen Riley since the car. I appreciate his graceful air. It soothes my embarrassment of being so clunky with my desires. I figure that the day before journeying with a strong psychedelic isn't ideal to ask him if he likes me back. It feels better to let it all go and allow the answers to unravel.

The next day, Ben picks us up in late-afternoon darkness and drives west to a house in Canmore. There, we arrange yoga mats in a circle in a large wooden living room. I create a cosy nest of blankets in my space and send my love to Conner, who is in Thailand on a university exchange. As two women pour the Amazonian brew into fourteen tiny glasses, a slither of apprehension drips into me. Ben places a reassuring hand on my knee then gives an I'm-with-you-you've-got-this-smile.

We drink the bitter potion in darkness, then recline on our yoga mats. As I concentrate on diaphragmatic breathing, the notion that I am a tiny body in a small house nestled amongst mammoth mountains dissipates. My life is a ripple in an eternal pool of love. The same chemical that our bodies produce when we're born, when we die, and each night we dream oscillates through my body. As others gag and retch, purging internal blocks, I swim in the icaros—shamanic songs from South America—that the two women sing from the centre of the circle.

Breathing deeply, I wait for the medicine to relieve me of my negative composts. Vomiting is to be expected. Nothing comes. Instead, I float in bliss. As I inhale from the base of my spine, every microgram of breath swims in my sacrum before passing through the fiery vortex of my solar plexus and basking in my open heart. Continuing to rise, each inhalation empowers my throat, opens my third eye, then stretches around my crown. Descending back down with each exhalation, the momentum of energy continues as it falls to my feet. There, with my next inhalation, it rises again. This time it zips through my body and shoots out of my head. With focused breath, I create a torus of energy flow. My body becomes a vessel for love. It cascades through me and finds those who need it most.

I feel so in sync with the world, I dissolve into the oneness of it. The others' experiences of paradise or torture is my own on a different day. In between the icaros, my mind flashes back to the windscreen's watery web. Time melts. I am experiencing the moment in the boot of Conner's car as the present while simultaneously breathing light through my geometric bubble. It is my awareness that trickles across the window. Suddenly it makes utter sense that our bodies die and decompose, but our souls exist forever.

Floating in a cosmic party of peace, I feel Laula, Lesley, and Stephen's essences drift into my sphere. But are they really here? Maybe if I sit up, I'll get an honest answer. I'm surprised at what I see. Perched at the edge of Ben's mat is a black jaguar peering over him like prey. I rub my eyes. My ego tells me I'm seeing things. It tells me to lie down. I do what it says.

I soon sense that Ben is spiralling. Deep, deep, down, he falls into a black hole of fear. It hits me that the black jaguar is real in this world we've all entered beyond the veil. He needs some loving. Later, I discover that jaguars are the only creature other than humans that purposely ingest the woody stems of the tropical caapi vine *and* chacruna leaves that create ayahuasca when combined. It's not here by mere coincidence.

I want to help Ben, but I don't want to interrupt his internal process for through the fear he cultivates strength and integrates lessons. Yet, I can't shake the feeling that I have something he needs.

At that moment, he whispers, "Jess, do you have that rose quartz?"

I smile and place a small pink crystal into his open palm. How lucky I am to have such open-minded friends. I think of Riley and the words he scribbled in my diary. Drenched in gratitude, I focus my energy on sending him waves of appreciation. *Thank you*, my soul sings. Then he starts purging. Momentarily I wonder if I caused it. The medicine is waning, starting to wrap its viny magic into the rationality of grounded thought. I realise I didn't cause Riley's purge. Assuming so is egotistical. It is selective perception causing me to notice his physiological state combined with a human urge to create meaning from patterns and connections.

An old friend once claimed, "Life is what it is. Not as it should be." His New Zealand accent floats through my mind, and though I don't agree, I understand why he thinks so. Our reality is moulded by our worldview. It's easier to accept this than judge it. With each breath, the light within me shines a little brighter with my newfound purpose to let love flow and rise by lifting others. I'm ready to embrace life without antidepressants.

Eventually, the medicine dwindles, the lights flick back on, and we nibble on fruit in the centre of the room. As Ben navigates slippery roads back to Calgary, I smile at silhouetted trees. The interconnectedness embodied deep within me is contrasted by early morning commuters beginning their voyage through the frigid city. The four of us have just embarked on an intense inward quest. Meanwhile, traffic lights flash orange, then red, then green. The world keeps spinning as though it doesn't know, or care.

Stars are souls gazing down upon us
from the place we reside
between being birthed and earthed.
We are born into this dream of life
with a stream of light
from the centre of our galaxy.
We are created to create.

Back in Kelowna, the email granting me a two-year working holiday simmers in my inbox. For the visa to commence I must leave the country to re-enter on it. I'm growing weary at the stale crystallization of breath every time I step outside. It burns my lungs and stabs my blood with frozen shards. I'd rather come back to warmer weather, so I book a ticket to Central America for six weeks.

Before I leave, Aimee invites me over for tea and introduces me to her two housemates—a witty brunette and her sensuous cousin. The girls are endearing, though their contempt for Aimee's young tabby cat, Lola, rattles me. As I envision streaming love onto the trembling creature, she leaps onto my lap where she curls up and purrs for the rest of the night.

Before I go, I catch up with Aimee again. It is the night of the Super Bowl, and the Kelowna I met in summer resurfaces in small baggies of white powder that are snorted in thick lines. With cold and clammy hands, I record the time that I swallow each tiny "parachute". I'm cautious of not having too much yet want to maintain my high. As serotonin and dopamine whiz through my veins, veiling my base emotions with an artificial fulfilment, I see how easy it could be to get lost in that world and vow to keep my head on my shoulders and feet on solid ground. Ronnie joins the party after work. Before we walk back to the hostel, Aimee offers us some ketamine.

"It's just the tiniest bit," she informs with genuine eyes that remind me of Courtney's loving gaze in the hotel all those years ago. "Enough to counteract the MDMA and help you sleep."

Halfway home, I levitate out of my body by a silver thread. From my bird's-eye perspective, I watch Ronnie and I walk, then lie in bed reflecting on the night. Aimee invites me to move in when I return from Central America. The house is cosy. Aimee is delightful. With my "yes", I understand that this this won't be my last high.

I awake in my Panama City hostel to a lanky Estonian man bouncing around the room. I'm drenched with sweat intensified by the ceiling fan's relentless compulsion to whir sticky air. The man introduces himself as Valter. I appreciate his fiery energy. His loud, persistent chatter is a little harder to swallow. Nonetheless, we become friends running across highways and getting lost on spontaneous adventures with the scent of coconut on our tongues.

Atop a lush jungled hill hosting breathtaking 360-degree views, a basketball-court sized Panama flag flutters in the wind. Rain splatters from muggy skies as monkeys, sloths, and toucans writhe in the thick green. From here, the cosmopolitan city feels conquerable. I'm a fan of the lenticular street art and want to explore more, but my flight back to Canada leaves Mexico in seven weeks. I've got to keep moving.

Gazing upon massive container cranes that look like metal giraffes overlooking prodigious ships clanking and humming towards the Atlantic, I proclaim, "That's the way I'm going...to Bocas del Toro."

Valter looks the other direction, pointing at pastel buildings and glistening steel skyscrapers towering over a misty grey fog. "I go this way. To Pacific surf towns!"

And so it is we say goodbye.

In my hostel in the tropical Caribbean archipelago, water swishes between cracks in wooden beams. Music blasts from the attached night club offering women free drinks. I ignore it, adamant for a drug- and alcohol-free trip. My brief frivolity in Canada was a fun gateway to befriend locals, but sobriety empowers my integration of healthy thoughts post antidepressants. As fellow travellers nurse hangovers in bed, I wake fresh and stroll secluded shores where tropical rainforests kiss shimmering seas. Leaping over fallen palm trees, it's a pleasant place for introspection. It's been seventeen months since I've settled somewhere for longer than a month. Soon that's going to change.

The air is thick from the unrelenting sun as I stroll across the border via a rickety old railway bridge. A stray dog trots past me as I stop and examine the silty river below. It moves effortlessly. Not belonging to Panama or Costa Rica, it just flows. A palm tree sways overhead as I wonder why mankind creates invisible boundaries. The wooden slates I amble over bridge the gap that separates.

At my funky beachside hostel in Puerto Viejo, the receptionist directs me to my hammock dangling amongst one hundred others in a massive gazebo. The kingdom of colourful mesh wraps positioned two feet apart is skirted by large lockers adorned with visionary art. I unlock one with a globe painted inside an eye's iris. *Earth is not a cold, dead place*, it reads. To my surprise, I find someone else's bag inside. I can't be bothered lugging my belongings to reception and then back again to get a different key, so I plonk my backpack inside. I return to a gorgeous, slack-jawed New Jerseyan scratching her head while examining my bag. I apologize and explain the receptionist's mishap. Her expression morphs into a grin that could melt the Arctic tundra as she becomes my new travel friend.

Long golden curls sweep away from her curious brown eyes that widen as we cycle through rainforests howling with monkeys. She's bronzed and beautiful—inside and out—and introduces me to two American guys. The four of us build sandcastles and splash in warm seas, then venture north to Monteverde, a relaxed mountain town perched beside an evergreen cloud forest. After a long, cramped day standing on back-to-back buses, one of the guys promises an epic adventure to two unique trees when we wake.

A thin mist drifts through the canopy as we follow the curly-haired Alaskan cutie to a horizontal ficus tree that's fallen over an empty riverbed. With roots stretching to the ground like wooden pillars, it's become a bridge. Climbing inside its hollow trunk, we ook-ook at nearby monkeys.

Our next stop is down a small forest trail to another quirky ficus tree. In strangling its host tree, it's created a one-hundred-metre hollow upwards tunnel. Using natural footholds formed from a lattice of entwined branches, we climb to the top and relish the lush canopy view. The cooling breeze is refreshing. I burst with joy.

After descending our wooden perch, we huff up a precipitous mountain swanking sparkly views of both the Caribbean and Pacific Oceans. We enjoy a picnic lunch then take a lonely rainforest trail home, guided by pink ribbons tied to trees. My legs shake as we pursue the dense green down and around. Eventually we gather in golden hour's glow. It seems we've done a loop. The group consensus is to climb up the peak then trail back to town the way we came. Soon jaguars will be on the prowl. We must be wise with sunlight's last rays.

Every fibre in my being wants to keep following the pink-ribboned path down. The hike upward is abrupt. I'm sticky. I don't want to take it. I squeeze my eyes open and shut in an attempt to sharpen focus. Inhaling deeply, I look to the trees for an answer. Does the trail lead anywhere? Or will I continue in circles? A gentle wind rustles through the leaves. Without words it whispers for me to turn back with the others. Begrudgingly, I swallow my need to lead and pant back up the mountain.

We later discover the pink-ribboned trail is an infinite loop. In daring the uphill battle, I unknowingly break a downward cycle of being afraid to depend on others in case they fail me. For so long I've been prisoner to the story "If I don't need people, people can't hurt me". Its stems are a defence mechanism from developmental lack of safety in primary school. My hyper independence has enabled me to seize many opportunities and cultivate a self-governance that is rich and fulfilling. But like left- and right-wing politics, independence and codependence in extreme states are equally detrimental because there is imbalance. In leaning into others and trusting that they can hold me, I create a new era of interdependence that aids connection by upholding my autonomy while recognising the value of collaboration.

*

Realizing you are off your path is the way to get back on it.

While my three American friends get cosy in Costa Rica, Valter and I reunite and venture into Nicaragua. At the crack of dawn, we hop on the first of five local chicken buses, coughing up dust that floats through the windows as we twist around bumpy roads.

On the second overloaded bus, Valter loudly proclaims, "I made up new song. It goes like this... *Duh, duh, duh. Everyone eats the dust...*"

He bops his head and sings to the rhythm of Queen's, "Another One Bites the Dust".

On our third bus-sauna, I chime, "I have the next line... *And, another black boogie. And, another black boogie. We're all eating the dust.*"

We joke like this until we pull into San Juan del Sur, a Nicaraguan party town nestled within a pristine half-moon bay. After finding a hostel on a street lined with bright Victorian buildings, we stroll to the beach to catch sunset. In the shimmering golden trail lapping at silhouetted boats, I see that Valter and I travel like the idiosyncratic fusion of water and earth. Our destination is solid, but our route is fluid. We often take wrong turns, but it's never an issue. Getting lost and trotting off the tourist track is all part of the ride.

Travelling with someone for a week divulges a myriad of faces not revealed for decades in one's hometown. It's like an arranged marriage because the future is concealed but you commit to being shaken out of your comfort zone which inevitably reveals your true nature. You've got to compromise for a smooth ride. On volcanic Ometepe Island soaring from the vast freshwaters of Lake Nicaragua, we cycle along rocky paths that coat my greasy sun-screened skin with silky red soil. Valter's hyperactivity is fun in small doses, but as we arrive in Granada—Nicaragua's oldest town—the time comes for us to divorce from our comradery. I can't stomach his need to chitchat at maximum volume. He doesn't understand my appreciation for stillness.

Our parting is peaceful, and with it I surrender to a stream of ephemeral encounters. By day, I explore enchanting cobbled roads with a group of Westerners. By night, they snort cheap cocaine. I tear up dance floors with them while keeping my nostrils and liver clean. Short stopovers in vibrant León and infamous Managua bring me to sunny El Tunco, where soft black sands glimmer beneath the sun and surfers flock to world-class breaks.

One afternoon, while the sun caresses me bronze by the hostel pool, I befriend Demi, a bright-eyed girl from Nova Scotia. Her accommodation doesn't have a pool, so she sneaks to mine daily to rejuvenate in the cool waters. I think it's hilarious.

As her angelic voice serenades us beneath the moonlight, I spontaneously invite her to join me at Shambhala Music Festival later in the year. My eyes crinkle with her straight-up "Yes." It's six months away, but I'm hopeful the plan sticks. I imagine us dancing in the old-growth forest dance floor described by Trey in Cuzco as I continue north into Honduras.

On a winding forest path sprinkled with fallen leaves, I follow the vanished footprints of the late Maya. The mysterious disappearance of the sophisticated culture makes the stunning temples and sculptures at Copán even more fascinating as I climb them. Running my hands over hieroglyphs carved into stone, I find myself in a solemn silence. I will never comprehend their story. Knowing this amplifies the tactility of mystery. It lingers on my fingers.

Trusting the journey is essential while travelling, with unforeseen obstacles lurking at every turn. My daily mantra is to stay present. My method is breath. Volcanic vistas roll me over the border to Guatemala, where I am charmed by thick-walled, single-storey buildings in colonial Antigua. As I ponder the romanticisation of wanderlust, my heart shatters at the beauty, bravery, and brokenness of the unravelling journey.

Sometimes I find it difficult to distinguish where I end and the world begins. It's a comforting sensation to feel my consciousness melt into the welcoming dream of collective awareness. I'm so content in this state that sometimes it's jarring simply having someone start conversation because it reminds me that I am distinguishable as a separate entity in another's eyes. Logically this makes sense. But spiritually, it overrides the glimpse of oneness in which I've surrendered. After stretching into this transcendental worldview, my mind cannot simply shrink or shrivel back into itself. And so, I'm left with a taste of feeling like I belong everywhere and nowhere, all at once.

While a skilled bus driver navigates sharp twists on sheer cliffs nearing Lake Atitlán, I discern that being a free spirit requires intention and surrender. We must know what we want yet allow life to deliver. As we descend into San Pedro, a party town slumped inside an ancient caldera, I vow to let and make life happen. Local women sporting colourful, embroidered skirts and shawls trail away from lakeside bars and beeping tuk-tuks. In their peaceful pace, I glimpse life before and beyond tourists' excessive consumption of liquified and powdered substance.

I stay in San Pedro just one night. I'd rather not stay at all, but it is where the bus delivers me and is my gateway via a small motorized dinghy to San Marcos, a pedestrian-only town across the lake. En route I chat with a wrinkled English lady. Years of joy crease her skin with character that seeps wisdom into the furrows. She explains she is heading to San Marcos to interview the owner of a spiritual study centre. I lean forward, grateful that she continues.

"There's a meditation garden with copper pyramids, and for part of the monthlong course, students go on a liquid diet and don't talk. I've spent my entire life travelling and have encountered nothing like it..."

I nod as we speed past wooden houses and soggy treetops submerged by water. It's a curious sight. I wonder why San Pedro's town centre is a steep climb with locals living in houses far from the shore.

As if reading my mind, the lady explains, "Lake Atitlán rises and falls in a fifty-year cycle. It takes fifty years to sink back to its lowest point, then fifty years to rise again. The Maya have known this for centuries. That's why town centres perch high above the water's edge."

"That makes sense!" I exclaim, gazing into the deep blue lake's glimmer on the horizon that is hemmed by verdant hills and striking volcanoes. "Where are we at in the cycle?"

"Right now?" She looks at the water then back at me. "Thirty years into the lake's rising."

"Ahhhh."

"When white man came, they built hostels and pubs along the water's edge thinking they scored the best views. They were wrong. The lake will continue swallowing many of these buildings, until eventually it retreats."

"And then the cycle repeats," I finish.

I farewell the lady on a tiny wooden jetty and follow a stony trail. It is adorned with wooden posts covered with flapping flyers advertising ecstatic dances, tantric yoga, breathwork sessions, and cacao ceremonies. I am wide-eyed yet calm. I soon discover that even the animals are at peace. One night a pack of stray dogs trot me back to the hostel after a local friend takes me to an acoustic set at a bohemian cafe.

It's ironic that San Pedro and San Marcos coexist on the same lake. I couldn't leave the former fast enough. I could stay in the latter for weeks.

*

The same sun melting into my morning,
is the tangerine dream being swallowed by your sea.

After bumping along a dirt track into Guatemala's jungle in the tray of a four-wheel drive pickup, I sit on the wooden balcony of my self-sufficient eco hostel. There I gaze upon the verdant canopy surrounding Semuc Champey. Candles flicker with the setting sun. I awe at giant ceiba trees stretching above the forest. Rooted in the underworld, the trees reach for heaven while their sturdy trunks exist in the world of the living.

The hostel owner stops in his tracks and sparks a conversation about synchronicity when he spots *The Celestine Prophecy* beside me. He then offers me a job taking travellers on adventures through the rainforest in exchange for accommodation and three home-cooked meals a day. I examine the darkening sky. The invitation is alluring. So damn alluring. There's a charm to being immersed in the genuine wilderness with limited WiFi and electricity. But my flight back to Canada is nonrefundable, and with dwindled savings I can't afford to buy another ticket. I also feel a strange obligation to be solid with my word of moving in with Aimee. I can't quite put my finger on why—perhaps I feel residual guilt for changing my mind with Blair—but it feels imperative.

Nonetheless, I daydream of settling beside turquoise waters cascading down tiered limestone pools. Most locals reflect and reinforce my joyful smile, but one throws an empty beer bottle at the back of the pickup as we drive past one afternoon. It shatters my heart into harrowing shards that tourism is already impacting the pristine environment and community relations. Living here could either help or hinder that. I'm not sure which.

With much internal debate, I bid the enchanted paradise goodbye and venture west to picturesque, pastel Flores with new friends. At 3:00 a.m. the next morning, we drive to the ancient Mayan ruins of Tikal. In pitch-black darkness we stroll to a massive stone pyramid then climb to a temple at the flat-topped summit and sit in silence. Morning imbues peachy-purple streaks. Birds chirp from the lowland rainforest canopy below. The mountainous horizon is silhouetted as the sun's ascent erases Venus and the stars. I absorb our guide's words as giant spiders crawl along the dense jungle floor and monkeys leap in the trees. My veins brim with wonder, even after leaving the ancient, once-thriving, now-deserted metropolis, and I cross the border into Belize.

On Caye Caulker, a small Caribbean island, dogs nap on the beach and reggae music infuses with the salty breeze. The coral coast's turquoise waters are advertised as relaxing, but I quickly loathe walking along the sandy stretch. Local men eye me like an all-you-can-eat feast, and I don't know where to divert my gaze. Between intoxicated travellers and leeching residents who didn't listen to my "No, I don't feel like talking or being sold a tour," I feel sticky and crave the peace and quiet of Guatemala.

Wooden slats poke into my back beneath the thin bottom bunk mattress as I meditate that night. I'm regularly lucid dreaming and am trying to now astral project. My dreams are deep on my eyelids when a drunk male stumbles into the dorm and unzips his jeans to piss on the wall. I jolt awake and feel my spirit enter my body from a few feet above me. It's the closest I've come to projecting out of my body into the astral plane. Years later, I'm still trying to make sense of it.

In the moment, another woman yells directions at him to the bathroom and then his bunk. He awakes with no recollection of his intoxication, and I leave Caye Caulker with a bitter taste in my mouth. Trailing up the coast of Mexico to Tulum where my flight back to Canada departs, I reflect on the eighteen months since I left Queensland. It'd been liberating to let my wings soar. Now emancipation comes by grounding my roots in solid ground. With sun-kissed skin, I land in Calgary and bus to Trey's university residence. I'm standing on my head, listening to Eckhart Tolle, when Trey returns home and his Mexican roommate exclaims, "Jess, your aura's expanded!"

I'm unsure what he means, but I feel lighter in observing my thoughts, instead of playing into the self-perpetuating drama of accepting mental knots as absolute. Instead of slinking off to the couch that night as I usually do, I sleep in Trey's bed. Wrapped in his arms, our limbs intertwine, and I feel safe cuddling him without shrinking with the density of ulterior motives. I relish that my body relaxes rather than tenses as our torsos mould into one. Despite Trey's mum growing very fond of me and often hinting that we'd make a great couple, our affections are always platonic. It's a turning point in me trusting that men value me for more than my physique.

How deep can you trust?
Will you let your walls crumble?
Can you open yourself to a galaxy of love?

Snowy mountains morph to desert as I rideshare west to Kelowna. There, I lug a black rubbish bag filled with my belongings from the hostel to my new home that is perched behind a jungle of overgrown grass. A mouse scurries between a pile of rubbish bags reeking of last year's escapades. Inside, Aimee welcomes me with a toothy smile. Another girl moved into the fourth bedroom while I was away, but a futon slumps in the dim downstairs lounge that I section off and make my own by sticky-taping a shower curtain to the ceiling.

Using some abandoned cardboard boxes as bedside tables, I set up my sentiments as the girls plan on getting high to celebrate my arrival. In my draughty room, I huddle over my bag, questioning my best next move. I need to eat before we go out, but the clock is ticking. The girls' feet are tapping to go. At the hostel, getting high is a prospect I can shut my dungeon door on. In my new home, the lines blur between having fun and losing self-control. How can I combine the part of me that is curious to explore the life my housemates live with my need to pursue healthy norms?

"Jess!" Aimee calls. "We're *readyyy*."

"Okay... Gimme a moment."

I swallow two heaped spoons of chia seeds, then allow myself one month of dabbling in altered states. One month will bring me to the fortnight of my twenty-third birthday. After that, I will not partake in regular drug use. As I skip past the downstairs bathroom, Lola leaps from the shadows and claws at my toes. It's like she's trying to stop me from running upstairs and swallowing the MDMA the girls have crushed with a credit card. I drop to my feet and hold my palm to her all-seeing eyes. She instantly softens.

"It's okay, Lola. This is only *temporary*."

Edging towards me, she slides her tiny silky body through my fingers and purrs. The delicate ripples of her vulnerability oscillate into my hand.

"Oh, you *beautiful* kitty. One month, then I stop. I promise..."

"Jess! You ready?" Aimee's cousin sounds impatient.

"Yes, beautiful. I'm coming!"

As I stroke Lola's black-and-grey-striped body once more her lucid chartreuse eyes penetrate me with the echo of my promise.

One month, Jess. That's thirty days.

I trust my tenacity to stop when I say I will. In the meantime, it becomes normal to take MDMA two or three nights a week. By day, I drop off resumes and rake the soggy clutter of rotten leaves dishevelling the garden. By night, I watch my friends' thirst for answers in small white baggies. Choosing to see the best in others and affirming their strengths allows them to step up and shine through positive reinforcement and increased self-efficacy. But it also overlooks addictive tendencies that spiral me into avoidance of my true feelings. It's like slapping an affirmation over trauma that continues festering on unhealthy, unexamined beliefs.

On spring's last snowy day, I hold my breath as cigarette smoke wafts through whizzing conversation in Aimee's boyfriend's lounge room. My focus lands on a slim friend. High as a kite on coke, she nods like a bobblehead figurine. With each frantic nod, she sinks deeper into the couch. I'm worried she might completely disappear. Skin and bones, she's wasting away one bender at a time. I yearn to reach out and touch her. I yearn to help her. But until she wants to help herself, there is nothing I can do but be a beacon of hope and hammock of support in her darkest hour.

Stretching in altered states makes me feel like a fairy. With retrospect, it is definitely serotonin triggering the release of oxytocin in my bloodstream. Inhaling love into my heart, I centre myself with the intention of it effortlessly flowing into the lives of those around me. I sense that I'm exactly where I am meant to be—for reasons beyond my egoic awareness—but two weeks into my "month of dabbling" I become drenched with fear. What if my innocent exploration cajoles dependence? What if I become the girl dissolving into the couch? No one enters the party scene with the objective to be addicted. It's a tendency that creeps in. I've only just waned myself off antidepressants. Altering my brain chemistry all over again isn't healthy for that integration. My meditation practice has recently slipped to the wayside. I've handed out a dozen resumes, but nothing tangible has solidified, and the stress of my waning savings tests me.

My pent-up agitation finds release when I'm home alone one afternoon. Grimacing at my cracked bedroom wall, I scream, "Why the fuck am I here?"

The words strike the wall. Then they lash back at me with a force throwing me onto the futon in a tight bundle. There, I weep until my sheets become a warm, salty puddle. I can't keep doing this. I can't keep getting high. I need a job. I need healthy norms. I need a friend who understands. A friend...

Stephen's huge grin morphs to genuine concern as we chat over Skype. He's recently moved back to Colorado and listens to my predicament from the shade of a lemon tree. I want to be clean, but I still have two weeks until I've given my word to cease. What if the day came and I can't do it?

His beautiful blue eyes brim with compassion.

"First of all, I love you, Jess. Big hug." Extending his arms, he draws his hands towards his heart as though holding me.

I exhale with relief, grateful to talk truth with someone who gets it and gets me.

"Secondly, you know what you're doing," he affirms in a tone that is soft yet stern.

I do, I think. Go as deep as I deem safe so that my curiosity is itched and I need not voyage here again.

"Thirdly, Molly is a pretty dirty drug. You never know what it's mixed with."

I nod. This premise strikes me. When asking "what am I putting into my body", I'd vowed to nourish myself with goodness. Drugs are detrimental to this journey. Plus, they steal $40 from my tight weekly budget that could go to fresh produce. Our conversation flows elsewhere, until the time comes to say goodbye, and Stephen gives another golden nugget to muse.

"The spiritual world shown by drugs isn't real, Jess. It's fake. We can get there, *we must get there*, by taking a sober route..."

Truer words have never been spoken. No one knows better than he who has walked it.

As the budding promise of spring adorns hillsides with brilliant chocolate-smelling yellow flowers, I am offered half a dozen jobs around town. My fear of scarcity suddenly blossoms into a smorgasbord of cafes and bars wanting to employ me. I've already said yes to late-night weekend work at a food stand downtown and the odd coat check shift at a rave lounge, but I can't shake the caring blue eyes of the redheaded manager who high-fived me during my interview at Marmalade Cat Café.

In my third week of MDMA exploration, I walk into the quirky café for my first shift. My manager smiles coyly behind bright-red lipstick and chuckles that her coworkers April-fooled her into thinking I'd taken a job elsewhere. She later opens a large drawer and jumps out of her skin at a wooden cat hiding amongst coffee tins. Apparently, the goal is to scare others by hiding the cat in creative ways. The shift sets the tone for the mischievous nature of my new workplace. I'm a natural fit.

On the final night of my thirty days, I end up at a bustling, sticky-floored nightclub dancing to '90s pop with Ronnie and my housemates. Just as I'm trying to discern if the month ends bang on midnight or the following morning, Ronnie pulls a skinny, orange-haired girl toward me and introduces her as Ella. She's recently moved to Kelowna from Perth and is out dancing alone. We invite her back to Aimee's boyfriend's house where dirty dishes fill every flat surface and cigarette smoke stains the ceiling. Aimee prefers partying there after discovering a skittish Lola licking plates used to crush drugs. Ella thanks us for being approachable amidst the club's cliquey vibe.

On a saggy, zebra-patterned couch, my eyes fill with tears as Ella discloses her father's recent suicide. As we get higher, a sinister energy warps our sphere. One boy living in the house starts sharpening a knife with a twisted grin. Aimee and Ella leave the room, perturbed by his volatility. With a heightened sense of awareness, I sit with him and chat in a friendly tone. He isn't threatening anyone in the house, and I don't feel in danger sitting beside him. I've always maintained a degree of sharp coherence no matter my mental state. So clearly, I see his actions are a subconscious way of stealing our attention and therefore energy by forcing us to be present with him and his potential danger. At the core, he just wants love. Eventually, I ask him to put the knife away because it's making me uncomfortable. Without argument, he does.

The following night, Aimee invites me to get high. Her chest visibly collapses when I decline. She knows about my thirty-day agreement, but I guess she assumed I wouldn't follow through with my word. To her, my integrity is a painful slap to all the fun we've shared.

*

Self-regulation and self-control are the greatest skills we will learn in life.
If we're not taking ownership of situations, we're allowing them to own us.

With a clearer mind, I replace my MDMA habit with meditation. With awareness centred in my heart, I check in with myself often by asking: *What would love do?* With slower brain waves, there is spaciousness between my thoughts and thus more room to select which notions I wish to invest in.

Sometimes I declare my intention unto the world, but more often than not I ask: *Where do you want me?* I start feeling my soul as opposed to feeding my ego, recognising the boundlessness of spirit and the impermanence of my physical form. Life is about value and virtue, not affluence and age. Breathing into the richness of each moment, I exhale love and trust what I need will appear. Every action has a deeper intention. For I am fuelled with the warmth of love as compassion expands inside my chest.

Every time Lola finds solace in my room, trembling with terror from my housemates chasing her as they spit ugly words, I imagine a pure stream of love flowing from my heart to hers. Slowly she softens, as I did, falling asleep in Trey's arms. As love overrides fear, she stops scratching and clawing. Instead, she pushes her tiny forehead against mine as she curls up beside me and gifts her healing purr.

As colour revitalizes the city and the days slowly warm, Ben and Trey come to visit. On a hike up Knox Mountain, the guys imply that Kelowna isn't the most fertile place to grow. The influence of drugs in the bikie run town is prominent. It's easy to lose one's way. I watch the lake meander through the valley and bite my tongue from screaming: *You guys led me here. You showed me this world. Six months ago*, I would have thrown fire, but in my commitment to respond rather than react I see that their stance stems from a will to protect me. They have a point. It isn't the most fruitful soil for spiritual expansion, but growth rises from within. I can stay *and* choose to thrive.

♥

My bond with Aimee is deep, so much so that it is rare to spend a day apart. She gives me feminine advice and a sense of belonging. I inspire her to cultivate positivity and purify her life, starting with borrowing her brother's truck to get rid of the stinking mound of rubbish festering outside. When the guys venture back to Calgary, I continue saying no to getting high. This forms a chasm between us. I'm sensitive to her spite. It feels like I'm being punished for honouring my wellbeing. With retrospect, I understand my actions are triggering because they elicit accountability for her own health.

She promises to help me decorate the house and hide Easter eggs in the yard for my birthday, which falls on 420—the national cannabis holiday—and Easter Sunday. As the day approaches, I keep checking the driveway for her car. She indulges in a three-day bender instead. I feed Lola all three days then collapse on my futon, letting the tiny creature press her paws into my heart. I miss Aimee. She's tasteful and driven. This spiky vibe isn't who she really is. It rekindles the feeling of losing Courtney to drugs, and my tears swallow me in an ocean of sorrow. Eventually I confide in Jacob. From Queensland, he heeds, "You have an incredibly deep soul, Jess. It's easy to get lost now and then when you swim that deep."

The day of my birthday, Aimee trudges home and apologizes for her absence. She acknowledges that drugs are impacting her wellbeing and hindering her growth. Peering into her vulnerable brown eyes, I exhale my hurt and forgive her. She's being real with me. This is the Aimee I know and love. I note that the desire to change is the challenging yet potent first step. Her fortitude to articulate it makes it even more powerful.

Aimee's birthday falls four days after mine, and I pop my head into her boyfriend's house before strolling to work at the food stand. It is a stale scene of my friends losing their shine as they converse about how many bags of Molly, K, and coke to order. My awareness to life's subtleties is sharpening. If I'm a musical note, my tone has changed. I am on a different wavelength and the chords created by being in the cigarette-reeking room are dissonant because I'm no longer in resonance. I seek counterparts that harmonize with my unique tone, without having to sharpen or flatten my natural timbre.

Gradually, the days are toasty enough to ditch long coats and sport bikinis. Aimee gets a new job and realises that her relationship is toxic. Their happiness depends on artificial highs. As soon as she stops using, they break up. With delight, I watch her inner light grow as she finds peace and enthusiasm on long mountainous hikes.

Perched on the front stoop one night, she turns to me and whispers, "You know how you always say everything happens for a reason? Well, I really believe that you coming into my life was for a reason. You've been such a blessing, Jess. Your positivity is contagious, and I don't think I could have gotten clean without you being here. When you stopped doing drugs, I realised it wasn't fun anymore. It inspired me to change."

My eyes smile as I search for the right words. It's been intense and cathartic for us both. I understand I can't save people, but something unhealed within me from my time with Courtney finds completion in Aimee's actions.

"Aww, Aimee...thank you. But—you need to acknowledge yourself too. You can't help someone if they don't want to help themselves. Trust me, I know from years of being a train off the rails."

"Really?"

"Yes. Something within *you* fuelled your transformation. Perhaps I inspired you externally, but you tapped into something internally. If you didn't have that will, nothing I tried would have gotten through."

Aimee's life continues to flourish as summer boils. We still spend quality time together, but the medicine has been absorbed, and I branch into other social pockets. As my self-practise solidifies, I feel clearer and calmer. Sometimes my selflessness is to my detriment, always putting other's needs before my own. I confuse the internal fountain of self-love with the ego's external need for validation, and this shows up as a bedroom with no mirrors and deflecting loving compliments out of fear of self-conceit. Eventually, I learn I must fill my cup before I can give to others. Eventually, I recognise that the more I receive the more I can give. But first the pendulum swings to the detriment of giving from an empty vessel.

As I feel clearer, Riley emerges from his sphinx-like cave, and we converse via long text messages every few days. His philosophical insights continue to inspire me into the best version of myself, and the less I attach to specific outcomes, the easier our connection flows.

Let your heartstrings harmonise with the world around you.

As tourists flock to Kelowna's glistening waters like bees foraging nectar, the café pumps from open to close. It's laborious to save on minimum wage, but friendly banter and jokes that we are the "aristocrat barista cats" add a lightness to hectic days. Over time it becomes my favourite workplace, especially when I'm on till. Meeting each customer with a genuine smile, I strive to bring self-awareness through eye contact. Only half of people meet my eyes. I savour the moments I catch the others and see presence click.

Sometimes, a lean middle-aged blonde woman busses tables for us amidst swarming rushes. Expecting nothing in return, Donna slinks into the dish station with a carton of dirty dishes then wipes tables for the swift turnover of customers. One afternoon, a dozen paper drink orders bank up while I steam milk and drink the aroma of roasted coffee swirling thick in the air. Lost in the labyrinth of my mind, I've reduced the orders to three when I feel a loving essence glide into my sphere. I look up. Donna watches me from a nearby table. The radiance in her magnetic blue eyes instantly dissolves my worries into steam from the milk wand, and I get curious to her story. Is she consciously sending me love? If so, why?

Slowly, we become acquainted as she orders fruit salad and black coffee. She seamlessly channels insights into bubbly chitchat, and I cherish her daily check-ins. One afternoon, in my small gap between jobs, Donna comes over with a bag of chic clothes gifted from a Los Angeles singer who frequents the café. Every cent I earn slowly accumulates to a ticket back to Australia, so it's meaningful to receive a glamourous new wardrobe. I don't care for designer brands. I appreciate that I've saved a few dollars and can discard some ragged items while enjoying quality time with Donna. Before leaving, she pauses at the bottom of the stairs. Looking from my housemate's closed bedroom door to me, she reassures, "Keep on doing what you're doing. You never know the difference you could be making in someone's life...."

Tension is boiling between two of my housemates. I find it challenging to be diplomatic while not getting singed from the flames. We seek ways to ease the strain with house meetings, but with both girls moaning in my ear about the other, I deteriorate in a no-man's-land of strife. One day, a friend comes around to mow our lawn and notices my strain. His eyes smile behind rectangular glasses as he prompts, "Hey, see those dandelion puffballs over there? Go kick them. All of them. You'll feel better once you do."

I leap off the front stoop and spin in circles until every fuzzy white seed whirls into the air. Then I burst out laughing. It doesn't matter if they're wishes or weeds. It matters that I've moved the tension through me, so it no longer lives inside my body.

※

One sticky afternoon, a man storms into the café as we are closing. He demands to see his brother-in-law who works the early morning bake shift. His glazed eyes tell me he is under the influence of something. Breathing into my abdomen—present to my power—I calmly explain that his relative isn't here. He shrugs and then demands a staff discount.

I meet his eyes and clarify in a kind yet stern tone, "Staff discounts are for individuals who work here."

He's playing the role of the intimidator described in *The Celestine Prophecy*. I refuse to give him the fight he seeks or be pulled into his drama by playing small. With power fuelled from within, my empowered stance is threatening to him because it doesn't depend on stealing energy from others externally.

"Okay, I'll have that chicken panini," he demands.

"Sure." I smile, maintaining eye contact. "That's $9.50, thank you."

I'm walking a tightrope that I've navigated as a skimpy barmaid many times before of standing in my power while not pushing intoxicated individual's ego too hard.

"What about my *discount?*" he roars.

"As I explained, staff discounts are for individuals who *work* here. Thus, the word *staff*. Even our staff don't get 50 percent off unless they're rostered on to *work* that day. The panini is our best seller. Our customers love it. Would you like it toasted?"

My awareness of his unconscious objective creates a shift in the interplay and interrupts his thievery of power. I sustain eye contact as his glaze evaporates with the ignition of an angry fire.

"You don't fool me," he barks.

I look at him doe-eyed. I'm not caving. Nor am I adding fuel.

He slams his fist on the counter, and then storms out of the café.

My co-workers congratulate the way I handled the situation, and we close up in peace. As I begin my short walk home, I have a hunch that he's lingering. I feel it in my stomach. Plugging in my headphones, I walk along the busy street with music pumping. Halfway home, I spot him yelling abuse at cars across the road. I continue walking with headphones in but turn the music down as he crosses the road and flounces into my peripheral. I'm acutely aware of his pace behind me, but continue walking with my shoulders back, head high, and a direct gaze. As I glance at my shadow for the first signs of him nearing, he mumbles something about slamming my head into the pavement.

Oh, hell no. I ain't taking none of that!

I halt and face him. Piercing through his egoic layers bundled with searing anger, I look into his soul with eyes that say: You cannot—*you will not*—touch me.

"Hi," I dare unwaveringly.

My acknowledgement of him has him jump back.

Internally, my heart beat hastens. Externally, I show no fear. We stand twenty metres from the hostel. My safety. My old home.

"Oh, it's—*you*..." he falters.

Before he can say another word, I stride towards the hostel's back stairs, knowing the situation will either escalate or unwind. He'll either follow me inside or walk away.

In the crowded communal kitchen, I announce what is happening. This draws half a dozen travellers to survey the intoxicated man slouched in on himself crossing back over the road. It's no longer just me he's up against. I've summoned an army.

Brushing us away, he yells, "Okay, okay, I'm going!"

Like the boy sharpening the knife at the party, his use of intimidation to capture people's energy stems from an innate human desire to be appreciated and understood. The method is warped. The intention is pure.

When all you know is a, b, c - it's difficult to fathom the rest of the alphabet.

"Jess, I want to talk to you about something before you leave."

The gracious café owner examines me with a twinkle in her baby-blue eyes. I'm about to venture west to Vancouver to meet Polly Jane, my childhood youth camp friend, who is visiting for three weeks.

"Yes?" I sing, impulsively wiping a milk stain off the metallic bench as the aroma of simmering borscht soup fills the air.

"You're the best hire we've had in a long time. I want to thank you for your hard work and outstanding customer service. We don't normally do this so soon, but we want to give you a raise."

I bow my head and thank her. My tight budget means I often scavenge customers' uneaten salads. Eleven dollars an hour is still tricky to live off, but every cent counts, and I leave Kelowna with a grateful heart.

Polly Jane beams at me from the arrivals gate beneath red-rimmed glasses and bright-green hair. Her animated "WOW" and "OOH" magnify my vivacious nature as we explore Vancouver. I am grateful to see a different side of the coastal city—a diverse fusion of zest, sophistication, and creativity amid beachfront heritage homes and tree-lined roads.

After a few days, we board a ferry to Vancouver Island and then bus to Tofino. En route to the easygoing surf town, I awe at bohemian boroughs thriving inside old-growth forests. It's easy to relax into a slower rhythm as whales breach on the glistening Pacific horizon and salty zephyrs ripple the surface of shores cresting in soft dreamscape hues. There are answers in the stillness and there is stillness in the answers.

After a buzzy weekend working all three jobs in Kelowna, Polly Jane and I venture to Banff. To my delight, Trey and Riley visit one afternoon. As we stroll through tall evergreens, birds tweet at snowy mountains peeking through the canopy, and golden-hour rays drizzle a reflective warmth. Earlier in the day, I'm struck by a bookmark with seven wolves and spontaneously get it for Riley. As I hand it to him, he beams and reaches into his pocket for a stunning turquoise howlite sphere. I later discover that it encourages emotional expression.

I am present to my unattached appreciation of him. It allows our connection to perpetually blossom as the four of us pillow fight in the blanket fort that we build in our empty dorm. In no longer forcing or pining for specific outcomes, a rhythmic flow ensues. I am taking the path of least resistance. This empowers my emotions to dance in an unshackled rhythm.

When Polly Jane and I bus back to Kelowna, I contemplate Riley's and my entwinement while watching a river glide parallel to the road. The occasional rocky outcrop causes glistening streams to separate and veer in different directions before merging again. These geographic formations are life's inevitabilities, lessons to be learned and forks in the flow prompting us to part before linking together again. We're all on a journey. But we take different routes.

After Polly Jane flies back to Australia, I plunge into a double-tempo beat with all jobs full steam ahead into Canada Day. The food stand stays open all weekend to accommodate swarming crowds, and I clock up a seventy-hour week working double shifts when my parents come to visit. They are happy entertaining themselves while I'm sweating and swirling amid honeyed aromas. On days I work only one job, we catch up over dinner. I'm not the girl they knew in Europe, and they note this transformation with crinkled eyes. Somehow, it's easier for our nearest and dearest to digest how we've changed after crossing an ocean of time.

Raise your standards, not your walls.

A few days later, Ben visits en route to a Vipassanā Meditation Centre, where he will sit in silence for ten days. His dedication inspires me to sharpen my own practise. With summer in full swing, deep breathing calms me amidst hospitality's hectic scurry. I find solace in stillness and often walk to City Park, where I envision love drenching the city with good vibrations. The ripples oscillate from where I sit beneath a shady tree to a wooden boardwalk packed with camera-happy tourists, to children leaping off a slippery blow-up slide, to expensive yachts sailing into the horizon.

Donna marvels at our team spirit at the café, and I walk to work with appreciation rippling through my veins. One of my co-workers, a witty chatterbox, and I meet Donna and an elderly customer to watch live music in the park every Wednesday. One balmy night, after the music ends, my co-worker and I stroll to a park behind the hospital and swing into the stars as lakeside houses twinkle reflections in the water.

"This is so therapeutic," she exclaims.

"Yippeeeeeee!" I agree, stoked that she is keen for a night swing. Daytime swinging isn't the same. Every time you get in a good groove, young children bolt over and you have to abandon it so they can have a go.

I explain to my co-worker that swinging reminds me of life's constant motion. For every down, there's an up. And vice versa. When I lose myself in a funk, the rhythmic pendulum brings me home. I'm reminded that nothing is permanent, our pain and our joy.

Without understanding why, I open up to my sapphire-eyed friend about my rape and its consequence on my sense of worth, my voice and my relationship to intimacy. By braving the prickly, knotted bulge of vulnerability, I create the space for her to do the same. The earth's springy blanket holds us as we sit cross-legged on the grass, and she confides that her first, and only, sexual encounter was not consensual. I feel the stabbing anguish of her story like it is my own. The withering torment of shrivelling into nothingness while grasping for reasons of why.

In that moment, I realise that the silencing of assault is more damaging than the act itself because it reinforces feelings of self-blame and distances victims from essential support. The lake's pleasant breeze suddenly feels scratchy as I'm inundated with the zap of understanding why Courtney and my bond ran so deep after she confided in me, why I distanced myself from Mama's parents with a roaring anger upon knowing they silenced their own daughter after her rape, and why I feel such an ardent pull to write a book and share my story. It's not about me. It never was. It's about creating new discourses around the importance of consent and the power of vulnerability, not as a weakness but a deeply important aspect of humanity to find one's voice again, move through heavy emotions, and feel the courageous opening into authenticity.

"I guess we're all fixing each other. Helping each other glue our pieces back together," my co-worker ponders.

"And if someone isn't helping us grow, they're showing us what we don't want, helping us grow deeper into ourselves by up-levelling our standards and boundaries."

"Breaking our pieces so they can be put back together again in a way that works," she clarifies.

I chuckle. It's the brittle kind to stop the tears from falling.

Sometimes we just need someone to listen. Even if they can't take the pain away or say anything to make it better, being heard enables the cathartic release we need to begin healing.

A light atop the two-storey homeless shelter periodically flickers. The electrical malfunction is common during my late-night food stand shift as we barbeque onions to reel customers in. As we wait for the 3:00 a.m. rush when nearby nightclubs close, tension weighs heavy in the air beneath an enigmatic full moon. The surge of customers comes then goes, and after thrusting the barbeque up a wooden ramp into the back of a rusty white van, my co-worker insists on driving me home. There's an eery vibe on the streets tonight. But the twenty-minute stroll helps me decompress before a short sleep and long Sunday shift.

"Are you sure?" the moon-faced sweetheart queries.

"Yes... Thank you."

As I turn away and take my first steps, intuition rustles my stomach with uncertainty. I silence it by telling myself it's a short walk on a well-lit road. The walk will be replenishing.

Crossing the highway, I turn my music down and glance over my shoulder. I don't want to draw in unsavoury experiences, so I tune into the feeling of safety in my body. Even as my nervous system settles, I can't shake the sinister sensation of someone following me. It's a question I often grapple: is intuition an inkling of something beyond our control, or is it us drawing things towards us with the law of attraction?

Halfway home, a lone man with a wide march appears before me. As I lift my gaze from my search for loose change on the footpath a stinging burn suddenly throbs in my right cheek. He's hit me.

"FUCK YOU!" he bellows.

I feel my skull pulse. Searching for his eyes, I can't see past his clenched jaw and jutting chin. I'm in shock. Yet instinctively, I continue walking to a small corner store across the road while alarm bells roar. This is an intimidator whose game I cannot crack.

Luckily, he too continues walking—away from me. With a road between us, I trust he can't hear my pounding heart. Outwardly, I remain composed. Internally, I wonder what prompted him to hit me. Maybe he lost his drugs and me scanning the pavement was a threat to him finding them.

I turn around to ensure he isn't following me.

The burly stranger's fiery eyes are on me.

"Come here!" he orders, pointing his finger to the footpath before him.

I don't budge. His command is nauseating because his confidence stems from someone else's obeying.

Breathing into my stomach, I appeal, "Hey, it's okay. We're okay."

His lip curls at something behind me. I turn around. A taxi approaches. With pronounced motion, I wave it down. It is occupied. It's not stopping. By sheer luck, the taxi indicates to turn down the street that separates me from the man. With its approach, we both run. We disperse in opposite directions. I know he won't just disappear, but the turning vehicle gives me a head start away from his angry hand.

Forty metres ahead of me, a guy plays with a sprinkler on a patch of lawn that fringes a tall apartment block. For months I've walked this street at 4 a.m. Not once have I passed another human.

Sprinting towards him, I blurt, "I don't know you, but I know you're safe. I just got whacked by some dude. I think he's lingering."

As I catch my breath, another guy pops his head over the first-storey balcony.

I verify the attacker is a stranger. The three of us look down the street to the aggressor's shadow. As I assumed, he's out from hiding and approaching. Then he spots the two men and bolts down the side street once more.

The man on the balcony runs after him, though I warn against it.

"No, fuck that," he disputes. "If he did this to you, he might do it to others. It's not okay!"

The man fixing the sprinkler walks me home as I calm my racing heart. The next day, I quit my job at the food stand. I also vow to listen when my intuition chooses to speak.

🍎

Trust yourself, trust the journey. The dots connect looking back.

A few days later, a lanky man with buzz-cut hair pokes his head between coffee machines amidst a hectic afternoon rush. The stranger smiles and waves as if we are friends. I look at him deadpan.

Yes? Is there something I can help you with? I've got drink orders coming out of my ass—can't you see I'm busy?

Then it clicks.

"Ben! Oh, gosh...hi!"

My once long, shaggy-haired friend has returned from Vipassanā. I fetch him my house key and blurt that I'll catch him after my shift. Summer shifts are nonstop, and I blur out anything nonessential to the task at hand.

We laugh off my not recognising him on an evening hike up Knox Mountain. The next day, thunder rumbles through pearly skies as lightning strikes the city in an electric embrace. People flock to the café for shelter, and the murmur of chitchat intensifies to a yelling, clanking pandemonium with a storm of people squished between occupied chairs. Just as we've made the final drink from a stream of backlogged orders, the power cuts out. The café empties. I'm still charged like the sky when Ben picks me up, and we drive to the shopping plaza to stock up on superfoods.

As we weave through the fluorescently lit mall, Ben grins at everyone we pass. I catch the infectious beam that he ignites in strangers, first a bowed-shouldered woman, then an elderly couple holding hands while they scuff along in a slow shuffle. In the stream of faces, I spot Ella's strawberry-blonde hair as she huddles with three others near a phone kiosk. When we met, her head sunk into her shoulders. Now, she holds herself with a straighter posture. Ben and I stroll over. Instantly, a man sporting a purple cap with a colourful eyeball pinned in the centre catches my eye. I remember him dancing with a unicorn horn on his head at the rave lounge, and he once tried coaxing me to give him free pierogies at the food stand. I feel him examine my colourful beach kimono as I eye the flattened pinecone wrapped around his neck.

I nearly choke on the smell of tobacco as he introduces himself as the "Peace Clown" and shifts a wooden staff from hand to hand. Adorned with chunky rings and crystal bracelets, he has a vertical labret and septum piercing with a silver chain curving from the latter to his ear. The expressiveness of his emerald eyes beneath thick, dark eyebrows intrigues me. He has the looks and persona of a Persian prince. Something in me is cautious. I perceive him as a leech, and it triggers me because he has no fear in asking for what he wants, while I stay shackled by my inability to express my needs out of habit of putting others first. The Peace Clown seeks a ride to a festival that Ben is going to that weekend, so we exchange contact information, then continue on our way. In subsequent months he becomes a pivotal part of the unravelling journey.

Tension builds in repeating melodic phases that boom from my friend's speakers as we wind through the Kootenay Ranges to Shambhala. As promised, Demi flies over from Nova Scotia and convoys to the festival with the guys. After bumping along a narrow dirt track, twilight darkens to an inky night as we enter a green paddock filled with rows of cars blasting music into a cauldron of sound. We're not even in, but the party's begun with lasers dancing above silhouetted trees and bass rumbling through the valley. Slowly our row is summoned to the gate and our tickets are scanned. I'm not ready to enter, not without the guys, so I snuggle myself into slumber in the back of my friend's car.

The next morning, I lug my bags through a wonderland of kaleidoscopic tents and market stalls where Ben meets me by a garden of sunflowers. Beaming humans garnish themselves in glittery face paint, metallic leotards, and furry tails. Some skip. Others strut. I falter. My senses are heightened.

At camp, I plonk my bag in Demi's tent and change into a slick, psychedelic bikini. The experience is already unparalleled, with my mind unravelling into the mountainous horizon. At 4:20 p.m. in Fractal Forest, a stage set within an enchanted old-growth woodland, the DJ flings perfectly rolled joints into the crowd from his setup in a burnt-out cedar stump. Trey is stoked. I'm already baked from the heat, so we follow the crowd to a cool river meandering through the forest and plunge in. People flock to the water like wild animals gathering at a water hole, with resplendent umbrellas and blow-up floaties adorning rocky shores. As sunshine licks my skin dry, we amble back to camp and layer up. Nighttime beckons with deep electronic booms.

Back in Fractal Forest, funky beats ripple through the trees and lasers slice open the canopy. It is decked with neon sunflowers and video-game-inspired visuals. Saucy leather cats, sparkly sequined pixies, neon totems, and jellyfish umbrellas spin around me. I yearn to melt into the music and let my body move unrestrained, but the first hip-shaking motion is hard to find with the guys watching for the moment I escape my cerebral chatter and let my body do the talking.

Amidst the bright lights and beaming smiles of fantasy creatures cavorting through the trees, I get triggered by the undeniable escapism of excessive drug use into wonky black holes that cajole illusionary realities. An unshackled joy connects us in booty-bouncing beats, yet 3:00 a.m. dance floors are dotted with dissociated people, wide-eyed and searching for truth. For this reason, I retreat before the others most nights. Camp is quieter. Camp is calm. Even amid the perpetual womp womp brmmm. On a deflating blow-up mattress, I come into the beating home inside my chest.

Oh darling, don't you know?
You're an artist, and you are art.

In a labyrinth of towering cedar trees, poetry hangs from leafy branches and a cool breeze makes netted hammocks and homemade dreamcatchers sway. I find a sunny patch in a cosy forest lounge and anchor myself in the intention to stay grounded and open. It's the first time I've been alone at the festival. I appreciate the rejuvenating stillness. It allows me to reflect on the journey leading me here, beginning with the Huachuma ceremony fourteen months ago when I questioned, "Where am I meant to be?" As I'm contemplating memory lane, I feel pulled to venture deeper into the grove's artful nooks. But golden hour breathes night's chilly promise, so I meander back to camp where the others await.

Later in the night, we're in Fractal Forest when a couple on stage sweeps me into a dark remembrance of my sexual assault. I'm slack-jawed as the lady in leather lingerie rips off the man's shirt then pushes him onto a chair, where he drools as she poses and struts. A sudden coldness pulls my stomach to the forest floor. Ben notices me spiralling. Their exhibitionism ignites the highly activated incomplete biological response of trauma in my body, which brings me back to the exploitation I felt by being filmed during unconsented sex. Later in life, I find tools to complete the somatic experience and move it through me. In the moment, I freeze.

Ben taps the guys on the shoulder and motions for us to move on.

"But the music's soooo good, man!" Trey reasons.

Conner looks from me to the stage, then shakes his head at Trey.

Ben concludes, "Nah, bro, Jess doesn't feel safe. We're going."

He links his arm in mine, and we walk away with the others in tow.

Away from the pandemonium, Ben asks, "Are you okay?" His chocolate eyes are loving and magnetic. In them I've always felt safe.

I pull him into a hug then nod.

I don't want to make a fuss, but I'm so grateful to be away from the lustful parade.

The next day, our final one, I wander back to the creative labyrinth of cedar trees. There I find a small box and a pile of blank paper with the instructions: *Write something you wish to let go of.* This is what called me.

Letting go isn't easy for me. My default is to clasp moments and stretch them into infinity. This inhibits presence because I'm holding on to the "safety" of what is known. Slowly, I'm learning to trust that anything happening—or not happening— is for my highest good, and that letting go creates space for new growth. I perch beside the box, mulling over all the things I wish to let go of and all that I already have—depression, unhealthy sexual patterns, fear of being me. I sit there for a long time, until finally I build the courage to scribble *the journey* and place it inside the box.

The moon blooms full that night. I feel succulent in a seamless golden leotard. Finally, I'm able to surrender into the bizarre, radically expressive, fun crowd. Finally, my body moves uninhibited. I'm liberated with the sensuous flow of my hips merging with groovy beats as basslines reverberate in my sacrum. Riley smiles every time I glance his way. The journey is unravelling.

I awake to an *untz untz untz wub* oscillating through the ground in predictable four-four beats. Rivulets of sweat trickle down my limbs. The tent is a sauna. As I reach for my water, a sudden knowing electrifies my entire body: it's time to go back to Perth.

To my surprise, I accept it wholeheartedly. My lack of resistance shocks me like a lightning bolt striking unsuspecting ground. It's been three years since I've spent more than a month in the world's most isolated city. It is uncanny that my intention in Peru *to figure out where I'm meant to be led me* to Shambhala, only to guide me back to Perth—the city I once ran from.

Emerging sticky from the tent, I perch on a rock overlooking the festival. Festivalgoers trickle back to camp after the last all-nighter as a distant DJ infuses reggae beats into heavy basslines. I feel uneasy in the looping *clicks* and *booms*. I can't help but wonder if audio geniuses target specific brainwaves with hidden messages wrapped in rhythmic loops. What if our deeper mental processes are being hacked and rearranged through trance states where our neural functions operate at peak?

On that same notion, it's possible for audio alchemists to tweak our subconscious by injecting sound with love. Standing there in Shambhala's final hours, I see that it comes down to intention. Like everything in life, our aims mould our actions. Artist's weave their soul into everything they create. When channelled with the right aims, we see lasting social change. This makes art our greatest tool for transformation and healing. Without it, society withers and wanes.

Sometimes pain is our greatest source of inspiration.
It is through art that our spirits rise.

I return to work pale and gaunt. A few days of catch-up eating has me feeling myself again, and I book a flight to Perth. Goodbyes are dewy-eyed and filled with strange truths. In my final week, my co-worker from the swing set pulls me aside as we close the café. Her topaz-blue eyes shimmer with infinite constellations.

"Jess, I have a confession."

I nod. My breath is calm. Nothing really surprises me anymore.

"When I first met you, I wanted to fuck you because I've always wanted to fuck a stripper."

I refrain from correcting her that I wasn't a stripper because she has more to say.

"Then I got to know you...and I felt *terrible*, because you're one of the sweetest people I've ever met. You coming to Kelowna has helped me grow in more ways than you'll ever know."

Peering into my soul with attentive jewels, she rubs her nose on mine. As she embraces me, I breathe love from my heart to hers. Then she leans in, flutters her long eyelashes, and gives me an innocent peck. Her lips are soft and tender. They tell me that her healing journey is just beginning, but she is going to be okay.

As I compile my belongings into piles of keep, gift, and throw away, Lola strides into my room. She swishes her tail with sassy independence. It's strange to think of the quivering kitten she once was. No more does she slink in the shadows or dig her claws into bare flesh. Lola spends more time with Aimee since she embraced sobriety, but visits me often to ensure her human subjects are behaving in an orderly manner.

Stroking her silky body, I explain that I'm leaving. "I'm really grateful we met…"

Lola purrs and presses her forehead against mine. Then she looks into my eyes as though peering into a crystal ball where she foresees the challenges, expansion, and lessons awaiting me.

"Hey? What do you see, Lola?"

She gives one more compelling gaze. Then she meows and prances away.

A philosophically infused rideshare brings me to Calgary, where Trey and Riley pick me up from a downtown café. A comfortable silence entails as we stroll along Bow River. I relish the calm of our trinity as we commune with nature, free from meaningless chatter tangling into futile noise.

That night—snuggled in the spare bedroom of Ben's parents' place in a prestigious hamlet just outside the city—a strange dream encapsulates me. In it, a beautiful 3D lattice engulfs me in bright geometry. Pulsating in technicolour, it rolls into me then morphs into a kaleidoscopic tube slide that I glide down effortlessly. As I twist and turn through the prismatic tunnel, occasionally and then often, it splits into two passages. I navigate the myriad choices of geometric tunnels forking into more tunnels without thought. It is pure flow. At the end, three women await my arrival. They are elated to see me. Initially, they dance like inflatable windsocks with no limbs and blurry faces, swaying with joy that the path I chose inevitably led to them. Slowly the details demystify, and the figures become Laula, Charlie, and Polly Jane. Together we dance until the dream fades into swirling patterns on my eyelids.

I awake with déjà vu rippling through my body as I contemplate the dream's meaning. It feels like a literal depiction of the unravelling journey, a path with multiple options requiring trust and flow. No matter the direction I veered, I end at the inevitable destination of home. The home that I discovered by asking a question in Peru, following its answer to Canada, where I was called back to Perth.

Sometimes life unfolds in mysterious ways.

Later, I climb Calgary Tower and awe at the 360-degree view from the ominous glass-floored observation deck. The city scurries into swaying prairies and lush foothills backdropped by fluffy clouds and the snowy Rockies. Gazing into the mountains, I wonder what awaits me in Australia.

As twilight imbues the sky in a peachy reverie, Trey and Riley collect me from the train station and we meet up with Conner and Ben for one final hang. Somewhere throughout the night, I find myself on Conner's parents' wooden decking with Riley. Amid pleasant chitchat, I peer into his magnetic green eyes. They shimmer with the soul of courtesy. Something in his gaze has me spontaneously realise that the mug magnet I bought in Slovenia was never meant for him. It is meant for me as a reminder to continue the path of cultivating self-love.

"I'm going to miss you," I croak.

"I'm going to miss you too," he concurs. "It's funny—"

"What is?"

"How we met, and how many times our paths have overlapped..."

I shake my head and grin. Is it really that bizarre? Or is it how the journey unravels?

⛵

The day after I leave balmy twenty-five-degree Calgary, a frigid Arctic airmass envelops the city, and temperatures plunge to subzero overnight. A freak snowstorm sucker-punches the city like a boxer knocking out the referee before the starting bell is dung. At the peak end of summer, the weather is out of character, even for the city's manic-depressive meteorology. With heavy snow collecting on trees that haven't yet lost their leaves, branches *crack*, *groan*, and *snap* under pressure, which topples thousands of trees. This causes power lines to fall and block roads, which congests traffic and stagnates flow.

Stephen once advised that it's best to let things flow. Paradoxically, we can't understand flow without first experiencing congestion. There's no clarity without confusion, no calm without conflict, no shadow without light, no healing without pain, no lesson without mistake. I often wonder if we should *let* things happen or *make* things happen. How do we know when to forge and when to flow?

"Trust," Stephen's voice soothes from memory lane. "Trust all that is. When I was incarcerated—stripped from everything and completely raw—that was all I had. Trust."

Can you trust yourself to do the work and steer into your destined horizon and then trust the mysterious undercurrents to carry you when you're tired and weary? Oh, the nuance of discipline and surrender. It is in this union we grow.

EPILOGUE

October 2015 - Thirteen months later

"Jess, you need to go home and finish writing your book."

An apple plods from a tree in the garden as I look into the Peace Clown's crisp mint eyes. His blue top hat perches by the windshield of my van, my beloved old Dotti we drove to Burning Man and then lived in for four long months.

"Why?" I plead. "Travelling is in my veins."

"Yeah, Miss...but travelling will always be there. You've gotta go home and finish this."

I divert my gaze to the redwoods in the horizon. I don't want to admit he's right. I managed to pump out my first, shitty draft in my nine months back in Australia, but I can't find the focus and structure to write with the road's endless adventures.

I trace my hands over Dotti's cold metal roof where his hammock dangles above my deflated air mattress. I recently discovered that his mother's job as a diplomat ensured a childhood split between Canada, Russia, Pakistan, India, Indonesia, and Egypt. It helps me perceive him in a clearer light, but I never *really* understand him until I later travel to India. Only then does his *buzzy* nature, love for community, and knack for finding order in chaos make sense.

I eye his tobacco pouch in the centre console and sigh. "Okay. I will."

"Promise?"

I hold out my pinkie and lock it in his, unknowingly binding myself to the unravelling journey of *The Unravelling Journey*.

For the following seven years, that's what I do. I sink my roots into Western Australia's creatively fertile soil, and I write. Sometimes I leave to sail through remote tropical islands on a dreamy wooden ship, explore crumbling jungle temples brimming with mystery, venture back to the world's largest temporary metropolis in the Black Rock Desert, visit my Canadian clan, and celebrate Wren and Lucas's love at a traditional Indian wedding. Sometimes the travel bug itches. I scratch it. But I never leave for more than three months.

In different homes in Fremantle, Darlington, and Scarborough, I stick it out and voyage into deep, icky, transformational, heartrending, aha, oh-no, private moments that are no longer hidden in the deepest crevices of my mind. Here they are, bared raw in these pages.

I wish I could say that once you've triumphed over depression, it never rears its ugly head again. But that's not how life unravels. Growing through our pain is part of our human experience. The dark days still come. Let them. We can't control what comes our way, but we can choose to grow through it.

It's important we override maladaptive patterns that resist and repress the entirety of our emotions. Instead let's armour ourselves with empowering tools to navigate the darkness while forming support networks to remind us of our strength on dreary days. There are highs when we fly. And there are lows when we grow. Some seasons are spiked with trials and tribulations, but potholes become portals if we let them. The inky darkness of the cocoon beckons us to transform into stronger, deeper, kinder, wiser versions of ourselves. Healing is a constant journey. We keep on unravelling.

Developing a daily gratitude practise empowers my mental wellbeing and makes me present to the richness of life. I've stayed off antidepressants but integrate stillness, movement, creativity, connection, and nature into each day. I walk along the beach often, still gazing into the horizon, still dreaming of distant lands. I still have the mug magnet from Slovenia. Inside it is a note that reads: *You are your own soul mate. Fall in love with yourself first.*

I still wish on shooting stars, fuzzy white dandelions, and perhaps I wished on Cumil's head (though I'll never tell you for sure) that this book might heal the hearts of millions. It's what drives me to open my laptop each day and scoop residual trauma into a potion that extracts the silver lining. You are the reason I sift through the rubble to find golden nuggets of meaning.

To anyone struggling with mental illness or the trauma of sexual assault: I urge you to seek help. All that grief, guilt, and gunk—it's not yours to carry. Can you let it go? The impulse to crawl up inside yourself and dissolve into the darkness...it passes. This is a rhythm allowing you to emerge with even greater light. Eventually the fog lifts, cleansing away all we do not need. On this fresh palate of possibility, we seed wisdom, feed happiness, weed what must be released, and breed the courage to rise again.

Thank you for being a part of the unravelling journey.

ACKNOWLEDGEMENTS

The Unravelling Journey is a project ten years in the making. From May 2013 to May 2023, it has been a deep and dynamic voyage that would not be possible without the following individuals.

Mama and Papa Bear, thank you from the bottom of my heart for being unwavering pillars of strength over the past decade. From the moment that I disclosed my vision of writing this book, to the red-eyed years of solitude knocking out multiple drafts, to the celebratory and stressful launch of Elemental Echoes (a fictional prelude for The Unravelling Journey), to the final months of editing and production, my heart overflows with gratitude that you've never let me doubt that I can lean on you in times of overwhelm. Thank you for showing up not just as loving parents, but also as solid friends.

Laula Perey, I can't thank you enough for instigating the journey, being the creative genius behind the title and having my back from day one. Friends like you are rare and treasured gifts. For you, I hold immense reverence and appreciation.

Blake Innes of HiveMind Press, I hold you in high esteem for your consistent and genuine support when the marathon became weary. Your novel publishing structure that puts autonomy back in the hands of artists is innovative and empowering. To have you by my side since 2021 with a loud "fuck yes, let's carry this project through to completion" has been a breath of fresh air. Your gentle fusion of considerate feedback and industry expertise has soothed my fears in the climb to publication. Thank you for bringing my vision to life.

To my eagle-eyed editor, Sasha Knight, words cannot articulate all you have done from the first developmental edit in 2018 to the second line edit in 2020, to the final copy edit in 2023. Five years of thorough insight delivered with an air of grace does not go unnoticed. Your professionalism in crafting a sharp and polished story shines like a gliding, diamond-studded swan. Thank you for facilitating my growth as a writer with kind-hearted encouragement and patient explanation. Your contributions are invaluable. I hope to one day meet in person.

Wren Jessica Richards of Ancient Rhythms Art, I truly appreciate your exquisite creative touch on the cover. Our four-month back and forth is a testament to your commitment to tirelessly produce something epic while pouring your beautiful heart into everything you do. I am blessed by your investment in The Unravelling Journey, both personally and professionally.

Ian and Ros Cleverley, Mathew Andrews, Daniel Campagnoli, Michael Barrett, Michelle Passmore, Kendra Lynn, Laula Perey, Tia-Rose Frecker, Pasan Tennakoon and Dr. Jae West, thank you for supporting me on Patreon between 2018 and 2020. Your generous financial contributions allowed me to focus on the developmental edit by covering my weekly groceries and coffee consumption. This is something I really appreciate. Additionally, your resolute belief that this book could enrich others was spiritual and emotional nourishment for me to give my all. I loved shared extracts of early drafts, behind-the-scenes footage and old travel journals with you.

To the anonymous literary critique from Writer's Victoria, I'm thankful for your honest manuscript assessment in 2020 that liberated me to see the gaps and blind spots in my work. I savour the opportunity for growth that knowledge brings.

Molly Schmidt and Alejandro Tuama, I cherish you helping me smooth and sharpen my work in our literary critique group, "1/3 of us is punctual". From our 2019 founding mission to empower each other to become published authors, to our passions igniting into a blazing inferno that finally culminated in 2023, I relish your constructive analysis on different snippets. I've loved watching you both flourish into successful writers. Thank you for helping me fan the flames.

Sammy Shaq, Christopher Lake, David Hammond and Zachary Anderson, I'm appreciative of your scrutiny and fortification on the extracts of Part I you respectively read in 2016, 2017, 2020 and 2022. Your keen discernment widened my lens on different constructions of meaning and gave structure to my writer's spirit. To also hold me in safe arms after delving into my past renders tender gratitude in my heart.

Mama and Charlie, I bow to your openness in our interview sessions and your trust in me sharing your battles and triumphs with mental health alongside my own. You both show profound courage under fire. I am immensely proud of your inner resilience and unshakeable resolve to thrive.

My favourite co-work buddies, Cass Cormack, Jae West and Brittney Tyrrell, I savour that you understand this means quiet focus, not buzzing chats. Thank you also for being loyal friends who've lovingly held me through my fears and continuously stuck feathers in my back.

Raven Brown and Cass Cormack, I'm beholden to your ceaseless support in the final months. Your honest advice and rapid-fire brain storm sessions got me to the finish line with warm rapport. Your help has meant so much.

Many thanks to Alexandra Nissen for editing my synopsis with keen perception,

Emma MacMillan for drafting up the blurb with passionate articulation, and Giles Roberts aka "Gino" for connecting me with Blake, which led to me being signed.

I am grateful to my housemates over the years—Emma Claudius, Jesse Derry, Mita Hill, Laula Perey and Callum Barton—for your patience every time I turned the dining table into my writing desk. Your kindness means a lot.

To the cafes and libraries of Perth, I relish the space to write, edit, network and plan, and not kicking me out when my constant presence felt like a squatter.

Thank you everyone who has been part of this wild journey. Whether we met briefly in passing, kept in touch, lost contact, included or not in this book, thank you for impacting the trajectory of my life. I am grateful for life's perpetual unravelling.

To the skies that sheltered me, the earth that held my roots, the trees that whispered secrets through dappled sunlight and the rivers that washed away my fears. To the mountains that stood sturdy and the winds that serenaded while carrying away my doubts. To nature, my gentle guide and steadfast friend, I honour you for colouring my life with wonder, beauty, imagination and creativity. Parts of this memoir are but a humble attempt to capture the magic you've brought into my world.

Finally, I pay homage to the darkness for being my mentor and guide. Though it sometimes felt like a shadow threatening to engulf me, I now see that without it, my light wouldn't shine as brightly. As Kurt Cobain once said, 'Thank you for the tragedy. I needed it for my art.'

But the true art lies not in tragedy, but in the power of transformation. I revel in the alchemy that turns wounds into wisdom, and pain into future fuel. So, dear reader, it is with deep gratitude that I thank you for taking this journey with me. Your presence, compassion, and willingness to bear witness has made all the difference in the world. Together, we have transformed the darkness into a beacon of hope. For that, I am forever grateful.

www.ingramcontent.com/pod-product-compliance
Lightning Source LLC
Chambersburg PA
CBHW011951090526
44591CB00020B/2719